BREACH OF FAITH

RANDOM HOUSE
NEW YORK

BREACH
OF FAITH

❧

Hurricane Katrina

AND THE

Near Death

OF A

Great American City

JED HORNE

Published in the United States by Random House, an imprint of The Random House
Publishing Group, a division of Random House, Inc., New York.

RANDOM HOUSE and colophon are registered trademarks of Random House, Inc.

Grateful acknowledgment is made to the following for permission
to reprint previously published material:

The New York Times: Excerpt from "Death of an American City," The New York
Times, December 11, 2005, copyright © 2005 by The New York Times Company.
Reprinted by permission.

The Times-Picayune: Excerpts adapted from "Carving a Better City" by Jed Horne,
The Times-Picayune, December 4, 2005. Reprinted by permission.

LIBRARY OF CONGRESS CATALOGING-IN-PUBLICATION DATA
Horne, Jed
Breach of faith: Hurricane Katrina and the near death of a great American city / Jed Horne.
p.   cm.
ISBN 1-4000-6552-6
1. Hurricane Katrina, 2005.   2. Disasters—Louisiana—New Orleans.
3. Hurricanes—Louisiana—New Orleans.   4. Disaster victims—Louisiana—New
Orleans.   5. Disaster relief—Louisiana—New Orleans.   6. Emergency
management—Government policy—United States.   I. Title.
HV6362005.N4 H66 2006   976.3'35044—dc22   2006046468

Printed in the United States of America on acid-free paper

www.atrandom.com

2   4   6   8   9   7   5   3   1

First Edition

Book design by Susan Turner

For Jane, who made this book possible

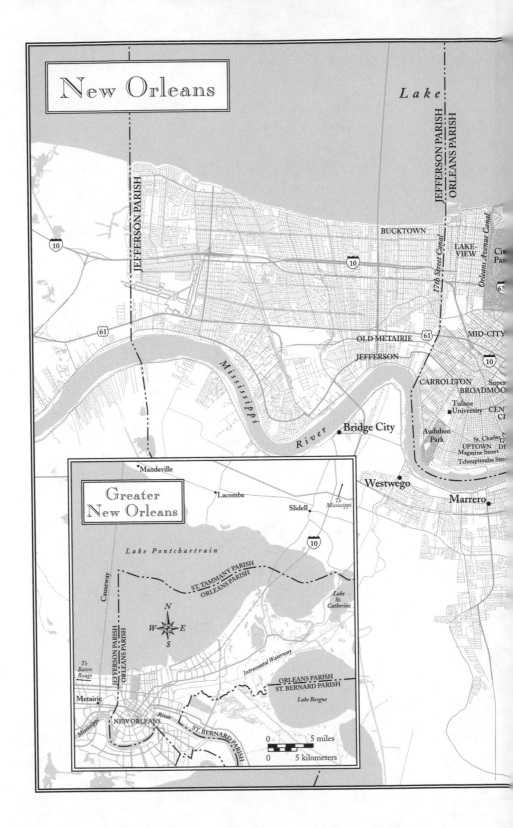

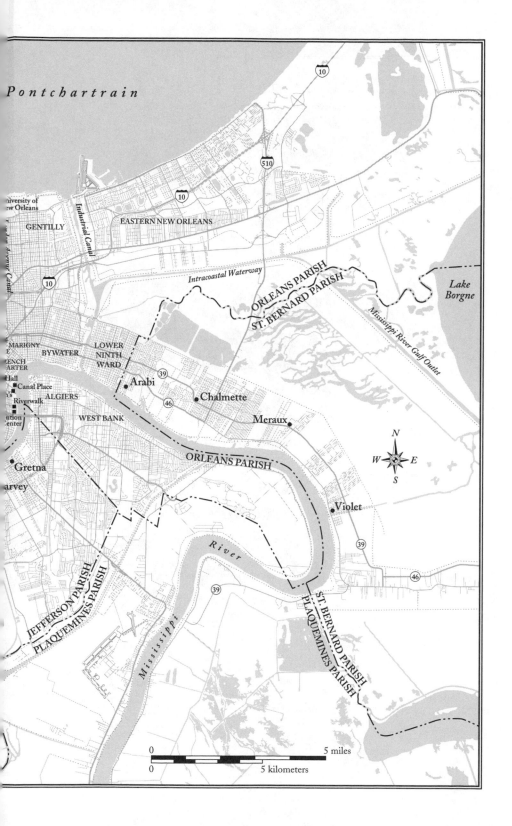

Pontchartrain

10

510

University of
New Orleans

Industrial Canal

GENTILLY

EASTERN NEW ORLEANS

10

Intracoastal Waterway

ORLEANS PARISH

ST. BERNARD PARISH

Lake
Borgne

10

Mississippi River Gulf Outlet

MARIGNY

BYWATER

LOWER
NINTH
WARD

FRENCH
QUARTER

Hall

Canal Place

Riverwalk

ALGIERS

WEST BANK

39

Arabi

46

Chalmette

Meraux

ORLEANS PARISH

N

W   E

S

Gretna

Harvey

Violet

39

46

River

39

JEFFERSON PARISH

PLAQUEMINES PARISH

ST. BERNARD PARISH

PLAQUEMINES PARISH

Mississippi

0   5 miles

0   5 kilometers

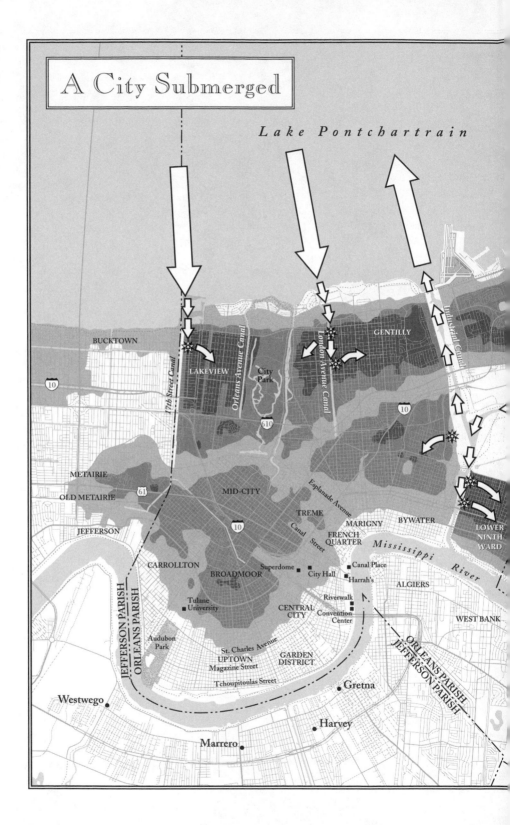

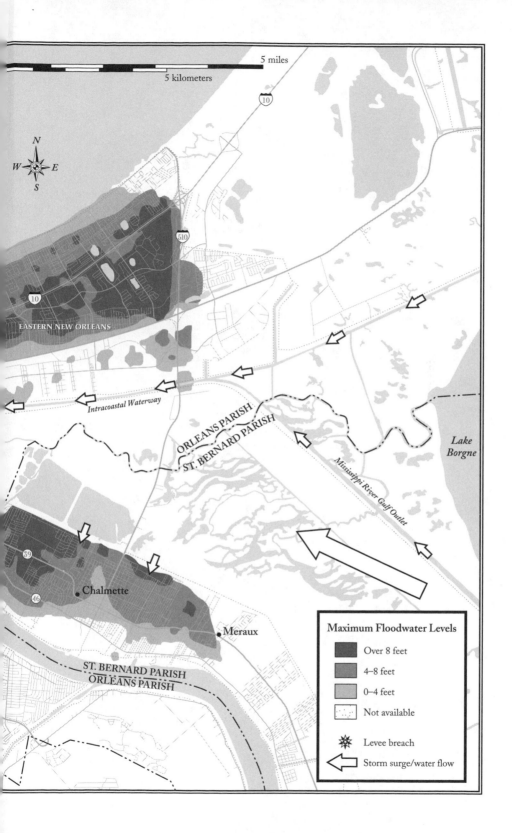

5 miles

5 kilometers

EASTERN NEW ORLEANS

Intracoastal Waterway

ORLEANS PARISH
ST. BERNARD PARISH

Lake
Borgne

Mississippi River Gulf Outlet

Chalmette

Meraux

ST. BERNARD PARISH
ORLEANS PARISH

Maximum Floodwater Levels

Over 8 feet

4–8 feet

0–4 feet

Not available

Levee breach

Storm surge/water flow

Contents

Maps *VIII*

Introduction *XV*

ONE *A Camille on Betsy's Track* 3

TWO *When Wallyworld Closes at Four* 22

THREE *An Imperfect Storm* 41

FOUR *Real Ugly, Real Fast* 48

FIVE *Decaf Cigarettes and Golden Carp* 73

SIX *Other Texans, Other Times* 83

SEVEN *Media in the Moment* 106

EIGHT *At Least Somebody Had a Plan* 120

NINE *Code Gray* 132

TEN *Like Bricks on Jell-O* 145

ELEVEN *Help Yourself* 168

TWELVE   *A Rockets Jersey and a Picture of Jesus*   187

THIRTEEN   *Reversal of Fortune*   200

FOURTEEN   *In Search of Common Ground*   218

FIFTEEN   *If They Can Rebuild Beirut*   232

SIXTEEN   *Crunch Time*   243

SEVENTEEN   *Sue the Bastards*   254

EIGHTEEN   *A Comparable Catastrophe*   275

NINETEEN   *Visions of a City Reborn*   288

TWENTY   *Blue Tarps in a Chocolate City*   306

TWENTY-ONE   *Shrink-Proof City*   315

TWENTY-TWO   *Safe Enough for Cows*   327

TWENTY-THREE   *Children with Bad Timing*   341

TWENTY-FOUR   *Failure Is Not an Option*   361

TWENTY-FIVE   *Summing Up*   374

Acknowledgments   387

Interview List   389

Notes   391

Index   401

Introduction

Katrina tore up lives as well as landscapes. A city below sea level was churned suddenly and convulsively by the hurricane that struck New Orleans in late August 2005. Rich people died along with the indigent. The pricey homes of the professional classes, both black and white, were destroyed, as were rickety cottages owned or rented by the poor. Millionaires and high-flying politicians were undone by Katrina, while other survivors found opportunity in the ruins of the city. That did not make Katrina an "equal opportunity destroyer," as some hastened to call it. Poor blacks did disproportionately more of the dying. And as the engines of recovery creaked into gear, people of means enjoyed advantages that had been theirs all along.

There is a comforting fatalism in thinking of Katrina as a natural disaster, or as God's will—whether that God is seen as a wrathful deity visiting retribution on a famously hedonistic part of the world or as the savior who once again spared New Orleans.

Katrina was an unnatural disaster—unnatural in its scale and destructiveness, but also unnatural in the sense that it was not limited causally to the forces of nature, to weather and geography and tides. (Of course, in an age of ominously rising temperatures and oceans, it may be that nothing about the weather is entirely a natural phenomenon anymore. I leave that debate to more knowledgeable writers.)

Both in its destructiveness—most of it tied to flooding—and throughout the early phases of the recovery that are part of the story chronicled in this book, Katrina has been essentially a man-made disaster. The levees that failed New Orleans were artifacts that, as much as the ruin of a Maya temple or the Great Wall of China, reflected the dreams and skills and politics of the society that built them. The relief effort and the recovery now under way have been only more obviously a manifestation of human agency—at a particular time and place in the lengthening history of a still-powerful nation.

Katrina taught us much about ourselves here in southeast Louisiana. It taught the rest of America a bit about Louisiana. This book is a skein of stories—about heroes, rogues, dreamers, doers—tangled together in the way that Katrina tangled the lives of its victims and survivors. But as a whole, these stories provide a lesson for America about itself. Because, for all that New Orleans lays claim to eccentric ways and a special place in our culture, it is at heart an American city, a great American city now testing the greatness of America to save it—for and from itself.

JED HORNE
New Orleans
April 2006

BREACH
OF FAITH

A Camille on Betsy's Track

T HE BIG OLD CAMELBACK HOUSE ON LAMANCHE STREET WAS HOME TO Patrina Peters, and had been for most of her forty-three years. Her parents lived in one of the paired front-to-back apartments that made up the ground floor—"shotgun" apartments in local parlance, because of their long, narrow layout. Zip, her brother's widow, had stayed on in the other downstairs apartment after Kevin's sudden death from a heart attack a year earlier. Peters and her two kids lived upstairs on the partial second floor that humped up on the backyard end of a camelback and gave this kind of house its name.

But if it was a cozy home for an extended New Orleans family, it was also a monument: to the self-reliance of Patrina Peters's forebears and to their standing in the city's Lower Ninth Ward, the rough-and-tumble working-class community some twenty blocks long and twenty-five blocks wide just downriver from the Industrial Canal. The waterway cut New Orleans more or less in half—a corridor of ship repair yards, steel fabricators, cold-storage warehousing, and the like that ran on a south-to-north axis from the

Mississippi River to Lake Pontchartrain. West of the canal, on the apron of land along the bank of the Mississippi River, lay the older and generally whiter parts of the city: Bywater, Marigny, the French Quarter, the downtown area with its business corridor and gentrified warehouse district, the Garden District, and then, farther up St. Charles Avenue, the sprawling heterogeneous swath of housing and universities known as Uptown.

There was more to New Orleans than these original settlements along the river's edge. As New Orleans was drained and landfilled early in the twentieth century, the city pushed out into the swamps, eventually reaching all the way to the lake, a shallow and brackish inland sea fifty miles long and twenty-five miles across. More recently, settlement had spread beyond the Lower Ninth into another, considerably larger welter of swampland and postwar subdivisions known as New Orleans East. People still spoke of wards in New Orleans, none so frequently as the Lower Ninth, mainly because it was geographically so succinct. But these political subdivisions—there were seventeen wards—for practical purposes had been supplanted in modern times by councilmanic districts, of which there were only five.

Peters knew what people said about the Lower Ninth, and she would hear a lot more of it on television in the weeks ahead. It would sicken and disgust her, the way the TV reporters figured everyone in the Lower Ninth was poor and on crack and couldn't get out of the way of a hurricane if their lives depended on it, which maybe they did.

Peters's great-grandfather on her mother's side, the Reverend Allen Thomas, had been pastor of the Battleground Baptist Church when it was in Fazendeville, a storied African American hamlet on a corner of the Chalmette National Historical Park a few miles downriver in St. Bernard Parish. The bulldozing of Fazendeville in 1964 was the final hurrah in a campaign by preservationists to bring the field to a closer semblance of its condition during the Battle of New Orleans one hundred fifty years earlier. Anticipating the end, the pastor moved his flock and his eleven children and *their* many children onto land he had acquired in the Lower Ninth. His sons were builders and cabinetmakers—the reverend himself sidelined as a roofer—and in due course, a swath of several blocks was dominated by his family and his followers. Two generations later, Peters's cousin the Reverend Eric Lewis was assistant pastor at Battleground Baptist. Her uncle the Reverend

Freddie McFadden III, a man who had found God after losing his spleen in a gunfight as a young man, presided several blocks away at St. Claude Baptist Church.

AND IF THAT DIDN'T PUT THE LIE TO THE LOWER NINTH'S IMAGE AS A REDOUBT of dysfunctional families mired in permanent poverty, Peters didn't know what would. Her mother, June Johnson, had managed a school cafeteria in her day. Her father, Edward Johnson, had retired as manager of a downtown U-Park lot. Peters herself had earned a degree in clerical studies at Cameron, a commercial college on Canal Street, and had worked as a cosmetology instructor at a beauty school until 1995. Then for four years, until her health gave out, she held down a job at Xavier University with the big AME janitorial service, a black-owned business that also cleaned buildings and cut grass for the Orleans Parish public school system. A plump, cheerful woman who pulled her hair to the back of her head and held it there with an elastic band, Peters had a foggy voice much bigger than her diminutive frame. Her epilepsy was manageable with medication, but a heart condition and a worsening case of Crohn's disease, a condition characterized by recurring intestinal inflammation, knocked her out of the workforce and onto disability in 1999. She was thirty-seven.

And so, while her downstairs kin watched TV that last Saturday night in August, and fretted over news reports of the huge storm winging across the Gulf, Peters headed upstairs, showered, and got into her nightgown. There had been a time when Trina, as everyone called her, had spent her Saturday evenings very differently, most every evening for that matter, a time when that Nina Simone voice of hers had been part of the smoky din of local bars and clubs—most especially when a storm was brewing in the Gulf. Storms were party time. In working-class neighborhoods still capable of civic occasion other than the late-night huddle along yellow slashes of crime scene tape, folks rolled grills right out to the curb when a storm was coming, and barbecued ribs and chicken for the whole block. After all, if the power failed, as it certainly would, uneaten food would just spoil. Merriment was already unfolding in the streets of the Lower Ninth and elsewhere across New Orleans as Peters took her medications and, by seven PM that Saturday night, was in her bed asleep.

She awoke the next morning to family dissension. Her mother had heard talk of a twenty-foot storm surge and Category 5 winds—winds above 155 miles per hour, the highest ranking on the Saffir-Simpson Hurricane Scale. That would make Katrina even worse than Betsy, the apocalyptic 1965 tempest that had uprooted trees and stripped roofs of their shingling all across New Orleans, deeply flooding the Lower Ninth Ward. June had fled Betsy with Trina, then a child of three, and could see no reason to do otherwise this time. Trina's great-uncle James McFadden, who lived just down the street, had been trapped on a rooftop by Betsy before extricating himself and joining in the Lower Ninth Ward rescue effort. "I'm not going to ride this one out," her mother said. Peters's way of dealing with the menace ahead was to stick to routine. All week, she had had it in mind to do a roast for Sunday dinner, with rice and gravy and peas and potatoes and salad, and she sure enough wasn't inclined to give that up for a long drive upriver to an aunt's place in St. John Parish.

But go, go if you need to, she told her mother, and take Damond. Damond was fourteen, a gangly basketball player already hitting the six-foot mark, but he was Peters's baby, and when she thought about the roast, she had her son in mind as much as any of the other people who would have relished it. Keia, her daughter, would stay behind. They'd eat the roast together and play a little gin rummy in the late afternoon—a nice little mother-daughter moment in an apartment refurbished with the new furniture Peters had bought just two months earlier, a whole household's worth. After all, moments like that were harder to come by and soon might be gone forever, now that Keia was twenty-four and about to graduate from college.

Damond fussed about the plan, and the roast was only part of it. He was the man of the house. He should stand by his mother and sister. But Peters would not hear of it. She and Keia would look after themselves. She would take no chances with Damond. As they loaded up the car, her uncle James came by to join with the others fleeing upriver. "Why you want to stay here, Trina?" McFadden asked. She recognized it as a man's teasing way of begging her to leave, and she answered jauntily, trying to cool him out: "I'm way upstairs. You go ahead. You go ahead, but we are way upstairs." When she saw his eyes starting to get watery, she tried a different tack. "I trust in God," she said. "Whatever God wills, it will be done." But her confidence was not contagious. Her uncle got into the car and looked back out at her through the open window. "I wish you were coming," he said. His voice was thin, and then he looked away.

By seven PM that Sunday evening, Peters was again bathed, medicated, and in bed, the last night she would ever spend in her family home, indeed the last time she would ever even want to think of the Lower Ninth as home.

It wasn't the morning news reports that did it. The mayor had made the evacuation mandatory, but he could do what he wanted. Peters wasn't planning to leave; she had already passed up her ride. And it wasn't the phone call from cousins over on Jourdan Road, four or five blocks away, to say that they were reconsidering their decision to stay put. In hindsight, Peters would remember being spooked as much as anything by a numerological coincidence: that exactly forty years separated 2005 from 1965, Katrina from Betsy. "You know, I think we made a bad decision," she said to Keia as the symmetry of the two events dawned on her. "I have a funny feeling about this."

And so that Monday morning—near dawn, but way too late—they started packing clothes, important papers, rounding up Peters's medications, her dentures. "I gotta have my teeth!" she joked with her daughter, trying to break the worsening tension that had come over Keia. The cousins called back, panicky now. From the upper story of their house on Jourdan Road they could see right into the Industrial Canal, beyond the earthen levee and the concrete flood wall that ran along the top of it, and what they saw was nerve-racking: "The water is, like, kinda rising," they told Patrina, "and it looks like it's about to come over the levee."

From the endless stories about Betsy, the memories of her uncle and so many others trapped in raging waters, Peters knew to share that sense of dread. The worst of it was realizing all this was just a prelude to the cyclone that lay ahead. The rising water would be storm surge funneling into the canal from the Intracoastal Waterway that connected to it from the open waters of the Gulf. Amplified by winds and rain, the surge would test mooring lines and knock barges against the massive concrete flood walls. But the eye of the hurricane was still miles way. At 6:10 AM, maximum sustained wind speeds had dropped to 121 miles per hour—Category 3 strength—as Katrina made landfall some fifty miles southeast of New Orleans, on the withered finger of land that separated the Mississippi River from the open Gulf. But the eye's distance hardly mattered, given the unusual width—four hundred miles—of the whirling disk that was Katrina.

From her upstairs rooms, Peters could see the trees toss mercilessly in the wind, and she could hear the bits of shingling begin to shred and fly against the walls of the house with a force that she knew would soon shatter glass. And then, suddenly the house shook with a concussive thud so violent that it knocked Keia back onto the bed and sent her mother scrambling to pull everything out of the closet so there would be room to shut themselves inside. In the months to come, many theories would be advanced as to exactly what sequence of events, what chain of natural forces and human failings, led to catastrophe in New Orleans, but to her dying day Peters, like many of her neighbors, would remain convinced that the thudding sound, a recurring motif in her dreams, was the sound of the Industrial Canal being deliberately dynamited. Why? To spare the fancier, whiter, upriver parts of New Orleans from the devastation that would have gone their way if the flood walls had ruptured on the other side of the canal. Hadn't the city's business elite done something like that during the catastrophic flooding of the Mississippi River valley back in 1927—blowing a hole in the levee and flooding rustic St. Bernard Parish, a realm of trappers and farmers, to ease pressure on the flood defenses at New Orleans? That was fact. History. "Everyone has a right to their opinion," Peters would say when confronted with differing views about the explosive sound she heard as Katrina struck—that it was an electrical transformer blowing up or, more probably, the impact of a barge as it was swept over the walls of the ruptured Industrial Canal and thundered like a giant empty oil drum onto the street below the levee.

Whatever its cause, the sound prompted Peters to peek down the stairs into the kitchen—maybe the stove had blown up—and see, to her horror, that raging water had torn the wall right off the back of the house, stripping her of any illusion that her family home, even in the recesses of its snuggest closets, could provide any protection at all. Just then the cell phone rang again: Deidra, one of the cousins, jabbering in such terror it was hard to make out the words. They were on their roof, a half dozen of them, Deidra screamed over the howling wind. The water had lifted their house right off the pilings and was carrying it down the street.

Peters called 911 and begged for help. Instead she got a scolding: "You didn't listen to your mayor? You should have listened to your mayor." And with that, the operator hung up. Now she reached her mother on the cell: "Oh, Lord, Mama, we're gonna drown. We love y'all, but we're gonna drown." With the whole upriver household huddled in a bedroom for the call, Damond had managed to wrench the phone from his grandmother and was speaking to Keia—his mother's sobs audible in the background—when the phone went dead. In an instant, it seemed possible, he had lost both his mother and his sister, women he should have stayed home to protect. Damond began punching numbers into the cell phone, desperate to reach someone, anyone, back in New Orleans who could attempt a rescue mission to Lamanche Street. No calls went through. He tried again and again to reach his mother or Keia. Nothing.

On a hunch that a mattress might float, mother and daughter managed to haul one out through an upstairs window and onto the camelback's lower front roof, water now lapping at its eaves. Neighboring houses had been wrenched free of their foundations and were easing out into the street. When a small cottage floating high in the water knocked up against their house, they heaved the mattress onto its more gently sloped roof and clambered aboard. The building swirled in the rising water and slid in behind the camelback, where it cropped up against a pecan tree, an old one that had been a fixture in the yard and in Peters's memories ever since she was a little girl and her mama had sent her out there to play. "It was like God said 'This is where I will anchor the house,' " she would later remember thinking.

On their rooftop mattress, Keia clung to her mother, and Peters, with one arm around her daughter, looped the other around a vent, the two women screaming, praying, weeping. At about nine-thirty, by Peters's wristwatch, the full fury of Katrina—the wall of the eye—made its closest swipe at New Orleans and the Lower Ninth Ward. The roar of the wind was unearthly, a banshee's wail and the deep and thunderous rumble of a volcano rolled into one, a sound so loud that even though her mother's mouth was inches from her ear, it was all Keia could do to make out the words of the hymn Peters began to sing at the top of her voice: "Come by here, Lord. Come by here, Lord. I need you, my Lord. Come by here." Trees and telephone poles had begun to bend and snap as though they were nothing more than stalks of dried grass; jagged slates of asbestos shingling whizzed past the two women on the roof, and so they buried their faces in the mattress ticking. For hours they would cling to each other like that, their muscles aching in a death grip they didn't dare loosen.

It was noon, two-and-a-half hours into this nightmare, when the entire roof blew off an adjacent structure and crashed into the water beside them. And with that, Peters came squarely to grips with a certainty: For all her prayers and hymn-singing and the love she had for her daughter, it was over for them. "Oh, baby, we're not gonna make it," she said. She kissed and hugged Keia. "If they find us, they'll find us clenched together." And then, there on the rooftop, they got ready to die.

THERE WAS THE HURRICANE ICON—THE DOUBLE-BLADED RED ROTOR TURNING slowly in the corner of Gulf Coast TV screens. And when the weather report came on that Friday night, there were satellite images of the storm as well, a vortex of whirling winds and thunderclouds coiling like a snake around an unblinking eye about a hundred miles west of the Florida Keys. The icon was an abstraction, but somehow it was the more unsettling of the two images: a double-bladed disk, the blades curved menacingly, like a streamlined swastika, to suggest a hurricane's counterclockwise churn. The TV people used it on their tracking maps, a ninja star sent skittering out across the Gulf to target possible landfalls. It was, to say the least, an imprecise science, this business of hurricane forecasting. As Katrina entered the Gulf, her range of possible landfalls extended from Louisiana at the Texas line all the way across the Florida Panhandle. Campeche, Mexico, could breathe easy, but not Morgan City, not New Orleans, nor Biloxi nor Mobile, nor Pensacola. Least of all Pensacola. Pensacola might have been closer to the eastern end of the storm's danger range, but Pensacola had forgotten how to breathe easy through a cloudburst, so frequently had the Panhandle come in for it during recent hurricane seasons. Of the six hurricanes that had hit Florida in the previous twelve months, two of them—both monsters—had sucker punched the Panhandle and the barrier islands meant to protect it.

There was fatalism in the way Gulf Coast towns dealt with hurricanes,

New Orleans among them. But as the season stretched on toward late summer, its period of greatest menace, the hurricane jokes and expressions of sophisticated indifference or resignation did not entirely conceal a sense of dread that crept over people who had been through their share of these things. Couples, without quite knowing why, would find themselves wondering again if New Orleans was really the place where they wanted to grow old. Or might it be time to unload the big, vulnerable house with all the gingerbread, and downsize into a condo in some bunker of a building? Just a thought. But one that did not go away after a big storm. Because unlike earthquakes, which tended to ease seismic pressure deep beneath the earth, at least for a few decades or centuries, the hurricane's gun to the skull was fully reloaded after each and every storm. It could happen again next year. Hell, it could happen next month.

By late Thursday, the snake in the satellite image had coiled suddenly tighter, and a disorganized tropical storm floundering east of Miami had reached hurricane strength, if just barely. In a matter of hours, Katrina tore across the tip of the Florida peninsula, feeding on a hurricane's usual diet: trailer-park housing, loose shingles, bug-weakened trees, poorly moored yachts. In one respect, Katrina revealed a freakish side: Forecasters had expected the storm to move west across the peninsula and at a snail's pace— maybe 6 miles per hour. Instead, inexplicably, it sped up to 12 miles per hour and shifted onto a diagonal course that carried it in a more southerly direction until the storm reached the Gulf shortly after midnight.

Scientists do not like to have their projections go wrong, but a fast-tracking hurricane is a friendlier beast than a slow one. A lingering storm has more time to tear up the landscape—and usually compounds wind damage with greater amounts of rain. On her tangent, Katrina was across Florida in a hop and a jump. About a hundred homes were damaged by buffeting winds or flooded out in the rain that followed. A 727 cargo plane was pushed along a runway fence like an unwelcome club patron shoved and shoved again by a bouncer. Six people died in Florida, half of them crushed under falling trees.

Katrina, in other words, had all the makings of a flop, a minimal hurricane, a Category 1 event. Her winds upon making landfall in Florida had been just barely above the 75 mph threshold that turns a tropical cyclone from seriously bad weather into an event worthy of at least grudging respect. In an age of billion-dollar storms, Katrina's ravages in Florida were pegged at a mere $600 million.

New Orleanians knew better than to revel in Florida's misfortune, but then, it being Friday night in the Crescent City, they reveled anyway, if only to escape the deep, sometimes unacknowledged, sense of unease that hung over the hurricane season. The gregarious among them streamed into the Superdome to guzzle beer with cheese nachos and watch the Saints blunder to a preseason 21–6 loss against Baltimore. Others crowded into bars in the French Quarter and the downriver faubourgs Marigny and the Bywater or gathered more privately on patios and terraces in Uptown and along the lakefront to sip wine, eat skewered shrimp, and commune around the topic of the storm, sometimes by sedulously avoiding it altogether. Because for all the merriment and distraction provided by the hurricane season's latest incarnation, there were other things to talk about. Donald Trump for one.

Among the real estate barons and everyone else who had come to measure their financial well-being by the vigor of the local real estate market, the big news in the morning paper had been Trump. The Donald—or at least his son—was behind a plan to build a $200 million luxury condo tower on Poydras Street. At seventy stories, it would be the tallest building in the city. Indeed, it would be the first major tower of any size since the oil crash of the mid-1980s. Overnight, the 1984 crash had ended a veritable frenzy of high-rise construction that had followed the belated discovery that you could actually build modern skyscrapers in the miles-deep muck of a delta city floating on silt.

Jazz clarinetist Alvin Batiste was booked into Snug Harbor that Friday night. Swamp rock blues sensation Coco Robicheaux had the early gig at d.b.a, another hot club. Kermit Ruffins, more commonly to be found at the ramshackle Vaughn's, way down Dauphine, almost to the Industrial Canal, had taken his trumpet up to Ray's over the River. Ray was Ray Wooldridge, a newcomer in a city often leery of them. Wooldridge had recently sold his interest in New Orleans's freshly minted NBA franchise, the Hornets, to concentrate on the high life. His club looked out over the river from the top

of the World Trade Center, the one built years before New York's at the insti-
gation of Clay Shaw. That gave it a certain dark cachet. Shaw was the hap-
less bon vivant and business leader who had been prosecuted unsuccessfully
on false charges: that he conspired with another sometime New Orleanian,
Lee Harvey Oswald, in the assassination of a president, John Fitzgerald
Kennedy.

Those of a religious persuasion celebrated more quietly, dropping to
their knees to pray that the city would be spared. It was a moment of supplication that quite quickly yielded to Christian guilt during the storm season.
Because when the misfortune you were praying to be spared was a Gulf hurricane, one city's salvation necessarily was perdition in the place where that
storm came ashore, as all of them eventually did, in Katrina's case more than
once. But even without divine intervention, there was reason to think New
Orleans might catch another break.

There had been the chance, more a faint hope, that Katrina would do her
damage to Miami and then weaken, perhaps even disintegrate, in passing
over the Florida peninsula. The odds looked better on paper than they really
were, because only on paper did Florida seem to interpose a storm-killing
landmass between Katrina's Atlantic origins and the Gulf, where she
yearned to quench her thirst for water, the warmer the better, a hurricane's
addiction. The reality, of course, was that south Florida was not dry land but
a swamp, and only more so in an age of rising seas. The Everglades were a
reservoir vast enough to fill pipes in Dade County, and Broward too. But, as
would be quickly demonstrated, no matter how many toilets were flushed
and Jacuzzis roiled up and scotches lightly watered in hotel towers along
Miami Beach, the Everglades were still wet enough to provide at least star-
vation rations to Katrina until she reached the Gulf. And now, as the evening
news made clear, she had. The red icon still rotated in the corner of the TV
screen, and the satellite found Katrina's coil of clouds a hundred miles or so
off Key West. The hurricane had not simply survived the Everglades, it had
been deeply refreshed in transiting south Florida.

As the ten PM news came on Friday night, Katrina's winds had stiffened
to 105 mph, Category 2 strength, and the storm was sidling away from the
Keys at 8 mph on a west-southwest trajectory. South was not necessarily bad
for Louisiana, though due north, a beeline to the Panhandle, would have

been better. The problem was the storm's westward drift. Hundreds of the nation's offshore oil platforms lay to the west, as did an appalling concentration of its refining capacity. And like a bull's-eye on all too many of the storm-tracking maps, New Orleans lay to the west—the Big Easy, once the richest city in America, "the city that care forgot," to use another sobriquet that seemed as old as Bourbon Street but that in fact first saw its way into print in a 1938 Federal Writers' Project guidebook. There were other handles on this strange and improbable place: "cradle of jazz" being one; "crescent city" another, reflecting the giant arc the Mississippi River made at New Orleans, in its sinuous and continent-long search for the sea. Now a majority black city, it was, on a per capita basis, one of the poorest, but New Orleans remained the center of the nation's most distinctive regional culture, a mix of music and food and parades and masquerade that many people, rich and poor, found irresistible.

MAYOR RAY NAGIN'S CONCERN FRIDAY NIGHT WAS THAT THE CITY THAT CARE forgot had forgotten to care. Here was this monster storm out in the Gulf, and everyone was watching the Saints game, he told TV reporters, his loose-limbed affability not quite disguising real concern. Nagin still wasn't calling for an evacuation, not even a voluntary one. That was an option he said he'd weigh the following morning at a meeting with emergency managers from across the area. But he warned people to be ready. And he got ready himself, arranging flights for his family to Dallas, should the need arise.

Kathleen Babineaux Blanco needed no convincing. As of Thursday, Louisiana's chief executive was still scheduled to go to Atlanta to be sworn in as the new chair of the Southern Governors' Association. A lifetime in Acadiana, Louisiana's soft coastal underbelly, had well acquainted the governor with the fury of hurricanes, and as she and her husband watched the weather reports, their initial concern had been to wonder if Katrina's projected landfall at Apalachicola Bay might make for messy weather in central Georgia and trouble with their flight. In hindsight, it would amuse Raymond Blanco—"Coach" Blanco, as he was usually called, both because he had been a high school and college football coach and because of his importance as one of his wife's key advisers—that the vagaries of a gathering storm could be so hard to predict. By midafternoon that Friday, Blanco formally declared a state of emergency in Louisiana and canceled plans to go to the governors' meeting. She placed the National Guard and state agencies on alert—a full day before Mississippi and two full days before President Bush did the federal equivalent, Blanco would find occasion to remind her critics.

There was still a chance the storm would turn. Hope for New Orleans was vested in a high-pressure system that had settled over the city and the Gulf Coast. Were that system to lift, as there was reason to think it would, a trough of low pressure easing southeast across the Great Plains could be expected to slide out over the Gulf in time to intercept the hurricane and steer it to a landing well east of New Orleans, somewhere between Biloxi and Mobile.

That's what Georges had done in 1998, deviating just hours before landfall from the worst possible course: right up the river and into Lake Pontchartrain, which would then have been lifted over the city's northern levees to turn New Orleans into Atlantis. Instead, just before dawn, Georges had bobbled ever so slightly and come ashore at Ocean Springs, a Mississippi coastal hamlet some ninety miles to the east. Ivan, in 2004, had also obliged New Orleans with a hook shot to the northeast, and had laid waste to barrier islands off Alabama and Florida before wading ashore to ravage Mobile, Pensacola, and Panhandle beachfront towns. Ivan had been the fourth major storm to clobber Florida in a single season. It being an election year, the quadruple whammy had been eerie enough to kindle political hope among Democrats of a superstitious bent. Fate, if not the Lord himself, seemed none too happy with the Bush brothers, not with Jeb, Florida's governor, nor with George W., then seeking to distract voters from the gathering winds of another catastrophe, the war in Iraq, and extend his lease on the White House by another four years.

By late Friday, Katrina's alarming shift to the west had been briefly checked, and it looked like Jeb might be in for yet another trip to the heavenly woodshed. The National Hurricane Center acknowledged an eastward shift in its projections for Katrina's landfall. Bar patrons in New Orleans still sober enough to grasp the implications raised their glasses to the weatherman, then drained them and headed for home.

• • •

MARK SCHLEIFSTEIN DID NOT NEED TO BE REMINDED OF THE WISDOM IN PREPAR-
ing for the worst. By profession and by temperament, he was one of the people who did the reminding. And that Saturday morning he was in good form.
News boxes across the metropolitan area framed the headlines above his by-
lined report on the storm's threat. He would repeat the message personally to
anyone who cared to listen as he and his wife, Diane, mingled with friends
after services at Shir Chadash Congregation.

Three years earlier, Schleifstein had led his colleagues at the local newspaper, *The Times-Picayune,* in putting together a multi-day report warning
that the city's storm-protection infrastructure—essentially a ring of levees—
was shockingly inadequate. In vivid detail, he laid out just how devastating
a direct hit by a major hurricane might be: "hundreds of billions of gallons
of lake water pouring over levees into an area averaging 5 feet below sea
level with no natural means of drainage," he had written in an article co-
authored with his colleague John McQuaid. "That would turn the city . . .
into a lake as much as 30 feet deep, fouled with chemicals and waste from
ruined septic systems, businesses and homes. Such a flood could trap hundreds of thousands of people in buildings and in vehicles. At the same time,
high winds and tornadoes would tear at everything left standing," they
wrote. A Red Cross official quoted in the series predicted a death toll of between twenty-five thousand and one hundred thousand—and this scenario
didn't even require levee breaches, just overtopping. The carnage would
leave corpses floating in the streets, others bloated and rotting in attics,
where people would seek refuge from the rising water, and then get trapped.
The filth and corpses would set the table for a wave of plagues and pestilence
of unparalleled severity, Schleifstein warned.

Some of his colleagues had snickered at the earnestness of Schleifstein's
doomsaying, as they did at his daily, sometimes hourly, interoffice e-mails
that forwarded National Weather Service updates on the latest dips and turns
of every approaching storm. And indeed, there was an obsessiveness in
Schleifstein's attention to hurricanes, that of an Old Testament prophet possessed of a vision and the need to warn his people. The office joke was that he
suffered ever so slight a pang of regret each time a monster storm bore down

on New Orleans only to pull its punch. If so, it was not out of any need for vindication. Schleifstein was too certain of the science behind his reporting to require that. A deeply religious man, an owlish gray-bearded journalist with a devoted wife and two grown children, he lived an observant, unpretentious life in a modest two-story brick house in the city's Lakeview district. Schleifstein's hurricane kit—candles, flashlights, and the like—was always at hand. As Katrina approached, he swapped cars with his son. Mike would take the good car, a Toyota Prius hybrid, and drive his young wife to Atlanta to stay with Schleifstein's daughter. Dad took Mike's junker, an old Mazda. They put Diane's car on the upper deck of a high-rise garage. Otherwise, Schleifstein had made no special preparations based on his premonitions of doom. As reporters and editors were expected to do, he would ride out the storm at the newspaper's main office, in an industrial district fast by the interstate and less than a mile from the Superdome and city hall. And Diane would be with him. He had lost that argument a few storms ago. She wasn't going to leave the city without him. Schleifstein's fate, whatever it might be, would be shared with the people he had been warning all these years.

On Saturday morning, one of the people Schleifstein warned was his rabbi's wife, heavily pregnant and a newcomer to New Orleans. Schleifstein had been on the search committee that recruited Rabbi Ted Lichtenfeld. True to form, in offering this man a congregation in New Orleans, Schleifstein had felt an obligation to caution him about what he was getting into. Schleifstein presented the Lichtenfelds with a copy of his series on hurricanes. The Lichtenfelds had pondered it and, to Schleifstein's delight, elected to come anyway. The rabbi had taken charge at Shir Chadash that very month, on August first. They were due to add the baby to their nursery—a son, the doctors had told them—in another several weeks. Schleifstein greeted the rabbi's wife and then got quite quickly to the point. "Y'all need to start thinking about where you're going to go," he told her that Saturday morning in New Orleans. "You don't want to stay on here."

What Schleifstein knew from his contacts at the National Hurricane Center was that, overnight, Katrina had taken on the trappings of a perfect storm, the Big One, an event long foreseen and dreaded and yet somehow impossible to fathom. Warm water, a hurricane's lifeblood, had been unusually abundant in the Gulf as Katrina took form in the mid-Atlantic early in

August and began working her way west. To the Cassandras of environmentalism, it was further proof, if proof were needed, that global warming was an onrushing reality, though Schleifstein had a more nuanced understanding of the way warmer seas both strengthened and inhibited hurricanes, by tearing at the swirling perimeter of what was called their "eye wall."

Whatever the reason, without doubt the Gulf was hot. Its usual influx of cool northern water from the Mississippi River had been choked off by a Midwest drought—the worst in twenty years. The drought had shrunk the Missouri River and, farther downstream, the Mississippi itself. And air temperatures along the Gulf Coast had been scorching in the preceding weeks, helping drive water temperatures above 85 degrees in many places. Not only was the Gulf water hot, the hot water ran deep—two hundred feet deep in one area sampled—thanks in part to the presence of a "loop current," an appendage of the Gulf Stream that had broken free and was rotating around the Gulf of Mexico, spreading the superheated water.

These conditions, eminently favorable for hurricane development, might have been checked by two countervailing forces: wind shear that can rip apart the upper levels of a swirling storm system, and dry air sufficient to sap the cyclone of its self-sustaining moisture. Instead, two days before landfall, for all her sprawling girth, Katrina had begun to manifest some of the nerve-racking precision of a tight and deadly tornado, a tornado not yards-wide like the funnels that spin across the dusty Great Plains but hundreds of miles in diameter. The hurricane had entered what meteorologists call the "eye-wall replacement cycle," spinning the clouds at its center—the fastest moving part of the whole dreadful machine—faster and faster until they flew apart, only to be replaced after a brief lull in wind velocity by a new eye wall, spinning as fast or faster still. The cyclone, in other words, had begun to pulse, almost to pant with thirst.

To slake that thirst, the Gulf had welled up into a dome of water as vast and wide as the storm itself, a huge and churning vortex that lifted sea levels yards above normal as the water was sucked skyward into the vacuum at the storm's very center. The strength of that vacuum was reflected in the plunging barometric pressures characteristic of a hurricane, 920 millibars in Katrina's case, one of the lowest readings on record. In deeper seas, the dome of Gulf water offered up to Katrina rolled over on itself endlessly like a boiling cauldron. But as the storm churned into coastal shoals, the bubble of rolling water would rise suddenly higher, knocking aside massive billion-dollar oil platforms and lesser jack-up rigs like flotsam. On such a course, within hours the dome of water would roll ashore, instantly crushing coastal communities. The direct storm surge would be a hurricane's most immediately destructive water, a towering wave that would first hurl houses and boats and parked cars and trucks and giant live oaks ahead of itself. Its forward motion exhausted within a mile or so of the shoreline, the surge would sweep back into the Gulf in an outrush powerful enough to uproot most anything it hadn't taken in the initial sweep.

New Orleans, many miles from the open Gulf, could assume it would not feel the brunt of that first wall of water. The city's doom—if it came to that—would lie in a secondary phenomenon: Even if the storm's eye glanced away from the immense lakes and the river that made New Orleans essentially an island, the dome of water in the open Gulf could drive huge tides through the narrow inlets that connected these waterways. And like an obese bather lowering herself into a bath, Katrina would slosh waves of water up against the sides of the tub—the Orleans levee system—overtopping it in many places, perhaps even breaching it in others.

And therein lay Katrina's—or any storm's—greatest threat to the city: not the winds, though they could be horrific, perhaps even powerful enough to twist skyscrapers off their foundations, an alarming new study had suggested. But skyscrapers, even toppled skyscrapers, were discrete phenomena that an otherwise intact city could then address. The worst-case scenario for greater New Orleans was the death-by-drowning of the city itself. With water filling a saucerlike landscape, much of it below sea level, the levees that ordinarily make that landscape habitable would become barriers against floodwaters ebbing back into the lake or the river and then into the Gulf. Every raindrop that fell in New Orleans, not to mention every gallon of treated sewage, had to be pumped up and over the levees and out into the surrounding water world. Swamp the pumps themselves or the electrical generators that power them, and New Orleans would become the large lake that Schleifstein and McQuaid had envisioned. Endless blocks of one-story cottages and ranch-style houses would be largely concealed beneath an expanse of oily water, broken only by downtown towers. The towers would stand like reeds along the river, the occasional bridge or elevated expressway looping up out of the water like the dorsal ridge of a giant sleeping alligator.

Katrina had that potential, the forecasters were saying. She was on a path of potentially maximum destruction, and since passing Florida her winds had jumped to Category 5 strength. For reference points of comparable menace, you had to hark back to the 1960s, to Betsy, the most destructive storm to have hit New Orleans in at least a half century, and to Camille, four years later, the most powerful U.S. hurricane ever recorded.

BETSY WAS A SLOW-MOVING STORM VICIOUS ENOUGH TO HAVE KILLED SEVENTY-five people—the greatest loss of life to a hurricane since 1957, when Audrey killed three hundred ninety in south-central and southwestern Louisiana. Betsy had flooded to depths of ten feet or more not just Patrina Peters's Lower Ninth Ward but vast stretches of the newly developed eastern New Orleans. And Betsy had been by no means a direct hit. The storm had trekked some seventy miles west of the city, west even of Baton Rouge. Camille, in 1969, plowed ashore about the same distance to the east of the city to make landfall near Gulfport, neatly erasing whole swaths of beachfront villas at Pass Christian, a summer retreat that had been favored by New Orleans gentry for a century or more. An entire apartment building at the Pass, the Richelieu, had vanished, along with a group of diehards who had stocked booze and decks of cards to ride out the storm. One family, that of a prosperous shipping executive, would never forget the post-storm sight of their place along the coast road at Pass Christian. Camille had left behind the slab—but only the slab—on which their spacious house had once stood, rather like a dance floor or roller-skating rink dropped from the sky into a tangle of brush and broken trees. Otherwise, about the only trace of their former retreat ever found was a chandelier, a memento of a time when they had lived in Germany. It fetched up in the sand-filled swimming pool to the rear of the house.

Camille was a top-of-the-chart Category 5 storm, meaning that it packed winds above 155 miles per hour as it made landfall. An hour's worth of the howling winds of a Category 5 storm, one scientist calculated, is equivalent in force to five atomic bombs of the size dropped on Hiroshima. Another measure of Camille's strength was this: Hurricanes feed on water, and as they hit coastal shoals, they ordinarily begin to wither and die. Betsy, for example, had weakened to Category 3 strength, with winds between 111 and 130 mph, by the time she made landfall at Grand Isle, about seventy miles south of the city, and began moving to the northwest. Flooding aside, Betsy at seventy miles' distance was still strong enough to rip off roofing throughout much of New Orleans. But Camille, two categories stronger as she came ashore, was still carrying enough water to cause record-breaking rains and flooding when she petered out on the far side of the Appalachians, hundreds of miles later. Betsy, though weaker than Camille, had been more destructive to New Orleans because the city lay on the eastern edge of the storm's circular wind pattern, invariably the more violent side of the giant counterclockwise centrifuge of wind and water that is a hurricane.

On Saturday, as Katrina bore down on southeast Louisiana, the emergency director in Jefferson Parish, the suburb just to the west of New Orleans, neatly wrapped up forty years of storm lore and tied a ribbon around it. Katrina, Walter Maestri said, was as strong as Camille and on the same track as Betsy.

TWO

When Wallyworld Closes at Four

T HERE ARE SEVERAL STEPS IN A STORM-PREP RITUAL AT LEAST AS OLD AS indoor plumbing: Fill the tub so you'll have water when electricity fails and the city's treatment plant shuts down; check flashlights and battery-powered radios; bundle important papers and financial documents and family snapshots into plastic bins and haul them to the second floor or, in its absence, the attic; gas up the car in case you decide to flee the city after all; keep a hatchet handy in case you don't—you'll need it if rising waters chase you into your attic and you have to hack your way out through the roof (assuming you still have one).

Ivor van Heerden had another pre-storm task to attend to, his boat. Years earlier, he had sailed it halfway around the world from his native South Africa, a journey interrupted by a job offer that eventually led to his current role as deputy director of the Hurricane Center at Louisiana State University in Baton Rouge. Summer was normally academia's off-season. Not so for van Heerden, a youthful-looking, tousle-haired fifty-five-year-old given to chino slacks and—the sailor in him—Top-Siders. Every storm was a source of fascination, a chance to measure the precision of his computer models against the reality of a pending cyclone and, as necessary, warn those in its path. By four AM on the Saturday before Katrina struck, there was no doubt that Katrina was a monster, but it remained possible, if everything went right, that the storm's greatest toll might be on the professional reputations of storm trackers, a competitive bunch.

And so, just ahead of dawn that morning, van Heerden checked his projections for the umpteenth time and issued advisory number sixteen. Weighing wind and storm surge against tide levels and the elevation of adjacent land, van Heerden had anticipated that Katrina would hit southeast Louisiana as a Category 3 hurricane and push the water in Lake Pontchartrain ten to eleven feet higher. Wave action might slosh over the tops of the levees, but they should otherwise be adequate to their task, van Heerden surmised. The levees, after all, rose fourteen feet above the lake's normal level. And the storm's rain component did not look to be apocalyptic. The combination of overtopping and precipitation would make for street flooding. The question then would be how fast that water could be sucked through the city's massive pumping stations, assuming they remained powered, and into the drainage canals that carried it back into the lake. That was the essence of the city's flood defense—levees to keep the water out and pumps to mop the over-the-top surge when the levees came up short. That assumed, of course, the levees did not break, but they had been built to exacting specifications under the supervision of the Army Corps of Engineers, widely regarded, and not just by themselves, as the best levee builders in the world.

Calculations complete, state authorities and fellow professionals duly notified, van Heerden hopped in a car and made the one-hour drive from Baton Rouge south to Madisonville, a self-consciously quaint village and marina on the north shore of Lake Pontchartrain at the mouth of the Tchefuncte River. Van Heerden wanted to get his sailboat out of Madisonville and up the Tchefuncte to a more sheltered mooring. In the process he would have a chance to supplement his storm projections with some additional data: water levels, as indicated on gauges he had tucked in among the brush and reeds here and there along the shoreline near Madisonville. He shared his data by cell phone with Mark Schleifstein at *The Times-Picayune* in time for it to infuse Schleifstein's page-one hurricane coverage in the Sunday paper. There was reason to expect even the lake's western half, the part farthest from the open Gulf, to rise dangerously. Then van Heerden went back to Baton Rouge, where he watched in growing alarm as the storm intensified. To judge from the tracks developed by forecasters all around the world and amalgamated into a spaghetti-like composite on the ever-handy hurricanealley.net website, Katrina was bearing down more and more surely on the New Orleans area.

Late that night, van Heerden completed two new computer runs—numbers seventeen and eighteen. Some level of flooding looked to be a certainty by then. The levees would be overtopped significantly, and the force of the water would contribute to "scouring," an erosion of the levee's land-side banks that, in a worst-case scenario, could lead to an outright breach. In any event, the pumping stations would need to stay at full-bore to keep ahead of the water spilling over the city's levees and into the bowl-like city.

After issuing the late advisories, at eleven PM, van Heerden ordered the Hurricane Center's staff of five to go home, and not without gassing up their cars on the way in case the storm moved a notch westward and Baton Rouge needed to evacuate. Van Heerden stayed on to play with a last couple of computer models. In one, he moved the storm's projected path to the western edge of the range—or "cone"—of possible landfalls. That put it in St. Mary Parish—Cajun country, more or less where Hurricane Andrew had made landfall to devastating effect in 1992. (Andrew, like Katrina, had swept across southern Florida before reforming itself in the Gulf and charging at Louisiana.)

From every angle, the results looked ominous, as van Heerden did not hesitate to tell the reporters now besieging the Hurricane Center with calls. The call van Heerden truly wished he'd get was from New Orleans mayor Ray Nagin. It appalled the scientist that Nagin still hadn't made his evacuation order mandatory. A call that did come through was from the Centers for Disease Control and Prevention in Atlanta. They had seen enough of van Heerden's projections to know that there could be severe health consequences from the anticipated level of flooding. Van Heerden agreed to participate in a conference call the next morning. Meanwhile, CDC wanted a favor: access to some of the GIS (Geographic Information Systems) data about New Orleans that van Heerden and his people had accumulated. It would help CDC anticipate likely flooding depths. Permission was readily granted. Next it was someone from the Department of Health and Hospitals seeking similar data. "So at least two agencies were getting their acts together," van Heerden said to himself.

BY MIDDAY SATURDAY, GROCERY SHELVES BEGAN TO BE DENUDED OF BOTTLED water and bread and nuts and fruit. Plywood seemed to fly out of the big building supply stores, but boarding up windows was not a universal enthusiasm, and hammering was scattered and intermittent in neighborhoods and commercial areas across the city. More commonly, homeowners taped windowpanes and sliding glass doors with an X-pattern on the assumption (largely discredited) that this would keep them from shattering. If taping was more superstitious than practical, like a hex sign on an Amish barn, it was ubiquitous. The hyperalert and the merely lazy were alike in already having marked their windows—the former because the hurricane season lasted from June through November, and here it was only the end of August; the latter because they hadn't gotten around to removing the tape from the city's last close encounter with rough weather, Hurricane Dennis, not so many weeks earlier.

The transition from concern to alarm had been sudden. A housing consultant named Raymond Breaux had been on his way to a Saturday morning funeral when a cell phone call from his wife snapped him to attention. The storm had reneged on its eastward shift, she said. The projected track once again fell right across New Orleans, with a landfall expected early Monday.

"I said, 'What!' " Breaux recalled, and the couple fell to planning an evacuation. But should it be to the east (Atlanta) or the west (Austin)? It was a decision requiring a blind guess at Katrina's eventual landfall, and it was only complicated by Breaux's mother, a frail ninety-two-year-old he would need to bring along.

His basic instinct was right. In the face of an onrushing hurricane, even the most elaborately stocked hurricane kit could not hold a candle to the best advice of all: Get out. Get out early and plan to stay away awhile. But in a city like New Orleans—an island, in essence, connected to the mainland by only four highways of any consequence—evacuation was more easily imagined than executed. And by early afternoon that Saturday, the highways were already starting to clog.

For years, New Orleans had talked itself into sitting tight through hurricanes by muttering that mass evacuation wasn't really possible. And it wasn't, not in the days when ferry service was the only way across the Mississippi or Lake Pontchartrain, and Interstate 10 had yet to link the city with dry land beyond the swamps to the west and east. And in the 1970s and '80s, after the river and the lake were bridged and the interstate went through, New Orleans still yielded to inertia. Even if highway traffic could somehow be kept from grinding immediately to a standstill during an evacuation, there were just a whole lot of New Orleanians too poor (or too sick or too aged) to fend for themselves, the thinking went. As the twentieth century gave way to a new millennium, there was still ample evidence to support this notion, including the census bureau's calculation that one out of every three New Orleanians had no car. The city's high poverty rate was one explanation, but the lack of cars also said something about the insular self-contentment of a city that, in a long lifetime, some of its residents never left for much more than a weekend away.

In recent years, the evacuation challenge had been addressed in a traffic-management concept called "contraflow." The idea was a simple one: for purposes of an evacuation, make the interstate and the causeway across Lake Pontchartrain one-way roads, with all lanes outbound from the city. Contraflow could be imposed all the way to Baton Rouge, for those fleeing west. And for those heading east or north into Mississippi and beyond, Interstates 10, 55, and 59 could also be made one-way.

Contraflow had been put to its first serious test a year earlier for Hurricane Ivan, and its failure had been massive and infuriating. State and local police had neglected to coordinate the conversion points, and motorists found themselves breezing onto contraflow lanes in Jefferson Parish only to have the interstate revert to two-way traffic flow and become a giant parking lot not so many miles up the road. Vehicles overheated and caught fire. Cars were temporarily abandoned, and traffic slowed further as men and women ran into the underbrush to relieve themselves. And who could blame them? The drive to Baton Rouge, usually ninety minutes, had become a day-long ordeal.

As a new governor, Blanco had inherited the contraflow plan that misfired so badly during Ivan, and she was adamant that it would work right this time. She had been on the phone with Mississippi governor Haley Barbour as early as Friday night to alert him of her intention to implement it. In rethinking the procedure, her people had come up with a phased-in parish-by-parish approach. When the governor gave the go-ahead, the coastal and downriver communities should leave first, it was decided. They were more seriously imperiled by storm surge and high winds. And if they didn't leave first, they might take to the highways only to be stuck in place behind the far larger throng of people fleeing the population centers of Orleans and Jefferson parishes. At any rate, that was how it was supposed to work under a regional plan the parishes signed off on. But regional thinking had never been much in vogue in the New Orleans area. Indeed, leaders in suburban parishes rather enjoyed scuttling tentative moves toward regionalism, the coded message being that regionalism was the hobbyhorse of the New Orleans (that is, black) political establishment, and that any changes that redounded to New Orleans's advantage would necessarily come at the expense of the people who, for a variety of reasons, had chosen to bail out of the city.

Whatever the motive, Blanco's redesigned and streamlined regional evacuation plan had collapsed quickly if harmlessly a month earlier, when Jefferson Parish, and Jefferson Parish alone, had decided that Dennis was too grave a threat to allow for any temporizing or cooperation. Without the governor's authorization, Jefferson Parish president Aaron Broussard had ordered an evacuation even before Orleans, let alone the truly imperiled communities farther downriver. If the predicted traffic jams did not immediately ensue, it was only because Orleans and the downriver parishes never found a good reason to order any evacuation at all. Amid ribald jokes about his "premature evacuation" problem, Broussard was rebuked, and vowed to do better. But as events would demonstrate, public ridicule did not permanently cure the man of a tendency to unseemly panic, followed by a histrionic defense of what he had done.

Dealing off the opposite end of the deck as Katrina approached, New Orleans mayor Ray Nagin sought to present himself as a study in cautious restraint when it came to pulling the trigger and making the evacuation order mandatory. By midday Saturday, after the meeting with his emergency operations people, Nagin was still inclined to hold off. There were reasons for his hesitation aside from a desire to leave the role of Chicken Little to Aaron Broussard. Mandating an evacuation carried legal implications and potentially heavy financial penalties if, for example, the big hotels and hospitals were forced to empty out, and they then sued the city because the storm went somewhere else. This was a mercenary consideration that Nagin at first admitted had been among his concerns but later, hauled before Congress in Katrina's aftermath, saw fit to disown.

In coming days, there would be an effort by FEMA officials to portray Blanco and Nagin as hopelessly at odds—a dysfunctional dyad at the heart of Louisiana politics. In fact, they had recovered reasonably well from a rocky start. Though both were centrist Democrats, in the governor's race Nagin had extended an unbroken record of endorsing candidates who went on to lose by backing Bobby Jindal, a boyish Republican whiz kid who had run the state's university and health systems. And there were other differences as wide as the Cajun prairies that separated where Blanco had grown up, in white rural poverty, from Nagin's black big-city boyhood. Tall and bald with a taste that ran to well-tailored suits in gray or black, Nagin had made his way as a corporate manager for the local cable TV franchise (Cox) before bursting onto the political scene as a reform-minded pro-business candidate. In 2002, in his first try for political office, he won the mayor's race.

Blanco, though prim and grandmotherly in demeanor, was the political pro, notwithstanding her pixie-ish haircut and burbly speaking voice. One of seven children of a vacuum-cleaner salesman turned carpet cleaner and tax collector in New Iberia, a Cajun town near the state's southern coast, Kathleen Babineaux taught school briefly before marriage to Coach Blanco turned her into a full-time mother with a brood that soon numbered six. After fourteen years at home, she took a job as district manager for the census bureau, and parlayed skills honed in door-to-door surveys by founding a small political consulting and polling firm in 1979.

Two years later she was her own client, in a race for the state house of representatives. She won, as she did every race over the next twenty years. By the 1990s the contests were for statewide offices. Blanco served as lieutenant governor under a conservative south Louisiana millionaire, Mike Foster, grandson of the governor Foster who had ruled Louisiana when the Supreme Court's *Plessy v. Ferguson* decision brought on the era of Jim Crow and legalized segregation. There had always been some question as to whether the political genius behind the Blanco juggernaut was Coach or his candidate bride, but there was no doubt their combined instincts were shrewd. After determining that U.S. senator John Breaux, a fellow Cajun and Democrat, was not running for governor, as had been rumored, Blanco took the plunge in 2003, artfully stealing the Democratic primary from two front-running white candidates who she assumed, correctly, would split the black vote. And in the runoff, with reconsolidated support from African Americans, she eased past Jindal, denying his bid to become the first U.S. governor who could trace his ancestry to India. (Within a year, Jindal had run successfully for Congress from a district centered in suburban Jefferson Parish.)

Blanco could not order Nagin to make his evacuation order mandatory, but she could coax. They were not close, but they had established a working relationship and Blanco was impelled by concerns graver than politics as she stood Saturday with Broussard for a press conference exhorting folk to flee the city, and then traveled over into Orleans Parish to do the same with Nagin. As far as Coach could determine, it was the first time a governor had ever come down to New Orleans on the eve of a hurricane and been that active in mobilizing an evacuation. Go door-to-door, she urged, looking into the TV cameras. Alert your neighbors, get them moving. Pack as if you're going on a three-day camping trip and there won't be a corner store for a hundred miles: food, water, clothes, toys for the kids.

And then there was nothing to do that Saturday but hold her breath and hope the contraflow would work this time. At four PM she gave the high sign. State police diverted cars and trucks still flowing into New Orleans, threaded plastic guardrails across the median strip, and directed them to cross over. Immediately the pent-up outbound traffic flooded all eight lanes in the widest parts of Interstate 10 through Orleans and Jefferson parishes. Congestion eased, and, for those who chose to avail themselves of it, the region's first successful contraflow was under way.

The smoothly flowing traffic was at first deceptive. If the cars were moving well, it was in part because there weren't enough of them. For all

Blanco's alarums and excursions, the word wasn't getting out there, or if it was, it wasn't sinking in. When a New Orleans state representative named Cedric Richmond called Baton Rouge to report that a throng of seven hundred had been merrily hooting and hollering at a local ballpark he'd visited that afternoon, Blanco got an aide named Johnny Anderson to begin calling African American ministers and urging them to mix an evacuation message in with their Sunday morning sermons: "Pack and pray."

She also had to find a way to get Nagin to make his order mandatory, and with help from Max Mayfield, head of the National Hurricane Center, she did. Nagin was eating a Saturday night supper with his wife and seven-year-old daughter when Mayfield got through to him by phone and in unvarnished terms told the mayor that this was it, the Big One, a storm with devastating wind power and surges that might well overtop some of the levees. The following morning, with Blanco again at his side, Nagin would make the evacuation mandatory. "Max scared the crap out of me," Nagin would later confide.

A VERY PREGNANT KATY RECKDAHL HAD OTHER THINGS ON HER MIND. "I LOOK like a Macy's parade float," she thought as she made her way on foot Saturday evening from her apartment to Matassa's, a French Quarter grocery store at Dauphine and St. Philip. Brothers John and Louis Matassa carried on the business their father, Cosimo, had never managed to escape, even after redefining midfifties rock and roll with single-mike recordings of rising legends that included Little Richard, Ernie K. Doe, Jerry Lee Lewis, and Fats Domino. The baby was due any day, Reckdahl told the Matassas. Any hour, maybe.

With Katrina coming, Reckdahl's doctor hoped she could hold off. You didn't want to be in a hospital when a hurricane struck. They tended to evacuate hospitals. And if a hospital was no fun, being stuck on a bus with a lot of ailing people was even less fun. Should she evacuate ahead of time? It might be too late for that, her doctor warned. What if she got stuck in some horrendous traffic jam and went into labor right there. Anyway, her partner in life, a trumpeter with the Treme Brass Band named Mervin Campbell, "Kid Merv" to his fans, had a gig that night. "Screw this evacuation stuff,"

Reckdahl would remember thinking. "We'll stick it out." She was leaving Matassa's with a Popsicle when she felt her contractions get suddenly serious. A friend drove her to the hospital.

IT DIDN'T TAKE AN IMPENDING BIRTH TO DISSUADE A LOT OF NEW ORLEANIANS from blowing town ahead of a hurricane, no matter how great the mayor's sense of alarm. For some it was a matter of protecting the house—from looters, if it came to that, more likely from undue damage if a window shattered or water started streaming through the roof, and buckets needed to be set out to catch it. For others, especially the poor and those without cars, evacuation was a daunting logistical challenge. But a lot of it was tradition. For all the fancy-pants forecasters on TV and the radio, no one really knew just what would happen, what confluence of meteorological factors would converge in the final few hours before landfall. And where science fell short, faith deserved respect. For some it was a faith in the divine, for others a faith in precedent. Storm survivors, like military generals, were forever doomed to relive their last great battle, and for many New Orleanians that battle had been Betsy, just as for Gulf Coast residents, now equally in Katrina's shifty eye, it had been Camille. They had survived those storms, they would survive Katrina, and they would survive at home, assuming home was a place that hadn't flooded or been blown away during Betsy or Camille.

Linda Usdin, a woman of reason as well as purpose, had survived both storms and was not one to quickly evacuate a city now only more heavily reinforced against floods than it had been in the 1960s. Poverty may have trapped some New Orleanians in a hurricane's path—particularly those waiting to replenish the household till with the first-of-the-month Social Security and disability checks they would need to get much distance from an end-of-the-month storm like Katrina. But many well-to-do folk were also inclined by long tradition to ride out storms at home. The Usdins were not the evacuating type, and in that regard they were typical of more than a few Uptown patricians. Linda's great-grandfather had made a fortune in coffee. Her father had retired as an eminent psychiatrist, and her sister had married a psychologist; her brothers were accomplished lawyers. A tall black-haired woman in her fifties, devoted to yoga, Usdin had earned a doctorate in public health at Tulane and was a consultant to foundations—Ford, Annie E. Casey—active in New Orleans community renewal. Her husband, Steven Bingler, was a community planner and architect with a national reputation for building schoolhouses that could serve double duty, as community and civic centers, museums, and the like.

You could not say Usdin was stupid or that, like many of the bedraggled souls seen on worldwide television staggering out of the Superdome days later, she lacked the wherewithal to get out of town. And yet, late into Saturday afternoon, she was among the substantial number of New Orleanians who intended to stay. Bingler was of a different persuasion, and it made for a bit of a clash. He had lived in New Orleans for decades, but he hadn't been born there and neither had he been born to wealth. A self-made man, perhaps he was less trusting of the old guard and their curious faith in the way things had always been handled, hurricanes included. In any case, he wanted out, if not for himself, then for their young daughters, Anya and Josephine, fifteen and twelve.

By nightfall, Usdin relented. This really did look like a bad storm. They would leave in the morning. Late Sunday they reached Houston, not without incident. En route, Bingler had been reaching for a ringing cell phone, the device on which he spent much of his day, in good weather or bad, when he rear-ended the car ahead. The air bags exploded from the dashboard. Houston would be the first stop on an odyssey that would take them city hopping all the way to New York.

An opposite marital dynamic prevailed in the home—a place to be proud of, right on the Lake Pontchartrain waterfront, in suburban Slidell—shared by newlyweds Thomas Yee and Thu Huynh-Yee. Yee, whose family operated the South China Seas restaurant in Slidell, a bedroom community about a half hour from downtown New Orleans, had no intention of leaving, though his parents already had. His wife wasn't one to take that chance. Yes, evacuation was disruptive, but so was life itself, from the perspective of a family that had fled Vietnam in 1976, when she was an infant, and arrived in New Orleans two years later. Yee was making good money as a chef in the family restaurant. His wife was a fast-rising branch manager with Chase in New Orleans. Their marriage, a year earlier in an elaborate function hall across the Mississippi from downtown New Orleans, had balanced Vietnamese tradition against emblems of the more materialistic American world in which they were making their way.

With Katrina in the offing, the old order swiftly reasserted itself. On Saturday, Thu's parents showed up at her home in Slidell, uncertain whether they were en route to a storm shelter or had just found one, thanks very much. And by day's end, with the arrival of another dozen cousins and siblings, they were a household of sixteen. If Thu had ever seen safety in numbers, one night of it was enough. On Sunday morning, she laid down the law. Thomas could stay behind if he insisted on it, but she was leaving and taking her family with her. Yee ceased to insist. At midday Sunday, the couple bundled Thu's mother into their Honda Pilot and her father into another daughter's car and, with a third car in the caravan, made the unorthodox decision to head east, toward Florida. There would be less traffic, less likelihood of becoming instantly snarled in the epic march of cars and vans and trucks streaming toward Texas. But of course there was a reason why the westward route was so favored: Katrina could always jog east again, in which case the Yees would find a hurricane chasing them as they made their run for the Florida line in search of Thomas's parents, said to have holed up in Tallahassee.

BEFORE LEAVING THAT SATURDAY AFTERNOON, LINDA USDIN HAD BEEN ON THE phone with a woman both she and Steven knew through their work, Saundra Reed. Usdin had been concerned about Saundra, the fifty-something matriarch of a goodly clan, with a decent job as a state social worker but, like many members of the black middle class, not without her share of burdens and challenges, among them a daughter on dialysis and a grandmother who was now in her nineties and fully in the grip of Alzheimer's. When Usdin offered her country place as a refuge, Reed accepted immediately, and by three AM Sunday morning, three of the countless vehicles toiling north on Interstate 59 toward higher ground in Mississippi would be carrying Reed and a dozen of her kin. They spanned no fewer than five generations. There was Big Mama, Reed's grandmother, more firmly in touch with the events of fifty years ago than with anything going on around her in the car. Big Mama was in the care of her only daughter, Reed's mother, Whilda, a spry seventy-five.

Reed's sister was aboard, a fifty-five-year-old nurse named Yeolonda, as were Yeolonda's three kids, one of whom had a wife and two sons with him. Reed's two children would round out the entourage, along with Bridgette, now fifteen, the granddaughter that Reed's son Aaron had given her before his early death. Oh, yes, and three dogs.

"When the family moves, we move en masse," Reed would remark, in reflecting back on Katrina.

They also lived en masse, the younger three generations anyway, almost like a kibbutz or commune in Central City, a low-income and crime-plagued part of New Orleans, not far from downtown. Central City was Reed's home; it was also her workplace as a community organizer. The sisters, Saundra and Yeolonda, lived right next door to each other on Baronne Street, between Third and Fourth, Saundra in a shotgun double that had been converted into a single-family residence, Yeolonda in a big, old two-story structure that had seen service, variously, as a brothel and a boarding house before she took it over.

Katrina bore watching, the sisters both knew, only more so with Big Mama to look after. You needed to get a jump on an evacuation, if it came to that, but well into Saturday they had sincerely hoped it wouldn't. A year earlier they had fled Hurricane Ivan, and it had been a nightmare: twenty-three hours on the road to Lake Charles, a trip that usually takes less than four hours. But by late in the week before Katrina struck, the possibility that they would have to leave again had begun to crop up more and more regularly in the collective conversation that was family life on Baronne Street.

"We have an unwritten routine," Reed said. "It's kind of like Christmas dinner: Everyone knows it's going to happen. Whoever gets a good idea, you notify the family."

The first idea was vertical evacuation, to a multi-story motel in eastern New Orleans. They had reserved three rooms when Yeolonda's oldest son, Whitman, put the kibosh on it. If it floods, the East lies even lower than Baronne Street, he warned. And then Linda Usdin had called, a white woman with a weekend retreat in Poplarville, Mississippi, a mere seventy miles up the road but a good few hundred feet in elevation. That would be perfect. They had been up there as guests, and loved the place. The lingering question was when to go. A consensus formed around leaving Sunday morning, after church. That left the rest of Saturday afternoon to stock up on food.

Reed's clan met the challenge with the recommended mix of urgency and merriment. "We were in a festive mood," Reed said of the group that set out for the Wal-Mart Supercenter over by the river, an outlet that had gone up on the site of a former housing project after a savage clash among preservationists, developers, and advocates for the displaced poor. "Everyone was going to bring what they wanted," Saundra said of their preflight shopping spree. "I took on the job of making sure we had enough." Hurricane food, she went on, is like picnic food: grapes, cookies, chips, cold cuts. "You also want to have cards, dominos, board games, flashlights, candles, and matches. We were going to buy great steaks and anything that could be grilled."

To their astonishment, the round-the-clock supercenter was closed. "That put me on high alert," Reed said. "Something's really wrong when Wallyworld closes at four on Saturday." Instead, they bought what they could at a smaller store and figured they'd get the rest in Poplarville.

Back on Baronne, they began monitoring the news nonstop. Suddenly the mayor was strongly encouraging a mass exodus. He was putting his family on a plane for Dallas the very next day, Nagin said, and he just might decide at that time to make the evacuation mandatory. They showed him on television with his police chief, Eddie Compass. The police were ready, Compass said; they'd be positioned around town to assist those seeking to leave, and some of the officers, Compass advised, would be stationed at supermarkets just in case anybody decided to help themselves in the anarchic interlude that always seemed to lie between a passing storm and the restoration of power, both the electrical kind and the civil kind.

There was some comfort in hearing Nagin's plans for his family. His decision to wait until Sunday backed their own timetable, Reed thought. If the mayor could wait a day, so could they. But by nightfall, she started to get scared. The mayor's wife would be flying. They would be earthbound. They had to get out and get out fast, she feared, if they were not to be snared in evacuation gridlock.

Midnight came and went, and still they weren't ready. Two hours later, they picked up Big Mama and Whilda at their home in the Gentilly district and were on the road, tailgating one another. They had timed their escape well. The outbound interstate was busier than it otherwise would have been but, thanks to contraflow, not jammed. They cruised along at 50 to 60 mph the whole way, the windows down on the Olds, Reed's car, because the air conditioner was busted.

By dawn's light, they saw that the borrowed weekend place was just as they remembered it: towering oaks and Southern pines, a big pond for Whitman's little boys to fish come sunup. And fish they did, hauling in a mess of bream and bass big enough to make a festive Sunday night dinner for thirteen. What they didn't yet realize—indeed what no scientist could have predicted with certainty—was that they had evacuated to what would soon be the very eye of the storm.

JAMES NOLAN, A WRITER AND FRENCH QUARTER RESIDENT, ALSO MADE A POINT of dining well that Sunday night, or as well as could be arranged. Nolan was a Camille survivor. You could say he was born to survive storms, his advent on the planet having occurred at the Catholic hospital Hotel Dieu, in the very teeth of the tumultuous but otherwise unnamed Hurricane of 1947. Elegant, intellectual, with an unthinned mane of reddish blond hair, Jimmy Nolan would be damned if he was going to evacuate for Katrina. Besides, friends were due for dinner: Claudia Copeland, a microbiologist, and her fiancé, José Torres Tama, a performance artist. Claudia and José would not let him down, not like Claudia's friends had let her down the night before. A blowout had been scheduled for Saturday, to celebrate the doctorate in microbiology that Tulane at long last had bestowed upon her. So many people had canceled because of the storm that Claudia was left with an untouched cake. Bring it along, Nolan urged. And so, with a bottle of Torres Diez cognac the cake capped off a meal that had begun with gazpacho and moved on to red beans and rice as only Jimmy Nolan knew how to prepare them.

AFTER HIS SATURDAY NIGHT GIG, KID MERV CAMPBELL HAD JOINED KATY Reckdahl on the obstetrics floor at Touro, a big private hospital a few blocks from the point where St. Charles crosses Louisiana Avenue, and the Garden District shades over into the larger, more amorphous district called Uptown. And at 4:13 AM, as his trumpeter father looked on, little Mervin Hector

Campbell, a vocalist, made his squalling New Orleans debut. Within hours, nurses were wheeling maternity ward beds, Reckdahl's among them, out into the hospital corridors to avoid the risk of shattering glass as Katrina blew out windows. And not long after that, as the citywide power failure outlasted the fuel supply for Touro's five generators, Reckdahl and Campbell found themselves in a blacked-out hospital, trying, in the pitch dark, to poke a mother's nipple into the baby's mouth so that Hector could begin nursing. Campbell had an idea. He lit up his cell phone screen. By its faint greenish light, the necessary connection was made, and Hector took it from there.

ELSEWHERE ACROSS TOWN, A MAN NAMED HENRY SHERROD HAD HUNKERED down to ride out the storm, a bit less joyfully. Sherrod expected to begin celebrations of another sort the following Sunday, upon his release from Orleans Parish Prison on a child support rap. The sentence had begun August third when, acting as his own attorney, he had failed to convince Judge Paulette Irons that he was not $1,300 behind in support payments to the mother of his firstborn. Pay stubs from his job at a west bank pawnshop showed that he was being garnisheed to the tune of $351 per month, Sherrod insisted, but Irons required that he come up with another $500 by the close of business that very day, and when Sherrod couldn't, he was packed off to jail for a month. Without explanation, the prison had cut off inmate phone service the previous Thursday, and so Sherrod and others on his tier spent the weekend out of touch with families and free-world contacts of any other kind. Indeed, the guards themselves had seemed strangely scarce. As the men gathered in the dayroom to watch TV news about the gathering storm, they could hear the roar and whine of trucks and cars fleeing on the interstate that bounded the western border of the sprawling prison complex.

Baton Rouge would get the biggest contingent. Others pressed on to Lafayette—the Cajun capital, a low-lying town frequently ravaged by hurricanes that came ashore in the state's midsection, but this time seemingly well wide of Katrina's path. Many evacuees did not stop short of the Texas line, some to lose themselves in the anonymity of Houston or Dallas. Others pressed on to Austin, the hill country, appealing not just because of the climb up off the broad coastal plain but because, especially for musicians, it had some of the feel of a second home. Cyril Neville of the Neville Brothers made it to Austin and was joined by Aaron. George Porter Jr., the bass player and guiding light of the Meters made plans to join them. Famed bluesman Clarence "Gatemouth" Brown made it as far as Dallas, where death would overtake him not many days later.

SEAN CUMMINGS—LEATHER-JACKETED, STUBBLE-FACED: THE VERY MODEL OF boutique-hotel chic—almost stayed behind, as did his father, one of the richer trial attorneys in a city crawling with that breed. Hurricanes could be good business for Sean Cummings's hotel. There was a venerable tradition of coming into the central business district from residential neighborhoods Uptown or out near the lake. Pack a suitcase with clothes enough to ride out a storm; bring a flashlight, a good thriller, a deck of cards. The bar business tended to pick up smartly on such evenings. There was a sense of safety in a big hotel, safety in the massiveness of the structure. Perhaps also a sense of safety in sheer numbers. If it got really bad, you weren't alone, and if you weren't alone, well, then maybe you'd see a faster response from emergency workers if the electric power went out or the streets took on a bit of water.

Cummings was enough of a New Orleanian to be skeptical of the direst predictions about hurricanes, and enough of an entrepreneur to see no point in not making what he could off bad weather. He admitted it: He had been lulled by good luck, by the way the hurricanes always seemed to hook east at the last minute, toward Biloxi or Mobile, the ones that didn't glide west and smash Morgan City. It was his general manager, one of the few female general managers in New Orleans's highly competitive hotel industry, who drew the line at Katrina. Amy Rimer had a bad feeling about this one. She didn't want a bunch of people to be riding out Katrina at the International House, a Camp Street operation of one hundred forty rooms. No more reservations would be taken, and it also meant clearing out the guests still there. On Saturday, Cummings and his staff began helping their clientele rustle up tickets, and then packed them off to the airport. By early afternoon on Sunday, the last of the guests were gone and Cummings was satisfied that all eighty of the hotel's employees also had headed home or to evacuation destinations far from the city. Now he could leave as well, and he did so, still bugged by the possibility that Amy's pessimism about the storm had need-lessly cost him a good few grand in lost bookings.

They were quite a caravan: Cummings in his Porsche; his father, John Cummings, in a hulking Ford 350 pickup that obscured his stature as a mul-timillionaire plaintiff's attorney and, with three thousand acres of undevel-oped land in eastern New Orleans, the city's biggest property owner. Sean had a buddy, Michael Miller, along for the ride. Amy, the hotel GM, was in the entourage, as was Kelly, another assistant to Cummings, in her Jeep—no doors on the vehicle, "but she did manage to save her surfboard," Cummings would note dryly.

Cummings, ever the contrarian, decided against heading west. Everyone was heading west. He throttled the Porsche east on Interstate 10 only to grind almost immediately to a halt. Ten hours later, the group had reached the seventy-mile mark on Interstate 59: Poplarville. A pine stand and a few mown fields were all that separated the stream of traffic from the borrowed cottage in which Saundra Reed and her family had holed up and were frying the fish her sister's grandsons had pulled out of the pond earlier that day.

Within another hour or two, the traffic had begun to fade, but so had the Cummings motorcade's fuel supply, and lines at the gas stations they passed were already beginning to lengthen. John Cummings, feeling, as he would recall, a bit like Big Daddy in *Cat on a Hot Tin Roof,* was running out of op-tions. The Ford 350 was about to guzzle its last few drops of gas when he pulled into a station near the Alabama line, with eight to ten cars backed up at every pump—save one. Cummings strode inside and would remember being struck by how completely the shelves in the station's convenience store had been picked clean—like locusts had passed. On inquiry, the station manager explained the unused pump. It was not broken; he was saving a last tank for his regulars, who'd come by in the morning. He figured the evacuees would drain the other tanks well before dawn. Cummings showed a number of greenbacks. The amount is known only to him, the station owner, and, of course, the IRS, but it was sufficient to make Cummings an instant regular. In whispered conversation with his son and others in their group, he advised that they ease on over to the freshly activated pump, saying nothing. Who knew what a group of panicky motorists might do in the wilds of Alabama if they saw a bunch of Louisiana license tags and needed to take justice into their own hands. The Cummings vehicles were all but gassed up when two other customers let it be known that they had been waiting longer than these interlopers. Cummings saw wisdom in letting their two trucks cut into his line. He did better than that. He stuck his credit card into the slot and urged both drivers to fill their tanks. And then he and his son and their associates got the hell out of there.

WITHIN TWENTY-FOUR HOURS, MOBILE SIGNBOARDS WOULD GO UP AT KEY JUNCtions across the interstate system that converged on southeast Louisiana, the lettering picked out in flashing amber dots against a black background: NEW ORLEANS EXITS CLOSED. Blink. NEW ORLEANS EXITS CLOSED—and suddenly, a name once evocative of elegance and devil-may-care good times, a haven of sophistication in the hardscrabble South, carried overtones of catastrophe: a Babylon, a Chernobyl. Blink. NEW ORLEANS EXITS CLOSED.

—— ⚜ ——

THREE

An Imperfect Storm

K ATRINA MADE LANDFALL AT 6:10 AM MONDAY MORNING AT BURAS, ERAS-ing that fishing hamlet near the mouth of the Mississippi. The town's most prominent feature, its water tower: gone. The levees that had offered at least brief resistance to the gathering surge: gone. Housing was reduced to splintered debris, as were the workboats and pleasure craft that had been the town's lifeblood.

A few miles away, at Empire, flotsam washed up against the lower reaches of the bridge that carried road traffic up and over the Empire Canal, high enough for seagoing spars to pass under. From the air, days later, the sizable island of this debris left behind after the waters retreated, looked like the usual shoreline mix of shattered timbers, trees, and unmoored buoys, with a tangle of seaweed thrown in. On inspection at closer range, the flotsam revealed itself to be not planking and telephone poles, but Empire's shrimp fleet: dozens of trawlers, flipped over, knocked on their sides, and shrouded not with sodden leaves but with their own torn netting. All told, coastal Louisiana's losses in fishing workboats and trawlers would come close to three thousand vessels. Three hundred wrecked vessels would have been catastrophic. The loss of ten times that many was unimaginable. And these were not skiffs. A good-size Gulf shrimp boat could run to sixty feet. All told, the fishing industry would sustain $2.2 billion in losses due to Katrina, a substantial part of it from the pulverizing of thousands of acres of oyster beds, some of them forty and fifty years old. The good news was that the shrimp populations would substantially rebound by year's end. The bad news, for the men and women who depended on the harvest for a livelihood, was that the main reason for the comeback would be the lack of trawlers left to ply those waters.

Within a day or two of Katrina, the crew on a navy landing craft working its way up the river would be astonished by the sheer volume of dead animals floating toward the Gulf—cattle, alligators, horses—that and the silence. The crew decided to go ashore near Buras to look for survivors in need of the boat's cargo of food and water, but then the silence was broken. Packs of dogs rushed the landing party and drove it back aboard the vessel, Rodney Blackshear, the navigator, said.

The losses to the wetlands that buffered Louisiana from the sea were equally catastrophic and far more dangerous to human settlement. Wetlands tamed onrushing storm surge, skimming a foot off the crest of the surge for every 2.7 miles traversed. Within thirty-six hours, Katrina had erased thirty square miles of Louisiana's coastal marsh, or about what ordinarily was lost in a year. Nineteen hundred square miles were estimated to have been sheared from Louisiana's coast in the past century as a result of rising seas and the oil industry's rough use of the marshes during the wildcat era of the early 1900s.

Within an hour of landfall the storm was chasing its own winds and surge on a northerly tangent that swelled the waters of the two vast, shallow lakes that lay between the open Gulf and the marshy shores of St. Bernard and Orleans parishes. The surge pushed across Lake Maurepas and Lake Borgne and on through the narrow inlet, the Rigolets, that led to the biggest of the three lakes, Pontchartrain. Adjacent to Borgne, another wall of water shot into the Mississippi River Gulf Outlet, a shipping channel built forty years earlier as a shortcut from the Intracoastal Waterway to the open Gulf. As the channels narrowed against steeper levees on their approach to down-

town New Orleans, the surge sloshed higher and harder, bursting into the Industrial Canal with the force of a water cannon that, in short order, blew
down the concrete flood walls above the earthen levees, and sent a Niagara
of water thundering onto the streets and through the doors and windows and
cracks in the walls of the houses that Patrina Peters and her neighbors had
called home.

Elsewhere, altogether indifferent to waterways it so easily overwhelmed,
the surge knocked down miles of giant fifteen-foot levees as though they
were nothing more than the walls of a child's sand castle on the beach.
Within an hour or two, all of St. Bernard Parish, twenty-one hundred square
miles of land and marsh, was underwater, as was most of the long swampy
extension of the city called New Orleans East. On the north side of the city,
the lake levees held, but the surge forced its way into the three major
drainage canals that were intended not to guard against rising water in Lake
Pontchartrain but to provide an aqueduct for the riptide of water propelled
back into it by giant pumps struggling to keep the streets from filling up. The
rising water in those drainage canals shoved aside levees and the concrete
flood walls that had been added above them for an extra margin of protection, and water swept through the Lakeview neighborhood and on into Gentilly, until it backed up against the undamaged west wall of the Industrial
Canal.

It would never be known exactly how many people died. The best estimate placed the toll at about 1,100, with another 231 lost in Mississippi. Nor
was it clear what proportion of the casualties died immediately, leaving the
rest to a lingering demise—by drowning, from exposure, from medical conditions that worsened lethally as men, women, and children attempted to
wade or swim to dry ground, perched on rooftops awaiting help that never
came, or succumbed to infernal temperatures and dehydration in attics
where the floods had chased them.

COMPARING HURRICANE WIND SHEAR TO NUCLEAR WEAPONS, EVEN THE SMALL
ones unleashed at Hiroshima, seemed preposterous at first, like childish hyperbole. And then, as the interstates and secondary highways were cleared of
fallen trees and flipped semis, it became possible to venture out along the

Mississippi coast, past Waveland and Bay St. Louis and Pass Christian, through Gulfport and on to Biloxi. Nuclear fire may be very different from a hurricane, but Katrina, though less deadly than Hiroshima's atomic blast, had easily surpassed it in the breadth and furor of the devastation. Little Boy had delivered shock waves and an incinerating heat to an area confined to hundreds of city blocks. Katrina erased neighborhoods across hundreds of square miles and wrought destruction in a surrounding area the size of Great Britain, ninety thousand square miles, all told. It tossed around giant float-ing casinos like dice on a craps table, snapped two-hundred-foot-tall pine stands with the ease of a scythe passing through dried hay, collapsed a mil-lion-gallon oil storage tank in Chalmette as though it were a beer can under a frat boy's loafer.

The surge—twenty-seven feet high as it reared up out of the Gulf in Mississippi's coastal counties—swept six miles inland and twelve miles up bayous and rivers before falling back in an outflow nearly as violent as the initial tsunami. In the metropolitan area, mile after mile of what had been residential neighborhoods—Broadmoor, Lakeview, Gentilly, eastern New Orleans, the Ninth Ward, and on into Chalmette and Violet in St. Bernard Parish—was simply rooftops poking above the dark and poisonous swill: a brew that mixed sewage, industrial chemicals, and gasoline with the waters that had flowed in from the lake. Five of the dead were people who had sur-vived drowning in those waters, only to succumb to bacterial infections they picked up from exposure to it.

Hotel skyscrapers, some with bedding sucked right out of the shattered windows and hanging from the sills, were one of the storm's signatures. An-other was billboards, arched over backward on bent steel girders until, like Caribbean limbo dancers, they were parallel to the ground they stood on. The coastal highway system, including sections of Interstate 59 seventy and eighty miles inland, was brought to a standstill by the tens of thousands of trees split, slashed, and strewn all over the macadam by Katrina's lashing winds and the even more devastating tornadoes they spawned. Waves and wind went to work on the major crossing at the east end of Lake Pontchar-train, the twin span that carries Interstate 10 from New Orleans on through Slidell, Mississippi, and Alabama to Jacksonville, Florida, and in short order the roadway's huge concrete plates had been knocked off the piers that supported them.

The wind and surge damage were immediately shocking. Houses were knocked apart as though hit by a wrecking ball as big as they were. Whole roofs were simply lifted up and tossed aside. Sturdier or more sheltered houses lost only their shingles or siding. But the more malignant destroyer of lives and property in New Orleans was quiet and insidious as it coursed through the city: floodwater. A house with the roof blown off could be rebuilt. Once the waters receded, a flooded property might look much as it did before the storm, except for the weirdly pale scum that coated plants, cars, and houses alike. But after marinating for a week or more in toxic waters, many such houses were going to prove unsalvageable. And parts of New Orleans would remain underwater for three weeks.

Early estimates were that two hundred twenty thousand New Orleans residences had been damaged and that seventy thousand to eighty thousand of them were beyond reclamation. Fifty thousand flooded cars littered the streets and median strips. It would be months, authorities estimated, before Entergy, the local utility, would be able to restore electricity to a city now trussed and hog-tied in a tangle of wires that had been torn loose by high winds and falling trees. And the city's water and sewerage infrastructures had also crashed—ancient and crumbling systems that New Orleans had been trying to nurse along for decades until it could figure out how to meet the billion-dollar cost of complying with EPA mandates. Mail service would be knocked out for months, and a half year would pass before the post could handle anything close to its previous volume. Cell towers had been toppled, killing phone service. As power failed and tanks fouled for lack of aeration and temperature control, the magnificent Aquarium of the Americas on the riverfront in the heart of downtown New Orleans would lose four thousand of the five thousand creatures that had lived there.

SANDBAGS ARE THE TRADITIONAL RESPONSE TO LEVEE PROBLEMS, WHETHER those bags are placed along the top to keep waters from spilling over, or packed into areas that are giving way in what's known as a breach or crevasse. Sandbags are part of Southern iconography. Generations of men and women have held them open to be filled by someone wielding a shovel, then passed them, hand over hand, up the levee to the people placing them at its brim. Sandbags were also involved in stanching Katrina's breaches of the New Orleans drainage canals. But the scale was a little different. Instead of being handed along bagging brigades, they were dropped from helicopters. Instead of being the size of a sack of potatoes, they were, well, bigger: seven thousand pounds the biggest of them, three-and-a-half tons sealed in gray canvas. Helicopters dropped six hundred of these bags a day. One breach took two thousand bags before the bags even became visible below the surface of the water. Desperate for more sand, the army corps broke into a local business and commandeered $580,000 worth of the stuff. By Wednesday, the waters on both sides of the breaches had "equalized," meaning the floods were no longer flowing into the city. It was filled to capacity, filled to a depth equal to the surface waters of the drainage canals and the lake beyond. New Orleans, in other words, had become a new bay, an arm of Lake Pontchartrain. Once plugged with sandbags, it would be weeks before the city was pumped out—"dewatered," in army corps jargon—by natural drainage through blown-away levees and, where needed, the application of hundreds of portable pumps.

There was an irony here. And it was only compounded by the revelation that federal officials as late as Tuesday were ebullient in their belief that New Orleans had somehow "dodged the bullet." The president saw fit to hop a plane from his Texas ranch to attend a fund-raiser in San Diego. Vice President Dick Cheney saw no reason not to be fly-fishing in Wyoming. Michael Chertoff, who as the head of the Department of Homeland Security was nominally in command of the nation's top emergency response tools, spent the day in Atlanta at a seminar on avian flu. The irony was this: In truth, New Orleans really had dodged the bullet. The eye of the storm had swept east of the downtown area, just grazing the farthest purlieus of eastern New Orleans. And though the storm surge may have been the vestige of the much stronger storm Katrina had been in the open Gulf, sustained wind speeds that maxed out at 121 miles per hour, as the National Weather Service eventually would conclude, made this hurricane barely a Category 3 event by the time it reached New Orleans. Supposing it had been a direct hit? Supposing it had been a Category 5?

EVERY DISASTER REQUIRES ITS MIRACLE, IN A CATHOLIC CITY, ANYWAY. THE prayers of Ursuline nuns were credited with a role at least as pivotal as the pirate Jean Lafitte's in assuring British defeat in the Battle of New Orleans. Katrina's requisite miracle involved the marble statue of Christ beneath the towering sycamores and oaks in the garden behind St. Louis Cathedral, the archdiocesan holy of holies and the centerpiece of Jackson Square—itself the centerpiece of the French Quarter. By night, the ancient vine-draped trees framed the giant silhouette of Jesus projected onto the cathedral's rear wall by the floodlight placed at the base of the statue. It was a kitschy touch but haunting in its way. The wrathful Katrina, clearly offended by any such challenge to her supremacy, toppled the trees, and they fell every which way, as though striving to smash the statue itself. It withstood the assault—a miracle, some claimed—but not without sacrifice. The marble thumb and forefinger of the outstretched left hand were knocked off, which gave rise to an instant legend: that they were the force that flicked the storm to the east, sparing New Orleans Katrina's very worst.

— ⚜ —

FOUR

Real Ugly, Real Fast

I T HAD ALWAYS BEEN A BIT OF A GAME—A GAME WITH NO WINNERS, BUT AT least most people knew the rules. Officially, you were on your own. A mandatory evacuation meant just that: Get out. Drive if you have a car—do whatever it takes if you don't: Call a friend, or someone from church. The city wasn't safe. Even the Red Cross had pulled back a few years earlier and announced that ahead of a hurricane it would no longer deploy volunteers and resources south of Interstate 12. There were New Orleanians who had to look at a map to even know where Interstate 12 was located. The answer: far away—across the causeway, the twenty-four-mile bridge over Lake Pontchartrain, and then nearly that far again into the northern wilds of St. Tammany Parish. With no Red Cross shelter, refugees running for cover were left with a collection of schoolhouses of dubious fortitude, and then, the Superdome. Maybe. Here the game got as intricate as poker, with city officials signaling as sternly as they could that even the Dome might not be available this time. That was partly to scold Dome refugees for what they had done to it a storm or two ago: seats and plumbing fixtures ripped out;

walls defaced with graffiti; fights; filth. Wherever culpability for that mess lay, the reference carried an ulterior message for anyone who needed reminding: You don't want to be Domed. The Dome is a drag. Make your own plans. Get out.

And then, of course, at the last minute, the Dome would be opened anyway, as it had been three or four times in recent years, and city buses and taxis would rumble downtown bearing the halt and the aged and the infantile along with the able-bodied, the overly fecund, the folk who just didn't get it together this time or who had too many kids to be able to impose themselves on a neighbor with a car.

There were rules for seeking shelter in the Dome: Bring enough food for three days, whatever that meant. And don't bring your gun. There were metal detectors at the entranceways, but of course wiseguys were guileful enough to get around them.

The Dome had been a wonder of the world when it opened in 1975, and in many ways it still was. An all-weather, temperature-controlled coliseum of more than seventy thousand seats, it had hosted a pope; it had picked a president (the first Bush); it had pulsed with the sounds of innumerable rock demigods and preachers who thought they were God himself. And thirty years and dozens of copycat domed stadiums later, it remained the NFL's favorite Super Bowl venue, thanks to its location right there in the middle of a downtown area dense with hotels and bars and restaurants. It was a short walk to Bourbon Street, where already well-marinated Saints fans repaired for postgame revelry, not any less raucous if the team, as usual, had lost.

Looking back from the vantage of three decades, architecture critic Nikolai Ouroussoff saw the Dome—like the Mulholland aqueduct in Los Angeles, or, closer to hand, the Orleans Parish pumping system—as one of the last great artifacts of a more heroic age of urban engineering. He admired the building's dash and optimism, the way it was sited with the whole cityscape in mind, and framed to be seen not just from the streets it towered over but from the ramps and ribbons of elevated expressways that coiled around and about it like fuel ducts and power cords in service to a colossal flying saucer that had just touched down.

Officially, all the city promised when it finally relented and opened the Dome in a storm was a warm, dry place. Real warm, and only dry for a while, until the inevitable electrical blackout killed the air-conditioning and people began to sweat and stink. Reality departed from this minimal promise, if not by very much. The city knew better than to think that the people straggling into the Dome on the eve of Katrina could be left entirely to their own devices. And so, on Saturday night, thirty-six hours ahead of the projected landfall, a cadre of workers with the state Department of Social Services (red vests) joined employees of the city's Office of Public Health (lab coats and reddish orange armbands) to begin manning phone banks and setting up a staging area on a loading dock in the rear of the Dome to receive evacuees with "special needs."

Sherry Watters was one of forty-three DSS workers who volunteered for Dome duty that weekend. A strapping and informal redhead in her thirties, single again after a recent divorce, she believed deeply in service to others, whether through the use of her law degree to help the indigent, or the less specialized skill set that would be required at the Dome. The idea was that the DSS people would register the new arrivals as they were dropped off: paralytics, nursing-home residents, diabetics, asthmatics, the terminally obese—in short, the usual gamut of just plain folks in a poor city like New Orleans. Once registered, the influx would be funneled to the OPH people at triage stations, to separate those who could tough it out at the Dome from those who needed to be sent on to hospitals.

The more disorganized or unscrupulous nursing homes began showing up Sunday afternoon and simply dumping off whole vanloads of residents, without so much as one staff person to shepherd them, Watters noticed. But some families did the same thing, either on purpose or by default, abandoning their elders while they nipped inside the teeming stadium to take a look around. By the time they remembered Grandma and headed back out to the special needs section, Grandma might have been whisked away, more addled than ever by the stress of the moment, and now alone.

Watters's later recollections would hinge on excesses and overload: the stifling heat, the cigarette butts, the empty water bottles, the glut of medical equipment—motorized wheelchairs, ventilators, you name it—simply abandoned on the loading dock as some of the poorer residents of the richest nation on earth were triaged and shunted off to other quarters. Later on, the excesses would be of human feces deposited in stairwells and shadows as the Dome's sewage system collapsed and a city of some twenty thousand began drowning in its own wastes.

But Watters's observations during her early hours in the Dome ran not to excesses but to deficits: not enough docs, for example. There were just two, as far as she could tell, with two nurses to assist them in processing the special needs people arriving by the hundreds per hour, starting late Sunday morning. There weren't enough forms to log them in; OPH had even run out of triage tags, adding to the risk of not knowing which patient needed what.

THAT SUNDAY, THE FEDERAL EMERGENCY MANAGEMENT AGENCY HAD SOMEone on the ground in New Orleans, one man, Marty Bahamonde, a gruff and graying career public servant who found himself shuttling back and forth from the Emergency Operations Center (EOC) at city hall and then across the street to the Superdome. What first alerted him to the scope of the challenge ahead was a very specific deficit: toilet paper. He was on a swing by the EOC when he heard Terry Ebbert, the city's "homeland security" director, ordering maintenance staff to scrounge up every roll they could find and get it over to the Dome. "It told me that supplies at the Dome might be a serious issue," Bahamonde would dryly testify before Congress eight weeks later.

He did not keep his concerns to himself. Though FEMA brass for a time would pretend to have been caught entirely unawares by the scope of the disaster unfolding in New Orleans, the reality was that Bahamonde made a point of constantly advising Washington of the gathering catastrophe, a catastrophe that had already been closely studied in a mock disaster drill a year earlier. FEMA had paid for the hypothetical "Hurricane Pam" study it would soon pretend not to remember, and the scenario would prove notably accurate.

Throughout the afternoon, Bahamonde shot digital images of the gathering throng at the Dome and e-mailed them to FEMA headquarters in Washington. "Medical staff at the Dome say they expect to run out of oxygen in about two hours and are looking for alternatives," he wrote in an e-mail to headquarters at 4:40 PM. An hour later he underscored the urgency of the situation: "This is going to get real ugly real fast." Shortly after sending that message, Bahamonde met with the National Guard detachment posted to the Dome to discuss the expected arrival of a DMAT, a disaster medical assistance team. For their part, the Guard assured him that three hundred sixty thousand MREs (military "meals ready to eat") were on their way, along with fifteen trucks of water. Reality came up a bit short: forty thousand MREs and five water trucks. In another indication that confusion was taking hold, the DMAT team FEMA had promised didn't show up at all that night.

AS PEOPLE BEGAN FILING INTO THE DOME'S SPECIAL NEEDS SECTION, AS AGOnizing for Watters as any part of it, was the need to extract the invalids from the clusters of friends and family who brought them to the loading dock and, unlike some of those dropping off the ill and the elderly, wanted to stick around. Police officers had contributed to the confusion by telling families, even large ones, that they could stay together with their special needs cases—and maybe even cash in on the airlifts and other services made available to the needy. In fact, the rules allowed only one family caregiver per patient, a protocol that required wrenching split-second decisions. Already haggard men and women were forced to make a Sophie's Choice: Who would stay with the children? Who, if anyone, with the ailing elder—and when would they see each other again?

At one point, Watters found herself struggling with an elderly dialysis patient. The woman had arrived in the company of her son and his baby boy, eighteen months old. Shortly, the young father drifted off with his son. "That didn't seem to bother her," Watters would recall. What bothered her was that she needed someone to carry her stuff, and there was a lot of it: three smallish suitcases, a box, two garbage bags crammed with bedding. "Now there was no one to help her." Not that it should have mattered. With or without her son to serve as her bearer, the woman had too much baggage to fit on the dialysis bus. She clung to her bags anyway, refusing to leave without them. Watters had an idea. Stacking everything in front of the patient, she began repacking the bags, discarding what could be done without, consolidating the rest into the two bags each bus passenger was allowed. Bags of bedding?

Out. Diapers and baby food? Out. Presumably they'd have them where she was going. But the Bible stayed, as did an equally important source of spiritual sustenance: her TV set, a small one.

For every able-bodied adult who abandoned an ailing friend or relative to the care of the special needs team, another would arrive—often with other family members in tow—looking for a loved one. The registration process having collapsed for lack of forms and because of the sheer number of patients flowing into the loading dock, workers found themselves trying to guess whether the person sought was in their care, or had been sent on to a hospital or another shelter. Conversations focused on diagnostics as well as physical appearance: the old woman with the mulberry birthmark on her face and the oxygen tank strapped to her wheelchair? That was easy. Other identifiers were more elusive: lung cancer and long gray dreads? Answers to "L'il Mama"?

Sometimes the best bet was to take seekers up to the second floor for a look-see among the patients huddled there. Sometimes it worked, and Watters would be witness to a tearful reunion. More often it didn't, and anxious and depressed families would return to the Dome's stadium area, muttering that it was pretty damn incredible that they could rebuild Iraq but they couldn't even get a few buses to begin shuttling people to Baton Rouge.

Inevitably, social workers bonded with some of their charges and kept an eye out for them. One of Watters's favorites was a tiny blind woman named Ms. Ruby, who sat up rigidly in her wheelchair on the chance that her daughter would spot her. Meanwhile, she'd like a Diet Coke, please. When Watters explained that the logistical challenges ranged far beyond the lack of Diet Coke, Ms. Ruby had a better idea: "That's okay, honey. Just call me a cab."

Twenty-four hours later, Ms. Ruby, all eighty pounds of her, would still be upright in her chair, but urgently in need of sleep. To get her to lie down, Watters would promise to "stay while she slept, and if her daughter showed up, I would make sure she saw her." Somehow it worked and the exhausted woman gave up her vigil, but not her sense of decorum. "I believe I'll take that nap now," she said to Watters, and in the blink of an eye, she was unconscious.

The communications failure that racked the relief effort was not limited to contacts between New Orleans and the rest of the world. The Dome, in its own way, was a Tower of Babel even among people speaking the same language. A Guardsman asking the blind Ms. Ruby for a visual description of her daughter was only ludicrous. The Guardsman barreling through the crowded special needs area in an electric cart—"Clear a hole! Clear a hole!"—was a real danger to at least two women in Watters's charge. "They're deaf," Watters yelled. In fact, one of the women was also blind. When the Guardsman continued shouting for them to get out of the way, another man in the cart up and slugged him, and the cart rolled to a stop.

The confusion of the special needs section was more than matched by the chaos within the Dome, though the specifics would be forever enshrouded in exaggeration and myth. And then at last, in the early hours of Monday morning, the Dome was beset by another kind of storm, Katrina herself.

From the sleeping area set up in one of the windowless halls that rimmed the giant stadium, at first Watters couldn't see the storm, but in the hours before dawn, she could hear it: the pinging and banging sound as the streetscape below was shredded and hurled at the Dome's metal cladding. From recessed doors leading out of the building, she watched the wind blow out the windows of adjacent hotels—including the Hyatt Regency, where Mayor Nagin and key aides lay on the floor to avoid the glass and other shrapnel flying through the now windowless suite they had taken over as city government's shelter from the storm. Exterior walls and roofing were peeled off tall buildings, like wrapping paper. The palms along Poydras Street bent double and touched the ground. And then, to Watters's astonishment, it was as though an invisible force of nature was pushed into the visual domain and made manifest for the first time: She could actually see the wind, Watters would remember thinking as another blast of mist and rain and crushed glass swept by.

Improbably, at the midmorning height of the storm, her cell phone rang. It was one of the boys she mentored through an after-school program called Each One Save One, a fourteen-year-old from the Lower Ninth Ward. He and his grandparents had evacuated safely some twenty miles upriver to Reserve, he told her, but he was almost beside himself with anxiety. A call had just come through on his grandmother's cell phone. It was his mother and his sister, they were on the roof of their house on Lamanche Street and they were saying they couldn't hang on anymore. "You have to do something, Ms. Sherry. There has to be something, somebody who can go down there and rescue them. Tell me you know someone with a boat, Ms. Sherry. You have to know someone."

For Damond Peters, the fear that he had lost his mother and his sister was compounded by a terrible sense of guilt. He never should have let them push him into that car heading upriver. He had failed his mother as a son and as the man he was trying to become, and he had failed his sister as well. The mix of grief and failure was almost impossible for him to bear, and for several minutes after the phone call from his mother, he could not think straight. Then he had remembered Ms. Sherry. She was more to him than a tutor. She was a counselor, as important to him as the teachers at his school, the Desire Street Academy, a strongly Christian private high school that had the backing of Danny Wuerffel, the Heisman Trophy winner and former Saints quarterback. As Damond despaired of getting back through to his mother on the cell phone, he had punched in Sherry's number and, on a fluke, got through.

Watters tried to be encouraging. She reminded Damond that his mother was a strong woman, and so was Keia. What else could she say? In her heart, she nursed doubts. She knew the Lower Ninth Ward and how badly it had flooded during Betsy, how many people had died there. Patrina Peters was strong, but hers were strengths of the spirit, not the body. An epileptic on a rooftop in a hurricane? A woman under treatment for Crohn's disease? Watters told Damond to be strong himself. People in the special needs station were yelling for her. They were nearly out of oxygen. "Be strong, Damond." And then she ended the call.

As Watters signed off, the wind that had contented itself with shredding the flags and chevrons circling the Dome's exterior terraces tore loose two air vents and then began to peel away long sheets of the rubberized weatherproofing from the convex twelve-acre rooftop that gave the Dome its name. Rain had begun to fall through the disintegrating roof and onto the floor of the stadium, when suddenly the lights went out, to screams and groans from the thousands of people encamped on the gridiron or sprawling in the tiered seats; the air-conditioning died, and it was as if the giant spacecraft that was the Louisiana Superdome had settled onto the dark side of a planet too near the sun.

Watters had seen no reason to fear for her personal safety. The Dome would survive most anything, she felt certain, though it was quickly becoming hellishly hot. She would later remember the sense of relief that came over her hours later that Monday as the storm subsided and she was able to step out of the Dome from time to time and pace the streets and sidewalks. A huge sheet of the rubberized roofing hung over the side of the arena like a wet towel. Drapery and even bedding flapped from empty window frames of the Hyatt Regency Hotel tower, and the streets were coated with shattered glass as though there had been a hailstorm—except that the streets were dry. Bone dry. Once again, New Orleans seemed to have survived a hurricane. Now, with the greatest urgency, it would be necessary to resupply the shelter or, better yet, begin moving the refugees back home or on out of town. Because along with the lowering levels of available food, medicines, and oxygen, morale inside the Dome was deteriorating rapidly. The situation was not improved by the efforts of the Guardsmen on duty—an insufficient force of about three hundred fifty—to impose order and calm. "The people were treated more as prisoners than evacuees," in Watters's view, "and some of them responded accordingly." One of the Guardsmen's rules was that people in the stadium area could not leave it. And smokers could not smoke. And the sewage problem was fast becoming a crisis.

"The hurricane itself was awesome, as the word was meant to be used," Watters would later write in an e-mail to friends. "Glass broke on the surrounding buildings. The light covers on the top of the streetlights were blown off. The Dome's flagpoles and clock tower shook and swayed. . . . Surprisingly no one panicked. Everyone still felt safe in the Dome."

But awesome, properly used, in due course gave way to awful, in the pedestrian sense of the word. And then suddenly it dawned on Watters that she was not simply biding her time and comforting special needs patients for a few hours of wretchedness until the buses rolled up to haul everyone away. On another break from the building, she noticed deepening water on sidewalks and streets that had been dry when she'd walked them just hours earlier. This was weird, like time going backward, a storm getting worse after it's over. What Watters didn't yet know was that although the storm had passed, the city's levee system was disintegrating. At a rate of millions of gallons a minute, Lake Pontchartrain was now pouring into a city below sea level.

AS AMBULANCES AND TRUCKS STREAMED TO THE DOME'S LOADING DOCKS, BEARing people who had been pulled off rooftops and other places of refuge Monday evening and all day Tuesday, Watters and her colleagues "became some of the first looters," as she put it. Dripping with sweat themselves, they were processing people who in many cases were chilled to the bone from their exposure to the elements. With no blankets on hand for the shivering influx that would soon drive the Dome's population above twenty thousand, the social workers ran through the corridors that wrapped around the central stadium, stripping curtains from skyboxes and corporate suites, tearing bunting from balcony overhangs—any fabric would do. To protect people from the slick and infectious wash of blood and feces and urine and floodwater coating the floor, the social workers stretched latex gloves and slid them onto their charges' feet to make long-toed slippers.

The denizens of the flooded areas were by no means exclusively poor and black. A white college president was in the mix for two long days. The Reverend Anthony DeConciliis had been inaugurated president of Our Lady of Holy Cross just three days prior to Katrina. He had taken shelter with other men of the cloth at a Catholic rectory—a refuge that promptly flooded while, ironically, his campus, like much of Algiers and other communities on the west bank of the Mississippi River, was more or less unscathed. Other whites streamed in from Lakeview, a prosperous neighborhood of stolid fifties-style ranch houses and more daring architecture thrown up by the city's nouveau riche. And even the Lower Ninth, while all but completely black, was not without its moneyed denizens, not all of them the thieves and drug dealers depicted by media. But few people of means wound up in the Dome by choice, and many with no means at all avoided the place just as scrupulously. They knew better. Indeed, days after Katrina had left a flooded city in ruins, desperately needy men and women would prefer to soldier on in wrecked homes rather than accept a National Guardsman's boat ride to the filth and squalor that they knew waited for them in the Dome.

Fats Domino broke stereotypes in two respects. He was a rich resident of the Lower Ninth, and he was a man of means who wound up in the god-awful city shelter, in his case the Arena, a smaller stadium next door to the Dome that was opened up to take the spillover. For reasons of his own, Fats had never been convinced by worldwide acclaim and substantial wealth to give up his home on Caffin Avenue, a few blocks east of the Industrial Canal. When big money, a peerless trove of musical memorabilia, and a growing business had crowded him out of one modest ranch house, rather than move to a classier neighborhood, he had enlarged his compound to include the property next door, a structure as unprepossessing as the first, except for the pink and cream paint job. Devoted fans could tell Fats's digs from other equally nondescript houses along Caffin by the stars that adorned his wrought iron fence.

Domino had prepared to ride out Katrina as he had ridden out every other hurricane, by cooking up a storm in his kitchen. But by late Monday, the only thing cooking in the kitchen was the witches brew of toxic floodwa-ters that had swept in around windows and doors, and Domino was on the roof, waiting to be rescued. In due course, plucked from his roof by the port's harbor police force, the musical legend was just another elderly black man with diabetes being tended by the special needs crew. There was a throng of people in dim light, a throng yelping and howling, if not as joyfully as throngs were wont to do when the great one settled down at his piano, a million-dollar smile on his face, fingers flashing diamonds. Watters listened more closely to the old man's hallucinatory ramblings, and then it dawned on her: Cracking from the strain of his ordeal, Fats thought he had been booked that night to play the Dome.

BAHAMONDE, THE FEMA ENVOY, GOT WORD OF THE LEVEE BREACHES AT ABOUT eleven AM that Monday morning at the Emergency Operations Center in city hall. Out near the lake, in the far northwest corner of the city, the Seven-teenth Street Canal had been breached, and the breach was "very bad," an evaluation that he immediately relayed to FEMA in Washington. At five PM, Bahamonde darted over to the Superdome to grab a helicopter ride out over the city. By seven PM, he was on the phone with FEMA chief Mike Brown and then with other FEMA brass to advise them that Katrina was a disaster on a catastrophic scale: The breaching was not limited to the two-hundred-foot gash torn in the Seventeenth Street Canal. A few miles to the east, the London Avenue Canal had failed, and a roughly equal distance beyond that, the Industrial Canal also had collapsed. Eighty percent of the city was underwater. The only access by interstate was from the west, Bahamonde advised, because the twin-span that carried Interstate 10 across the eastern end of the lake had been decimated.

The Dome already sheltered twenty thousand people, and a flotilla of boats was needed to rescue thousands more trapped on rooftops and balconies all across the city. Moreover, there were thirty thousand tourists stuck in downtown hotels with no power. Windows had blown out of Charity, the huge public hospital near the Dome that, by dint of constant practice treating gunshot and stab victims in a singularly violent city, had one of the best trauma centers in the world. As for the other twenty-seven hospitals in the region, Bahamonde hadn't even been able to make contact, let alone assess whether they were functioning. Brown thanked his aide for the update and said he would contact the White House. In congressional testimony, it would be confirmed that he was as good as his word. Calling the White House—in this instance the Crawford, Texas, ranch where Bush was vacationing—was Brown's way of cold-shouldering a boss he considered incompetent, Homeland Security chief Michael Chertoff. Chertoff was at first widely assumed to be lying when he claimed that the first he heard about a levee breach in New Orleans was Tuesday. Incredibly, it may have been true.

Bahamonde would remember Ebbert, the local homeland security chief, pulling him aside before he went to bed that Monday night. "You've done this before," Ebbert began. "What do we need to do now?" Bahamonde's advice: Make a list of priorities and communicate it to state officials and to FEMA. "Consider it done," Ebbert said, and Ebbert's warnings to FEMA and requests for aid and supplies soon augmented Bahamonde's. And then Blanco added her voice to the chorus crying for help, with the Monday night call directly to Bush and her beseeching and oft-quoted assessment of

Louisiana's predicament. "We need your help. We need everything you've got," she told the president.

In the months to come, Blanco's cri de coeur—"We need everything you've got"—would be analyzed two ways: as an unambiguous expression of how desperately Louisiana needed the maximum possible infusion of troops, buses, earthmoving equipment, and whatever else could be mustered to fight an unprecedented catastrophe, or as an inarticulate whine from a governor too ill-prepared to know what she needed. If it was the latter, that was consistent with the very definition of a catastrophe offered by no less an authority than Joe Allbaugh, the Bush loyalist who had been rewarded for fund-raising during the 2000 campaign with a job as FEMA's director. An emergency qualified as catastrophic, Allbaugh told *The Times-Picayune* in 2002, when it overwhelmed state and local resources, requiring the federal government to inject itself rather than wait passively for properly filed requests. Allbaugh in making that remark had been talking about "a half dozen or so contingencies around the nation that cause me great concern," one of them being a major hurricane in New Orleans. The irony was that Allbaugh's tenure at FEMA had been marked by a systematic assault on the resources and funding of an agency that he told Congress he considered little more than "an oversized entitlement program."

From the state's emergency command post in Baton Rouge, one of Blanco's earliest indications of just how grave the peril was in New Orleans was a phone call early Monday from state representative Nita Hutter to report that she and much of the rest of St. Bernard's parish government were stranded on the second floor of a building in Chalmette, eight miles downriver from central New Orleans and the only town of any size in the parish. The first floor was essentially a fish tank, Hutter advised, and out the windows there was water of comparable depths as far as the eye could see. Hutter's call compounded the urgency of an appalling and nearly simultaneous report to Blanco that the state National Guard's Jackson Barracks, right on the line between Orleans and St. Bernard parishes, was underwater.

To complement a coast guard rescue operation then gearing up, Blanco ordered the state Department of Wildlife and Fisheries to deploy the boats it customarily used to knock around in inland swamps and open waters— about one hundred thirty would be mobilized, along with two hundred fifty fisheries personnel. She also called Sam Jones, in her Community Programs office, and told him to begin recruiting private boats, a volunteer force already stirring. Then came word, this time from Ray Nagin in his windowless bunker at the Hyatt Regency, that more than powerful storm surge was at play. The breach had been detected in the Seventeenth Street Canal levee and seemed to be getting worse. In short order, Nagin would no longer be able to make calls out, though his Blackberry would still allow for text-messaging. Along with its levees, the city's communications infrastructure had begun to crumble, and soon the city would be almost completely cut off.

Ivor van Heerden, the LSU hurricane expert, was at the state Emergency Operations Center at about seven PM Monday evening when he got his first intimation that the situation might be worse even than his troubling computer runs had led him to believe: "We're at the EOC. The storm has passed and everybody is congratulating themselves, saying things like, 'We got off easy this time'—and this guy comes up and asks if we know why a nursing home is flooding in St. Bernard Parish. 'Well, it shouldn't be flooding,' " van Heerden told the inquirer. "The surge event is over." All van Heerden could think was that rain water had begun to pond in low-lying areas—which in itself stretched credulity, since Katrina had not been particularly rainy, as hurricanes go.

What infuriated van Heerden in hindsight was that officials at some level already knew why that nursing home was flooding. As early as midday Monday, emergency personnel were informed of the breached Seventeenth Street Canal. "Why didn't they tell the media," van Heerden wanted to know. "We could have warned the hundreds of people who died in their attics."

"If we had got the word out—radio was still on the air, landlines were working, some cell phones—if they had put word out, it wouldn't have taken long to say, 'There's a big flood coming; go to bridges or high ground; untie your boats.' "

By the time word did begin to reach media, night had fallen. In a conversation with Mark Schleifstein at *The Times-Picayune* Monday evening, "homeland security" director Terry Ebbert confirmed that there was a still-smallish breach in the Seventeenth Street Canal. The news was posted immediately on the paper's website, and a front page story would make the paper's Tuesday edition. But van Heerden's first inkling was a sketchy CNN report, a little past two AM Tuesday: One of the canals connecting to Lake Pontchartrain—the report wasn't specific—had been breached. It was noon Tuesday before van Heerden got the details. He called his wife immediately and told her he'd be picking her up as soon as he could drive over to the house. Be ready. Within an hour they had parked van Heerden's four-wheel drive vehicle in Madisonville and were in a little inflatable dinghy with an outboard motor, checking van Heerden's water-level gauges. The water in the Tchefuncte River was already six feet above normal—and to van Heerden's horror, it was still rising. Given breached levees, the flooding in a below-sea-level place like New Orleans wouldn't stop until the water in the city was the same height as the swollen surface of the lake. In short, as van Heerden realized, New Orleans was doomed. By cell phone on the way back to Baton Rouge, he warned state officials and contacts in the media of what he had discovered, then called the Hurricane Center to order runs against laser imagery of the city's topography that showed the consequences of four-foot, five-foot, and six-foot lake levels. "Flood New Orleans," he said, ordering his people to simulate the catastrophe already under way.

Van Heerden's instinct was to go back down to the city with Hurricane Center personnel for further documentation of the disaster. Unfortunately, someone thought to check in with LSU administrators, who panicked. The city was on fire. Riots had broken out everywhere, to judge from the breathless cable news reports. LSU forbade the trip. Van Heerden consoled himself by posting high-resolution satellite imagery of the flooding on the Hurricane Center website. That too was met with official resistance in the form of an e-mail advising that there was a pricey fee for tapping into the satellite imagery and that it must otherwise be taken down. Van Heerden played hardball. In an e-mail to the French company that owned the imagery, he advised that he was going on *Larry King Live* within minutes—as indeed he was—and would go public with word that profiteers had denied Louisiana the data needed to more fully assess their peril. The French backed down, the image could remain on the website; indeed, they gave permission for free use of an updated image that was posted on September second. It was a fascinating glimpse of the disaster for van Heerden because, under close scrutiny, it revealed not just the massive breach at the Seventeenth Street Canal, but additional breaches all over the failing system.

The day after his *Larry King Live* appearance, Wednesday, van Heerden saw the need to shift from a research mode to active operational support for officials in charge of the emergency effort. That required the approval of the state Board of Regents, which was secured, and van Heerden would have gone aloft that same day for additional reconnaissance, but for an annoying development. To signal his concern, President Bush had decided to drop down below cloud cover on his way to Washington from his ranch in Crawford, Texas, and gaze upon the ruined city from Air Force One. Presidential security required ridding the sky of all other aircraft, a blow to the gathering momentum of van Heerden's research that did nothing to endear the president to him.

Until he could get up in the air, van Heerden digressed to water sampling from a borrowed coast guard boat that got him all over the lake and into the Industrial Canal. By Sunday, he was airborne at last, surveying the extent of flooding in day-long sorties while scanning the levee system for breaches. He stopped counting at twenty-eight.

BAHAMONDE WOKE TUESDAY MORNING TO WORD THAT HIS BOSS, BROWN, WAS helicoptering into the city that morning, not with supplies and emergency personnel, but with an entourage that included Governor Blanco and Louisiana's U.S. senators, Mary Landrieu and David Vitter. Nagin needed to be on hand, to meet with Brown and convey with all due urgency his sense of the city's priorities. To make that happen in a city with a rapidly atrophying nerve system of cell phones or landlines, Bahamonde got into sneakers and shorts and waded in waist-deep water to Nagin's rooms at the Hyatt Regency. From there it was back to the Superdome to introduce Nagin to Brown. Formalities attended to, Bahamonde pulled Brown aside. The situation was beyond intolerable, he advised. Food and water had all but run out, along with oxygen for the special needs people. Bahamonde was blunt. It was, very simply, a worst-case scenario. This was FEMA's man on the ground—Brown's "eyes and ears," as Bahamonde characterized their professional relationship—telling FEMA's boss precisely how dire the situation had gotten. Thus apprised, Brown got back into the helicopter and took off for Baton Rouge.

A day later, landlines, cell phones, and many other forms of communication had failed, but Bahamonde's wireless Blackberry was still working, and so was his sense of urgency. "Sir, the situation is past critical," he messaged Brown from the Superdome. Public order was an issue, what with an increasingly angry, dehydrated, and hungry crowd of refugees trapped by rising water. Lives also were at stake, Bahamonde cautioned, with relief workers estimating that they would begin to lose special needs patients "within hours."

Brown's response: "Thanks for the update. Anything specific I need to do or tweak?"

Three hours later, Bahamonde got another response to his increasingly desperate effort to pull his boss's head out of the sand, this time an e-mail from Brown's press secretary scolding Bahamonde for demanding the big man's time and attention. Brown was doing MSNBC's *Scarborough Country* talk show that evening from a studio in Baton Rouge and really needed to put a good meal in his belly beforehand. They had reservations at Ruth's Chris, a steak house much favored by politicos and lobbyists. "We now have traffic to encounter to get to and from a location of his choice," press secretary Sharon Worthy messaged Bahamonde, "followed by wait service from the restaurant staff, eating, etc. Thank you." Bahamonde was outraged and his message back to people around Worthy made for sarcasm as savage as it was vivid: "OH MY GOD!!!!!!!" he began. "No, won't go any further, too easy of a target. Just tell her that I just ate an MRE and crapped in the hallway of the Superdome along with thirty thousand other close friends, so I understand her concern about busy restaurants. Maybe tonight I will have time to move the pebbles on the parking garage floor so they don't stab me in the back while I try to sleep, but instead I will hope her wait at Ruth Christ [*sic*] is short. But I know she is stressed, so I won't make a big deal about it and you shouldn't either."

It wasn't that Brown lacked a sense of priority, it just seemed a bit skewed. One of numerous e-mails he blasted to friends and staff sought help finding a dogsitter for the family pooch back in the Washington area. In another, he powwowed with aides on how to counter media probes into the rumor that he was, in fact, fired from his job supervising horse-show judges for the International Arabian Horse Association, his station in life before Bush crony Joe Allbaugh pulled strings with the White House and landed his buddy the top job at the nation's emergency management agency.

Terse messages from Brown to Bahamonde did not preclude more expansive exchanges with those seeking to curry the FEMA chief's favor. That Monday, as New Orleans drowned, he took the time to answer a message from a FEMA cohort who had seen him doing a TV interview and wanted him to know that "you look fabulous and I'm not talking the makeup." Evidently the sycophant was talking clothes. Brown's reply: "I got it at Nordstrom. . . . Are you proud of me? Can I quit now? Can I go home?" But not all of Brown's correspondents were as complimentary about his sartorial style: "Please roll up the sleeves of your shirt . . . all shirts," one handler implored him. "Even the president rolled his sleeves to just below the elbow. In this crisis and on TV, you need to look more hardworking. ROLL UP THE SLEEVES!"

It was just a moment, one stupid moment in the first major test of the giant Homeland Security bureaucracy that the Bush administration had built after 9/11. These were the people who were supposed to protect America not just from predictable, well-foreseen disasters like hurricanes but sudden ones, like earthquakes and dirty bombs insinuated into the bowels of the New York City subway system.

On Thursday, seventy-two hours after Katrina's visit, evacuation of the Dome would still be in the planning stage, further evidence, as Bahamonde would suggest in a message to a FEMA colleague, that "the leadership from top down in our agency is unprepared and out of touch. . . ." What Bahamonde called "cluelessness" was one problem. The rub was the "self-concern" that the top echelons of the bureaucracy seemed to have substituted for any sense of obligation to the taxpayers who funded their ample paychecks.

FORTUNATELY, AS FEMA BRASS DITHERED AND DINED WELL, AN ARMADA OF small craft had begun fanning out over the flooded city, an impromptu and unofficial rescue mission that nicely complemented efforts by the coast guard, harbor police, and Blanco's wildlife agents. It was an impulse as old as the sea, and seemingly as inexorable. On Monday, and only more urgently on Tuesday, in bayous and back bays, at fishing camps and in the driveways of suburban homes all over south Louisiana, people with boats cranked them onto trailers or strapped them to the roofs of cars and trucks and headed for the disaster zone, for New Orleans—unless they were already there because it was home. An informal flotilla estimated at three hundred craft would work Katrina's aftermath in New Orleans, not counting the coast guard vessels and the boats put in service by the state Department of Wildlife and Fisheries. No one told the self-appointed captains to mass on the edges of the flooded city and launch their boats. No one had to. In a culture built on fishing and intimately familiar with hurricanes, no one needed to say a word. There was a sense of duty in responding to a flood. Also, truth be told, a sense of high adventure, and there were those among the boatmen who enhanced the moment with a swig of liquor and the swagger that came with strapping on a sidearm as well as a life vest. There would be desperate people in a city underwater. There would be a need to keep order.

A shipyard carpenter and crabber who had handcrafted his own pirogue, a low-sided canoelike boat popular with swamp fishers and trappers, Stephen Ford settled for the liquor. He made no bones about it: "At the time of the storm, I was drunk." It was all part of riding out a hurricane, and Katrina was looking to be a vicious one, especially in the Lower Ninth, Ford's home. He had been a fourth-grader when Betsy struck, and now, at fifty, he still remembered it well: "It wasn't as scary a storm as Katrina."

Ford had shooed his wife and their two daughters out of the house on Roffignac Street and on to a relative's place in Baton Rouge. His sons were older and on their own, one of them trying to make it as a musician, the other at Fort Campbell, on the Tennessee-Kentucky border, en route to Iraq. His wife and all four of the kids got through to him by cell phone, urging him to get out, but Ford was not about to leave his home unguarded. Even in a storm like Katrina, especially in a storm like Katrina. He had no lack of affection for the good people of the Lower Ninth. Bar patrons called him the Crab Man and bought the blues he netted in the area off Florida Avenue known as the Florida Walk. But Ford was realistic: "People will clean you out if you leave your house during a storm."

Houses were already floating up off their foundations Monday morning when he saw his neighbors Kevin and Clinton down the block and hollered at them to come on over: "Water coming up fast, man." As the men started running, the water was knee-deep. By the time they got to Ford's house, it was surging up over the stoop and in through the front door. Ford had tethered his pirogue in the alleyway alongside his house, but there was no time to fool with that. Instead, he grabbed his Bible and some bottled water and a battery-powered TV. The tandem surges from the Gulf and the failing Industrial Canal filled his house to the ceiling as, in the nick of time, the men hoisted themselves up into the attic and fell back on the floor, panting from their exertions.

"Like I say, I was drunk. I grabbed the Bible but I couldn't read it," Ford said. Instead, ducking his head to keep from whacking it on the rafters, he stumbled over to the little stained-glass window up under the eaves at the front end of the attic, and pushed it open. It startled and dismayed him to see two of his toolboxes bobbing in the swill that had eased them out of the shed. He figured the weight of the tools would have sunk the boxes. The force of the current was equally surprising. The wind was from the north, but the water seemed to be pushing into the Lower Ninth from the south, as if it came from the river. "It puzzled me," he said. "The wind was laying sideways, going against the direction of the water." And under assault by that same wind, it was as if the attic roof had started to breathe, Ford would recall. "I was thinking to myself, If this roof blows off, we won't survive— so many small objects like missiles blowing around." Somehow the roof held, and Ford could only thank his maker. "The Lord allowed us to be protected and stay dry," he said. Hours later, the surge and some of the wind abated and the water settled back to the depth in which the Lower Ninth—and the corpses of scores of its former residents—would marinate for weeks to come.

To escape his confinement and see if he could be useful, Ford fished the mooring line of his pirogue out of the water and pulled the swamped boat into reach. His first stop was his parents' house. They had evacuated, leaving behind another of their sons to guard the place. The pirogue Ford had built for himself, twelve feet long and a mere twenty inches wide at the gunwhales, was a tricky proposition with only one crabber aboard. It took some cussing to get his brother to settle down and not capsize the boat, and even then it proved impossible to make much headway against the lingering winds. Ford gave up on trying to ferry the man back to Roffignac Street and instead dropped him off at another house chosen at random from among those still standing.

Ford then headed out again, this time along Alabo Street, which is where he encountered Shug, clinging to the limb of a tree. Shug, short for Sugar Boy—his Christian name long since retired from service—was a test of Ford's own faith. More bluntly, Ford despised Shug and all young men like him. "This dude, he's a hustler, up to no good in his life," Ford said. One glance at the roof of Shug's house—or rather, the lack of one—explained how he had happened to fetch up in a tree. Shug had been there for six or eight hours, he said, and at one point, as someone else's house floated past, a corner of the splintered structure had snagged on his clothing. Shug had been pulled out into the still raging water, and after breaking free of the house had fought his way back to the tree. Something about Shug's ordeal opened Ford's eyes. "I used to think he was a piece of tissue paper doing nothing to help the community," Ford said. The shared experience of the storm had altered Ford and his view of people like Shug. "He was a man; he was surviving."

"God opened my eyes to many things during the storm," Ford went on. "He allowed me to see the humanness of everybody and what I needed to do and how I needed to be—at least a snapshot of how I should be." What Ford first needed to do was get Shug out of the tree and into the pirogue without tipping it over. Come in over the bow, not the side, Ford told him. Lie down in the bottom of the boat, then pull yourself upright. But then, where to put him? Ford did something that would have been inconceivable to him a day earlier. He decided to open his own home to Shug and dropped him on Roffignac Street. Kevin and Clinton could look after him.

And then the Crab Man was off again, to Charbonnet Street this time, where he spotted a man hanging on to a pipe, a man submerged to his neck and, as he plaintively revealed, unable to swim. That man was humble and grateful when Ford finally got him into the boat and then to a house on Lamanche Street where people were willing to let him inside. But the next man Ford tried to help—a huge three-hundred-pounder trapped in a tree—

swamped the boat, and when Ford told him it just wasn't going to work, that he'd have to wait for one of the bigger boats starting to prowl the Lower Ninth, the man broke down. "It hurt my heart to see men in this condition," Ford said. "I never served in nobody's war—I was in the army but not war," he went on. "I had never seen a man that looked like he was at his wits' end, crumbling under the pressure, sinking in a whirlpool. It made me sad and it made me feel strong."

Ford soon swapped the delicate pirogue for a flatboat he spotted in a neighbor's yard, loaded about four dozen army rations aboard—from a stash donated to the household's hurricane larder by his soldier son—and continued his rescue work. To keep dry against the still-intermittent rain, he put three garbage bags inside one another and punched holes for his arms and head to make a poncho. The rain was a nuisance. The flying cockroaches were a pestilence of an altogether different variety. The billions of them that lived in a town such as New Orleans had been forced up out of their usual haunts—behind walls, under stoves and refrigerators—and now the entire population was swarming over the surface of the drowned city, pausing wherever they could, an itinerary that included Ford's boat, his face, his garbage bags, and the clothing underneath them. Snakes were the more menacing phenomenon, though they could be avoided altogether unless you had the misfortune to fall into the water. They were everywhere, knots of them, clinging together: water moccasins, black snakes, rattlers, floating in brine that had swept them from coastal marshes into a city that was not supposed to be prowled by wild and poisonous animals. The clusters of them reminded Ford of blackbird nests.

In one of her last calls before the cell service went dead, Ford's wife had told him to be sure to check up on her cousin Jackie, on Lamanche, and so he did, arriving to find her trapped on the roof and sobbing such that she could barely catch her breath. He gave her one of his garbage bags to stop her shivering. It took a while, but when Jackie finally realized she wasn't going to die, she got "bossy," Ford was amused to recall. She demanded to be taken to her ex-husband's place, a few blocks away. Ford obliged, dropping her off in the attic for who knows what postmarital melodramas.

The wildly varying emotional condition of those he tried to help prompted Ford to get strategic in how he approached them. The man lying stomach-down over the crest of his roof appeared to have given up, if in fact he wasn't dead. Ford wanted to come on gently. He announced himself with a song, something by the Temptations, on the chance it would rally the man's spirit, which it did. Earlier in the day he had tried to rescue two women on a rooftop off Lamanche Street, only to find that fallen wires blocked him from reaching the backyard where the floating house they were riding had fetched up against a pecan tree. He had told them he'd be back, and now, hours later, he was, but the older of the two women, the one he knew as Trina, was in a bad way.

The Temptations might have worked for the younger woman—only later would he learn her name: Keia—or maybe something by Jeffrey Osborne. But with Trina Peters in mind, Ford tried a hymn: "Great Is Thy Faithfulness." It carried over the water as he paddled toward them across the drowned and silent blocks. Keia heard it first over her mother's anxious and distracted chatter. "Hush, Mama," she said. "That's the man. Praise, God, he's come back. I told you he would. I told you!" And with that, Keia began to clap her hands and shout. Maybe it was the wrong song. Peters remained disconsolate as the hull of Ford's boat brushed up against the shingling. Greeted by the daughter as a guardian angel, Ford found himself barking at her mother like a drill sergeant: "You're a grown woman; you are not a baby. You need to be strong for your daughter"—any foolish thing that came into his head, in hopes that it would piss Trina off enough to snap her out of her mood of helplessness and despair. Keia would remember the sense of overwhelming relief—"an indescribable feeling"—that came over her as she settled into the boat with her mother, and this virtual stranger, Stephen Ford, began to paddle off. Within a few blocks, Ford knocked the air conditioner out of a second-floor window and helped the women climb inside, with apologies for not being able to carry them farther, not with so many more people still trapped on rooftops. Peters and her daughter, trembling by now from exhaustion and exposure, stumbled into the room and over to an old-time iron-framed bed, where they collapsed.

By Tuesday morning, Keia was so dehydrated she began to drink mouthwash, and for breakfast they ate toothpaste. They rummaged through the house and found men's cutoff shorts—khakis for Keia, green ones for her mother—to substitute for the sodden garments they had pulled off on arrival the night before. Suddenly the air was filled with the *whap-whap* of helicopter rotors and the shouts of survivors drawn back onto rooftops by the dawn. Keia found some balloons in a drawer full of party favors, blew them up, and waved them out the window. But it was a boat that came to their rescue, not a chopper, one of the Wildlife and Fisheries boats. It took them across the breached Industrial Canal to Poland Avenue, a ridge of dry land that rose up out of the inky floodwaters in a gentle swell like a whaleback. They had reached the natural levee, the part of New Orleans—once the city in its entirety—thrown up above sea level by the Mississippi River during eons of flooding and sedimentation. From Poland Avenue, this natural formation stretched along the riverfront all the way to the city's Uptown end, a strip of land perhaps a mile wide, if that, and less than eight miles long. The vast rest of New Orleans, a city of 468 square miles, had been won in a struggle with swamps and open water. It had been drained and filled and leveed and now it was underwater again, as perhaps it was always meant to be.

Peters and Keia found themselves among a thousand survivors at the Poland Avenue landing spot, some stunned and weeping, others galvanized by need and opportunity. A food store was cracked opened like an oyster shell and those who wanted clothing as well were directed through the smashed window of a sporting goods store with a supply of tennis sneakers in the latest styles. The looting was driven by necessity and there seemed no reason at first that it not be orderly. It would also be thorough.

Peters and her daughter finally got a lift downtown in an army truck, and by early Tuesday afternoon, they were two among the thousands of sodden, sometimes ailing evacuees filing through the Dome's entrance. In their borrowed cutoffs they must have looked like two old men, Keia would remember thinking—except that her long hair had exploded wildly from the doughnut form she had used to pull it to the back of her head. She and her mother climbed a few rows up into the tiered stadium, as far above the seething, reeking floor as they could get before their legs gave out and they sank into plastic seats. It was from one of the Dome's balconies far above them, they were cautioned, that a man had leapt to his death—or was he pushed? The stench, the heat—conditions in the stadium were appalling, but Keia hardly noticed, so intently were her thoughts fixed on the process that finally seemed under way: getting out of the city altogether. Mother and daughter might have dozed off in the fetid air had Peters not glanced down just then and seen—could this possibly be the same woman?—the friendly redheaded white lady who had been so good to Damond. "Miss Sherry! Miss Sherry!" Peters called out the name, then mother and daughter together, and sure enough, the lady from the Each One Save One mentoring program looked up and saw them.

It was quickly clear to Watters that Ms. Peters was in a bad way and needed to be evacuated on a priority basis. But even as she jogged up into the bleachers, she called Damond, knowing how important it would be for him to get word that his mother and sister were alive. The call went through. That was propitious. But the boy did not pick up and so Watters left a callback number. The more urgent task, she realized, was getting Trina the medical attention her many health problems required. "Whatever you do, don't get separated," she warned Keia, after delivering them to the special needs area and arranging for one of the doctors to hook up an IV drip. With that, Watters had moved off to cope with other crises.

Trina was trembling all over and her eyes were starting to roll back into her head, but she must have heard Watters's warning to stay together, because she hooked her fingers into the belt loops of her daughter's khaki shorts and wouldn't let go. Keia read her mother's familiar symptoms for what they were, the onset of an epileptic seizure. No, just a panic attack, a passing medic insisted, and arguing with him proved futile. Watters would know better. Keia found herself torn between the need to stay with her mother and the temptation to go in search of Watters. She was verging on panic herself when Watters's rounds brought her back within hailing distance. In an instant, Watters had Peters on a gurney and properly medicated against the worsening seizure. She handed her cell phone to Keia, who dialed Damond's number. This time he answered. Keia pressed the phone to her mother's ear, and the last words she heard as she was rushed onto a medivac helicopter was her boy saying he loved her.

❖

FIVE

Decaf Cigarettes and Golden Carp

PATRINA PETERS AND HER DAUGHTER WERE PART OF A RESIDUAL MIGRATION of some thirty-five thousand people who staggered in from all over town on foot or in trucks that converged on the Superdome. By Tuesday night, five thousand of them had joined the twenty thousand who had been trapped in the Dome since Sunday, and authorities were waving newcomers on to the Ernest N. Morial Convention Center, a kilometer-long collection of exhibition halls and meeting rooms that sprawled along the riverfront some fifteen blocks down Poydras Street from the Dome. With no provisioning whatsoever in the form of food or water, the convention center proved even less suitable for mass habitation, and within a day most of the twenty thousand refugees who had been sent there—some of them stiffening under blankets draped over them as they expired—were forced out onto the sidewalk by the appalling stench, the backed up toilets, and fears of violence. And when one group of men, women, and children heeded the mayor's mandate to get out of New Orleans and began a hike on foot across the soaring Mississippi River bridge to the suburbs, they were met by an armed constabulary that fired shots over their heads and forced them back to where they had come from. Jangling with racial overtones, it was a confrontation that would be the focus of animosity on both sides of the color line for as long as anyone could remember it.

FOR A WORLDWIDE TELEVISION AUDIENCE, THE LASTING IMAGES OF KATRINA would be panoramas shot from helicopters for the most part: the housing tracts flooded right up to their rooftops, the collapsed buildings, the shattered Interstate 10 twin-span at the eastern end of Lake Pontchartrain, the throngs milling and seething outside the Superdome and the convention center. For those on the ground, the survivors, the indelible imagery was more idiosyncratic and personal. Roy Mullet, an auto mechanic in eastern New Orleans, would not be able to forget the water moccasins, several of them, that glided out from behind an aunt's life jacket as he and his son and a cousin encountered her corpse snagged in flotsam, and then pulled it aboard their search boat.

For Jon Kenyatta, a Web designer, it was the strangely perplexing sight of golden carp in the waters covering a downtown street below the office where he had been trapped for days on end, a spiritual sign to him that somehow it was time for life to go on. For James Nolan, the writer, it was the infuriating sight of his sink faucet run dry and the realization, two days after the storm, that now he really would have to leave his otherwise comfortable French Quarter digs. For one hundred dollars, he bought a seat on a hijacked school bus that had pulled up in front of the Monteleone Hotel near the Canal Street side of the Quarter, and in due course he was being intercepted at a drop-off point and deposited at the Baton Rouge home of his friend Andrei Codrescu, the writer and NPR radio commentator with the signature Romanian accent. For a week, Nolan would dazzle the house full of refugees with his cooking, then decamp for Florida, then Barcelona, to wait out the mess back home.

Norman Jones, a slight, wiry man with a bald head and a civil service job in maintenance at the LSU school of dentistry, was struck by the sight of a woman's corpse sucked halfway down into an open manhole, but no farther because of the amplitude of her breasts. Another indelible image was that of a young man of twenty-three or twenty-four, his hand clapped over a bullet hole in his chest. The word was that he had been nailed while stealing, whether by police or a vigilante was uncertain. Other storm casualties had simply expired by the side of the road as they attempted to join in the long march from all over the city toward higher ground along the riverfront.

After taking shelter in the second-floor office of a lawyer friend in the Mid-City section of New Orleans, Jones had watched through the window on Tuesday as floodwaters slowly rose over his Toyota 4Runner. His trek to the convention center took him through a schoolhouse in Treme that had been seized and occupied by survivors. In a curious blend of anarchy and postapocalypse communitarianism, disparate families had laid claim to different classrooms and generally stayed out of one another's way. "When you go to the bathroom, go together. There be people in here who are playing for keeps," Jones advised some teenage girls, daughters of a couple who had ridden out the storm with him in the lawyer's office and then joined him in the trek toward the riverfront. But in fact, the spirit of mutual assistance prevailed, and so far as Jones knew, no acts of violence marred their two days at Craig School. To feed those bivouacked inside, a Samaritan had set about the business of cooking up edibles from the school's thawing freezer—fish sticks, pizza (one-half pie per classroom)—and for one of the evenings, Jones spelled him as chef.

He finally reached the convention center on Thursday. Perhaps it was the sight of the young man with the chest wound, perhaps it was Jones's own nervous system honed taut over the half century he had lived in a town such as New Orleans, but at the crack of what sounded like a gunshot just after entering the center, he dove onto the floor and lay there, prostrate, until he could be certain bullets were not flying overhead. Instantly, a National Guard detachment wheeled up to the door, M16s raised, lights probing the shadows of the blacked-out hall and the throng inside. Whatever the sound, the Guards could not trace it to its source, and so they drove off, leaving Jones and the herd of refugees to the squalor and chaos of a building that would loom large in the mythology that built up around Katrina and the suffering that followed.

Jones did not find the convention center less than repulsive during his two nights there, the thousands of people, the stench for lack of working toilets. But murder and rapine? The worst of it, in Jones's experience, truly was the stench. He searched carefully for an unfouled swatch of floor big enough to lie down on, but couldn't take it for long and headed outside with his friends to sit on the curb and wait for the fabled buses to arrive. Around dawn the next morning, he gave up. Instead, Jones accosted a city worker he spotted in a tow truck. How much would he want to drive them to Baton Rouge. Immediately. The driver said $500, and they offered $1,000 just to be sure he knew they were serious. Eventually he agreed to do it for $200, perhaps, Jones would surmise, because they were the first people to ask and he was eager to get out himself.

For Gregory Richardson, the indelible memory of Katrina—one of them, anyway—would be the spectacle of whole neighborhoods of trapped flood victims hollering for help from rooftops and upper-story windows as a police boat towed the craft he was in toward dry ground in New Orleans East. Another, weeks later, would be the sight of his father's corpse in the house Richardson grew up in, a house on Egania Street in the Lower Ninth Ward. Soldiers had marked it with an *X,* indicating that they had located the corpse weeks earlier and should long since have removed it, an oversight that a grieving son found unconscionable.

Richardson was black but hardly poor. A real estate investor, he owned four dozen rental units and had ensconced himself, his wife, and her father in a fine home with a swimming pool in the city's Lake Barrington subdivision, in eastern New Orleans.

Richardson had grown up in humbler circumstances. As a nine-year-old, he had ridden out Betsy in the house on Egania Street, the house where his father would die forty years later trying to ride out Katrina. Richardson's wife had thought better of staying on in New Orleans for Katrina. She and her own father, a vigorous ninety-year-old, evacuated to her sister's place in Atlanta. Alone in the night, waked up by shrieking winds of almost unimaginable intensity, Richardson suddenly wished he had gone too. But by nine-thirty Monday morning, the worst of it seemed to have passed. Richardson reached his wife by cell phone and, as they talked, walked over to the front door to look out. A stretch of privacy fencing had blown down. That could be easily repaired. And the good news was that the streets seemed to be draining nicely. And then, oh my God: Richardson saw the wall of water, "like a tidal wave coming right down the road." He had the presence of mind to dart to his truck and retrieve a hammer, a flat bar, a couple of chisels, a screwdriver. In the few seconds it took to run back inside, rising water had covered the floor of the house. Richardson grabbed some bread and a bottle of water and, once in the attic, called his father to tell him to do the same thing. It would be their last words.

Within three hours, Richardson had five feet of water in his house and knew that it would be over his head if he were to step outside. The lull at the center of the hurricane had passed, giving way to fresh torrents of rain and wind gusts so fierce they lifted the roofing plywood up and down. "If it tears a hole in the roof, the wind will blow me away," Richardson thought. To monitor the rising water, he kept an eye on a ground-floor door he could see from the attic's folding stair. As the water reached the top of the door, he realized the only way out was through the roof, now that the wind had died down enough to make that feasible.

Richardson lay on his back and settled into the task, chipping and cutting away at the plywood and its overlay of shingles. "I am lying down and the debris is falling in my face. It took me a while; I had to rest my hands." Richardson lost track of time but estimated an hour passed, maybe an hour and a half, before he had made a hole big enough to squeeze through. His roof was steep, and Richardson slipped at one point and tumbled toward the water lapping up under his eaves. He bent the gutter, but it stopped his fall into waters alive with snakes washed up out of Bayou Sauvage and the wetlands to the east. Gnats and mosquitoes were torment of another sort, and to escape them Richardson ducked back into the attic. It was too hot for insects in there, almost too hot for Richardson. He must have slept awhile. When he next stuck his head through the hole in the roof, night had fallen. He stepped out onto a dark island in a pitch-black sea, barely able to make out the roofline of the house next door. The insects quickly drove him back inside.

By dawn's light on Tuesday, Richardson climbed back out onto his roof and was confronted by his first clear look at the utter devastation, not just of a neighborhood but of a way of life, the way of life hard-won by New Orleans's black middle class. Every house within sight was damaged, some catastrophically. "One neighbor's brick wall is on the ground; another neighbor, half her roof is off. Chairs from my backyard are floating." It threw into question Richardson's sense of himself, as a man of prowess and accomplishment—forty-eight rental units: God only knew what was left of them. "I'm thinking, I'm gonna die."

It did nothing for Richardson's self-esteem to conclude that he was the only man in all of eastern New Orleans foolish enough to have disregarded the order to evacuate. And then, he heard a sound, the tapping and ripping sound of another roof being breached from the inside out, and in due course the house two doors down hatched another human, Richardson's neighbor Charles Richard. "That you, Charles? Someone else around here too stupid to get out of town?"

From their rooftop perches, the men ribbed each other and waved at passing helicopters, which sometimes seemed to slow before zooming off and away. All day they kept it up, and when it was dark, to keep from falling asleep and rolling off their roofs, they resolved to talk each other through the night. It wasn't necessary. The gnats and mosquitoes would have kept a zombie awake, and soon the men were driven back into the infernal heat of their attics to escape the insects.

By Wednesday morning, Richardson was out of food and water and knew he was going to have to risk the dark water. From a gap between houses, he could see people floating by on makeshift rafts. A group of women had pulled the door off a refrigerator, taken out the shelves and drawers, and loaded the box with children and an elderly gent. The sight put Richardson in mind of an unhung door out in his shed. They could use it as a raft, or at least a sort of kickboard, he told his neighbor, something to keep them from drowning. And anyway, what was the alternative? Another forty-eight hours growing light-headed on a rooftop for lack of food and water? Richardson eased himself over the edge of the roof and into the drink. The water had receded enough to let him into the ground floor of the house. He found a small canvas satchel and threw in muscle relaxers, medicines for back spasms, and a few items of clothing. He put his wallet, keys, pager, and about $900 in cash into a freezer bag and then tossed that into the satchel as well. With the door as his lifeboat, he paddled over to his neighbor's house and propped up a ladder so Richard, a man of about sixty, could get off his roof and join him in their attempted swim to safety.

They had left the Lake Barrington subdivision in search of higher ground when they brushed past a corpse, a man they guessed to be in his forties, facedown in the water. A snakebite victim? Electrocution? Simple drowning? None of those possibilities made them any happier to be hanging their hindquarters in murky water and kicking as hard as they could. It came as a considerable relief, then, to spot a decent-size boat stranded at an interstate on-ramp—a timely find since by then both men's legs were cramping badly. They had rounded up fence palings to use as paddles and were easing the boat back into the water when two couples with three children between them clambered aboard. In due course, a police boat came abeam of them and offered a tow to dry land. It lay to the south along Read Boulevard, they were told, where that thoroughfare met Chef Menteur Highway, once the main route across the swamps to the Mississippi coast and points east, in the era before interstates. At Chef and Read, they became part of a small throng of stunned and anxious survivors waiting their turns to get on army trucks for the lift that would make them part of the far larger, and perhaps even more anxious, throng milling in and outside of the convention center.

Stepping off the truck at the convention center, with an urgent need to relieve himself, Richardson pressed through the hordes of people, in search of the toilets. Another indelible memory: the widening plumes of acrid urine that spread out from under the bathroom door and across the carpeted convention hall. That was more than Richardson cared to deal with, and so he found a less fetid if more public spot in which to relieve himself, then headed back out to the curb. Since Guardsmen had brought him to this place, Richardson assumed there might be some semblance of civility, maybe even the orderly distribution of food and water. But the evacuees had been left to themselves, while the military, openly fearful of the throng, barricaded itself in another hall down the way. It was an engineering unit not trained in crowd control, its commanders would say days later when asked to explain the unit's timidity and reclusiveness. In due course, helicopters piloted by soldiers equally wary of the people they were meant to help began off-loading crates of water and food rations, but from an altitude that guaranteed many bottles would burst open on impact and that the starving evacuees would have to chase after the scattered MRE packets like pigeons competing for slop leaking from a city garbage truck.

It disgusted Richardson to see sneering young men hawking eight-ounce cups of water for five dollars a pop, but he pulled out a twenty and gratefully bought four of them. Twenty-four hours had passed since his own provisions ran out, and the cold water he poured down his throat felt like it was splashing directly onto his lungs and his heart on the way to his belly. To his astonishment, Richardson caught the scent of barbecue and became aware of a more honorable distribution system: Ten men, mostly in their twenties, were grilling looted chicken on a lineup of about three dozen looted grills. Richardson queued up and stood in line for two hours. There was jostling and shoving, but Richardson finally was rewarded for his patience with a chicken leg and a fresh bottle of water.

In due course, Richardson and his neighbor ran into a couple of men they knew, and for safety, the four of them decided to band together. While media accounts would wildly overstate the levels of violence at the convention center and also at the Dome, there was no mistaking either shelter for a picnic. "You would doze off, and you'd hear screams and running, people running and hiding," Richardson said. "When guns would go off, about two hundred police and soldiers would come in from all directions through the crowd, then they'd go back out." That happened about three times Wednesday night, Richardson said. Cops would charge in, frisk a few people, and then retreat without arresting anyone. Richardson was particularly disturbed by the sight of a young girl crying, maybe twelve years old, her clothes hanging off her in shreds, her mother wailing beside her: "Why would they do this? Who did this to my baby?" A rape victim? A girl roughed up in a turf war among peers? One characteristic of a collapse of social order was the way the lives of strangers were laid bare, and yet were still shrouded in mystery. The extreme intimacy was death itself, death in a crowd. Richardson had seen corpses along Convention Center Boulevard, slack-jawed old people, mostly, people who had survived a drowned city only to expire in the heat. One stricken family continued to wheel the corpse of an elderly woman around in her wheelchair. That stayed with Richardson, the sight of the corpse being wheeled round and round.

On Thursday, he and his friends began to keep a distance from the convention center and found themselves at the river end of Canal Street, the grandest commercial boulevard in the South in the era before flight to the suburbs had drained the life out of it. Desperate for water, Richardson slipped through a shattered window and into a convenience store, his heart pounding. "I never stole anything in my life," he said. On a second visit, to Richardson's great dismay, he was confronted by an unexpected police detail. But when they saw that he and his associates had taken only food and water, they stepped aside.

On one of his forays up Canal Street, Richardson ran into a man from his father's block in the Lower Ninth. The man said he had been the next to last person to leave and that he didn't think the old man had made it. Richardson told himself it couldn't be so, then burst into tears anyway.

"Friday night, I'm trying to sleep a little. One of the four of us, Verdell, he had a hip replacement. He went to take a crap, and when he squatted down, he dislocated his hip. We heard a loud scream. We cleaned him up and got him to the front of the parking lot." Two hours later, a medic came to their assistance. He asked for their belts, wrapped them around Verdell's feet, and told Richardson and another man to grab him under the arms and pull. Verdell is screaming in pain. "I said, 'Why don't you give him a shot? Why don't you take him out of here?' The guy said, 'Look, this is the best we can do.'"

And then, a day later, it was over, an end somehow as coarse and abrupt as all that had gone before. Herded onto a bus, Richardson begged to be dropped at an airport, any airport, or at least to be told where the bus was heading. At eight AM the next morning, after an all-night drive, he found himself in a line of what he estimated was a hundred buses, at the gates to a military base in Arkansas. Some of the people told him they had been sitting outside for a day and a half, waiting to be admitted onto the base. With $900 in his pocket, Richardson had options. He turned on his heel and simply walked away from the base in search of an airport. A police car stopped, and the officers quizzed him on what he was up to. He seemed to ease their concern that he was a troublemaker, but when he asked for a ride to the airport, they turned him down. As soon as the cruiser was out of sight, he stuck out his thumb, a black man on white turf, hitchhiking for the first time in his life.

To his surprise, an elderly gent stopped, a white man, and agreed to take him to the airport. Six hours and $600 later, he stepped off a plane in Atlanta, in the clothes he had been wearing for a week. His family hugged him anyway. Lord! Did they hug him.

A BIT LIKE ONE OF THOSE JAPANESE COMBATANTS WHO EMERGED FROM HIDING in remote Pacific islands decades after the armistice, Jon Kenyatta, the Web designer, was one of the last people to be evacuated from the convention center, in part because he had rather enjoyed being stranded in his workplace, at least for a time, and the peace that isolation had brought with it. He had ridden out Katrina in his Canal Street office not to defy the evacuation order or to prove a point but because, with a music festival looming in two weeks and a hell of a lot of work to get done, he had scarcely taken note of the gathering storm. Enisled in the building circled by golden carp, he had rolled cigarettes out of decaffeinated tea and subsisted on edible desk-drawer detritus: plastic packets of soy sauce, Sweet'N Low, and—the pièce de résistance—ketchup. By week's end, the flooding along Canal Street had receded to the point where Kenyatta could descend to the ground floor, open the door, and suffer the bedazzlement that came with bright sunlight and his first street-level exposure to humanity in the post-storm era. The sight was amazing to him. Within several blocks of his office, Canal Street looked like nothing so much as a carnival parade route. But instead of little children on stepladders waving their arms and yelling for float riders to throw them some beads, as far as the eye could see, the median strip—or "neutral ground," as locals call it—was thick with media crews and cameras on tripods.

SIX

Other Texans, Other Times

W HITE AND BLACK, EXHAUSTED AND HUNGRY, THE NEW ORLEANIANS were still huddled in a shelter the day after a terrible hurricane when the president, a Texan, stood among them, turned a flashlight onto his face, and said he was there to help. The hurricane was Betsy. The president was Lyndon Johnson. Forty years later, the memory for those who had lived through it was sharpened on the stone of another Texan's presidential performance. As thirty billion gallons of water poured into New Orleans on the day after Katrina made landfall, Bush could be found in San Diego, for VJ Day anniversary observances where he strummed on a gift guitar with country singer Mark Wills. The post-Katrina era was three days old before Bush cut short his Texas vacation and on Wednesday headed back to Washington. The photo op was not LBJ among the people. It was Bush in the clouds, peering out the window of Air Force One as it dipped over New Orleans to provide the commander in chief a glance at the worst disaster in American history. Why Bush political tactician Karl Rove allowed that shot to be taken—a study mixing impotence and indifference in equal parts—will remain one of the curiosities of the Bush years. True, in an age of violence and lawlessness, sheltered throngs weren't what they used to be. Neither, in the eyes of many New Orleanians, were Texas presidents.

FOR THOSE NOT CAUGHT IN THE MAELSTROM, IT COULD BE DIFFICULT TO GRASP just how uniquely appalling that first week was in New Orleans. No American city of comparable size had seen anything remotely like it since the San Francisco earthquake of 1906. The terror attacks on New York had been confined to Lower Manhattan. A day after Katrina, four-fifths of New Orleans was underwater, four times Betsy's floodplain, an area seven times as big as all of Manhattan. And the wretched masses huddled at the Superdome and the convention center were only the visible part of a ghost city of homeless New Orleanians—perhaps a quarter of a million in number—now scattering across the nation. Stunned by what she had seen earlier in the day, Blanco had gone back to the Dome a second time Tuesday, to get a better feel for conditions on the ground than had been possible while accompanying Mike Brown and the senators on their quick trip to the Dome's copter pad. This time she brought her husband, but no media. It was a chance to talk to people in the crowd, some angry, more of them scared. One man thrust a baby at her, apparently half-hoping she would take the infant. Addicts scattered in the crowd had begun to go to pieces for lack of drugs, but the Blancos' overall impression was of an anxious but still orderly throng—provided evacuation could be arranged quickly. It was, of course, inconceivable to the governor that it would take most of the week before a significant federal relief effort had been mounted.

The hurricane was the least of it, and the flooding, vastly more devastating than the hurricane, was not the end of it. Each passing day seemed to mix a new horror into the catastrophe, a new pestilence. To the misery in the Superdome was added the pillaging of the city—on a scale that was at first only more terrifying for being impossible to control or even measure, in the absence of a meaningful police or military presence.

Then, to floods and the sacking of New Orleans was added fire. Warehouses and shopping malls had been set ablaze, whether by accident or design hardly seemed to matter. The French Quarter had burned more than once in its history, most recently in the early nineteenth century. Would this densely packed cluster of ancient buildings be touched off again? And of course, firefighters were as helpless as cops in a city that was both underwater and out of water. With trucks hamstrung by flooded streets and dead hydrants, helicopters took to the air, trailing giant buckets that could be dipped in the river or the lake and dumped on the biggest blazes. But most fires simply ran their course.

By Wednesday night the looting was so wanton—even hospitals were under siege, by both addicts and patients dependent on life-sustaining medicines—that Nagin ordered city police, those among them who hadn't deserted, to leave search and rescue work to others and join the fight to retake the city. The desertions were only one part of the problem; more than a few police had joined in the looting themselves, with some of them heedless of TV cameras rolling as they helped strip the Wal-Mart that Saundra Reed and her family had visited in search of pre-evacuation provisions, only to find the place ominously closed. Mostly the looting by police was to resupply the force, as was permitted under the city's disaster plan, but jewelry and Cadillac Escalades—two hundred cars were taken from a downtown dealership— were not quite the same as canned goods, bottled water, and batteries. Yet more dismaying were media reports—at first unquestioned—that helicopters had come under fire as they attempted to airlift food to evacuees and carry off the sick and aged. Rescue boats also were scared off by gunfire, though upon review, most of it turned out to be shots that had been fired into the air in a misguided effort to summon help.

Much would be made of how Katrina tore the veil away to reveal the persistence of poverty and race-based disadvantage in America. If so, the storm did at least some good. But in truth, what may have seemed startling from a distance came as no great surprise on the ground. Middle-class New Orleans may have been numb to poverty's pain, but the troubles poverty brought upon its victims and the city in which they lived were very much in the forefront of local political concerns. So much so that the related question of whether the Bush administration and its feeble relief effort was "racist"— a topic dwelt upon in the national media—seemed sort of beside the point. From the perspective of black New Orleans, much about America was racist, and so surely a Republican administration elected with scarcely a nod to the black vote it didn't need was not going to have the interests of a black city like New Orleans at the top of its agenda. Bush and other whites could and did deny it. Mrs. Bush spoke up to say that as "the person who lives with him," she knew that her husband "cares about people," an assertion of Bush family values that was undercut by the famously callous remark by the president's mother. Barbara Bush suggested that maybe losing one's home, all earthly possessions, and perhaps a relative or two was not necessarily such a bad thing, a cleansing experience for the great unwashed, if you will. "So many of the people in the arena here, you know, were underprivileged anyway," Mrs. Bush offered as she toured the Astrodome, "so this is working very well for them."

Of course there could be no reconciling one camp with the other on an issue as fraught with passion as race and class. The numbers spoke of an unbridgeable divide: Bush had garnered 8 percent of the black vote in 2000, and even after leading black sons and daughters to war, his status as commander in chief got him only a 3 percent uptick in support among blacks in 2004. This was, after all, the man who had made a point of repeatedly declining the standard NAACP invitation to address their annual convention. And after Katrina and the administration's bungled response, a CNN/*USA Today* poll showed that while 60 percent of blacks saw race as a factor behind the delayed response, only 12 percent of whites held that view.

Million-album-selling rapper Kanye West discomfited fellow celebrities at a Katrina telethon four days after the storm by bluntly asserting: "George Bush doesn't care about black people." Actor Colin Farrell posed the hypothetical question: Would the federal response have been so lethally incompetent if those in need of rescue had been standing on rooftops in the Hamptons?

Of course not, though the better hypothetical might have been white folks stranded on rooftops in Des Moines or Waco, because the Hamptonians probably could have mustered their own damn helicopters, and anyway, a lot of them would have been Democrats.

Master P, the Louisiana rap mogul, spoke in tones more typical of the people on the roofs and flooded streets of New Orleans when he responded to Kanye West in an interview after the Katrina telethon, with the observation: "We gotta save people. We need George Bush, we need the mayor, we need the governor. I've lost people. I know how real it is."

And yet for days on end, those needs went unmet. And the question that would be asked, and asked again, once people had time for reflection, was why. Republicans in the House of Representatives, in a report on the fiasco that pulled no punches, would speak of a "failure of initiative" on the part of the administration, including the president and the signature creation of his presidency, the Department of Homeland Security. But again: Why? Why the failure of initiative? Some of what made parties to the discussion irreconcilable was a lack of semantic clarity. Did racism require conscious if not active enmity? Cross burnings? Lynchings? Or was it enough to diagnose a failure of empathy at the heart of the Bush administration, a simple inability on the part of country club Republicans to act with the aggressiveness and confidence that would have brought them more quickly and effectively to the aid of what they perceived to be a troubled black city with a reputation as kind of a strange place? Was an administration that didn't need to care about blacks the same thing as one that didn't care about blacks, and was that indifference racist or political? Was an administration that had made some high-profile black hires an administration that, paradoxically, had somehow retarded progress toward racial equality? The answers were obvious—and they were opposite, depending on your political bias, which as often as not depended on your skin color. But the questions wouldn't go away.

Related themes were at least as interesting, and probably more fruitful as a way of getting at the particulars of the botched Katrina response, because they arose in Bush administration policies more explicit than its racism, real or alleged. One was the administration's deep deference to the private sector, both as an abstraction and as a collection of well-heeled campaign donors at the top of American corporations. Government was perhaps inevitable, the Bush camp conceded, but it was antithetical to "freedom," and the nation would be better off with as little of it as possible. Not only was big government an open door to debilitating socialism and the "welfare mentality," the private sector was infinitely more efficient, the argument went. And as proof, it was necessary only to mention the Pentagon's fabled $700 screwdriver and other icons of government waste.

The less-is-more approach to government had been part of the Republican right's credo at least since the Reagan presidency. That Bush had betrayed it by creating in Homeland Security a bureaucracy bigger than anything since the glory days of LBJ's Great Society programs was an irony that spoke to the virulence of another obsession that had shaped administration policy and that would factor into the Katrina response: terrorism and the need to eradicate it. Terrorism had turned a born-again neocon into a spendthrift president wallowing in red ink. That terrorism had also turned a conservative president into an aggressive agent of government intrusiveness into private lives—domestic spying, detention without trial—was as startling to civil libertarians on the right as it was to those on the left. But what mattered in the narrower context of the Katrina response was that both tenets of the Bush faith—the small-government mantra and the conviction that the nation's gravest threats were posed by the likes of bin Laden, not Katrina—had conspired to gut the nation's disaster response bureaucracy in the name of making the nation safer.

FEMA funding had been cut, and cut again. As further evidence of the Bush camp's indifference to FEMA's once-close attention to natural disaster, the agency's top echelons had become a roost for political cronies, with little or no expertise. Joe Allbaugh's claim on emergency management skills was the fund-raising prowess on Bush's behalf that was rewarded with the FEMA directorship. He had greased the skids for a college roommate to succeed him, and Mike Brown's résumé was paltry even before it was revealed by *Time* magazine to be fake: He had not been an "outstanding professor" at Central State, he had been a student; he had not overseen "emergency services" in Edmond, Oklahoma, he had been an assistant to the city manager, an internship; and his decade with an Arabian horse-breeding association—something he omitted from the résumé—reportedly had ended with his being fired. As Katrina struck, five of FEMA's top ten posts were occupied by people with no disaster experience, while fourteen of the top twenty-five slots were filled by temporary hires or by people doing two senior jobs at the same time.

Katrina was a test of Bush's faith in smaller government and his fixation on foreign terror, and rarely does history grade a presidency so quickly or so harshly. Because if Homeland Security and its stepchild, FEMA, was what stood between America and the next 9/11, then, as New Orleans learned the hard way, America was in deep trouble.

FEMA's failings, most of them reflecting simple ineptitude in the art of mustering available resources, were extravagant, outrageous—one wanted to say fabulous, except that they were also deadly. There was the USS *Bataan* hospital ship mobilized to the Gulf ahead of Katrina, then largely ignored by FEMA in the critical first week after landfall, its one-hundred-thousand-gallons-a-day water-making capacity untapped, its six hundred hospital beds empty, its six operating rooms idle. "I can't force myself on people," the *Bataan*'s captain Nora Tyson grumbled as she waited for FEMA to put her vessel more fully into service. There were the three U.S. Customs Black Hawk helicopter crews marshaled to Crestview Airport in Florida and, to their disgust, wasted in ferrying press around the disaster zone for a couple of days, rather than being allowed to participate in the rescue work.

At several junctures, it seemed as if what was left of FEMA's staff had been reduced to the pettiest and most timid kind of bureaucratic thinking. On the eve of the storm, the state Department of Wildlife and Fisheries had appealed to FEMA's headquarters in Denton, Texas, for three hundred rubber rafts to rescue flood victims—a request later upped to a thousand rafts. The word from Denton: "Request denied." In their wisdom, the FEMA operatives had decided rubber rafts were an imperfect response; there might be debris in the water. Harry Lee, the mercurial and hard-charging sheriff of Jefferson Parish, was mystified when FEMA suddenly put the kibosh on the volunteer boat brigades that had turned up in the storm's immediate aftermath to begin plying the flood zone in a search for survivors. Lee had been mustering them at points of entry to the city, when word came down that FEMA would not let them in. The situation in the city was, in FEMA's view, unsafe. "No shit," muttered a boat captain as he backed his trailer out of line and prepared to leave the scene.

Members of the Florida Airboat Association called FEMA to find out where they should deploy their resources, a traditional component in hurricane response. Three days later, FEMA had not called back, and the airboaters were on the phone to the Florida congressional delegation, seeking intervention. Now at least they got an answer. Volunteers were not allowed into the disaster zone because it was, as Sheriff Lee had already been advised, unsafe. "We cannot get deployed to save our behinds," Robert Dummett, state coordinator of the Florida Airboat Association complained.

The federal government itself was rebuffed by FEMA. The Department of the Interior, with hundreds of boats available for rescue work, had not been able to get a callback from FEMA, the Senate Committee on Homeland Security and Governmental Affairs would learn during hearings in January. Even the Red Cross, deeply seasoned by service in combat zones around the world, was held back for a time on grounds of safety. If aid workers were on the scene, people might begin to think it was safe to stay on in New Orleans, FEMA told the Red Cross. And perhaps it might have become safe to stay, but without the Red Cross, it was surely less so. The federal obsession with safety struck survivors as belated, if not deeply hypocritical, given that it was failure of the neglected federal levee system that had brought catastrophe upon New Orleans in the first place.

A deadly extreme of bureaucratic inanity was reached out at the airport when Dr. Mark Perlmutter, an orthopedic surgeon from Pennsylvania who had come down as a volunteer, was ordered to stop giving chest compressions to a dying woman because he wasn't registered with FEMA. Not for lack of trying. Perlmutter had spent the previous day on the phone with FEMA trying in vain to arrange certification. "I begged him to let me continue [the chest compressions]," Perlmutter said. "People were dying, and I was the only doctor on the tarmac. Two patients died in front of me." But the coast guard official in charge of the medivac location knew FEMA's rules to be inflexible. "I asked him to let me stay until I was replaced by another doctor, but he refused," Perlmutter said. "He said he was afraid of being sued. I informed him about the Good Samaritan laws and asked him if he was willing to let people die so the government wouldn't be sued, but he would not back down. I had to leave." FEMA explained itself in terms that were, if nothing else, entirely consistent with the mindless policy enforced on the tarmac. "We have a cadre of physicians of our own," spokeswoman Kim Pease said. "The voluntary doctor was not a credentialed FEMA physician and thus was subject to law enforcement rules in a disaster area."

Not that local officials were blameless in all this. Both Nagin and Blanco had made plenty of mistakes and, in hindsight—or under congressional prodding—were obliged to admit them. Nagin's failure to stock the convention center with food and water before opening it as an overflow shelter the day after the storm, struck the Senate Committee on Homeland Security and Governmental Affairs as particularly egregious. The list of provisions for the convention center that Nagin claimed to have rushed to FEMA's attention had not turned up among eight hundred thousand documents reviewed, according to the committee's chairwoman, Senator Susan Collins, a Republican from Maine. At the state level, transportation secretary Johnny Bradberry, much lauded by Blanco for designing the successful contraflow evacuation plan, had taken no action at all in response to an instruction from state legislators that he develop evacuation plans for people without cars. The failure to evacuate nursing homes led directly to the deaths of seventy-five residents, Collins charged while grilling Blanco two days after Nagin's appearance. Blanco pointed out that the evacuation plans were in place, which was true, but some of the nursing homes just hadn't acted on them. Mississippi, by contrast, had instructed the state agency that finances nursing homes simply to mandate their evacuation, Governor Barbour told the senators. Barbour's support for the presidential administration of a fellow Republican was not unflinching, however. When it came to FEMA, he echoed the complaints from Louisiana about the agency's failure to come through with promised supplies of food and water.

EVEN MORE THAN THE WAR IN IRAQ, KATRINA ALSO LAID BARE THE SHORTCOMings of the Bush administration's rigid top-down management style. A chain of command meant to free the president from distracting minutiae and allow him to implement a grand vision of conservative reform, instead seemed to put him out of touch and out of reach, as Governor Blanco discovered in several initially unsuccessful attempts to speak to Bush by phone. A decisive moment, his aides would later reveal, turned not on the president's assessment of field reports from government operatives on the ground but on his exposure to a tape cobbled together from news broadcasts the rest of America had been watching all week. History does not record whether the tape included the radio interview in which a grizzled, half-unhinged Mayor Nagin howled at federal and state officials to be done with media ops and get something done: "I don't want to see anybody do any more goddamn press conferences," Nagin snarled in a phone interview with radio commentator Garland Robinette. Bush had just been on the air, as had Blanco, to say that the forty thousand troops she'd asked for were on their way. "Put a moratorium on press conferences," Nagin continued. "Don't do another press conference until the resources are in the city. And then come down to this city and stand with us when there are military trucks and troops that we can't even count. Don't tell me forty thousand people are coming here. They're not here. It's too doggone late. Now get off your asses and do something, and let's fix the biggest goddamn crisis in the history of this country."

Indeed, for a while that week it was hard to turn on a cable news channel without some local politician cursing or sobbing on camera. Mary Landrieu wept publicly for her people, as did many Senate colleagues after a speech in which she said, memorably, about underfunded flood-control measures: "Washington rolled the dice, and Louisiana lost." And Eddie Compass, the New Orleans police chief, sobbed on Oprah's show after giving her audience a recklessly exaggerated depiction of post-Katrina New Orleans as a city witness to "little babies getting raped." Jefferson Parish president Aaron Broussard wept on his own behalf, for losing his home, and on behalf of a colleague in parish government whose mother, in Broussard's dramatic (but partly invented) rendition, had expired after waiting all week in a St. Bernard Parish nursing home for a rescue team that never came. "Every day she called him and said, 'Are you coming, son? Is somebody coming?' 'Yeah, Mama. Somebody's coming to get you on Tuesday. Somebody's coming to get you on Wednesday . . . on Thursday . . . on Friday. And she drowned Friday night." The truth was horrendous enough, but it had nothing to do with the failed federal relief effort: Emergency manager Tom Rodrigue's mother, Eva, ninety-two, was one of thirty-five residents of the St. Rita's nursing home who died when the place was inundated in the storm's earliest hours. St. Rita's operators would be charged criminally by the state for failing to evacuate the facility ahead of time.

Rage and self-pity having failed to quicken the federal disaster response, public paroxysms gave way to another strategy, hyperbole. Nagin used his Oprah moment to report that "hundreds of gang members" were raping women and committing murder at the Superdome, a fiction, as it turned out. And with another camera whirring, he advised that the eventual death toll could be north of ten thousand. In fairness to Nagin, FEMA had rushed out and bought twenty-four thousand body bags after Katrina struck—further evidence of chaos in that agency, given the hundreds of thousands of body bags already stockpiled at army bases around the country and the thousand on hand at the coroner's office right there in New Orleans, almost exactly as many as the disaster would require. Had more thought been given to buses than body bags, maybe we wouldn't have needed even the one-thousand-plus bags that eventually were used, one pundit suggested.

Grasping at last the gravity of the problem, both in New Orleans and in the nation's ebbing confidence in his own abilities, the president winged back over Louisiana air space Friday morning. This time, Bush was emboldened to touch down at Armstrong International, the New Orleans airport, for a meeting with Nagin, Blanco, and various members of the state's congressional delegation.

That morning in Mobile, ten days before Mike Brown would be eased out of FEMA's top job, in disgrace, Bush had clapped him on the back and declared, memorably, "Brownie, you're doing a heck of a job." But the massiveness of the federal failure was already coming clear to others in the White House, and spin control was reaching hurricane velocity. Brown attempted to blame the fiasco not even partly on his own incompetence but on a "dysfunctional" relationship between unnamed Louisiana politicians (Blanco and Nagin). The blame-casting blew up in his face, though in February he would try it again, this time laying all the sins of the administration's failed response at the feet of his boss, Michael Chertoff—a man so useless in crisis that Brown said he couldn't be bothered to brief him on what was happening in New Orleans. Rove—at least those in the Blanco administration would assume it was Rove—came up with a more artful strategy for the president.

Step one was to deplore "the blame game" and declare it over and done with, an exercise in petty politics unworthy of a great nation at a time of tribulation. Step two was to try to win it. In an effort to push blame back down the chain of command to the state and local level, defenders of the president and FEMA seized on two themes, one apiece for Nagin and Blanco, and started to work them hard. Nagin's problem was the discovery of parking lots filled with city and school buses. Who was Nagin to so loudly condemn FEMA for not rushing buses to the Dome and the convention center? He should have used his own damn buses in the evacuation. Or so the counterattack went. Blanco was taken to task for the long—indeed, permanent—delay as she pondered Bush's curious offer to "federalize" the Louisiana National Guard. What was her problem? If she wanted Bush to help, she should have gotten over herself, stepped aside, and let the army take over the state's military assets, critics charged. Doing so, the argument went, would have brought all available troops under one seamless command structure for maximum efficiency.

The bus issue, like the buses themselves, could be called a nonstarter. By the time anyone paid them much mind, the parking lot where many had been stashed was deeply swamped, as was most of the city, and for those buses that had been pulled up onto the levee, where they stayed dry, there were no drivers. But suppose that before the storm and the flooding, New Orleans for the first time in its history had attempted not simply to order an evacuation but to engineer one, using city buses. Assume for the moment that the plan had actually worked, that decrepit buses had not broken down, that ill-paid drivers had agreed to abandon their families and labor all Saturday and Sunday and on into the night ferrying evacuees—somewhere. Mississippi was the nearest high ground, but it was also the storm's likely landfall. West to Baton Rouge, then, or Lafayette, or maybe right on into Texas. There was, of course, no place big enough to receive a nomadic city of one hundred thousand stragglers envisioned in this retrospective scenario. And this number would have grown only larger the moment the city announced it was willing to drive the needy out of town, and carless residents stopped looking for rides on their own. And for those who somehow missed the city-managed evacuation, there would be no buses left to do the one thing they were always needed for when a storm was brewing: shuttling the stragglers and the ill and the aged to the Dome.

Buses were best not mentioned in playing the blame game with Blanco. The issue didn't work against her. Indeed, she could use it against the feds. She had begged all week for FEMA to make good on a promise to round up the armada of coaches needed to evacuate the Dome and the convention center, something that had barely been started as Bush touched down that Friday, five days later.

In ways that suggested he was all over the situation, Mike Brown had been immediately attentive to Blanco's concerns when they met in Baton Rouge on Monday, just hours after the hurricane struck. And he had promised the world: five hundred buses to evacuate the Dome, an allotment of $26,200 for each destroyed home. "Don't worry about costs," Blanco remembered him saying, "and be sure to get eight hours of sleep." That had amused Blanco, a woman who rarely logged a consecutive five hours of sleep even without a catastrophe to worry about.

Indeed, sleep seemed to figure prominently on Brown's list of concerns. On inquiry, it turned out the buses would take some time to reach Louisiana, he cautioned. Drivers can only work twelve-hour shifts, he said. When Blanco nudged him a bit and asked if, under the circumstances, maybe two-driver crews could be assigned so that one could sleep while the other drove, Brown blandly observed that some buses had that arrangement. And some didn't. Nonetheless confident that the buses would soon arrive, Blanco that same Monday ordered an aide to line up shelter for the twenty-five thousand people who would shortly be rescued from the Dome. Because the overflow would surely spill all the way into Texas, she got on the phone with Governor Rick Perry to arrange for use of the Astrodome as a temporary shelter. It would become clear that Brown's talk about the buses had been just that. Talk. Two days would pass before he even issued the order that started them on their way from distant states to New Orleans. When Wednesday rolled around but still Brown's buses hadn't, Blanco stormed into the Emergency Operations Center office demanding to know who on her staff could figure out how to round some up. Tour and school buses were duly commandeered, but many of their drivers, alarmed by overblown media reports of violence in New Orleans, handed over their keys to Blanco's people and refused to make the trip themselves. Which made for further delays and a search for substitute drivers. No, buses might have been Nagin's problem, but they were also FEMA's. It would take something else to push Blanco back on her heels.

What the Bush people came up with was the idea of trying to get her to hand over formal command of the state militia. It might seem to have been an arcane technical issue, but the political possibilities were tantalizing if, in seizing control of the 13,268 Louisiana National Guard troops—or at least the 6,000 or so not already called up for service in Iraq—Bush could seem to be stepping in forcefully and cleaning up a mess of Governor Blanco's making.

Ambushed by the president on Air Force One with his request to relinquish control of the Guard, Blanco smelled a rat and stared him down. She said she'd want to discuss the matter with him privately. Her temporizing prompted Nagin to slam his hand down on the table and suggest that she and the president get it over with right then and there. He could wait. The governor and the president repaired to a private room.

Federalizing the Guard would do nothing to put more troops on the ground. Indeed it might reduce the federal commitment, Blanco feared. Moreover, federalizing the Guard had a very real downside, as Blanco had come to understand. Once merged with the regular army, the Guard would no longer be available for one of New Orleans's most urgent needs: policing a city and the looters who were sacking it. A law passed in 1878, the Posse Comitatus Act, forbade federal troops from getting involved in the policing of U.S. civilians unless the Riot Act had been invoked, which it hadn't been in New Orleans, and wouldn't be. (The prospect of fuzzy-cheeked regular army recruits training assault rifles on the desperate and volatile storm survivors still milling about in New Orleans was a prospect even the Pentagon found nerve-racking.)

Rather than turn Bush down cold—he was the president, after all—Blanco temporized by demurely asking for twenty-four hours to consider his request, and the Air Force One meeting moved on to other topics. That night, the White House tried again. Back in Baton Rouge, Blanco was in a midnight session with advisers when Bush chief of staff Andy Card called and told her to look for a fax, a memo of understanding that needed only her signature to accomplish the transfer of command that would federalize the Louisiana Guard. Certain by then that she had been right all along in sensing political gamesmanship rather than strategic concerns behind the federalization riff, Blanco didn't sign then or ever. The House committee reviewing the Katrina debacle would concede that federalizing the state militia would have provided no advantages at all.

Bush's aides, of course, denied that anything so petty as partisan politics played a role in their minuet with Blanco, one of the last Democratic governors in a part of the country that Republicans had come to think of as a core constituency—worse yet, a Democrat who had signaled her disgust with Bush's FEMA by hiring the well-regarded Clinton-era FEMA boss, James Lee Witt, as an adviser. (The day after the meeting with Bush, she would put Witt in charge of the state's emergency response.) As proof of White House impartiality, the president's counsel Dan Bartlett would insist that "the same discussions" about federalizing the state militia were under way with Mississippi governor Haley Barbour, a Republican who had headed the national party. But that was a falsehood, if one was to believe Barbour's people. "No such request" was made of Mississippi, the governor's press secretary said. In any event, Mississippi didn't federalize its Guard.

Blanco, like Nagin, would be faulted for many things about the way she handled Katrina. Critics called her indecisive, a weak leader in a time of crisis. Her grandmotherly tones did not well serve the purposes of ringing oratory, though she would avoid Nagin's gaffes as a public speaker, a litany that would grow beyond his wild exaggerations on Oprah to include his clumsy declaration that God was angry at George Bush and that it was divine will that New Orleans remain, as he put it, "a chocolate city." But whatever Blanco's failures of leadership, she did not lack a shrewd instinct for politics. Nonetheless, the coming assault, she conceded in hindsight, caught her off guard—not the monkey business aboard Air Force One about relinquishing control of the Louisiana National Guard; she had been tipped off to that possibility the night before by General Blum, chief of the National Guard Bureau, and he had cautioned her against doing it, she said. No, the first scent of blood in the water—and the blood was her own—had come two days earlier. Queries to her press secretary, Denise Bottcher, were the first intimation that something was up. Why hasn't the governor signed a disaster declaration, one news service wanted to know—when in fact Blanco had declared a state of emergency three days before Katrina struck. When calls like that persisted, Bottcher started asking reporters where they were getting their leads. The answer: "high White House sources," Bottcher said.

From the perspective of the governor's staff, it was a systematic disinformation campaign with, many assumed, Karl Rove putting the falsehoods into the minds of a reliable stable of Republican stalwarts, and then making them available to the media as talking heads. The shock was only greater because the knife in Blanco's back contrasted so markedly with the way things had started out. Late that week, and only more so as the months rolled by and the finger-pointing continued, it was wrenching to think back on the love fest that had been Blanco's Tuesday press conference with Mary Landrieu and Brown.

> BLANCO: Director Brown. I hope you will tell President Bush how much we appreciated—these are the times that really count—to know that our federal government will step in and give us the kind of assistance that we need.
> LANDRIEU: We are indeed fortunate to have an able and experienced director of FEMA who has been with us on the ground for some time.
> BROWN: What I've seen here today is a team that is very tight-knit, working closely together, being very professional doing it, and in my humble opinion, making the right calls.

Stepping out of a Black Hawk an hour later in New Orleans, Brown had also lavished praise on Nagin, commending him on the comprehensiveness of the list of the city's needs that had been forwarded to FEMA, a moment hard to reconcile with the federal government's later attempt to blame both Nagin and Blanco for the fiasco by insisting that they hadn't been specific enough in their requests for help.

If there was any satisfaction in Blanco's handling of the Guard takeover flap, it was this: Manipulation of the issue by her enemies may have cost her some support, but it had done nothing to shore up Bush's plunging approval numbers. On his next trip to Louisiana, three days after the meeting aboard Air Force One, his people resorted to the politics of the calculated snub, and failed to inform Blanco of the visit in advance. Indeed, they denied that he was coming at all. The governor was at the airport, preparing to leave by helicopter to meet with evacuees in Houston, when her aides determined that the president was about to arrive. She canceled her trip, and met the president instead. But there were other prices paid for not having friends in high places. By year's end, though Mississippi had incurred just a fraction of the damage—61,386 severely damaged homes compared with 204,737 in Louisiana—on a per capita basis, the Magnolia State had secured three times Louisiana's share of the congressional allocation designated for community development block grants, a prime vehicle for funneling billions in disaster aid to the two states.

The imbalance owed as much to Barbour's Republican clout and to Mississippi senator Thad Cochran's seniority and legislative skills as to White House maneuvering against the Democrat governor of Louisiana. But that made it no more palatable to the people of Louisiana. "It makes me sick to my stomach," Blanco would say in an unguarded moment in late January 2006.

THE WEEK'S HARSHEST EXCORIATION OF A LOCAL OFFICIAL WAS RESERVED FOR Aaron Broussard and was meted out not by anonymous spinmeisters in Washington but by Broussard's own furious constituents. As president of Jefferson Parish, Broussard essentially was mayor of the thicket of strip malls and housing subdivisions immediately west of New Orleans. Critics found opportunities to suggest that Broussard's hand on the tiller of parish government was just a bit unsteady. But there could be no accusing him of inconsistency. He had come under fire earlier in the storm season for breaking ranks and ordering the "premature evacuation" ahead of Hurricane Dennis. With Katrina, not only would he order an evacuation, he would signal once again, by activating the parish's "doomsday" plan, just how seriously everyone should take hurricanes. Developed after Hurricane Georges in 1998, the plan, in the face of a Category 4 or 5 hurricane, ordered the entire parish government and some seven hundred parish vehicles to hightail it many score miles to the north, to a schoolhouse in rural Washington Parish. Critics were prepared to concede that the parish could survive at least briefly—perhaps permanently—without the services of many low-level functionaries. But when it was understood that Broussard had also ordered pump station workers to evacuate—a move that instantly shut down drainage operations throughout a parish that was far less flooded than Orleans—the outrage was tempestuous. It did not help Broussard that among the few areas that did flood was Northline Avenue, a stretch of palazzi and mere mansions much in vogue with Jefferson's richest burghers.

It made for quite a dustup, only more so after it was revealed that the parish's longtime emergency manager, the esteemed Dr. Walter Maestri, had ignored Broussard's evacuation order and assigned crews at the parish water treatment plant to ride out the storm. Next it was the president of the East Jefferson levee board, Patrick Bosetta, who was publicly assailing Broussard for pulling the pump station operators. In the face of mounting public scorn, the flight-prone Broussard at first stoutly stood his ground. Pump crews would have drowned or been electrocuted had Katrina made a direct hit, he argued, and anyway the pumps wouldn't have worked against an onrushing storm surge. For good measure, he announced his intent to sack Pat Bosetta. When the furor failed to die down, lawsuits were being readied, and prospective rivals for the parish president's job began joining in the clamor, Broussard conceded that the doomsday plan might benefit from "tweaking." To return them more quickly to their posts, perhaps essential workers could be evacuated to a less far-flung shelter.

By late October, foreseeing a personal doomsday of the political variety, Broussard was reduced to pleading his case in four full-page ads published over eight days in *The Times-Picayune* at a cost of $38,000. He also followed Mike Brown's lead toward a more rough-and-ready approach to fashion. His way of rolling up his sleeves was to doff a risibly unconvincing toupee and begin appearing in public unshaven and in a baseball cap. It is uncertain who paid for the baseball cap, but rather than commit campaign funding to pay for the ads, Broussard billed the parish for them. They were part of an effort to keep the public informed on hurricane issues, he declared, not a self-serving exercise in spin control—and anyway, he said when quizzed, he could probably get FEMA to chip in. It was an opportunity for emergency management that FEMA quickly and respectfully declined.

Issues of command and control would also crop up among personnel of the city's port. There, a Broussard-like zeal to evacuate appeared to have been felt powerfully by a woman named Cynthia Swain, the safety director with the semi-autonomous Port of New Orleans. Swain's yearning to flee to Texas was not shared by harbor police chief Robert Hecker, her underling according to the port's command structure but a man who had spent a decade in the chief's role after twenty-eight years of service with the New Orleans Police Department. Hecker had moved swiftly after the storm passed and breached levees flooded the city. By Monday evening, harbor police boats were plying the drowned streets of the Lower Ninth Ward, plucking screaming survivors off rooftops. His men were still at it Tuesday afternoon, to the enormous relief of Fats Domino, one of the neighborhood residents they rescued. But late that evening, Swain ordered Hecker to abort the rescue mission and leave the city, consistent with her mandatory evacuation order for port personnel. Hecker refused.

"She panicked, I guess." That was the opinion of Frank DeSalvo, the attorney Hecker decided he'd better retain when state and local agencies began probing the matter. Swain's boss, port director Gary LaGrange, was prepared to give her the benefit of the doubt. After all, at the time Swain gave her evacuation order, rumor had it that Canal Street might soon be under ten feet of water, a not entirely unreasonable expectation, though a false one. Meanwhile, gangs of looters were menacing the city, and about that there could be no doubt.

Hecker and a couple of officers decided to defy Swain and attempt to keep looters out of key port properties, including two cruise ship terminals—assets critical to the economic well-being of the port—and the harbor police armory, which was heavily stocked with weapons Hecker definitely didn't want to see in looters' hands. On a tip that it was being plundered, they also rushed to the Riverwalk, a long shopping arcade above the downtown wharves, but the three officers were no match for a gang of twenty-five, who were moving systematically through the upscale shops, helping themselves to Sharper Image hardware, designer clothing, and the pricier lines of New Orleans memorabilia. Other officers, hearing that Hecker and his cadre were still on the job, began getting in touch. Hecker said he could not order them to join him, but he made no secret of the gratitude he would feel if they elected to make themselves available as "volunteers." Three weeks later, Hurricane Rita was menacing the Gulf when Swain struck again with an evacuation order. This time Hecker articulated his defiance more fully. In DeSalvo's words: "That's when he just openly told her, 'I'm not following your orders. Perhaps you didn't get the message, but you're no longer in command of my police department.'"

By late September, Hecker was under internal review for insubordina-tion, an outrage in the eyes of many who saw him as the hero, Swain as the story's goat. For them there was consolation in Swain's predicament: She was also under investigation by the state attorney general's office for possi-ble malfeasance.

Anything short of canning her would be a cover-up, DeSalvo thundered. And just to complicate Swain's legal exposure, he filed a whistle-blower lawsuit on Hecker's behalf. In early February, probe completed, Hecker was reinstated without penalty as harbor police chief. In sparing Swain the axe—much to DeSalvo's disgust—the port offered a face-saving analysis of events. She had never formally given the order to disband that she then tried to fire Hecker for defying, port officials concluded. Ergo, no insubordination on Hecker's part.

The mudslinging and petty rivalries tended to obscure that there had been standout performances before and after Katrina struck. The National Weather Service had operated at a peak of precision, accurately predicting the storm track within fifteen miles, as many as fifty-six hours before it made landfall. (On average, storm track projections made forty-eight hours before landfall are off by one hundred sixty miles; twenty-four hours out, they're typically off by eighty-five miles.) Moreover, two days before Katrina hit New Or-leans, the weather service had anticipated its wind speed within 10 miles per hour. Nor was the service less than prophetic in decoding what those numbers meant. "Most of the area will be uninhabitable for weeks . . . perhaps longer," the service said in a Sunday release that bluntly predicted "human suffering incredible by modern standards," even without a breach.

Unlike FEMA and the Bush White House, the coast guard acted on those insights and, within hours of the city going under, was pulling people off rooftops and other places of desperate refuge and coptering them to safety with a quiet efficiency that certainly lessened the loss of life. Twelve hours ahead of landfall, the coast guard had staged double its usual squadron of aircraft at inland airfields across the South. Helicopters available to the coast guard's eighth district, which stretches from New Mexico to Florida, including Louisiana, were increased from fifteen to twenty-nine; fixed wing aircraft were increased from four to eight. The district ordinarily had sixteen cutters at its service. That number was increased to twenty-four. All did not go perfectly, however. Even before Katrina's landfall, the coast guard's New Orleans computer hub crashed, snapping the district's link to other coastal ports. Phones and faxes continued to function, however.

WHAT THE MEDIA WANTED, OF COURSE, WAS A STAR—SOMEONE ON WHOM TO focus the yearning for effective leadership that seemed so sorely lacking among the many politicians jabbering, finger-pointing, and blubbering on camera. And briefly, at least—for as long as he could put up with it—the media had their man in Lt. Gen. Russel Honoré, the commander of Joint Task Force Katrina. In a landscape crawling with double-talk, he was blunt, action-oriented, and, after a delayed start, capable of results. Governor Blanco would long recall the sense of relief she'd felt two days after Katrina, upon seeing Honoré stride into the state Office of Emergency Prepared- ness—here at last was the cavalry—and then the sense of astonishment upon learning that the commander of Joint Task Force Katrina, this toweringly tall cigar-chomping soldier from her own part of Louisiana, had arrived without his army. The delayed start was troubling to more than the Blanco team. FEMA operative Phil Parr believed he had contrived an effective plan that would have evacuated the Dome by helicopter Tuesday night. He had se- cured permission to begin the deployment when the troopless general said no—and for reasons that were never meaningfully explained.

But if those wobbles could be overlooked, by week's end, Honoré was walking tall. Six-foot-two and given to mirror-lensed aviator glasses and the brandishing of cigars the length of a billy club, he called the storm "evil" and did not hesitate to reveal the awe in which he held it.

Honoré, the Pentagon's second-highest-ranking African American, had taken the measure of Katrina as he raced on Tuesday from Atlanta, where he lived, to the tristate hurricane command headquarters set up at Camp Shelby in Mississippi. It staggered him to learn that the storm's wind band had been two hundred fifty miles wide and able to shred New Orleans's electrical grid while the eye was still more than one hundred miles away; that the storm had killed people simultaneously in Mississippi and in Georgia, places separated by a six-hour drive.

Honoré remembered barely being able to keep his car on wind-buffeted

Highway 20 as he tore toward Camp Shelby. He arrived to find the base reeling as if it had been nuked. Power and cell service had crashed along with what seemed like half the pines in the adjacent De Soto National Forest. Down on the coast, his most lasting impression was of a huge steel barge, the underpinnings of an otherwise-decimated floating casino, that had been flipped out of the water at Gulfport, Mississippi, and onto U.S. 90—or what used to be Highway 90, by then beachfront.

Honoré thought about Katrina in much the same way he had taken stock of the enemy during combat in Iraq and Kuwait. "It did a classic battlefield maneuver," Honoré said. It compounded the force of its attack with an element of surprise. The feint was to enter the Gulf as a paltry Category 1 storm, its energies seemingly sapped during the transit across Florida. And then, having ramped up suddenly to monstrous strength, "It surprised the hell out of people in Mississippi, because they thought it was coming to New Orleans."

Honoré could only respect how Katrina had seen fit to scramble the region's communications networks, because that, he said, was exactly what he would have done in the first phase of an all-out attack. And Katrina had gone on to dice key highways and the region's rail lines—just as Honoré would have done. "We try to use overwhelming military power to shock and overwhelm the adversary," Honoré said.

Honoré loved to rattle off the stats and superlatives: that two hundred fifty thousand refugees had descended on Baton Rouge, instantly turning a sleepy state capital into the largest city in the state; that forty thousand people would have died had the twenty-eight-foot storm surge that slammed into Gulfport instead been unleashed in a direct hit on New Orleans; that there were more helicopters available to Joint Task Force Katrina than deployed to Iraq and Afghanistan combined.

But if Honoré could sound gung ho, he could also be a voice of moderation, a commodity in short supply just then in New Orleans. Had snipers outside the Dome really begun shooting at helicopters? Honoré was there and he had a different explanation: An army personnel carrier had driven over a plastic water bottle at an inopportune moment and the popping sound was mistaken for gunfire. The pilot heard it and flinched. Someone in the crowd yelled "Sniper!" and an urban myth was born. But were there people out there desperate enough to start shooting at a helicopter trying to rescue them? Honoré wasn't going to rule that out.

As much as he was the darling of the media, Honoré was also their scourge. The TV crews were wild for a little face time with the man in the black beret and aviator glasses. Honoré put up with some of it—and then wrought revenge by dressing down reporters at his briefings. Inevitably, the press dwelt on the atrociousness of the federal response, the failure to vacate the Dome and the convention center for days on end. "Okay, reporter," Honoré snapped during one such inquisition. "How many people did you take out? How many people did you give water to?" And why had it taken the military so long to bring in the buses when TV crews were in and out of the city at will? "Where were we going to find the buses at, mister? You're confusing what you can do with money in your pocket and the corporate sponsorship of some news company with taking care of twenty thousand people with no water in an unsafe environment. Don't confuse that, okay?"

A lot of it was bluster. When the aviator glasses came off, there could be a twinkle in Honoré's eye. In a sense, Joint Task Force Katrina had brought him home, and he seemed to be enjoying himself. He had grown up during the segregation era in Cajun country: a farm in Pointe Coupée Parish, out on the Louisiana prairie. That made him a country cousin, but no bumpkin. He had spent two weeks in Charity Hospital after getting cracked in the head with a baseball bat during otherwise happy summer trips to New Orleans. It hadn't soured him on the city. Not by any means. He had sent one of his four kids—two boys, two girls—to college at Loyola. Kimberly had evacuated her apartment in Kenner and joined her big sister in Florida—leaving extra helpings of food for her pets, on the assumption, widespread among evacuees, that she'd be back in a couple of days. Well, it didn't work out that way, and her father was getting barraged with almost daily e-mails to rescue Gumbo, the cat, and Hammie, the hamster.

"I've got eighty helicopters in the air and we're trying to evacuate twenty thousand people from the convention center, and she's e-mailing me every day about her cat," Honoré growled.

And then he went and got them. "The good news is they were okay," Honoré said. "The cat was living large in that place."

SEVEN

Media in the Moment

THERE CAME A MOMENT, MIXED IN AMONG SOME OF THE VERY FINEST MO-
ments of his career as a newspaper photographer, when Ted Jackson
was ready to throw down his cameras and walk away from photojournalism
in shamefaced disgust. The nosiness of his calling, the implicit voyeurism,
the way news photography fed on human tragedy without seeming to alleviate the suffering. There was nothing new about this ethical conundrum, but
Katrina threw it into high relief, and Jackson, a man of deep religious faith,
was tortured. There had been the cluster of women and children trapped on
a front stoop in rising water below the St. Claude Avenue Bridge into the
Lower Ninth Ward. Jackson had come across them Monday afternoon as he
scoured the city for images of what seemed like a subsiding storm. He had
ventured out into the water to try to help the women and children reach the
ramped roadway, only to discover that the current was more than he could
handle. He begged the women to stay put, not to attempt to swim to higher
ground; he promised that he would notify authorities of their dilemma
(which he soon did). And when a man cursed Jackson and told him not to be

taking their picture if he couldn't help them, Jackson fired off some shots anyway. They should talk about it over lunch someday, he told the man. Meanwhile, it was his job.

A day later, he found himself on another elevated roadway, Causeway Boulevard this time, where it rose up over Interstate 10 in Jefferson Parish. Ambulances were dropping off medivac cases there, and as Jackson and a cluster of TV camera crews stood by, a helicopter clattered into position to pick up a woman with a broken hip. EMTs hopped out, snapped a gurney into its upright position, and began trying to ease the woman onto it. There seemed to be a problem with the gurney. The wheels wouldn't lock, and so every time the EMTs got ready to hoist her aboard, the damn thing would begin to rattle away from where it needed to be.

"Can someone help us?" The EMTs were hollering at anyone within earshot: a moment of crisis, a touch of excitement. And so the TV crews did what TV crews do, which is not to play EMT but to zoom in on the woman's face, contorted in agony.

Jackson had photographed wars, in Iraq, in Bosnia. He had photographed death and dying. But the choice that confronted him—whether to chronicle the event or break right through the frame and take action—had never been so vexing, only in part because this disaster had hit so close to home. Maybe if he had been alone with his thoughts he would have acted differently, but somehow seeing the ethical challenge play out in the automatic responses of the camera crew made it harder to ignore. Jackson put down his cameras—great shot or not. He picked the woman up and helped ease her onto the gurney, and that was when the impulse overcame him, to just chuck a thirty-year-career and $10,000 in camera gear and start walking. It didn't much matter where. "My honest-to-God thought was to just walk down the interstate and go home."

Months later, reflecting back on this moment, Jackson remembered an old joke photographers told each other in the days before digital cameras: "If you saw someone about to be killed and had to choose between saving a life and the Pulitzer Prize–winning shot . . . what kind of film would you use?"

Jackson was not the only photographer Katrina inspired to deeply probe his professional ethics, nor were photographers the only part of the media brigade to come under review. Reporters, even from some of the big papers that for a decade had been exhaustively critiquing their own and their rivals' work for signs of racial and gender insensitivity, proved shockingly comfortable reviving stereotypes that were both unflattering and, as it turned out, false. Rumors of gang rapes and wanton murder needed to be repeated only two or three times before reporters decided the rumors had been corroborated, and repeated them in print—the story of the asthmatic child, for example, reported by one paper as having died in the convention center and then been simply abandoned on the floor by police and, apparently, the child's own parents. No such death was ever confirmed by authorities, nor were the even more widespread reports of babies getting their throats slit at the Superdome. Of course, it did not help the cause of reliable journalism that, for reasons of their own, the city's mayor and his police chief were repeating some of these same rumors as fact.

Caught up in what for many was the biggest story of their careers, reporters dipped their pens in purple ink. The aggregate portrait was of a city gone mad, a black city, a city of depraved men and women who would walk away from asthmatic children and leave them to die, if they didn't violate them first. "It just morphed into this mythical place where the most unthinkable deeds were being done," a National Guard spokesman, Ed Bush, said. Media critic Michael Eric Dyson would speak perceptively of "a conceptual vacuum" that opened up as government help failed to arrive. The vacuum quickly filled with lies and legends. "There were reports of an infant's body found in a trash can, of sharks swimming through flood waters on Canal Street, of hundreds of bodies stashed in the Superdome basement," Dyson wrote. A doctor showed up to start processing the bodies. "I've got a report of two hundred," he told a Guardsman in charge. The real total was six: a drug overdose, the suicide Patrina Peters and her daughter had heard about, and four deaths from natural causes.

Some of the rumors were spun from whole cloth: that a hundred corpses—or was it twenty?—had been lashed together in Chalmette to keep them from simply floating out to sea. A delegation of reporters and photographers hastened to Abramson High School in eastern New Orleans to inspect the remains of six hundred people thought to have drowned there after seeking refuge in the school gym. The actual total of corpses: zero. Some rumors had a toehold on reality. The rumor that police superintendent Eddie

Compass had mutinied like others under his command was substantiated by the sight of the superintendent's cruiser on the interstate heading toward Baton Rouge. Yes, the chief's car had left the city at high speed, bearing Compass's very pregnant wife to an appointment with her obstetrician. Nagin was believed to have treacherously bought a home in Dallas, when, in fact, he had rented one as a place of refuge for his wife and younger children. Jefferson Parish sheriff Harry Lee was rumored to have checked out altogether: dead. How that one got started remains obscure, the once exceedingly stout Lee having survived stomach stapling so successfully that the attendant weight loss left many of his constituents with the impression that he would live forever.

Rumors like that were mostly harmless. Others had a virulence that actually slowed the relief effort. Incredibly, FEMA's mistaken assumption that rioting was about to sweep the Superdome late Tuesday inspired the relief agency not to augment its efforts to ease the misery, but to yank its people from harm's way for several hours. The same impulse led to an overnight suspension of boat rescue missions amid fears that craft and FEMA personnel might be hijacked by the stranded folk they were trying to pluck from rooftops and attics.

Other myths and rumors were counterproductive in subtler ways. A street-level activist named Dyan French Cole, a.k.a. Mama D, set back Louisiana's effort to win the sympathies—and loosen the purse strings—of Congress when her rambling appearance before the House committee investigating Katrina included a full-throated testimonial to her belief that the levees had been dynamited as part of a plot to drive blacks from the city. But she was not alone in her conviction, and fellow adherents to it ranged far above the social station occupied by Patrina Peters and others of the working poor whose homes were knocked asunder by the raging water.

So persistent was the rumor of a deliberate breach—no matter that it eradicated prosperous white communities as well as black ones—that lawmakers would still feel compelled to quiz Nagin about it during his testimony before a House select committee on Katrina in mid-December. Connecticut representative Christopher Shays began by gently scolding Nagin for some of the trouble he'd gotten himself into by making reckless remarks to reporters, then he cut to the chase: "First, do you believe [the levees] were blown up by the government?" Shays demanded. "And second, do you believe they were blown up?" Nagin knew better than to deny an otherwise sympathetic Republican the simple clarity the issue required: "I do not believe that the levees were blown up," he said quickly.

THERE WERE MOMENTS IN THE ENDLESS WEEK THAT WAS WHEN THE LIFE THAT hung in the balance was Ted Jackson's. He and another photographer managed to contact an evacuee friend of theirs, a woman who had reason to believe that her home in Jefferson Parish was unflooded. Not only was it unflooded, it might even have had power and water, no small consideration after a week of twenty-four-hour days without a change of clothes or much chance to shower. They could use it if they could get to it, she said, and once on the premises, Jackson had slipped in through a back window. He was coming out the front door to let in his colleague when a gunman's voice rang out and Jackson dropped swiftly to the ground, as ordered. A retired cop, clearly thrilling to the opportunity to relive his glory days, had decided that Jackson and his buddy were looters. Jackson could feel the itchiness of the man's trigger finger. Shoot-to-kill orders against looters were tacit but highly motivating among certain elements, an opportunity to work out ancient racial grudges. Jackson was saved by his pale skin and by his fast-talking friend just then coming around the corner of the house and somehow able to make clear in very short order that they knew the owner and had even been advised to look out for "Al," the retired cop in the neighborhood who was doing such a good job looking after folks' property. Al put down his gun, and Jackson's heart began to beat again.

A gun to the head was an extreme. There had been other kinds of menace in the week since Jackson had told his editors at *The Times-Picayune* that he really wasn't sure he wanted to take them up on their request that he sit in the lead truck and document the newspaper's evacuation to higher ground that Tuesday morning. It had been a tumultuous departure, a time of snap decisions and mounting tension as it became clear that the water already covering the newspaper's parking lot was rising, not falling, as it should have been twenty-four hours after a hurricane. In short order, even the big circulation trucks would no longer be able to negotiate the high water.

The publisher's immediate subordinates had been at loggerheads, with some contending that professional valor required toughing it out in place. The story is here, one newsroom manager argued, what kind of newspaper would flee the biggest story of the millennium? But the rebuttal was equally succinct: What's the point of staying here if we can't reach or leave the building? Why print a paper if we can't circulate it? Operating on their own imperatives, the circulation people had favored the news managers with the courtesy of an invitation. The trucks were leaving in about fifteen minutes, circulation said. If the newsroom wanted a ride, they should climb aboard. If not, that was the newsroom's business. And suddenly the publisher had made his decision. Ashton Phelps assembled the staff in the paper's cafeteria, water streaming through the ceiling from an upstairs office that had lost a huge plate-glass window to Katrina's winds: Drop everything, the publisher said; get on the trucks. And Jackson had been urged to take the catbird seat, an honor he respectfully declined.

A small cadre of about a half dozen reporters had also elected to stay on in the city, but they had gone their own ways, and so Jackson found himself alone in the parking lot. Just what his options were was not immediately clear. The day before he had borrowed a boat and with a reporter named Brian Thevenot had headed out into St. Bernard Parish, the two of them reaching up to swat at traffic lights and overhead signs as they cruised down Judge Perez Drive in about ten feet of water. But that boat was nowhere at hand. What was available was a little inflatable Zodiak that belonged to a photographer with the good sense to have evacuated New Orleans. It would do, but not very well, and so it seemed almost miraculous to go around to the back of the building just then and find a flat-bottomed aluminum fishing boat bobbing in the water on the other side of the fence that bounded the newspaper property. "God has sent me a boat," Jackson said to himself. God, however, had not sent oars. Jackson grabbed a broom. And then he remembered the oars in the Zodiak and used the broom to paddle over and retrieve them. They didn't fit the oarlocks and, of course, were much too small for the fishing boat, but Jackson had been a Boy Scout. His MacGyver moment, as he called it, was the inspiration to pull the laces out of his boots and use them to lash the oars into place. Every so often they broke, and Jackson would tie them again and press on.

Jackson couldn't get the *Titanic* out of his thoughts and the stories of the lifeboats pulling away from the drowning men, women, and children. People are going to want my boat, Jackson said to himself. And he was right: People on rooftops bellowed at him as he passed, they cursed him and they begged. But in mulling over the ethical implications as he set out, Jackson had found clarity: If people were in the water, he would pick them up. If they were on rooftops or highway overpasses, he had a job to do, and it wasn't ferrying people around.

Not every ethical decision could be so stark. Jackson had fought a riptide along Carrollton Avenue, an arterial roadway that ran from City Park to the university section at the upriver end of St. Charles Avenue. He reached a sprawling shopping center on Carrollton, about two miles from the paper, in time to watch looters swarming in and out of the smashed storefronts like maggots in a dead cat's mouth. He knew better than to move too close to a crime scene. The looters might be obsessed with their goodies, but Jackson had a hunch they would not hesitate to take action if they sensed that he was documenting them. Just then the bootlace oarlocks broke, irreparably this time, and Jackson had to wonder if he was going to drift right into harm's way. That was when he noticed the looted sneakers floating all around him. Dozens of them, unboxed and found wanting by the fashion-conscious, he decided as he scooped a few pair into his boat and stripped them of their laces to make new oarlocks.

He was passing an access ramp and overpass at Palmetto Street when he tuned in to the mutterings of the men trapped there and realized they were talking about his boat. "If we work together, we can take it from him," he heard them say. Jackson paddled faster. The men plunged in after him, and Jackson paddled faster still, eventually shaking off the posse. But there were others ahead as he made for Airline Highway, men and women on bridges. "You just gonna shoot me and not save me?" one man howled at Jackson as he framed a shot. That encounter aligned Jackson's moral compass more exactly. He might be under no obligation to rescue people, but if he wasn't going to rescue them, neither was he going to photograph them, he decided.

It came almost as a relief to ditch the boat after helping to load the woman with a broken hip into the helicopter. From Causeway at the interstate, Jackson hitched a ride on an army dump truck to what was known locally as the "i-ten/six-ten split," the junction where Interstate 610 peels two or three lanes from Interstate 10 and carries eastbound traffic above the very heart of Lakeview, the prosperous, largely white neighborhood of reclaimed swampland that had flooded as deeply as any part of the city.

The split had become a staging area for the slew of private boats that had mustered from all over the region, as outdoorsmen of every description—trappers, fishermen, crawfish farmers—dropped whatever they were doing, threw their small craft on trailers, and came to the assistance of a city in distress. Again, Jackson put out his thumb and shortly was bounding along a block of ranch houses so deeply flooded that the wake of the boat that had picked him up was lapping water into the gutters under their eaves. Now the captain cut his motor and yelled across the rooftops: "Hello? Hello? Anyone there?" And like an echo, there came an answering cry: "Hello! Over here! Hello?" Jackson shot one man as they approached his rooftop, put down the camera, and helped with the rescue. At last, the mix of professional and humane obligations felt right.

In the next house over, he encountered his first corpse, that of an elderly gentleman who, trapped in the attic, had managed to punch a hole through his roof. When a boat came by and offered a rescue, his neighbor said, the man had refused to go, not without his sister. She was wheelchair-bound on the ground floor, which had to mean she was dead. By the time the neighbor came back with help, the man had become delirious, waving a broom handle to fend off the team trying to save him, and shouting: "You said you were coming back, and you killed my sister instead." Now on a third pass, Jackson was able to get up on the roof, peer into the hole, and see that the man had expired. He holstered his camera.

The dead were beyond helping, and anyway the newspaper generally did not publish pictures of hometown corpses, out of respect for their survivors. It was the living who ate at Jackson. "Someday you're gonna need help and nobody's gonna come for you," one man howled as the boat plowed on toward another victim more urgently in need of rescue. And Jackson had no doubt it was true.

By Wednesday night, Jackson and a photographer buddy he had run into had found floor space in a *Houston Chronicle* reporter's hotel room at the fashionable Windsor Court. He woke up to coffee and the whine of the rumor mill: Riots had broken out at the Dome, they were saying; cops were stealing cars all over town, siphoning gas. That kind of thing. The Dome was within walking distance. Jackson decided to give it a go. He was stopped two blocks from the stadium by National Guardsmen. "You don't want to go down there," a Guardsman advised. The place, he said, was "a zoo." But on inquiry, the soldier conceded he had heard nothing about riots. In short order, an AP photographer recognized Jackson, pulled up alongside in his Jeep, and said get in. The rumor had undergone a change of venue: The rioting was at the convention center. And so off they went.

They thought of parking in a multi-story garage, to keep any rioters from trashing the Jeep, then thought better of it. They could hear pandemonium in the garage, the sound of windows being bashed, tires squealing. You could call it looting, or you could call it young men liberating available means of transportation after three days of broken promises that the government would soon bus them to safety from a disintegrating city. Farther down the boulevard, Jackson, now on foot, could see the convention center throng, a crowd of twenty thousand roiling in front of the blocks-long building too badly fouled to be tolerable indoors. He continued his approach, on guard with each step against the possibility that the mob might suddenly spot the cameras slung over his shoulders and tear after him.

Then suddenly that's exactly what was happening, and too quickly for Jackson to take to his heels. But instead of attacking the photographer, the crowd rushed forward to embrace him, and in short order Jackson was being pulled and pushed along by men and women desperate for him to chronicle their misery and a nation's shame. Here was photography not simply tolerated but put to use by and for the victims of a disaster. In that moment, Jackson could not have been prouder of his profession. He was shown dead bodies, and he was told horror stories. He was asked questions: How was it possible that they were still here, uncared for, days after the storm? If he could get there, where was the army?

There was much that astonished Jackson in what he saw at the convention center that day. The absence of rioting was just a part of it. There was also the unexpected way in which a group of young men had taken it upon themselves to police the crowd, keeping people on the sidewalks: "If you don't stay on the sidewalks, the buses won't come," they shouted as they walked back and forth along the curb. But the buses hadn't come. Nor had any other emblems of order or civility. Indeed, what stayed with Jackson more powerfully than anything else he saw that day was this: the utter lack of help; the lack of any government presence whatsoever. No food. No water. The woman who had grabbed him most possessively to show him around was Angela Perkins. Her picture, by another of the photographers with Jackson, would appear the next morning over four columns on the front page as *The Times-Picayune* managed to move past exclusively online publishing and began printing at least a limited run on paper from a borrowed press in Houma. Perkins had slumped to her knees and wrung her hands in supplication. "Help us!" she howled. "Help us!"—an icon of need in a city begging for mercy. Jackson was on autopilot by then, his fingers moving over the camera, adjusting the settings, firing the exposures as fast as he could frame them. But he could scarcely see what he was shooting through the tears that stung his eyes.

INEVITABLY, THE EFFORT TO DEBUNK WILDLY EXAGGERATED REPORTS OF RAPE and carnage at the Superdome and elsewhere around town was followed by a counterstroke: a campaign by women's groups to show that, indeed, in a city that recorded a rape every other day in the best of times, there was no lack of them during the period of chaos. In December, in a powerful radio interview that mixed sobs and anger, a Ms. Lewis came forward—she chose to withhold her first name—with an account of her own ordeal, a rape at gunpoint as she tried to sleep at a center for the elderly run by Redemptorists in the Irish Channel. Another woman, a hairdresser who called herself Anastasia, said she was raped in a parking lot next to a McDonald's on Gentilly Road some few days after the hurricane. Anastasia reported her assault to police, but Ms. Lewis did not. Sex crimes unit chief David Bennelli acknowledged that the sensitive, personal nature of sexual assault meant that many victims had never come forward. If and when they did, Bennelli said, the incidence statistics would be adjusted accordingly. But for the time being, he had no way to meaningfully alter the record long since in hand: two rape attempts at the Superdome and another two rapes elsewhere in the city immediately after Katrina, one of them Anastasia's.

The cause célèbre of rape victims was Charmaine Neville, the jazz vocalist whose father and uncles comprised the Neville Brothers, perhaps the quintessential New Orleans musical combo. Neville, a local icon herself—with waist-length dreads and a physical presence as stunning as her voice—reached the media encampment on Canal Street after three days in Ninth Ward floodwaters, and immediately went public with word that she had been raped while stranded on the roof of a schoolhouse where she had sought shelter. Details of Neville's storm saga would engender much chatter and some skepticism among Web bloggers of an antifeminist bent, and in some accounts of her ordeal she would speak, as the mayor and the police chief had, of pandemic rape among the storm survivors and also widespread murders. But the core account of the sexual assault she knew firsthand remained consistent, and, months later, while willing to talk openly about it, she was regularly reduced to tears.

Her point in going public was complicated, a double-edged message: partly a warning to other women and an exhortation by her example not to suffer in silent shame; partly—and this was unusual in feminist discourse on the subject of sexual assault—it was an appeal for the public to understand her assailant and other men like him. "What I want people to understand is that if we had not been left down there like the animals that they were treating us like, all of those things wouldn't have happened," she said in an interview with New Orleans archbishop Alfred Hughes on WAFB-TV out of Baton Rouge shortly after surfacing. The men driven to rape were themselves victims of the chaos in which the whole city found itself, Neville was saying. They were not the monsters of depravity evoked in media accounts.

Neville had performed in the week before the storm to a late-summer smattering of the regulars who would ordinarily pack Snug Harbor for her weekly gigs. She was more than a vocalist. She was a cult, a way for her devotees to signal allegiance to a particular duchy within the musical dynasty called Neville. "The Brothers" were her father, Charles, and her uncles, Art, Cyril, and Aaron—he of the impossible falsetto and the Top 40 radio hits. A half century earlier, "Tell It Like It Is" had made for fleeting fame but not very much money, given the exploitative industry practices of the day. Aaron had followed his brush with the big time with hard time, on criminal convictions rooted in theft and drug addiction. And then, in middle age, it had all turned to gold. Aaron hit the charts with solo material and, in collaboration with Linda Ronstadt, successes that revitalized The Brothers and their funky offshoot band, the Meters.

Charmaine was the freer, jazzier side of the family tree—freer musically, which led her from a role as a wah-wah girl backing up The Brothers to virtuoso solo work in jazz and world music styles. She was free with her money, performing gratis for charities and even local school fairs, when not circling the globe on paying gigs. And in addition to her two blood sons, she had raised a baby with AIDS that she nursed until death. She was also free with her mouth. It had pleased Charles none too much when her advocacy of better services for foster children had led to her revelation that she had been fobbed off on the foster care system in her own youth. And one brother would be just as uneasy about her rushing forward to announce the rape.

Charmaine talked too much, was the general view among the Nevilles in the city's Uptown district, which is where most of them lived, but not Charmaine. Like Fats Domino, she had stayed true to the Ninth Ward, and like many of her neighbors, she would remain convinced that the levee breaches were a calculated assault on one of the city's more marginal communities. "I don't care what anyone says: They blew the canal. They blew it in 1927 and when my mother was young, during Betsy. I heard the explosion," she said months after Katrina over coffee in LaPlace, a river town some twenty miles west of the city, where she was living an exile's existence between European tours and gigs back in New Orleans. Others in the family also saw a malevolent design in the disaster. Shortly after the storm, her cousin Cyril Neville appeared at a Katrina benefit concert in New York in a T-shirt inscribed with the words "Ethnic Cleansing in New Orleans," a not very oblique reference to the assumption that the breached levees had been a deliberate effort to pare down the city's black majority.

As for so many flood victims later depicted by the media as hopelessly trapped by poverty, age, or illness, Neville's decision to ride out the storm at home was a case of inconveniences blended with a pinch of inertia, the roux in many a New Orleans recipe for good times and bad times alike. Her car was on the fritz. One of her sons headed over from Houston on Saturday to pick her up, only to get hopelessly snarled in the evacuation contraflow plan. It would have been shocking if neighbors had not come to the assistance of a woman as public-spirited and outgoing as the singer down the street, and they did. But taking the remaining seat in a full-up car would have meant leaving elderly neighbors behind—Bill, the single guy in his sixties who lived on one side of her place, and the deaf couple, both in their seventies, on the other. And so Neville turned down the ride and took in the neighbors, whites as it happened—a datum of no particular consequence to the black woman who had taken them in, but that cut against the grain of another media stereotype, that the city's storm-racked downriver reaches were monolithically black. She put the elderly couple on an air mattress. Bill got a pallet on the floor; Neville slept on the couch, or tried to. "I stayed because of my neighbors," she said. "They didn't have a way out, and their houses were lower than mine."

A few feet in elevation made no difference, as it turned out, and as Katrina sucked the windows out of one side of Neville's house and water surged in under doorways and through chinks in the weatherboards that fateful Monday, she tied a rope around her waist and the waists of her elderly neighbors and began wading through the chest-deep water. Within a block, they had reached Drew Elementary over on St. Claude Avenue, the main artery between the French Quarter and the St. Bernard parish line. A janitor was on hand, and Neville had to overcome his initial reluctance to let the three-story school serve as a shelter. By day's end, there were, by her estimate, four hundred people inside.

By nightfall on her second day at Drew, at least some of the people who had found refuge in the schoolhouse were settling in. It was "a beautiful night," as Neville would recall, thinking of the weather and the conviviality among survivors who had gathered on the roof. They had rigged up a makeshift grill and were barbecuing some of the fixings gathered from the school's larder and on trips back to Neville's house on Pauline Street—for bedding, food from her freezer, batteries, a radio. And when everyone had eaten their fill, the group fell to singing before drifting off to sleep in various nooks and crannies of the school. Neville stayed up on the roof, amazed by how bright the stars were, unnerved by how dark the sky was, in a city without electricity.

"And later that night is when I was attacked," she said quietly. There on the roof, she woke to a hand on her mouth and a knife to her throat, she said. The ultimatum was as trite as it was easily enforced—in essence: yield or be killed. And her assailant made her understand, Neville said, that she would be violated sexually whether or not he killed her first. She did not know the man, she said, and in the perverse way of memory under stress, she could recall only one thing about him beyond the knife to her neck and his threat to pitch her off the roof—his glistening and even rows of teeth.

EIGHT

At Least Somebody Had a Plan

"H E MUST HAVE BEEN FIVE OR SIX. HIS SKIN WAS JUST FLAKING OFF." FIRE-fighters see a lot of burns, so Ukali Mwendo knew this was from the sun, not flames. A civilian might have had a hard time telling the difference. "He had no shirt, so his skin was just peeling off from exposure." His skin was not the only part of his body that had gone dry in a city engulfed in water. "The little boy was crying. His body had stopped producing tears, so he was just heaving."

Much would be said and written about the scandalous performance of police and other "first responders," to use the fashionable term: desertions, looting, incompetence. Some of it was true. There were also claims of heroism among cops and firefighters and emergency medical technicians—brave and selfless rescues and lesser acts of service, some of them true, many embellished. Mwendo would not claim to be a hero. He looted some, if that is the right word for what it took to keep body and soul together and on duty. He also came up against terrible situations that he couldn't do anything to ease. The little boy, for example. Just one pathetic face in a throng of hundreds of people baking on an interstate ramp near the Metairie line. Four days had passed since Katrina. President Bush at that very moment had been at the airport, ten miles and a world away, talking with Nagin and Blanco.

Mwendo did what circumstances and the fire chief required him to do. He drove on, continuing the survey of a city in extremis, a hazardous materials specialist looking for chemical leaks. "We couldn't do anything. We didn't even have a first-aid kit on board. That was back at Engine 20. And there were just too many people—hundreds of them on the interstate."

In another part of the city, on the second floor of a nursing home that police had taken over as a barracks, Friday was also the day that a thirty-one-year veteran officer, Lawrence Celestine, put a gun to his head and pulled the trigger. His commander, who watched helplessly, said Celestine had been driven over the edge by the deep sense of betrayal he felt in the face of the desertions and looting by police. Eventually, ninety-one officers would resign or retire and another two hundred twenty-eight would be probed for leaving their posts in the moment of crisis. Without doubt it was a police force in meltdown. Three hundred police cruisers were flooded, as was Jackson Barracks, the National Guard post, with forty boats and twenty-four high-water vehicles that NOPD's hurricane plan counted on for joint rescue missions. The day after Celestine did himself in, the NOPD was rocked by a second, more private suicide, that of Paul Accardo, a public information officer, who drove out of town before blowing himself away. Within four weeks, as a step toward rebuilding the shattered department, Mayor Nagin would encourage and accept the resignation of his police superintendent, the voluble Eddie Compass.

Mwendo, like most first responders, stayed on the job, rattled by much of what he went through, but not broken by it. He was a thoughtful man of imposing stature: six-four, divorced, kids grown and gone. He had his mother to worry about, what with her cancer. A cousin had picked her up at her apartment on Sunday, the day before the storm, and driven the seventy-seven-year-old to Atlanta. That had meant interrupting her treatments, and it worried Mwendo.

Born in a downtown housing project, the Lafitte, Mwendo had raised a fist in the glory days of the Black Power movement. Now, at fifty-five, he was more focused politically on somehow getting reparations for slavery's descendants. Meanwhile, he had his fire department job to do.

He had been with the department for twenty-seven years, the last fifteen of them with the hazardous materials division (hazmat). The fire department was divided into three platoons, twenty-four hours on, forty-eight hours off. "For some of my coworkers, the fire department is their life. I just follow orders. I am one of those firefighters they say has a bad attitude. I do my twenty-four hours and go home."

Mwendo's twenty-four hours were due to end Sunday, but then the governor declared a state of emergency and he was ordered to stay on the clock, as he would for eight days straight. A hurricane was coming. Mwendo and his crew knew it as well as anyone who had spent the weekend playing cards, watching TV, and now and again summoning to mind the fine points of the hurricane preparedness plan that was reviewed at the onset of each season—with PowerPoint presentations, roundtable discussions, booklets, briefings, and the like. "We were as prepared as any computer simulation could prepare us," Mwendo would say sardonically, noting that as the storm finally struck, all that careful planning went "right out the window."

His company, Engine 7, had been evacuated to the Park Plaza, a down-at-the-heels Canal Street hotel. From his room on the tenth floor, Mwendo had been able to see the vaults and crypts of St. Louis No. 1 Cemetery, the city's oldest, and he could see the palm trees that had been planted along Canal Street as part of a recent beautification effort, a lot of them now snapped or pulled right up out of the ground, like weeds. He could see the hotel swimming pool, which was empty as Katrina swept past New Orleans on Monday, and overflowing on Tuesday, a swirling sinkhole in a city rapidly filling with floodwater and sewage.

The chunk of the hotel roof that had flapped in the wind Monday night finally broke free and crashed to the street on Tuesday, but the Park Plaza had some kind of generator, so at least there was emergency lighting in the hallways. And for a few hours on Tuesday, the hotel phones continued to work, which was more than could be said for the fire department's radio channel. With firefighting's chain of command fractured along with its communications grid, Mwendo was not sure how word reached the Park Plaza that they should transfer to Engine 23, Uptown on Magazine Street, or who gave the order. Maybe it was just the rumor that Engine 23 hadn't flooded and a herd's impulse to go somewhere dry. Mwendo assumed they'd be coming back to the hotel to sleep and change clothes. "All I had was my tennis shoes and the dark blue NOMEX fatigue uniform. So I went with the clothes on my back." Plus his New Orleans Fire Department ID. "I always keep that on me."

They reached Engine 23, or was it Grand Central Station, a little before noon. At any given time, there were maybe eighty to one hundred people in there, milling about, coming and going. Their frequent destination was the Wal-Mart by the river, on Tchoupitoulas Street. Fire trucks would return loaded with soap, toiletries, boxes of cold cereal, water, clothing, batteries. Firefighters also returned laden with what Mwendo politely called "nonsurvival" items. "Guys were on the phone calling their good buddies to get a pickup truck over there before it was too late," Mwendo said. The police led the way, from what he had heard. "They moved the civilians out of the store and then went on a looting frenzy." And, yes: "The fire department joined them." Now and then someone would call in a fire or a hazmat situation, but there was no responding, not with the streets flooded like that.

As the Wal-Mart shelves, clothes racks, and gun and jewelry cases were stripped bare, officers with the NOPD's third district, flooded out of their usual haunts in the city's Gentilly district, lighted upon costlier goods: Cadillacs and Chevrolets. No matter that the third district's entire motor pool was high and dry in a downtown garage, the officers commandeered two hundred vehicles, some of which were privatized by officers with no greater act of public service in mind than getting their own tender behinds to Baton Rouge or Texas. Criminal probes would end some careers, but the stolen Cadillac Escalades would become emblems of a big-city police department's breakdown in command, as severe as any in memory.

While firefighters and cops looted the Uptown Wal-Mart at a stroll, EMTs across town cruised the aisles of the flooded Wal-Mart at Read Boulevard by boat. One of eight medics stationed in a disused BellSouth building along with about two dozen firefighters from Engine 36, Drina Freitas woke up Monday to find most of eastern New Orleans underwater, her ambulance included. Three of the firemen had brought their jet skis to the BellSouth building, and in short order they had skimmed out over the flooded city and rounded up a half dozen powerboats that had been lifted off their trailers by the storm surge and set afloat, many with keys in the ignitions and gas in the tanks. Rescuing flood victims from the mostly low-rise housing in the east was not a problem. The challenge was getting people out of the boats once they had been brought to a two-story structure or an interstate ramp. "We would have to throw them bodily out of the boat," said Freitas, a curly-haired, heavyset young woman of twenty-six from the New York City suburbs who was working her way through Tulane med school.

Freitas had tossed three cans of SpaghettiOs and a gallon of water into her kit upon reporting for duty the weekend before the storm. Now, as supplies dwindled, she pondered the ethical implications of breaking into a vending machine on the BellSouth premises. By Wednesday, the boat trip to Wal-Mart occasioned no such scruples. This was survival. Freitas's boyfriend, Jay, another EMT also posted to the BellSouth building, had made it up onto the roof of the building that same day and had managed to text-message their supervisor. "What's your plan?" Jay typed. But there was no plan, and when Jay reached another supervisor that evening, same thing: no plan. Then Jay got lucky. Another attempt at communication with the outside world reached a buddy of his named Cedric Palmisano, a flight paramedic who happened to be doing helicopter rescues from the Superdome. Palmisano told the EMTs they had ten minutes to get to the nearest interstate overpass, and shortly they were rising into the sky, slack-jawed with amazement as they saw for the first time that it wasn't just eastern New Orleans that was underwater, but almost the whole city.

Freitas was soon working in the Dome's special needs section, alongside the likes of Sherry Watters, the lawyer/social worker and counselor to Damond Peters. Freitas was strangely comforted to encounter in her very first patient a familiar face, a vagrant French Quarter drunk her ambulance had tended to in the past. Freitas and the seven EMTs in her group had been warned to find a safe place to sleep, given the tensions and occasional eruptions of violence beginning to course through the throngs at the Dome. And because they were in city uniforms and carried paramedic bags further identifying themselves, the EMTs thought to try the compound in which police—some lying over the hoods of cruisers, with guns drawn—had barricaded themselves. The smell of barbecue wafted from the compound, but the police weren't sharing, either food or space. Freitas's group wound up dining on army rations and sleeping on the helicopter landing pad once darkness fell and the day's rescue missions were suspended until dawn. Before nodding off, the EMTs and military personnel guarding the landing area bartered for necessities. Freitas was out of cigarettes. Socks bought cigarettes. She still had a can of SpaghettiOs, but no can opener. "There was a kind of a prison trade there," she said. "Nobody had a full set of anything. One guy had extra pants he traded."

Within a day or two, Freitas and her cohorts had scrounged a jacked-up pickup, commandeered a postal service eighteen-wheeler, and made it across the river to the drier Algiers district, where they based themselves out of a residence for the elderly, which was operated by the Little Sister of the Poor. Freitas did not know him, but Mwendo was also briefly among the four hundred cops, firefighters, and EMTs holed up there.

FOOD WAS NOT A PROBLEM FOR MWENDO, THANKS TO THE WAL-MART RAIDS, but to fuel their trucks, the firefighters had begun prying (or sledgehammering or hacksawing) the locks and siphoning gas from the underground tanks at service stations—the pumps being useless for lack of electricity. On Wednesday, Mwendo's unit moved for the fourth and final time, to Engine House 20 in Algiers Point, the wedge of land that stuck out into the river, directly across from the French Quarter. Engine 20 was an older building on high ground and with lots of space. Using the generator aboard the hazmat truck, Mwendo's team soon had lights. They also had WWL, both the TV channel and its talk radio station, the only local broadcaster that stayed on air for the duration. Not that much of the WWL audience was left in town, and few who remained had a way to tune in, but for those who had power, Mwendo among them, it was a lifeline: "It helped us understand what the state and federal government were doing. It also played a key role in helping keep morale up. You know, to see some daylight at the end of the tunnel."

The men spent that first day at Engine House 20 clearing trees, organizing supplies, and piling trash and debris from around the station house. Being hazmat specialists, it fell to them to keep the department supplied with fuel by continually replenishing Engine 20's five-hundred-gallon diesel storage tank. Other tasks included monitoring air quality and surveying the city for leaks and other chemical problems, the mission Mwendo was on when he came across the sobbing, sunburned boy.

"Everywhere we went, people were running up to us, asking for help, directions, food, water. When we could, we would give them water. We were looking for protection ourselves. We got reports that people were belligerent, rushing our vehicles, throwing objects. I didn't experience any of that. I think there is a grain of truth in this because I have seen it before, but in that atmosphere, there was a lot of embellishment."

The firefighters made a point of getting back to the station house by sundown, so as not to miss the food. It was almost the opposite of looting—reverse looting—the way people from the neighborhood, local restaurant owners, anyone with a freezer full of food that was just going to go bad, brought it to the station house. "Tuna steaks, swordfish, oysters, shrimp, you name it. People brought lots of food—more than we could eat. They brought cat and dog food, ice, and clothing. Civilians thought we were doing relief out of the firehouse. Some people even came by offering to help with the rescue work."

After a full meal, there were beds upstairs for all the firefighters, though Mwendo preferred a ground-floor sofa. "The beds weren't long enough for me."

As Mwendo and his team arrived back at Engine 20 Wednesday evening, they could see a big chemical warehouse burning on the waterfront, directly across the river. There was no fighting that fire. "The best we could do was get personnel and air monitors close enough to begin to figure out what the chemicals were." Fires were reported elsewhere in New Orleans, also in Jefferson Parish, and under terms of a mutual aid agreement, Mwendo and company were meant to respond. They didn't. They couldn't. The only upturn in their situation was that late Wednesday the team began to reestablish intermittent radio contact with the department. Beyond that, the best the hazmat team could do in a city that was beyond hazardous was to cruise the streets looking for points of intervention.

Snatches of what he saw were graven in Mwendo's memory: the people surging down Canal Street toward the convention center, floating their belongings ahead of them in tubs and plastic chests. The packs of dogs roaming the city. "For some reason, those dogs looked bigger and hungrier than ever before," Mwendo said, but he and his mates were not attacked.

The suspicious suitcases turned out to be an anticlimax of another sort. "One was on the neutral ground of Canal Street. We responded with the National Guard, the New Orleans Police Department Bomb Squad. The first one was empty. Then there was another one that was by the aquarium. When we opened it, it turned out to be filled with somebody's clothing. They must have just left it there."

Checking empty suitcases in a drowning city?

"I guess the thought was that the city was vulnerable. It was prime time for a terrorist strike."

But the principal and persistent chemical threat that Mwendo could do something about was running out of gasoline. "For our unleaded vehicles, we would suck fuel out of the underground storage tanks at gas stations." Firefighters come equipped with "universal keys"—power saws, chain cutters—whatever it takes to break a lock. Not all the fuel wound up in fire and hazmat trucks. "Some people's friends may have gotten some gas and supplies, but mostly we held on to it for ourselves."

Mwendo hadn't given much thought to his apartment. Because it was in Algiers, and the levee breaks had been across the river, he assumed it was at least relatively dry. On Thursday, he went by the Seine Street building and confirmed his hunch. He wanted to get some extension cords and his collection of *Amos 'n' Andy* DVDs because he knew the others back at Engine 20 would get a kick out of them. He also wanted to change his clothes. Oh, God, did he want to change his clothes—for the first time in a week. People in the apartment complex across the street, there must have been two hundred of them, spotted him—a man in uniform, an upholder of civic order—and there was no end to their questions. "I guess they figured I am the expert. So whatever I told them, people did."

From his Black Power days, Mwendo knew enough about community politics to have some good ideas. "I started organizing people in teams of twenty-five and put one young lady in charge. That way, when the National Guard got there, things would go smooth and there wouldn't be any rioting." Except that the National Guard had other things to do and never showed up at that particular location. Meanwhile, Mwendo shot back over to the fire-house and returned with some of the extra food people had been dropping off. By Friday, buses were starting to pick people up from an assembly point at the Algiers ferry landing. The ferry service itself had been knocked out, but the landing was plied by water rescue units. They needed only to cross the river and cut into the devastated Industrial Canal to gain access to a flooded world that stretched from the Lower Ninth Ward on into eastern New Orleans, farther than the eye could see. Then they'd return to Algiers with those they had rescued. Numbed and shuddering, angry and howling—they came in all varieties.

Drina Freitas and the EMTs also returned by day to downtown New Orleans. She was posted to the convention center when the big Chinooks showed up and finally began hauling off the sickest and frailest refugees. It reminded her of Mardi Gras, what with the throngs and the long lines of peo-ple waiting, not for parades but for a ride out of the hellhole in which they found themselves. "All day I would look at the military guys in the Chinooks to see how many fingers they were holding up. Then I would count off from the line and send them to the helicopter. I tried to keep the families together." But it wasn't always possible, particularly when the "families" numbered in the dozens and included self-designated kin who had paid for the privilege of pretending they were related to someone whose medical needs might be a ticket out of town.

Freitas's duties also brought her into contact with the MASH unit the military had set up in tents inside one of the convention center halls. "They had two chicks that were, like, eighteen years old running the place," Freitas recalled. "They didn't know what they were doing: bags of fluid on the ground, IV catheters on the bed. The military is supposed to be organized."

At one point some of the big shots from Washington came through—Senate majority leader Bill Frist, for one—and wanted their pictures taken alongside paramedics. The sentiment was not reciprocated. "We're all dirty-mugging the camera, just mean-eyeing it," Freitas recalled with a chuckle. But the real nastiness lay ahead, as Freitas and others on her team started re-sponding more systematically to calls for service. There were five hundred calls on one particularly grueling day—mostly people still trapped by flood-water, or family members frantic to know something about a missing relative. Freitas would come to recognize the "vomit kind of smell" that meant a corpse was inside. Other survivors would be "loopy, exhausted, dehydrated, and sick" by the time the EMTs got to them. "We found one elderly couple. He was dead; she wasn't. He had been dead for three or four days, and she knew it." The worst of it was the look on the old woman's face as she was led away, her husband's corpse left behind for the coroner to retrieve.

BACK IN ALGIERS, MWENDO FOUND THE STATION HOUSE WHERE HE WAS BASED to be a window onto the perverse and myriad ways a disaster like Katrina tears up a city like New Orleans, and Mwendo jotted down some of his observations in a notebook:

- Lawrence Martin, fifty-seven years old, comes looking for eighty-seven-year-old mother, Alzheimer's case. Wanted help getting her evacuated. He was crying.

- Fritz Windhorst (longtime state legislator) calls the firehouse. Wants us to know he's doing his part, bringing supplies to L.B. Landry High School.

- Lady who lives next door to firehouse calls asking someone to check on her dog.

Mwendo decided to take that one on himself, along with Eddie Holmes, the department's assistant superintendent. They dutifully broke into the woman's house, and sure enough a dog started barking in the back bedroom. The men dragged mattresses from another bedroom and held them up like shields, needlessly, as it turned out. "The dog ran for cover as soon as we opened the door." Mwendo and Holmes left food and water and headed back over to the firehouse.

And then that Sunday, the next in the endless stream of inquiries from family members was for Mwendo himself: his mother, calling from Atlanta. The ride had taken it out of her, and the suspension of her cancer treatments had set her back. "She was calling to say good-bye. She said it was her time. She was ready. She had made peace with God and this planet."

Mwendo couldn't take it. "I broke down and cried like a baby. I hadn't cried all week. I couldn't talk, I was crying so bad." Holmes approved an emergency leave, someone drove Mwendo to Baton Rouge, and he caught a Greyhound to Atlanta, arriving Monday. "My mother was still at my cousin's house. My ex-wife and I walked into the room at the exact same time. She was glad to see both of us. She said, 'Okay, I'm ready to go to the doctor.' " By midweek she was hospitalized and on an IV. By Friday she was dead. "It was just me and her there when she expired," Mwendo said. "I can't help but think that's the way she wanted it."

FREITAS WOULD WORK NONSTOP FOR A MONTH. SHE WASN'T ABLE TO GET through to her folks until the end of the second week. Her mother was beside herself with worry. It hadn't registered with Freitas until then how grim a portrait of her world was being painted by the media. "I had no idea. I hadn't seen the news."

"I think I'm safe," she said to calm her mother. "Don't worry. Now let me talk to Dad."

MWENDO STAYED AWAY UNTIL EARLY OCTOBER, COMBINING FUNERAL LEAVE with a previously scheduled vacation. Upon return he took a berth aboard the huge cruise ship that FEMA had rented for millions of dollars a week to house essential workers, a vessel that in normal times whisked fun-lovers off on seven-day Caribbean cruises past Cozumel, Grand Bahama, Jamaica, and the like, at a quarter the price. It was moored in the river alongside the convention center, a luxury vessel adjacent to what had been a locus of unutterable misery, both as an impromptu shelter and then as a trauma hospital. Hazmat shared shipboard quarters with firefighters, cops, the National Guard, regular army personnel, air force, EMS workers, and city employees and their families, including a lot of little kids, too many little kids. "I understand why most cruises are just seven days," Mwendo quipped.

For the cops on-board the cruise ship, Eddie Compass's ouster as superintendent, the very day Mwendo returned to his duties with the fire department, held the promise of a new beginning. But the scandals were not over. On October eighth, with the eyes of the world still on New Orleans, camera crews on Bourbon Street taped three white officers wantonly beating an elderly black man—a retired schoolteacher, as it turned out. The officers, one of whom was photographed lunging at the cameraman, said the retiree had been drunk and had resisted arrest, a disputed contention. In any case, the police violence was inappropriate, Interim Superintendent Warren Riley ruled, in swiftly suspending the officers.

Mwendo continued to work a nonstop schedule. "We were told the hazardous materials unit can work as much overtime as we want and that the federal government is picking up the tab." The problem was that the feds would pick up only the overtime, under provisions of the Stafford Act, governing emergency response. How the base pay would be covered by a city without revenues was another problem as yet unaddressed. For Mwendo, to keep working was an act of faith. "I haven't seen any of the checks yet, but I trust them," he said of his paymasters.

"I love New Orleans. Working every day, this is my contribution."

New Orleans was still in utter disarray, but that morning, as Mwendo made his rounds a week after returning to duty, the city offered up a throwback to the old order that had seemingly been lost forever, the era of secret passion and private death in a famously violent town. Mwendo was traveling from the French Quarter out toward New Orleans East to spot leaking barrels, or any other kind of chemical hazard that might be exposed now that the floodwaters had mostly receded. But on Elysian Fields Avenue, two men in street clothes flagged him down. They had been cleaning out an apartment behind the Phoenix, a men's bar that had been popular with enthusiasts of nipple clips and leather clothing. "We got human remains, badly composed," one of the men said to Mwendo. Sure enough, the men had come across a trunk stuffed with mothballs and a shriveled corpse. "It was clearly dead before the hurricane," Mwendo concluded as he waited around for detectives to come and take charge of the scene. "At least somebody had a plan."

NINE

Code Gray

THERE WERE MANY THINGS THAT WERE INFURIATING AND UPLIFTING AND simply strange about riding out Katrina at Charity Hospital, downtown New Orleans's huge depression-era monument to poor people's medicine. There was the look on the face of the profoundly aphasic patient, a man essentially incapable of speech, and the tears that fell silently from his eyes and the way he shook his head when one of the doctors had led him over to a fifth-floor window so he could look out onto the flooded streets below. There was the huge migration of people through those streets and past the hospital doors, people in search of shelter, men and women wading in chest-deep water, little children pulled along in rubber tubs and on inflatable mattresses, a whole city of them washed out of their homes and heading for the Superdome a block or two away. There was the ritual of the peanut butter jar that got passed around—at God knows what risk of contagion—when hospital staff gathered for support meetings each morning at eleven. And there was the five PM prayer and gospel meeting conducted by a Bible-thumping security guard on the ramp where, a week earlier, EMTs had routinely pulled heart attack patients and gunshot victims out of ambulances. But nothing was quite so bizarre, or quite so infuriating, as learning via CNN on Wednesday that Charity Hospital had been completely and successfully evacuated.

As the talking heads cheerfully intoned the false report—just another symptom of how completely the city's communications system had fallen apart—the reality was that twelve hundred staff and patients were still trapped in Charity, with rapidly diminishing supplies of food, water, and medicine. And large numbers also languished at University, Tulane, and the VA Medical Center, additional components, both public and private, of a downtown medical complex a stone's throw from city hall. Lunch at Charity, the day after it reportedly had been evacuated, was a bowl of cornflakes, served dry, and a packet of peanut butter. Supper was a roll and canned green beans served cold. Fluids were the graver concern. Like the rest of the city, the hospital had no running water by then, or electrical power for that matter, and temperatures on the upper floors had risen above 100 degrees. With bottled-water supplies rapidly dwindling, someone remembered the Peace Corps rehydration solution: a quart of water mixed with three packets of sugar (for taste) and a packet of salt (for electrolytes).

What was the right word for the relief effort, when the government finally realized it was still necessary: anemic? Kiersta Kurtz-Burke was a doctor—how about perniciously anemic? Malignant? How else would you describe a Thursday afternoon encounter with a National Guardsman who, in full regalia, stepped at last from a heavily armored vehicle to tell the exhausted doctor it was "too dangerous" to evacuate her patients—an assessment based on overblown rumors of rampant violence in the area. "We're being told to leave. We'll be back at nine AM."

The doctor may have been ravaged for lack of sleep and food. She may have been standing in papery surgical scrubs next to a man kitted up as if to invade Baghdad, but she had not lost her sense of irony. "Why not oh-six-hundred military time?" she snapped back at him. "We're working all night. Why don't you?" And all the soldier could do was repeat his orders. We'll be here at nine AM—another day would pass without the United States of America finding a way to assist New Orleans's biggest hospital.

Yes, Kurtz-Burke was bitter about it. These are people who go to Fallujah, she thought. These are people capable of gathering intelligence on the ground. And yet in a storm-racked American city, they are entirely the captive of rumors: that the patients, perhaps even the Charity staff, are a pack of wild dogs, when in fact, against all odds, security remained intact. As the army kept Charity waiting that Thursday, helicopters were evacuating critically ill patients from Tulane University Medical Center, the private hospital right across the street. The conjoint bigotries of race and class were part of it. Kurtz-Burke knew that, just as surely as she knew that most of the uninsured patients who depended on Charity were black. But she couldn't help wondering if the relief effort's pathetic excuse for a military response wasn't rooted in something else: Iraq and the huge diversion of resources that war entailed.

New Orleans had been doing its birthing and dying at Charity, its ailing and its mending, nonstop and mostly on the government's dime, for about as long as the hospital's older patients had been alive. The mayor had been born in Charity, though one could confidently assume that he would not now seek its services except in the direst emergency. The violence in New Orleans's back streets had made its trauma center and emergency rooms as skilled as any in the South, and a mecca for interns with the gumption to endure permanent battlefield conditions. There was a prison floor in Charity for inmates from the parish lockup a few blocks to the north. The hospital's emergency rooms were backed up with uninsured patients afflicted with conditions ranging from measles—who could afford to visit a doctor?—to heart attack and diabetic shock. Clinical trials were administered from Charity, a giant petri dish in which to study the pathologies of urban life.

Kurtz-Burke's domain was rehab. She worked on Five West, which is where they brought the stroke victims and the head-trauma patients and the spinal cord cases within a few weeks of their initial hospitalization—two weeks after admission for the easier cases, eight weeks for the ones clinging to life, the ones that Kurtz-Burke fought to rescue from what otherwise might be quadriplegia or worse. There was a bit of history in that designation, Five West—a mystery to solve, once you realized that it was the fifth floor not of the building's west wing, but of its north wing. The *W* had once stood for something else: "white," Kurtz-Burke had been told. West's counterpart in the postsegregation era was, logically enough, the hospital wing called "East"—at the south end of the building, the wing where black patients had once been treated.

Here was a poser to toy with in idle moments—not that there were many in a place like Charity. If the *W* stood for "white," had the *E* once been a *C* for "colored," or a *B* for "black," as Kurtz-Burke had been told? Had hospital officials drawn a horizontal line through the *C* to make it an *E*, or had they shaved off the rounded right-hand protuberances of the letter *B*? It would have been like Charity to improvise in haste and not to care all that much about racism's delicate nuances. Charity was all about getting the job done, and young doctors loved it—those who didn't hate it so much that they got out just as fast as their residencies allowed.

"There was such a tremendous history there," said Kurtz-Burke, who had done everything she could to escape an internship that landed her for a time in the bland, insurance-driven world of a Sacramento hospital. Getting back to New Orleans meant getting back to a big-city public hospital. Charity came with "no frills" but offered, in Kurtz-Burke's view, "tremendously good care," and not just for trauma patients. From obstetrics to open-heart surgery, "we never turned anybody away," Kurtz-Burke said. "Insurance or not, it didn't matter. I met people from all walks of life, mostly poor—artists, musicians, writers, service industry workers. All of them didn't have insurance.

"And the people who worked there were lifers," just as she intended to be, Kurtz-Burke said. "It lured you back—the bravado, the adrenaline, the drama. You got hooked. Any place else was boring. We used to laugh about how chaotic it was there." And not just inside the building, which was completed a few years after its source of inspiration, Huey Long, was gunned down in another of his creations, the state capitol in Baton Rouge.

On the Tuesday six days before the storm, Kurtz-Burke had been on the sidewalk, passing from one building to another, when shots rang out and a group of kids scattered under the interstate. Kurtz-Burke found herself bending over a twelve-year-old in his school uniform, solid blue pants and a white shirt—except that the shirt wasn't white anymore; blood was soaking into it. The boy was incredibly lucky. The bullet had entered his right hip and had exited from his lower back without smashing a vital organ. Two hours later, Kurtz-Burke had tried to check up on him in the emergency room. He had been patched up and sent back to his home in the nearby Iberville pub-lic housing project.

That weekend, Kurtz-Burke's number was up, and so she was the faculty member on call as crises developed and interns needed guidance. If your working life was a continuing emergency, a storm in the Gulf didn't count for much, and so when a young intern told her the hospital was going to Code Gray—hurricane emergency status—she had to ask what that meant. There was no cause for panic, she felt. Charity had weathered plenty of Big Ones in its sixty-six years. Kurtz-Burke's husband, Justin Burke, also a doc-tor, was less encumbered that weekend and had been convinced by a friend to evacuate to Baton Rouge. He took Titus, the pitbull-boxer mutt they had rescued from the streets of their Mid-City neighborhood.

Code Gray had done its thing by Sunday evening as Kurtz-Burke made her rounds. Staffers had set out mats on the floor to sleep on, and TVs were rigged up in the hallways, giving the giant hospital some of the feel of a slumber party. The elderly woman easing toward kidney failure and due to start dialysis the next morning was attended by her husband, both because it comforted her and because it provided him shelter from the storm. So too the young woman keeping a vigil beside her husband, a twenty-two-year-old who had suffered brain damage in a car crash. The most worrisome of the patients Kurtz-Burke looked in on was the young man who had come in just that weekend riddled with bullets. The wounds on his arms and belly were under control, but he was still bleeding from a hole in his neck that seemed to have become infected. "We didn't know him too well yet either, so we were watching him closely," Kurtz-Burke would recall.

Overnight, the storm shattered two dozen windows, most of them on the fourteenth floor, where residents bunked, and soon enough Katrina's hori-zontal bursts of wind and rain had flooded corner rooms to a depth of five inches. With an industrial broom she retrieved from ER, Kurtz-Burke was able to muscle the water out over a fire escape and onto the streets below. And by six AM, as she made her morning rounds, the storm had calmed down. She assumed it was the eye passing over the city. "Good," she would remember thinking to herself, "we're halfway there."

One of the lessons that would stay with Charity staffers was just how de-pendent on electricity modern medicine had become. The lights flickered and went out at around eight Monday morning, and the generators kicked in, power enough for the emergency lighting in the hospital's endless corridors, but other electrical demand was suddenly unmet. Elevators froze in place, air-conditioning died along with the refrigerators critical to the maintenance of medicines, plasma, food, and the corpses in the hospital morgue.

Tubercular patients ordinarily were kept in isolation through negative air pressure in their rooms. When the electricity failed, so did the pressurizer, exposing other patients, and staff as well, to TB.

Power packs in the portable blood-sugar monitors couldn't be recharged. Blood pressure cuffs were electronic, not to mention the dialysis machines. Even the pill dispensers were electronic, though they could be busted open with a screwdriver. A patient on blood thinners because of a clot in his lung needed to be checked continuously, or thinning could shade over into hemorrhaging. The surest way to monitor the woman easing toward kidney failure would have been to check her potassium levels, electronically.

"It was like suddenly being blindfolded and handcuffed in terms of how we practice medicine," one young doctor said.

An ER specialist had come to work equipped with three small portable generators, basically the size of car batteries. They were good for low-power functions, but not for ventilators. And so, on fourteen-hour shifts, ER and ICU nurses in charge of some twenty-five dependent patients fell to the challenge of working the bellowslike "ambu" bags by hand, a task both tedious and nerve-racking.

Ambulances were still able to negotiate downtown streets on Monday afternoon, and Charity's first post-storm patient had arrived at about one PM—a nineteen-year-old with multiple gunshot wounds. He was sent on to nearby University Hospital, a smaller part of the Charity system since the 1990s, when the state took it over from the Daughters of Charity and renamed what the nuns had called Hotel Dieu. University, it seemed, still had generators sufficient to power its operating rooms.

A University Hospital doctor named Lynn Harrison had reason to doubt that power would last very long. After terrible rainfall flooding in 1995, University had moved its emergency generators ten feet aboveground, but the switch boxes and circuitry were still at ground level, behind a flood wall only four feet high. A prominent cardiothoracic surgeon, with degrees from Yale and Duke and numerous published papers to his credit, Harrison, sixty-one, had seen his wife and daughter off to Texas ahead of Katrina, Mrs. Harrison and the cats in her black Corvette, their daughter and her husband in a VW Jetta with two dogs. On Sunday, Harrison had come to realize the storm was not digressing from its beeline toward New Orleans, and, on duty for the duration, he made a pallet of some padding he'd pulled off a gurney and turned an empty office into a bedroom. He'd be fine, Harrison figured. Hospitals were big, solid buildings.

Harrison woke up to the low moan of what sounded like a gargantuan woodwind instrument, and realized the storm was approaching. But the office lights still worked, and cool air continued to spill from the ceiling ducts—"those things we take for granted," Harrison noted in a journal he kept fastidiously. Breakfast was being served when the district's electrical service crashed, and in an unwelcome and somewhat mysterious interval before the hospital's generators kicked in, dietitians roamed the corridors, serving the meal by flashlight. Every patient who could be safely discharged had been sent home the previous Friday, leaving a residual population of 234, plus two or three times as many nonpatients, counting staff and family members, who had come to the hospital for shelter. Twelve of those remaining in the hospital were the heart patients of special concern to Harrison. Fearing the hospital would not have power for long, and that staff would no longer be able to communicate by the usual beeper networks, Harrison found himself running through the halls of the hospital, checking to see that ambu bags were beside the beds of patients—including a smattering of premature newborns—unable to breathe on their own. His concern proved prophetic. At 9:15, the cellars flooded, soaking the switch boxes and circuitry, and manual ventilation began, a process that would be unrelieved for fifteen hours, until a small gas generator could be installed on the roof.

And so it went at hospitals throughout the city. A mile or so uptown from Charity at Memorial Medical Center, a private hospital run by the giant Tenet chain, thirty-four corpses would be recovered after the storm had passed, a toll so high it would provoke a criminal probe by the state attorney general, amid rumors that doctors had euthanized terminal patients by overdosing them with morphine and other routine end-stage palliatives. The probe continued, but no indictments had been handed down a half year later.

Back at Charity, staffers with the strength to make the climb drifted up onto the roof of the building Monday night, to commune with one another and savor the cool air and gaze vacantly at the dazzling display of stars in a suddenly cloudless sky. They did not know that elsewhere in New Orleans, residents were gazing less willingly into that same firmament, people trapped on rooftops in parts of the city to the east that had already gone under. Tuesday morning, Charity and University woke to discover that they too were islands in an inland sea that stood four- to six-feet deep. Contact of sorts was maintained with the mainland. The Code Gray team—including a group of doctors mostly from the ER—was in touch with FEMA, and after the team's exchanges with the feds, they would report to their colleagues— groupings of one hundred fifty to two hundred crammed into the hospital lobby.

For all the disaster drills and dry runs—a singularly inappropriate word to describe their present predicament—no one had ever planned on an evacuation taking longer than a day, let alone two days. And here they were scrambling to improvise care for four hundred fifty patients, forty-six of them critical. Still more were on the way, including the woman who gave birth in a nearby discount hotel and then surged to Charity through the deepening flood, holding her baby, Mariah, and the placenta above the black water.

Like a terminal patient, the hospital's vital functions had begun shutting down, one after another. Unrefrigerated blood had gone bad. Medicines were running out along with food and water. Morale too had begun to disintegrate when an ER doctor—he had been a medic in Vietnam—stood up at one of the Code Gray meetings, the one on Wednesday afternoon, and found words that somehow pulled the shattered group back together. "The rescue effort is officially a cluster fuck," he began, in an Alabama drawl thicker than crankcase oil. "They don't know what the fuck they're doing, and we don't know when the fuck we're gonna get out of here." His suggestion was this: "I need you to prepare right now to be here another week." The preparation he called for was mental, psychological. There was nothing much to be done in the way of reprovisioning themselves physically for even another day. "The only thing we have control over right now is inside these walls," the man continued. "We have twelve hundred people here. I want everybody to take care of everybody else. Go up to people and ask, 'What can I do for you? Have you had a break? Have you sat down?' We are an island."

The same gritty resolve found expression in bedsheet banners that began to hang from upper-story windows around the hospital wards. The first of them had been coy, a collaborative effort meant to get patients involved: "Five West Got the Thunder. We're not Going Under." Some gave way to cruder sentiment: "Get us the hell out of here."

Of course it did not help anyone's morale, patient or physician, to be so entirely in the dark—ignorant about the relief effort, such as it was, ignorant about the medical crises that continually presented themselves. One brain tumor patient had begun to behave worrisomely on Thursday. A simple electrolyte abnormality from dehydration? Or was he suffering from hydrocephalus or stroke? Normally, such a patient would have been whisked off for a CAT scan, given an EKG, or at least had some lab work done. Kurtz-Burke put him on IV fluids. What else could she do? By Friday he was vomiting. Kurtz-Burke stayed the course: more IV fluids, and he began to stabilize.

To Kurtz-Burke's delight, the new patient in Five West, the multiple-gunshots victim with the hole in his neck, forced himself up off his bed and, with help from a physical therapist, learned to walk again in the five days after Katrina. "He was tough. 'I want to walk,' he kept saying through the hole in his throat." But the doctor's interactions with most patients were far less promising. Day after day, the question on every patient's mind was, when would they be rescued, and for many of them, particularly those helplessly dependent on medical services, it was a question fraught with fear. It appalled Kurtz-Burke not to be able to provide an answer. "All I could say was, 'I won't let you die or starve, and I won't leave you. You will go first.' "

Some of them had a clearer fix on their dilemma than others. Kurtz-Burke would recall sitting up Thursday night with a quadriplegic. He had heard the *whap-whap* of helicopter rotors and surmised, correctly, that critical patients were being evacuated from Tulane Medical Center. "I remember sitting with him in the waning light, and he said, 'All the other hospitals are evacuated, I think.' 'Yeah, they are,' I said. Everybody knew the score," Kurtz-Burke would say, thinking back on that heart-to-heart with the quadriplegic. "We had poor people. We were going to be last. Nobody had any illusions about that."

It may not have hastened the arrival of help, but Charity did find ways to dispel the false report that the hospital had long since been evacuated. Some of the hospital's telephone lines were still working, and Kurtz-Burke had been able to maintain contact with her husband in Baton Rouge. He called *The New York Times,* and they ran a story on Charity the next day. And Kurtz-Burke talked to Dr. Sanjay Gupta from CNN, setting the news service straight. Fellow staffers text-messaged additional contacts, and word began to get out: Official chatter about a successful evacuation was, in a word, "bullshit." But even friendly media were still capable of fear-mongering and distortions, some of it outrageous.

From inside the building, it was easy enough to dismiss radio reports that Charity had been taken over by looters. But then somebody in the hospital pharmacy told Kurtz-Burke that inmates in the hospital's fourth-floor prison unit had shot the guards and taken over the floor, which proved harder to dispel. Other rumors ranged from the improbable—that George Bush was en route in Air Force One to personally spearhead the evacuation—to the fabulous: that sharks were finning through the flooded streets, snacking on refugees trying to wade to safety. At a morning meeting that Thursday, Kurtz-Burke pronounced a ban on rumors and urged her colleagues to respect it. "If you didn't see it, don't say it," she begged. But it didn't entirely quell the jitters. At one point, the woman running the hospital's day care center had come running down the corridor, screaming, "They're shooting at us!" What she had heard was the sound of shattering glass as patients and staff broke out windows for ventilation on the stifling floor above.

Meltdown took various forms. A prison guard had to be subdued and his medications adjusted after he paraded through the hospital on Wednesday afternoon ordering every floor to be ready for evacuation in thirty minutes. A little after midnight Thursday morning, Kurtz-Burke slipped into a conference room to call her mother. She was assuring her that her beloved doctor-daughter was safe and sound, when another woman from the day care center burst in, shouting at Kurtz-Burke to turn off the flashlight she had used to find the phone and dial the number. Couldn't she hear the gunshots! The doctor strained her ears. No gunshots, but she could hear helicopters. At last the big Chinooks and Black Hawks were starting to arrive in force.

His own hospital's resources verging on nonexistent, the head of Charity's ICU, Dr. Ben De Bloisblanc, began moving his most critical patients toward Tulane—some by canoe, others by high-water truck. One twenty-three-year-old was in transit when the doctors realized they needed to insert a chest tube to keep him breathing. The operation was performed, of necessity, without anesthesia. They had lost one patient earlier in the week, and they lost another on the roof at Tulane while they waited overnight for the helicopters. It was a convulsive expiration that drew all available staff into an anguished circle around a patient whose death they could only watch.

University Hospital also heard the helicopters and began moving patients by flatboat toward the helipad, a distance of seven blocks followed by a hike up eleven flights of stairs; residents carried those who could not walk. The most critical patients were whisked away, some of them only to be returned to the Tulane helipad after medics discovered that the Superdome did not have the dialysis machines now desperately needed by kidney patients. Others didn't get that far. Hospital guards turned them away so the Tulane staff could be evacuated. Some doctors and patients retreated to University or Charity. Conditions at the former had continued to deteriorate alarmingly. Harrison, a fastidious man who normally showered two to three times a day, had begun to smell like "Pecos Bill after a few years with the coyotes," as he put it.

Mealtimes featured such abominations as cold canned ravioli over uncooked rice. The menu was only slightly improved when a passing coast guard helicopter splashed University's roof with two hundred pints of water, thirty cans of potatoes, and a six-pack of Friskies cat food. Half the cans of beans and all the cat food exploded on impact. "Too bad about the cat food," Harrison wrote that night in his journal. "I bet it would have been good on crackers." The journal was Harrison's emotional release. Another entry: "Duane [Edwards, University's chief operating officer] put a sledgehammer to the windows in the board room and his office. We did get some breeze." And then the capper, as University ground toward complete dysfunction: the report Thursday on CNN that it, like Charity, had been successfully evacuated the day before. "They were wrong time after time," Harrison noted.

For Kurtz-Burke, Thursday was greatly leavened by the arrival of her husband, on a break from volunteer work he had been doing in the medical facility set up for refugees at LSU's Pete Maravich basketball arena in Baton

Rouge. His wife had tried to talk him out of coming. "Don't come in just to come in," she said. But Burke was not to be dissuaded. In fact, he and a buddy were going to see if they couldn't do something to alleviate Charity's woes—maybe even pull off a bit of a rescue, he intimated. Kurtz-Burke was deeply skeptical, only more so when she came to understand that her husband's accomplice in this mission of mercy was a Texas cowboy-type named Randy Faulkner, who claimed to own an outfit called Gulf South Search and Recovery. Charity security was by then a no-nonsense proposition. The flak-jacketed guards were heavily armed and just a bit full of themselves after a week on red alert. "We all have armbands," Kurtz-Burke warned her husband. "They'll never let you in."

She had underestimated her husband as surely as he had overestimated the Texan. At seven AM, Faulkner had arrived at the Maravich Arena not with a fleet of ambulances suitable for a mass evacuation but in a pickup truck with a cooler of water in the back and a stash of protein bars. Faulkner had bulled his way around checkpoints at entrances to New Orleans by pointing to Burke and announcing that the doctor was on an emergency visit to resupply Charity. When flooded streets finally stopped them, they flagged down a high-water truck and convinced the out-of-town cops aboard to drive them a ways farther. When the water became deeper than the truck could handle, the cops handed the rescuers off to a New Orleans Police Department SWAT team, which took them by boat to the Charity ambulance ramp. And yes, there they were, security guards swaggering about in flak jackets, assault rifles at the ready. Burke was thinking this might be more than even the best Texas blarney could overcome, when someone called out his name: "Justin, my man." It was Pierre, one of the guards. He had been working at Charity forever, as had his wife, Rita, another guard, and somehow Pierre remembered Burke from the doctor's days in the emergency room during medical school.

Burke's arrival was timely. Word came late Thursday that the hospital really was going to be evacuated the next day, and Kurtz-Burke and her husband set to work sawing up doors and conference tables to make spine boards, there being just one hundred in the whole hospital. To prepare the patients for destinations unknown, staffers wrote out medical discharge summaries by hand, in triplicate—one copy for the hospital, one for the rescuer, and the third for the patient. It was pinned to his or her clothing, along with three days' worth of medications and a recent medical history. After five days in hundred-degree heat, some of them were fading fast. The brain tumor patient had become unresponsive, and the woman in renal failure was nearly incapable of making urine. But staff too had begun to lose their battle with microbes running rampant through Charity. Diarrhea was epidemic. In the absence of working toilets, the staff had lined buckets with biohazard bags, which were then dropped down an old service elevator shaft to distance patients from the filth. If the problem was simply a full bladder, many staffers preferred to relieve themselves on the emergency stairwells that ran down the hospital's exterior walls.

At a review of the evacuation plan during Wednesday's Code Gray meeting, an intern had posed a question: "What about staff who are on IVs? Do they count as patients or employees?" In truth, it was getting hard to tell. They count as patients, the ER doctors had decided.

Kurtz-Burke was standing on the hospital's ambulance ramp at about eight-thirty Friday morning when the relief so long delayed hove into view: a flotilla of fan-powered swamp boats. Each could hold at best a couple of patients on spine boards, so the evacuation was going to take hours. Shoving aside dead bodies in the ER morgue to make room, staffers set up an assembly line that snaked down flights of stairs and out onto the ramp. Eight hours later, the last of the patients from Five West was eased into a swamp boat, and screams of jubilation coursed the length of the assembly line. Now it was time for the staff to leave, and as the boats pulled up, calling out the number of vacant seats—two, two, six, four—Kurtz-Burke was reminded of nothing so much as the rides at Disney World. Before taking her own place aboard one of the boats, Kurtz-Burke and her husband dashed back up the five flights of stairs to the rehab unit, driven by a terrible suspicion—groundless, as it turned out—that someone might have been left behind. She scrawled a note to no one and everyone: "We were here. We survived Katrina," and left it on the desk. And then she burst into tears. "It was the first time I cried—for relief, for joy, for sadness, for my whole life, for my city." She had a sneaking suspicion she might also have been grieving for Charity Hospital itself.

TEN

Like Bricks on Jell-O

ALARM HAD GIVEN WAY TO FEAR AND THEN TO HORROR AS KATRINA SWEPT toward Louisiana and then across the landscape of public awareness in the wider world. Dismay had engendered compassion as well as anger once the full scope of the catastrophe registered. Ivor van Heerden was buffeted by all those feelings and by another, curiosity. Why had the levees failed? What had gone so terribly wrong? Had the hurricane—not all that strong a storm as it made landfall—simply overwhelmed stalwart levees? Or was there an inherent flaw in their construction—something that should have been foreseen? And if so, was it due to flawed engineering, or were these failed levees fitting monuments to Louisiana's famous corruption? Had some contractor cheated the government and the public by cutting corners to save money? Or had the army corps itself, ever under the gun to trim its own budgets, tried to do the job on the cheap?

Answers to these questions lay buried in the earth as well as in the archives of the army corps, and it might be months, even years, before a forensic probe of that magnitude could be completed. But within a few weeks of Katrina's passing, van Heerden's curiosity had begun to harden into preliminary convictions about where the blame might lie, and it had begun to get him into trouble.

As deputy chief of the LSU Hurricane Center, van Heerden and his colleagues had pioneered well-regarded computer models that could predict where and with what force a hurricane's storm surge was likely to strike. By his reckoning, the army corps had been misinformed—or perhaps they'd been lying, politics and tort law being what they are—in their confident early assertion that, of course the levees had failed; the flood walls above them had been overtopped by surges much greater than they'd been designed to resist.

"The breach at the Seventeenth Street Canal levee, a levee–flood wall combination, is about three hundred feet long. It's believed that the force of the water overtopped the flood wall and scoured the structure from behind and then moved the levee wall horizontally about twenty feet, opening both ends to flow," the corps would declare in a public statement released within three days of the disaster. Not only did van Heerden's field data convince him the corps was wrong, he was not afraid to say so loudly, and media gave him every opportunity. Even before the storm struck, he was the go-to guy for local reporters and TV crews. In the storm's immediate aftermath, his tousled hair and distinctive South African accent were on every network and cable news channel.

Katrina had triggered a media-feeding frenzy, and van Heerden, as the most knowledgeable and iconoclastic sound bite in Louisiana, was the chum in the water. CNN, *Meet the Press, The New York Times, Time,* they all wanted a piece of him—which was fine with van Heerden, because he did not see his role as purely scientific. Van Heerden was a man with a mission: to wake up Louisiana to its peril, and Washington to the need for a far more serious commitment to coastal restoration and storm protection. It made for a sleep-depriving kind of celebrity. The BBC would want to go live at 2:15 in the morning van Heerden's time. And the phone never stopped ringing.

It could be called a matter of scholarly dispute, but the intensity with which van Heerden and the corps soon ratcheted up their disagreement suggested that professional reputations were at stake, not just fine points of hydrology. And in due course, van Heerden began to suspect that more was going on behind the scenes than was apparent in his give-and-take with talking heads speaking for the corps.

Van Heerden was not sure of the exact moment when LSU's expressed delight in its hard-charging and telegenic hurricane expert turned to anxiety that he was a firebrand who might jeopardize federal research grants. Maybe it was the *Larry King Live* appearance, in which van Heerden went public with the contention that, as he put it, "the wheels were coming off" the FEMA relief effort, notwithstanding the president's backslapping vote of confidence in Mike "Brownie" Brown earlier that same day. Or maybe it was van Heerden's public disclosure that the president and Homeland Security chief Chertoff were misinformed or simply lying in their contention that the challenges posed by Katrina were unprecedented and couldn't have been anticipated. In fact, as van Heerden pointed out on national TV, the whole scenario—levee inadequacies, widespread flooding, and mass death—had been not only anticipated but simulated in the "Hurricane Pam" disaster drill a year earlier.

How did van Heerden know? He had participated in the drill. How did he know FEMA was aware of it? The agency had sponsored the exercise and paid handsomely for it. It would be months before the president's prior knowledge was confirmed in the tape that showed him being officially briefed on the afternoon before the storm, warned that levees were likely to be breached with catastrophic consequences. But with the hurricane-induced fog still obscuring who knew what when, van Heerden's pronouncements through the autumn of 2005 deeply antagonized the corps and its champions in the Pentagon.

It was great publicity for LSU, and then suddenly van Heerden was ordered to stop. In early December, one of the vice chancellors, a man able to sever an untenured associate professor's contract with the university by simply snapping his fingers, advised van Heerden that it was time to put a cork in it. No more interviews. Van Heerden was furious but had no choice other than compliance, which meant canceling the twenty television appearances then pending.

If there was a certain zealousness in van Heerden's approach to both science and the attentions of the media, it could not be laid off on sheer egotism. The son of progressive white South Africans—his mother was a bookkeeper; his father had risen high in the nation's education ministry—van Heerden had seen more than his share of government oafishness, or worse, in its dealings with the disempowered. It deeply offended him to realize that the catastrophe in New Orleans was an entirely avoidable event, a man-made event—not at all the "act of God" that the federal government (and the insurance industry) wanted people to think it was. "The bottom line is, a hundred thousand families lost everything because they believed what the federal government had told them," van Heerden said over coffee in Madisonville in early December. "They evacuated like they were supposed to, and now they can't go home. They're broke, they're being sued by mortgage collectors. . . . The federal government owes these people not just an apology, it needs to bail them out."

Maybe so, but for van Heerden to translate his opinion from rhetoric into hard science, he had needed more than a hunch to support his claim that Katrina's flooding was a man-made disaster. The army corps showed no inclination to concede the point, certainly not without a fight. The levees failed because they had been overtopped, and they had been overtopped for the simple reason that they were not built to withstand a storm as strong as Katrina. That was the army corps' position. And the army corps should have known what it was talking about. After all, it had built the levees.

Yes, but van Heerden had built the storm surge models on which his reputation depended, and that of the LSU Hurricane Center. And the models showed that Katrina, for all the wind and swollen water, would not have raised levels in the drainage canals above the flood walls. There had been no overtopping, which meant the levees had failed for some other reason, most likely because they were improperly constructed.

But how to prove it?

Van Heerden, of course, was not the only scientist bedeviled by the levee failures and hell-bent to solve the mystery behind them. The National Science Foundation had tapped Berkeley engineering professors Ray Seed and Robert Bea to lead a forensic team. And the army corps was doing its own investigation, a dubious proposition in the minds of rival scientists, given the corps' role in the construction of the levees and possible culpability in their collapse. But the American Society of Civil Engineers had pledged to review the corps' exercise in self-examination. And van Heerden himself would soon be ably assisted by LSU colleagues and others who would constitute a state-sponsored cadre called Team Louisiana. Separately, the U.S. attorney for New Orleans had announced a probe after spotting possible corruption in the design and maintenance of the levee system. But from the ubiquity of van Heerden's mug on television—often with the Seventeenth Street Canal breach as a backdrop, or a view of him pacing the levees with or without a camera crew in tow—it came to seem as if he were on a one-man crusade to find the truth about what was being called the most catastrophic failure in the history of American engineering.

His dealings with the media cut two ways. Media used him as the available incarnation of scientific inquiry into the collapse, and he used media to shape the national conversation about the disaster in ways that kept a finger pointing toward human error. From time to time he was also assisted more directly by the work of newspaper reporters as eager as he was to expose the truth and, if appropriate, indict the guilty.

Bob Marshall was one of the reporters who joined the hunt, and the call to his desk at *The Times-Picayune* in late September was one of those tips a journalist lives for. A woman named Mignon Marcello was on the line. Some nine months prior, right around Thanksgiving 2004, Marcello had noticed water in her backyard on Bellaire Drive, the Lakeview street closest to the Seventeenth Street Canal. Of course, it could have been anything: rainfall in a poorly drained dip in the yard, a leaky water main. But it had become a nuisance, and if Marshall needed to talk to someone else on the block with a soggy backyard, he should try Gary Breedlove and Beth LeBlanc, Marcello told him. Their stories, which jibed, were highly suggestive. More annoyed by the water than concerned about its source, they had called the Sewerage and Water Board, the city agency responsible for pumping and drainage, and in due course the Water Board had sent someone out. This was not potable water, the Water Board's man determined. That ruled out a leaking main. Neither was it infiltration from the brackish lake; the salinity levels were too low. It had to be coming from the canal, the man said. Which made it somebody else's problem, if indeed it should even be considered a problem. New Orleans, after all, was a damp city. A little water in your yard? Get used to it.

Marshall wrote for the sports pages, but that did not mean his interests were circumscribed by quarterback trades and league standings. Marshall's specialty was a column that dwelled on outdoor adventure in general, hunting and fishing in particular, and along with great tips on where to bag ducks and hook stripers, he had kept a drumbeat of attention to environmental issues, not least of them the dire peril that coastal erosion was bringing upon Louisiana. His knowledge of marine ecology had prompted news editors to recruit Marshall onto a reporting team whose eight-day presentation warning of threats to global fisheries had won *The Times-Picayune* the Pulitzer Prize for public service in 1997. And yet, by no stretch of his imagination did Marshall—or his editors—think of him as an investigative reporter, the type of journalist who knew how to take a tip like Marcello's and worm his way into the city bureaucracy in search of documentation. Without that kind of corroboration, the tip would never be anything more than a suggestive but unverified anecdote.

Marshall had been far from New Orleans when Katrina struck. His first glimpse of his hometown's ruin had been of front-page pictures on a newsstand as he and his wife emerged from the wilderness after a week-long hike in Glacier National Park. Back in the office, he had asked to be assigned to the team of reporters who had stayed on in New Orleans after the paper was forced to evacuate, first to Houma, Louisiana, and then to Baton Rouge. Marshall was denied. There were stories more obviously within his purview that needed doing, and they were better done from Baton Rouge—an assessment by helicopter, for example, of how badly Katrina had eroded the coastal wetlands. On another occasion, Marshall found himself writing a requiem for Blackie Campo's operation down in Plaquemines Parish, Campo being a fishing guide and boat-launch proprietor who had figured in Marshall's column over the years.

But between these assignments, Marshall pursued a growing fascination with the levee failure and, in due course, with the mystery of Mignon Marcello's sodden backyard. If the Sewerage and Water Board had come out, as she claimed it had, then there would be a work order filed away somewhere describing the visit. Marshall tracked down an attorney for the Sewerage and Water Board and asked to see the document and others related to it. They were public records, after all, and under Louisiana law—albeit, a statute often observed in the breach—the Sewerage and Water Board had three days to hand them over. They didn't. Marshall surveyed his options. In order to ratchet up the pressure a notch, he would have had to file a formal public records request, a first step toward a possible lawsuit forcing the Water Board to surrender the documents. "But who would I sue—which agency?" Marshall asked himself, as he pondered the total disarray of city government since the hurricane.

Instead Marshall went another round with the Water Board attorney, who treated him to some blunt talk: "People get nervous, Mr. Marshall. There are lawsuits swirling all around this." That said, the attorney promised he'd make sure the Water Board coughed up the documents that afternoon. Again there was a delay, but eventually the attorney came through, and Marshall had what he was looking for: the work order. It confirmed Marcello's account. The Water Board had indeed come out to Bellaire Drive and later concluded that the water was coming from the canal, not from some busted water main or sewer line.

Then, one afternoon Gary Breedlove, Mignon Marcello's neighbor, walked Marshall through the wreckage along Bellaire Drive near the breach, telling him which wrecked house had been whose. In several cases, the force of the water had swept cottages clean off their foundations. But Breedlove also pointed out three fresh slabs that workmen had been racing to finish framing in the days just before Katrina interrupted them. If the workmen were at the framing stage, that meant they had also driven pilings to stabilize New Orleans's sodden soils. And the site preparation had included yanking out two huge oaks just yards from the toe of the levee, said Breedlove, who had watched the work progress as he walked his dog, sometimes pausing to chat with the construction crew.

Marshall checked in with his sources at the corps to ask about the implications of what Breedlove had told him. Uprooting big oaks close by the levee was not a great idea, the corps conceded. Hell, letting big oaks even grow alongside a levee was ill-advised, given how handily the root system provided pathways for water to work its way through the soil. And hammering in pilings? Not good. Pile-driving was like a small temblor within the loosely compacted soils of a man-made levee. Pile-driving could weaken a levee. And why hadn't the corps done anything? It's not our jurisdiction, Marshall was told. The corps might have taken responsibility for building the levees, but maintenance of them, once constructed, was one of the tasks that still remained with the local levee board. Maintenance centered principally on grass cutting, but the pantomime of a more formal review of flood-system integrity was enacted once each year when the corps and the levee board conducted their annual tour of the levees. In late November, colleagues of Marshall's named Frank Donze and Gordon Russell would expose this as the travesty it had degenerated into over the years: essentially a hasty drive-by of small portions of the 169-mile levee system, culminating in lunch and much merriment at a west bank restaurant: crab cakes with champagne dill sauce and a dessert of white chocolate mousse with raspberry coulis.

VAN HEERDEN'S EASY GIVE-AND-TAKE WITH THE PRESS WAS NOT REPLICATED IN his dealings with the corps. He had made no secret of his skepticism about the corps' claim that the levees had been overtopped. As one scientist to another, he called the corps early in September and left word that he thought their analysis was flawed. The corps ignored him, but van Heerden was not one to be ignored. To carry his message up the political food chain, van Heerden called John Barry, the New Orleans writer whose bestselling account of the 1927 flood, *Rising Tide,* had come into a revived shelf life in Katrina's aftermath. Van Heerden had met Barry not in New Orleans but in Washington as a fellow guest of Tim Russert on *Meet the Press.* What he needed, van Heerden told Barry, was a contact at *The Washington Post*— someone who could bring the story of the levee fiasco and the corps' role in it to the attention of the Beltway intelligentsia. It was time, in other words, to "let the cat among the pigeons," van Heerden told the writer.

Barry put van Heerden in touch with reporter Mike Grunwald. Grunwald got interested enough to come down to New Orleans, and in short order van Heerden was escorting yet another journalist along the well-trod path to the collapsed flood wall atop the Seventeenth Street Canal levee. Grunwald's front-page story, co-authored with Joby Warrick, was to that point the fullest elaboration of van Heerden's insights to appear in the nation's capital. The drainage canals that failed had not been overtopped; they had collapsed well shy of the maximum load of water they were designed to carry.

"This was not the Big One, not even close," van Heerden's colleague Hassan Mashriqui, an LSU storm-surge expert, told Grunwald. Human error turned "a problem into a catastrophe," he added. In short, try as the corps might to portray the disaster as an act of God, it had human fingerprints all over it. The LSU group also played up a related theme: that the seventy-six-mile channel that the corps had dredged through the eastern wetlands as a shortcut for ships traveling between New Orleans and the Gulf, was directly implicated in the flooding and levee failures.

The Mississippi River Gulf Outlet—or "Mr. Go," as it was known locally—had been decried as an environmental threat even before the waterway was dredged to its thirty-six-foot depth forty years earlier. But the early indictment had been a general one: that the shipping channel would sluice in salt water and upset the delicate ecology of wetlands not already destroyed in the dredging. Valuable shellfish and trapping industries would be decimated—as indeed they were—and finned fish would lose a fertile breeding ground. The channel cut miles off the older and still very active route that required ships to exit Louisiana via the mouth of the river. But over the years, Mr. Go had proved both expensive to maintain and difficult to confine within its original borders. Not only was dredging constantly required, at an annual cost in the millions, but the channel had sprawled ever wider as saline waters killed off the marsh grass and cypress stands that had once defined its banks. The capper was that very few ships actually used the channel—fewer than one a day.

Destroyed wetlands were high on van Heerden's list of environmental atrocities that exposed New Orleans to hurricane threats, but the data from Katrina suggested a much more specific culpability. Mr. Go had acted like a funnel for storm surge that had risen quickly higher as it was channeled past the junction with the Intracoastal Waterway in eastern New Orleans, and on into the Industrial Canal near the city's very heart. Surge had moved through Lake Borgne at approximately three feet per second, accelerating to six feet per second at the mouth of the funnel, and then to eight feet per second as it neared the city and overwhelmed the Industrial Canal flood walls.

The national press attention imbued van Heerden's corps-bashing with legitimacy. Building on the momentum, he met with Blanco's people and pitched them successfully on the idea of a state-sponsored forensic study, the effort that would be mounted by the group dubbed Team Louisiana. Van Heerden's storm-surge models would be incorporated into the study, with his hypotheticals now grounded in the data on actual water levels that he had gathered. But he needed more, in particular a clearer sense of exactly when and in what sequence the various levees had been breached. To that end, Team Louisiana came up with its "stopped-clock program." Notices tacked up on the doors of flooded houses and published in *The Times-Picayune* offered fifty dollars to people who would advise researchers of the exact moment when the rising water had fouled and stopped their clocks.

On prowls throughout the floodplain, van Heerden was not above slipping into an abandoned house on the chance he'd find a clock—a mission that subjected him on at least one occasion to an encounter with the corpse of an old man in the wheelchair where he had died, a profoundly distressing moment in a season that for van Heerden, as for many residents of southeast Louisiana, was a wild gyration between anger, resolve, and deep depression. From the frozen timepieces, it was possible to re-create the order in which the levees were breached. Building on that data, it became clear that some of the breaches had occurred before the water had peaked, and some afterward, as it began to ebb—further proof that the surge hadn't knocked the flood walls down; they had failed for some other reason.

In van Heerden's view, this evidence pointed to underlying structural failures. Two explanations jumped to mind. One was that the soils beneath the levees were unstable, as might be expected of drained swampland. Swamp soils were likely to be full of everything from rotting wood to alligator carcasses. At the London Avenue Canal, it was immediately clear to van Heerden from the hillocks of sand that had blown out from the sides of the levees as they failed, that these ramparts had been built above an old beach, which greatly augmented their instability. The other key variable was the depth of sheet piling, the huge interlocking iron plates that were driven into the levees and, in theory at least, deep enough below the levees to provide an impenetrable barrier to water migrating horizontally from the canal. Under that scenario, the flood walls had collapsed because the sheet piling beneath them—twenty-foot lengths, according to the corps' design memoranda— did not go deep enough to get past the unstable peat and sand, both of which siphon water out of canals, especially canals that in recent years had been dredged deeper than the piling that lined them.

Now all of a sudden the callback number on van Heerden's cell phone was the corps'. Maybe they should work together on the forensic probe, the corps suggested. Van Heerden arrived full of questions for a dinner with some of the corps' brain trust. It was not a productive encounter. The exchange of information, as he would tell it, was one-sided at best—an accusation with which the corps concurred, though by their lights it was van Heerden who was holding back. "The only thing we learned is that the corps people liked to eat steak," van Heerden said. It was particularly frustrating to him to make no progress on a matter that might be absolutely critical to any wholehearted effort to find out what really went wrong: pulling up the sheet pilings to determine their actual length and condition. The corps, in its understandable zeal to haul in tons of gravel to buttress the levees where they had been breached, seemed to be doing more to bury evidence than expose it to scientific review, van Heerden thought. The sheet pilings were not the problem, the corps insisted. They had been driven to depths seventeen feet below sea level. Maybe fifty feet would have been better, but at seventeen feet, they were not going to be the smoking gun.

Eventually the corps would start opening its files on levee construction to public review, but before that happened, van Heerden had strong reason to believe the corps was not dishing up unimpeachable data. While he waited for the corps to get a lot more candid about its performance in constructing the levees, the state Department of Transportation and Development (DOTD)—the part of state government that interfaced with the levee boards and that was nominally sponsoring Team Louisiana—came up with a "design memorandum." This was part of the paper trail generated in the early phases of the levee engineering process, and it called for sheet piling to a depth of ten feet, not seventeen. The only documentation more decisive would have been the corps' "as-built" records—the paperwork detailing what had actually gone into the ground—and the corps was not coughing them up.

Whatever the corps' motives for being so reluctant to pull the sheet pilings—and in his blacker moods, van Heerden had his suspicions—not knowing exactly what lay below the levees became intolerable to the detective in him. It was then that someone tipped him off about an alternative way to get at the sheet pilings: sonar. The same X-ray-like technology used to descry underwater objects—be they the hull of the *Titanic* at the bottom of the North Atlantic or a school of sea bass below a charter fishing boat plying a Gulf shoal—could provide readings on how deep the pilings had been driven. By eight o'clock in the evening, van Heerden had secured the go-ahead from the state DOTD to hire a contractor with sonar gear. The next morning they were out on the Seventeenth Street Canal, dinging sound waves into the levee's underpinnings and listening for the varying echoes as the waves ran up against pilings—or didn't.

The army corps took some readings of its own, and now at last there was some cooperation—or at least the appearance of it. Both van Heerden and the corps submitted their readings to the same analyst for interpretation. The analyst's assessment conformed more or less exactly, not with the depths the army corps claimed, but with those specified all along in the design memorandum. Bob Marshall got a call from van Heerden, clearly keyed up by the day's developments: "Guess what, Bob. They're only minus ten."

From the Seventeenth Street Canal, it was on to the London Avenue Canal and the breach at Mirabeau Avenue. The design memoranda for these levees had called for sheet pilings to be driven twenty-six feet below sea level. They'd also specified that the flood walls be in the shape of upside-down *T*'s, to provide subterranean crosspieces that would greatly stabilize the structures. Instead, the sonar readings showed I-shaped flood walls, fused to the sheet pilings but without the anchoring crosspiece. And the pilings once again were a paltry ten feet, the sonar analyst said.

There was a reason why van Heerden called Bob Marshall at *The Times-Picayune* to share the early returns of the sonar readings. He owed him. In another coup for an investigative journalist, some weeks earlier, Marshall had unearthed the soil tests that were made in the early 1980s as engineers had pondered ways to raise and fortify the drainage canals—a process that had led to topping the levees with the flood walls that eventually failed. And, after overcoming some initial resistance, Marshall had won his colleagues over to the idea of sharing this scoop with van Heerden—and the scientist was keen to see them—in order to get his comment and elucidation before the paper published the story.

The soil tests identified varying layers of sedimentation and decomposed vegetation in the former swampland below the levees. Aside from being a critical piece of the puzzle, the test results were also a redemption of sorts for *The Times-Picayune* team, after being scooped in their own backyard—and by a TV network at that.

Do you mind if NBC comes along? That had been van Heerden's question one afternoon when Marshall was making plans to meet him at the Seventeenth Street Canal breach for another look-see. Marshall was not enamored of the idea of sharing the moment with TV, but there wasn't much he could do about it, except make sure that his own interview with the LSU scientist would not be part of whatever NBC was out there to film.

And it wasn't—at least not his questions. But as van Heerden rattled on against the backdrop of the breached flood wall, he had things to say. Some of it would have been old hat to Marshall's readers: that, in van Heerden's view, the levees had not been overtopped, they had collapsed—flopping over like the tailgate on a pickup truck. And van Heerden trotted out his view that Katrina had been barely Category 3 strength—not the huge Category 4 or 5 storm that the army corps was so quick to excuse itself from failing to manage.

But then van Heerden mentioned something not yet part of the public discourse on the levee failure: legal action in the early 1990s that had stemmed from a contractor's problems dealing with the unstable soils below the Seventeenth Street Canal. NBC had no reporter present on the scene; they were simply after footage of LSU's hurricane guru walking the levee and moving his mouth. But the questions van Heerden answered were being posed by an unheard, off-camera presence: Bob Marshall. It galled him more than a little to see NBC air not only the first reference to the uncertain soils but also the first reference to the legal action, a 1994 arbitration proceeding.

The plaintiff, a subcontractor named Pittman Construction, had been seeking an extra $800,000 from the corps to finish putting the flood wall on top of the Seventeenth Street Canal levees. Pittman's contention was that the site analysis had been flawed, and as a result, the sections of flood wall were slipping out of alignment. They weren't anchored adequately—further evidence that their underpinnings were unstable, van Heerden suggested. (In the end, the judge had denied Pittman the money and dismissed the suit.)

Abashed by NBC's coup, Marshall was all over Pittman. Formerly based in Franklin, Louisiana, the firm had moved to Baton Rouge. But the man Marshall realized he needed to reach was a consulting engineer named Herbert Rousselle. Rousselle was an adjunct professor at Tulane, Marshall determined. Tulane, clobbered by Katrina to the tune of $180 million in damages, had shut down for the semester. Marshall thought he had tracked Rousselle to an office address in Metairie—only to discover, on arrival, that the office had flooded. Marshall left a note on the door and fired off some e-mails asking Rousselle for an interview. They disappeared into cyberspace without an echo. And then one day, Rousselle called. He had just read a story by Marshall's colleague John McQuaid quoting Bob Bea, one of the Berkeley engineers reviewing the levee failures for the National Science Foundation. Rousselle didn't think that highly of Bea: something of a glory hound, he cautioned, harking back to when he knew Bea as an engineer with Shell Oil. You want to talk soils, come by my office, Rousselle said. And in two shakes of a lamb's tail, Marshall was out the door.

Rousselle had the entire file: the five hundred borings the corps had done in order to develop a cross section of the soils underneath the levee. Perhaps "soils" was not quite the right word for what the tests showed. Loam was in limited abundance. Instead, as Rousselle freely acknowledged, the levees had been built over a mishmash of sand and clay and rotting vegetation variously referred to as marsh or peat. Sinking a sheet pile into peat was like trying to make a fork stand up in salad. Marshall had an indelicate question: Had it occurred to Rousselle and the firm he worked for that the unstable soils might jeopardize the integrity of the levees themselves? No, Rousselle said, that really wasn't the issue. Pittman had been concerned about the tolerances involved in lining up the sections of flood wall. Period. Flood safety was someone else's problem.

The minute van Heerden got wind of the soil samples in Marshall's possession, he began agitating for a look. And Marshall's editor and fellow reporters were frankly just a bit uncertain whether that was a good idea, given van Heerden's cozy relations with some of their competitors. But in the end, the reporters needed van Heerden at least as much as he needed to see the subsoil cross sections. And so one afternoon, Team Louisiana was invited up to the newsroom. Van Heerden and three colleagues gathered around a table, and Marshall rolled out the cross sections. There was a moment's silence, and then heads began to shake in disbelief. "No way," one of the men muttered. Another, Radhey Sharma, an expert in geotechnics, had this to say: "We tell our students all the time, when you see these materials, don't rely on them. Keep going down until you get some better strata. This would never work." A more vivid reaction was elicited by Marshall from J. David Rogers, a University of Missouri engineer: Building a flood wall on that kind of foundation was like "putting bricks on Jell-O."

But one among many unanswered questions was this: How had the corps—an organization esteemed around the world for its levee-building expertise—presided over such a fiasco?

Soon enough the corps had moved beyond invitations to eat steak. Col. Richard Wagenaar, commander of the corps' New Orleans district, saw fit to present himself personally at LSU for a one-on-one discussion with a gadfly who didn't seem to be easily swatted away. Van Heerden found the corpsman refreshingly frank and tried to reciprocate. "I said, 'We aren't enjoying this, but the corps keeps saying the levees were overtopped and the sheet pilings run to minus seventeen, and we know that's not so.'" The scientist in van Heerden was staking his claim to empirical fact, to truth. But his agenda was a little longer than that. There was a political side to him that would not be denied. "What was driving us was this," he would say in summary, looking back on a struggle that soon would poison his relations with LSU and jeopardize his job. "Somebody's got to take responsibility."

Van Heerden was no fool. He knew what side his bread was buttered on, and as an untenured associate professor, he knew his bread was buttered rather thinly. He might be cofounder of the university's increasingly high-profile Hurricane Center, but LSU could fire him at any time. That was the downside of the footloose course through life that van Heerden had charted for himself. The upside was the independence of mind that came with having relatively little to lose. No comfy endowed chair awaited him, no matter how well he played his cards, no Nobel Prize. At fifty-five, van Heerden's chief asset, aside from that sailboat at Madisonville, was the self-respect that he would lose if, for the first time in a knockabout career, he betrayed his principles.

Van Heerden had grown up in Johannesburg and was just seventeen when he arrived at LSU for graduate work in geology, a time—the late 1970s—when the virus of environmentalism was at its most contagious. Van Heerden had focused his studies on the Atchafalaya delta west of Baton Rouge, the enormously feral web of wetlands, bayous, and rivers that would have been the Mississippi's natural course to the Gulf if heroic efforts had not been mounted—by the army corps, as it happened—to keep it on its old path past the wharves and grain elevators and refineries leading to New Orleans and, seventy tortuous miles later, the open sea. The wilds of Louisiana were a crash course in the importance of environmental management and coastal restoration, and back in South Africa, van Heerden took a government job in that area before jumping to the private sector and, for a time, running a large marine diamond mining operation.

By 1989, he had accumulated enough savings—an amount more or less exactly equivalent to his accumulated restlessness—to cash them in and go sailing. He bought the boat and set off around the world with his wife. In December 1990, they had docked in Grand Cayman and flown to Baton Rouge for Christmas with friends, when van Heerden ran into an old comrade in arms, Paul Kemp, head of the nascent Coalition to Restore Coastal Louisiana. "This is right up your street," Kemp told van Heerden. "We need you. You need to come back."

The needs of Kemp's coastal restoration project coincided nicely just then with van Heerden's need to replenish his exchequer, and yankee greenbacks had an allure not matched by rand. Van Heerden decided to give it a go for two years as director of the coalition. Fifteen years and another wife later, he was raising two daughters and serving as the founding codirector of the Hurricane Center and its public health affiliate.

All this was on his mind a few days after Colonel Wagenaar's visit with him at LSU, when van Heerden got the call that summoned him to the vice chancellor's office. The conversation's point of departure was also its bottom line, reiterated as van Heerden was shown the door: The Katrina story was dead, he was advised. Let it go, Ivor. Get your goddamn face off television.

The Katrina story was dead? As van Heerden sat in the vice chancellor's office, he was juggling no fewer than thirty requests a day from major news organizations for a bit of his time, a phone interview, a studio appearance, another trip down to the Seventeenth Street Canal. He was swamped under more than two hundred daily e-mail inquiries, sometimes a multiple of that number—and he tried to answer as many as he could, based on the conviction that fostering public awareness of hurricane research and the forensic probe of the levee failures was an integral part of the Hurricane Center's mission. Van Heerden could only assume that someone had gotten to the vice chancellor, not an assumption that could be explored overtly, of course. A university bureaucrat would not freely acknowledge having been cowed into compromising free speech, even that of a lowly associate professor. What the vice chancellor did not hesitate to say, however, was that van Heerden stood to jeopardize LSU's life-sustaining flow of federal dollars, research grants and the like. Their importance had been reflected in LSU's recent hiring of former NASA administrator Sean O'Keefe to run the university—a man far better credentialed as a Washington insider than as an academic. Bad enough to be trying to run a university in the last Southern state with a Democrat for a governor. LSU hardly needed a junior professor running around insinuating that the army corps bore culpability for an act of lethal negligence.

Van Heerden instantly agreed to stop talking to media. It was that or his job, he realized. For all his recent face time on television and the minor celebrity that came with it, he spoke with the authority vested in him by LSU and, by extension, the state DOTD probe. That authority could be withdrawn by the vice chancellor. Indeed it had been. Overnight, people accustomed to reaching van Heerden by phone on the spur of the moment—people like Marshall and his colleagues—found themselves routed to a university functionary handling requests.

But van Heerden was not without political wiles of his own. For one thing, he and the Hurricane Center had brought an enormous amount of favorable publicity to LSU. Academic colleagues, those not made envious by his high visibility, frankly told him so. For that matter, so had Governor Blanco's people, in congratulatory e-mails sent to van Heerden after he testified in early November in front of a Senate committee probing the Katrina debacle. State Attorney General Charles Foti, who endowed the DOTD forensic probe with his office's legal authority, had sent two attorneys along to Washington to provide backup for van Heerden, as they had at other moments in the probe. Now van Heerden had to tell Foti's office that he no longer could do media. Foti, a former Orleans Parish sheriff and a master of media himself, could be expected to feel van Heerden's pain and regret his being sidelined.

A week later, van Heerden got an e-mail from LSU administrators saying go ahead. Another someone had gotten to them. Foti? Blanco? Van Heerden had no idea. The restriction on media interviews was lifted. It left van Heerden wondering if the forces opposing him—some in the interests of grantsmanship, some out of egotism and envy—had merely given ground in a tactical retreat and would now muster themselves for a run at getting him fired outright. Paranoia on van Heerden's part? Possibly so, but these were trying times, and tensions ran high.

The drumbeat of revelations about the levee failures and insinuations as to who was at fault finally stirred the corps to a showy public response. December eighth, a Thursday, was selected as the day the sheet pilings were to be pulled. The announcement was accompanied by buzz tantalizing enough to guarantee a fully mobilized media presence. The levees where the pilings were to be pulled would be managed like a crime scene, reporters were advised, and the evidence handled accordingly. Media would be tolerated, but credentials needed to be in order. Whatever nods were made to proper forensic procedure, the upshot was something of a circus, with reporters and camera crews and corps PR teams tripping over one another on the gravelly slope of the levee.

The fanfare could be chalked up to the corps' avowed commitment to "transparency." Hey, this whole investigation is a completely open process, a corps information officer would insist, without irony. But after so much resistance by the corps to even routine document requests, skeptics were muttering that the obstreperous show of transparency on this occasion had to mean that somehow they'd already made sure the pilings were not going to be the mere sixteen-footers Ivor van Heerden had detected by sonar, sheets that ran to only ten feet below sea level. Design specs had called for them to be twenty-three feet, which would put the in-ground end seventeen feet below sea level—clearly not deep enough, as catastrophe had shown, but twenty-three-foot sheets might at least counter accusations of fraud.

Van Heerden, as it happened, was not present. He was in Holland with the local CBS affiliate that, following the lead of *The Times-Picayune,* had decided to examine the complex and vastly more reliable flood-control system created in that low-lying country after the devastating floods of 1953. There was an irony here. A century earlier, the Dutch had sent a delegation to New Orleans to learn state-of-the-art flood-control techniques from Baldwin Wood, inventor of the giant pumps that still drained New Orleans. The trip had been necessitated by Wood's breezy refusal to accept a contract that would have required him to do the traveling. If the Dutch wanted state-of-the-art pumping equipment, they would just have to come to New Orleans to get it. And so they did. A century later, America had relinquished its place in the forefront of flood-control technology and, after Katrina, had lost the confidence of New Orleanians and the respect of the wider world. The richest nation on earth hadn't managed to protect a major city from a storm that had passed far enough to the east to have posed what should have been a manageable, if not minor, threat.

There were aspects of the Dutch system clearly relevant to New Orleans, none more so than the giant surge-killing gates that had been erected at key North Sea inlets. The gates were ecologically healthier than the intractable earthen dikes some of them had replaced, because, except on the rare occasions when they were closed, they allowed tidal give-and-take between the sea, freshwater lagoons, and the brackish marshes that, in Holland as in Louisiana, lay between them. A gate at the Rigolets, the narrow strait at the eastern end of Lake Pontchartrain, would be a critical improvement, van Heerden had decided. The gate was one item on a multibillion-dollar menu of improvements that would have constituted a flood defense against even Category 5 hurricanes. Instead of authorizing it, Congress had repeatedly nipped the army corps budget in ways that left incomplete even the Category 3 defense prompted by Hurricane Betsy.

Van Heerden also saw a critical advantage in a measure already available to Louisiana levee boards and the army corps, indeed already installed at Jefferson Parish drainage canal outlets within a mile or two of Orleans: pumping stations placed right at the lake's edge, not miles into the city's interior, as in Orleans. Pumps near the center of the city lifted water up into canals and then had to push that water many miles toward the lake. Pumps at the lake's edge would suck water out of the city, a far more efficient process. They would also double as gates, denying a surging lake easy—and deadly—access to the heart of the metropolis. As one Dutch engineer had said in summarizing the philosophical underpinnings of the Netherlands' flood barrier: Better to take the battle to the enemy, the sea, rather than letting that enemy penetrate your lowlands before mounting a defense against it.

But the galling thing to van Heerden was that New Orleans would have easily stood up to Katrina, indeed to a much stronger storm, if only the existing system had been built and honestly maintained to its own specifications. That it wasn't, that the seepages along Bellaire Drive and at Mirabeau Avenue weren't seen as red flags signaling that something was going radically wrong, that trees were allowed to take root and grow tall, that pile-driving was tolerated at the foot of the levees, was outrageously derelict on the part of the Orleans levee board. But it was the army corps that had overseen flood wall construction and the installation of the sheet piling, and, come to think of it, it was the army corps that regularly bestowed citations for excellent maintenance on the levee board. The corps had also approved plans by the Sewerage and Water Board to dredge the Seventeenth Street Canal, a move that came under suspicion after the flood. The dredging was meant to speed the flow of water as pumps pushed it toward the lake. But it also deepened the canals and ate into the levees in ways that probably contributed to the seepage under the sheet pilings.

Van Heerden still hadn't found the smoking gun, but he had a hunch where it was hidden. The design memoranda in 1989 for construction of the London Avenue Canal flood walls had called for the inverted T shape and for twenty-three-foot sheet pilings. A year after the 1989 designs, when it came time to put flood walls on the Seventeenth Street Canal, someone had decided to cut a corner, van Heerden surmised. The inverted T had become a simple, less stable I shape, and the sheet pilings only needed to go to minus ten feet. And here was the crux of the matter: What was good enough for the Seventeenth Street Canal suddenly was deemed adequate for London Avenue, notwithstanding the engineering studies that dictated longer sheet piling and the more rugged inverted T-wall design. The 1989 memo was simply overridden and the cheesier construction practices approved retroactively. But why and by whom?

IT WAS A WINTRY DAY BY LOCAL STANDARDS, WITH TEMPERATURES SINKING toward 40 degrees, chilly enough to erase all thought—even here at the very site of the Seventeenth Street Canal breach—of tropic seas and wicked cyclones. For local reporters who owned such garments, the chill was an opportunity to dig back into closets for down vests or overcoats. Others, less well equipped, walked about briskly flapping their arms against thinner shirts and jackets, or prayerfully clutched paper cups of coffee with two hands, in order to warm them. No one moved more briskly than the numerous military personnel, in black boots and camo-patterned uniforms. Energized both by so many milling civilians and by the imminent arrival of the district's top dog, Gen. Robert Crear, they hopped up and down the levee, greeting one another and executing small errands. Others leaned over the plastic tape and gave interviews to media restricted from the levee's higher altitudes and the heavy equipment assembled there.

The print reporters and still photographers were a motley bunch, baggy-eyed, wan—unashamedly haggard in the harsh light of a day on which they had to get up early. By contrast, the TV people positively glowed. Some of them were already orange with makeup; several were got up in the uniform of their trade: careless, even ragged slacks and footwear below the spiffy bib and tucker that would be visible on camera. Where is Metairie? a newswoman asked a corpsman from behind her makeup mask. And, told that Metairie was the part of Jefferson Parish directly across the canal, she double-checked her bearings: So this is St. Bernard Parish?—a question that embarrassed her, St. Bernard Parish being many miles from the world-famous levee breach where she had been sent that morning to update her viewers on the disaster in New Orleans.

A soldier with the name Starkel on his shirt—Lt. Col. Murray Starkel, the corps' deputy district engineer—briefed her privately on the proceedings, all part of an effort to figure out what had failed and why. What he did not need to say, because everyone well knew it, was that this particular part of the probe, and the reason people such as she had been encouraged to be present for it, had been shaped by the infuriating Professor van Heerden and his claim that the sheet pilings were somehow shorter than they were supposed to be.

A day earlier, the corps had cut out four-foot-by-four-foot chunks of the concrete flood wall at both ends of the breach and hustled them off to a laboratory, Starkel explained. The lab techs would analyze the strength of the concrete and of the rebar—the reinforcing metal bars—underneath it. Today's mission, the occasion for all the hullabaloo, was to pull up the pilings, the long, flanged sheets of interlocking iron that were driven through the levee and deep into the ground—but how deep?—to reinforce the walls of the levee and keep the water in its proper channel. To that end, a one-hundred-foot boom crane had been mustered. It towered over Starkel and the unsmiling crew of civilian workers slouched against it, waiting to get on with the job. The whites among them came primarily in two varieties, this being the South: Willie Nelson clones, with ponytails hanging below their hard hats, and GI Joes—with tattooed arms, and heads cropped close or shaved. For the blacks in the crew, a job with Boh Brothers was too good a break to mess up with a fashion statement. Pillars of their communities, they were dressed and barbered conservatively: steel-toed boots and matching shirts and pants in khaki or dark blue.

Now Starkel stepped back up onto the levee, took hold of a microphone, and cleared his throat. Opening remarks ended with an exhortation to his troops and all others present to be conscious of safety: "Please try to leave in the same condition you arrived in," he said, eliciting chuckles and, from the smokers, coughs.

Indeed, the corps' concern for the safety of New Orleanians was thorough. Cellophane-wrapped safety glasses and earplugs were being pressed into the hands of reporters and camera crews as they arrived and registered at a table set up near a break in the fence that surrounded the breached levee. The safety gear was quickly pocketed and, in any case, entirely unnecessary.

The pile driver, suspended from the hundred-foot boom crane, did its magic by vibration, not hammer blows.

Now Starkel introduced General Crear, who used the occasion to tout recent achievements by the corps district he commanded from Vicksburg: the life-saving efforts in the early days after the storm; the installation to date of some sixty thousand blue tarpaulins—"FEMA roofs"—on storm-damaged houses in Louisiana as well as along the Mississippi coast; the removal of nine million cubic yards of debris (about 40 percent of the job). And the corps was fast at work on the levees, Crear announced, not just along the Seventeenth Street Canal, but at London Avenue and the Industrial Canal and along the coasts of St. Bernard and Plaquemines parishes, where miles of corps-built earthworks had simply washed away in the storm.

"We all want to know what caused the system to fail . . . but also what parts of the system did well," Crear added, by way of reminder that though the corps may have presided over the destruction of a major American city, it had also built some pretty terrific levees in its time.

A PR lady working with the corps leaned toward a reporter: "I made a bet they're gonna be twenty-three feet long." The reporter asked how much she bet. The answer: twenty dollars.

"What I do now is give the order to pull the pile," General Crear said, and then he said it: "Pull the pile."

It was 8:10 AM. Within minutes, first one and then another of the pilings at one end of the breach slid up out of the muck almost to its full length. For a few minutes, the pilings stood there wobbling in the air like reeds along a bayou. Their flexibility was surprising, suggesting to the uninitiated that in place belowground they were more like a foil lining than an unbudging rampart. After a pause, the pilings were pulled all the way up into the air and set down on timbers lying on the muddy levee. Tape measures were duly produced and run from one end of the pilings to the other. General Crear bent over the squatting engineers huddled around the tape, then rose, took the microphone, and announced the results: One piling measured 23 feet, 6 and ⅞ inches; the other 23 feet, 7 and ⁷⁄₁₆ inches.

Take that, Professor van Heerden.

ELEVEN

———— ⚜ ————

Help Yourself

I T'S SAFE TO SAY THAT EARL FARRELL—FOR PRESENT PURPOSES, HE WILL BE called Earl Farrell, because he is fifteen and about to commit a felony offense, and because Earl Farrell is not his real name—would have declined evacuation from New Orleans even if Angelina Jolie had rolled up in a black Chrysler 300D with tinted windows, pushed open the door, and said, "Get in." Big storms were a special time in the New Orleans that Farrell called home. A short, well-built kid with a big grin and close-cropped hair, he was not one to miss out on the fun. In due course, however, it would be Farrell himself at the wheel of a car, or more precisely a hot-wired Jeep, because good times had started to wear thin in a flooded city without electricity or tap water, and it was looking like time to join the hundreds of thousands who had already gotten out.

Technically, Farrell's neighborhood was a part of Uptown, but on the wrong side of St. Charles Avenue and not far enough from Canal Street to be the Uptown known to millionaires and carnival royalty. The corner butcher shop was better stocked with candy and cigarettes than with sirloin steak, but you could at least get chicken and catfish and lesser cuts of beef. Prompted both by need and by the sense of license that set in with a hurricane, Farrell made it his business to pay a call on the corner store. It took some doing. Fortunately, there was a tire iron in the car he had hot-wired—a different car; the Jeep came later—and driven over to his girlfriend's that Monday after the wind had died down and before the floodwaters had begun snaking through the streets in that part of town. Showing up in a hot car was mostly about showing off—a romantic gesture, but then the damn thing wouldn't start up again and they all fell out laughing, Farrell, Lakesha, and her friends Tania and Brenda.

Tire iron in hand, Farrell got himself up onto the roof of a building next to the store and then was able to hop onto the meat market roof, peel up some shingles, and then pry apart the planking they'd been tacked to. Soon enough he had a hole he could fit through. Lakesha tried it too, but her leg got caught, and she said that was it: "I ain't crawling down through no roof." Tania was game, though, and pretty soon they had a regular little bucket brigade going, with Farrell handing stuff to Tania, chops and chicken legs, mostly, and Tania handing it up through the hole in the roof to Brenda and Lakesha. When they had all they needed, they put the meat in a big ice chest and one of the men in the area set up a grill and barbecued for the whole neighborhood.

Of course it could be argued that Farrell and his accomplices were simply acting in emergency-response mode, that people needed to eat, that the food would have spoiled anyway, with the electricity out, and so on. But that is not an argument that much interested them, not when there were so many other stores to loot, food stores, clothing stores, the Rite Aid down on St. Charles Avenue, the Winn-Dixie on Claiborne, a Payless shoe store—"beaucoup stores," as Tania put it. And from the look on her face days later in Baton Rouge, and from the excitement in her voice, you could tell that their afternoon and evening of marauding had been just an amazing experience—a peak experience—for a bunch of kids without too much in the world.

Not that the looting was limited to kids. Grown men were doing it—men they knew and who knew them. They got to the Rite Aid too late to see it, but someone said the first wave of looters had used one of the security guard's guns to blow the locks. Rite Aid was an effing bonanza: hair gel, beauty products—and that stuff costs. The Pampers department was depleted in a trice. Lakesha rifled through the packets of snapshots waiting to be picked up and found some of her own ready to go. One of the neighborhood men brought the same precision to his looting of a pawn shop on Freret Street and did not leave until he found an item he had hocked some days earlier.

In other words, everyone was doing it. From what Tania had heard—or wanted to hear: "The police were saying, 'Go to it.' " It would come as no surprise to Tania or any of the rest of them to learn, as they later did, that police had not only condoned the looting but had participated lustily in it, notably at the Garden District Wal-Mart, where fellow looters and reporters watched in amazement as uniformed officers hauled off jewelry, electronics, DVDs, and other valuables.

There was just so much stuff to steal, a bounty of stuff, so much that it took garbage bags and garbage cans to get the stuff back to the house. One store had a smallish opening that you had to squeeze through. Farrell gashed his hand getting through there. But he got in. Tania had a little wagon she dragged along to carry the loot. "We knew it was wrong, but we did it anyway. All the neighbors were doing it," she said. Indeed the competition for the good stuff could be intense. She remembered a small clothing outlet—"this itty-bitty store"—and the way some of the women would "jump all over you to get a purse. They were pushing each other out the way to get their clothes."

There were exceptions. Lakesha's mother, Ramola Burnes, was against looting. While the others were out carrying on, she snatched up a grandchild and set off with a handful of folks to see if they couldn't find a way to get out of town, something she had put off doing ahead of the storm because the man in her life had been due to collect his pay on the first of the week. The group returned a while later, defeated by the rising water between them and the still unflooded parts of Uptown, that and the weird darkness of night in a city without electricity and only a little sliver of a moon. On Tuesday, the gas service went the way of electricity: no more stove, no hot water. And then no water at all, no matter how far you opened the tap and cursed or prayed. It was time to get out. But how?

Some of the young people went up on the roof and tried to wave down passing helicopters. No luck. And then all eyes turned to Farrell. "Everyone knew he could hot-wire cars," Lakesha said. Some of the men started jollying him into doing it for them. It did not take much of that to turn a fifteen-year-old's head, and Farrell agreed to jack enough cars for the whole neighborhood, including the elderly paralytic and his sister who lived across the street. They were a special concern of Lakesha's mother's. She helped load them into a passing skiff, and then pushed it along as the small throng followed Farrell.

The seas did not part for this fifteen-year-old Moses, but he was able to lead his people through thigh-deep water to a social services center a couple of blocks closer to St. Charles Avenue and another block or two toward Canal Street. The center's parking lot held great promise, a bunch of cars, beaucoup cars, up to their hubcaps in water, which was not too deep to drive if you went slowly so as not to swamp the motor. The flood by now had spread across four-fifths of the city, but this was close to its southern edge, St. Charles Avenue. From there to the river, perhaps another twenty blocks, the city was dry. But from St. Charles to the lake, a distance of several miles, the city was underwater. And in some places it was nearly twenty feet deep.

With the others looking on expectantly, Farrell tried to hot-wire one of the cars in the social services center parking lot: wouldn't start. The next car came alive, but then got hopelessly hung up on something below the surface of the water and stalled out as Farrell tried to power it off the snag. The men lifted the car bodily out of the way. Then someone came up with the bright idea of breaking into the social services center to look for keys. Farrell followed a rock through the window and came back out with a handful. One key worked, and the group was possessed of the first component of what would become a three-car caravan.

There are different strategies for hot-wiring cars, and Farrell knew several. To mobilize the Jeep that had caught his eye, he reached under the dash and tore away the plastic sheathing. He touched the red wire to a black one and beamed back at his ragtag entourage as the motor kicked in. The third, a sedan, had a metal plate under the steering wheel column to frustrate jackers such as him. Well-schooled by an older brother, Farrell was undaunted. He pulled out a flat-head screwdriver and grip pliers, slid the screwdriver into the ignition, and used the pliers to turn the cylinder until it broke and could be pulled out. He then stuck the screwdriver back into the ignition shaft and fired the motor.

THE COMMANDEERING OF AUTOMOBILES WAS COMMONPLACE IN THE DISINTE-gration of the social order that followed Katrina across the city. After reaching Canal Street from the flooded Ninth Ward where she was raped, Charmaine Neville and some confederates had hot-wired a school bus first commandeered and then abandoned by another group of refugees. The singer barreled upriver to Donaldsonville, where her group was taken in by a church that had turned itself into a shelter.

FROM A DIFFERENT PART OF THE SOCIOECONOMIC SPECTRUM OCCUPIED BY Farrell and the girl he sought to impress, a Massachusetts lawyer named Peter Berkowitz, his wife, Brunilda Groennou, and son, Ernesto, also found themselves caught up in looting before managing a belated escape from disaster. Berkowitz and Groennou had brought Ernesto to enroll at Loyola, only to be turned around by the university and warned to flee New Orleans the very weekend they arrived. Through a combination of bad luck and canceled flights, they wound up riding out the storm in a French Quarter hotel, and then, evicted from the hotel amid warnings that the city was about to be covered in floodwaters, they walked to the convention center, a dozen blocks away, with a group of about fifteen dislodged hotel guests, American tourists, mostly, with a few British and Australians thrown in. The convention center was not yet the mass refugee center it was about to become. Indeed, Berkowitz's group was alone there and wondering how best to escape the predicted deluge, when they spotted an exterior staircase that rose from a parking lot at the easternmost end of the blocks-long exhibition hall. It led up to an exterior walkway perhaps thirty feet in the air that ran across the back side of the Riverwalk, a shopping arcade oriented toward the tourist market.

The walkway would be their home for the better part of a week, their shelter from floodwaters that never reached that part of the city and, in due

course, a respite from the agitated and ailing throngs that shortly overwhelmed the convention center and the streets surrounding it. They had only
just reached the walkway when Berkowitz and his party noticed a man with
a rifle and a duffel bag climbing the exterior staircase and trying the glass
door to the mall's rear entrance. Finding it locked, "he simply smashes out
the door with the butt of his rifle and walks in," Berkowitz wrote to his
mother in a letter that eventually was posted on the Internet and constituted
one of the more nuanced accounts of the ethical issues that cropped up in
Katrina's aftermath. "Maybe half an hour later, he marches past us and is
gone. His duffel seems a bit fuller." Berkowitz and his group exchanged
glances, then they also slipped inside to look for provisions. "Some time
passed and then the person with the rifle returns again," he wrote. "This time
we notice he is a cop and he is with four other cops and they all have
[fire]arms and duffel bags. And their only purpose is to get whatever they
can. And that really opened the mall for us. We gathered food, drinks, and
explored the stores. Some other tourists appeared and joined us. We took
chairs and tables out of the mall. The police had 'opened up' Foot Locker
and other stores, so there were shoes and clothes available for the taking. I
wandered through looking for bedding and ways to set up camp. I took the
covers off some kiosks to use as a bed. Bruni," he wrote, referring to his
wife, "found some semi-cushioned furniture, and we took cushions. One day
we found pillows in a store."

By the next day, Wednesday, the throngs fleeing the floods, or rescued
from them, had begun to mass at the convention center, and a steady stream
of people was flowing up the staircase and into the mall in search of what
they needed. Berkowitz and others in his group helped distribute looted provisions among them, and when the military helicopters began buzzing the
place and dumping pallets of army rations and bottled water onto the street,
they helped distribute that too, the packages and bottles that didn't explode
on impact after being pitched off aircraft held nervously high above the
crowd. And then things started to get truly sour.

"It was maybe . . . Thursday that some people on the street are yelling
about dead bodies and toss a body wrapped in a sheet on the side of the Convention Center just below us. A little later, a wheelchair with a dead woman
appears there as well," Berkowitz wrote. "Everything is rumor. People are

saying that the dead woman in the wheelchair was bludgeoned to death in the Convention Center. At the same time, hordes of people are coming up the steps past us and into the mall. They are breaking into all the stores, smashing cash registers, etc. There is desperation all around. And anger. And violence."

Racial tensions had begun to roil the community that had set up house-keeping on the walkway, a group now grown to maybe eighty, some of them black. Scornful references were made to "the people down here," noted Berkowitz, who had worked as a civil rights lawyer in Puerto Rico before moving to Massachusetts. One white woman on the walkway began jabber-ing that the blacks were just biding their time before surging up onto the walkway to slaughter the whites. The hysteria was reaching its peak, Berkowitz wrote, when "a black man stands up and says: 'Why do you think these people want to kill you? They are surviving just the same as you. Sur-viving just the same. Just as desperate as you. They don't care anything about you.' . . . That calmed people down and made them feel particularly foolish."

It was Saturday, after five days of this, before Berkowitz and his family were able to get onto one of the buses evacuating the convention center, and it was east Texas before they were able to convince the Guardsmen to let them off. A volunteer family took them in and offered them showers and a place to sleep. "They were kind, concerned, and really wanted to help and do the right thing," Berkowitz wrote. "As we talked it was also clear that they were religious conservatives, racist, homophobic, etc. East Texas. Kindness and hatefulness on the same plate."

The next day, Berkowitz and his wife and son managed to hitch rides back across the Louisiana border, to Shreveport, and catch a flight to Boston. Berkowitz's account, and the placidly candid way in which he told it, ad-justed the impression fostered by television footage and commentary: that the looting was the work of wild gangs, mostly of black men, who had whipped themselves into a murderous frenzy as they tore through the streets, hurling bricks through plate-glass windows and grabbing everything in sight. "Crazy black people with automatic weapons are out hunting white people and there's no bag limit!" author and New Orleans native Michael

Lewis wrote, satirizing the racial paranoia in a sometimes hilarious account of a visit home in the storm's early aftermath.

EARL FARRELL AND HIS UPTOWN ENTOURAGE HAD MADE IT TO BATON ROUGE, not without incident. They had been only a few blocks from the social services center parking lot—Farrell in the Jeep; a neighbor, Mr. Richie, in the van; and Lakesha's brother-in-law in the sedan—when they were stopped at a National Guard checkpoint, a moment of considerable tension. But if the checkpoint soldier noticed the wiring hanging from below the dashboard of the Jeep, he chose to make no mention of it. Nor did it seem to concern him that a fifteen-year-old was at the wheel. The Guardsman waved them through the checkpoint and they quietly began to breathe again. Three hours and one breakdown later—that car was abandoned—Farrell and friends could see the spire of the state capitol rising above the river. Their first stop was a shelter Lakesha's mother had heard about. No room. But she had another number in her purse, that of a man who had figured for a time in her late mother's life, her stepfather, as she thought of him, the Reverend Bishop Frank Washington.

A tall man with long gray hair combed Al Sharpton–style behind his ears, the bishop had packed a lot of living into his seventy years, and his achievements were impressive, not the least of them the sobriety he had regained since leaving New Orleans after many years of what he considered wantonness and sin. Another achievement was his ascension to the rank of bishop and first vice president of the Louisiana Free Will Baptist Association. The bishop's church was a white wooden shotgun in a run-down part of town. He had put a steeple on the roof and gutted the interior to make room for pews to seat his flock of about seventy-five. There were three more pews and an old sofa under the carport. A ranch house behind the church served as his fellowship hall, and across the street from it was the bishop's residence, a brick ranch painted lime green. Out front was a brown van with BANKS COMMUNITY OUTREACH BAPTIST CHURCH written on it. The compound made for a sacred place, only more so by contrast with the crack house next door, the bane of a bishop's existence. As the reverend held forth, cars pulled up to the house next door, and young men stuck their heads in the windows, and then the cars left again. Other young men could be seen lounging by the door.

The Reverend Bishop Frank Washington had gotten into the shelter business inadvertently. A group of thirty or forty evacuees had simply shown up on the Monday that Katrina was playing havoc with New Orleans, and they had asked to stay the night. Washington saw fit to secure the permission of his congregation, and it was a good thing he did so, because a month later the refugees were still on hand and the Red Cross was showing up twice a day with meals. They also sent over medical people from time to time look in on the refugees.

The role of churches is to give, the bishop said, chiding fancier churches as too interested in the material realm. But, to be blunt about it, he was not all that impressed with the homeless New Orleanians lounging around his grounds and crashing under his roof, sometimes in pairings not sanctioned by the church or the laws of marriage. Most, he said, were inner-city kids from the housing projects, and they needed help. Ramola Burnes was a good woman, he had decided. But the kids with her? Washington spoke as a diagnostician of ailing souls. He called their affliction the "project mentality." "You go through life with that attitude," he said with prophetic resignation, but not without compassion. Sidelined mothers, missing fathers, and never quite enough cash in the household till, "these kids will go out there and get what they need," he said. "No one's there to purchase it for them. You get what you can where you can from who you can." And unfortunately, where a lot of the kids were getting it while staying with Washington was from the house down the street that sold crack and marijuana. He had seen them in there, and he let them know he wouldn't care to see them in there again.

When Washington alluded to the seamier side of life, he knew whereof he spoke. He had been a police officer in the sixties in suburban New Orleans, and a boozer and a gambler and a womanizer nonetheless. "I was a drunk, and I followed people who drank," he said bluntly. "I had a religion, it was the religion of the streets: alcohol, women, gambling. That was my religion and I did it religiously. There's nothing that the young people do that I didn't do, short of robbing banks and killing people."

In 1970, at forty-five, he moved to Baton Rouge and kept up his wicked

ways for another seventeen years. A heart attack while hunting rabbits triggered an out-of-body experience that brought Washington to God and, in
due course, to his third wife. The church was an avocation verging on a full-
time job. "I don't take a nickel from the church," he said. He had started
Banks Community Outreach Baptist in 1994 with six parishioners, and now
the church covered its own bills. The bishop paid his bills through employment with the Winnfield Funeral Home, bagging bodies that had recently
given up the ghost, and bringing them back to the parlor. Harboring the
evacuees was a Christian duty, he said.

But not a permanent one. Within a month, the church would revert to its
usual purposes. Washington's parishioners had decided they wanted the
place back, and the Red Cross had weighed in with a timely option: the
larger, more formal shelter FEMA set up in Baton Rouge, on the campus of
Southern University. The truth was a little more complicated than the simple
coincidence of travel trailers and a congregation's yearning to recover its accustomed haunts. Someone had leaned too hard on a church sink and it had
broken off the wall. A mirror got smashed. The biggest problem was the
crack house and the kids who wanted to hang out there. Washington had imposed an eleven PM curfew and declared the house off-limits. "Anyone going
over there was going only for one thing."

His stepdaughter's gripe was that the reverend put them out with no notice. Just: "Pack up your bags, it's time to go." Farrell and Lakesha and Tania
decided they were well rid of him, but it would have been better if they still
had the van Mr. Richie had driven from New Orleans. Washington had
blessed the continued possession of it. He had deemed it a "survival van,"
not a stolen van. But now it was gone. Someone had been driving it in Baton
Rouge when they met up with a cop, and fearing the law might take a different view of their claim on the vehicle, they had bolted from the van and dis-
appeared.

STOLEN CARS WERE ONLY ONE MEANS OF ESCAPE FROM THE CITY AFTER KA-
trina. One man walked to Baton Rouge: seventy miles. Put aboard planes,
others stepped out onto the tarmac hours later in Omaha, Salt Lake, Min-
neapolis, Norfolk, Chicago. An elderly gentleman named Mr. Lee, propri-

etor of a Chinese laundry in the French Quarter, was told to step out onto the river levee behind Café Du Monde and wave something blue. Spotted by the pilot, Mr. Lee and his wife were whisked off to Baton Rouge in a corporate helicopter arranged by a fast-rising son in the oil business. Henry Sherrod's evacuation was a bit less graceful. The day after Katrina, five days before his month-long sentence for failure to provide child support was set to expire, he was rousted from his second-floor cell in Orleans Parish Prison by guards wielding shotguns and wearing body armor. The city was going under, inmates were warned. Mute warning of another kind was embodied in the dazed inmates—one bleeding from the scalp, another from a gash in his shoulder—who stood on exhibit as Sherrod and others were herded through the prison's reception tier and into boats. The bleeders had exploited the chaos of the moment by trying to escape, guards intimated. Fourteen inmates would do a better job of it, hopping over walls and swimming to freedom from a prison that verged briefly on anarchy. A rumor that inmates had made a hostage of their warden, newly installed Sheriff Marlin Gusman, would gain wide currency in the several days before it was dispelled.

Sherrod's boat ride was a brief one. He and some five hundred inmates were ferried to a nearby overpass above a six-lane expressway that swept past the torn and battered Superdome, visible a half mile in the distance. Six hours later, mutinous for lack of food or water and arguing at gunpoint with guards who would not let them stand to stretch, the inmates were on buses to distant prisons, Hunt Correctional, in Sherrod's case. Three weeks would pass before he attracted the attention of overwhelmed prison officials and convinced them that he had paid his debt to society and should be released. Sherrod was lucky. A half year later, many other inmates—including scores who had not been convicted of the crimes they were set to be tried for when detained—would still be lost in the prison sector of a criminal justice system that, for all practical purposes, had collapsed.

AFTER FLEEING NEW ORLEANS BEFORE DAWN SUNDAY IN THEIR THREE-CAR caravan, Saundra Reed and her extended family had designs on Baton Rouge, but first that meant getting out of Poplarville and the borrowed cottage, now entirely enmeshed in fallen trees, where they had taken refuge. As she drifted off to sleep that Sunday night, after feasting on fish her nephew Whitman's boys had angled out of the pond, Reed had been plagued less by thoughts of the coming hurricane than with the need to get her older daughter, Andria, to a dialysis center. She was due the next day for the first of her three sessions a week, but that could be postponed until Tuesday, if the storm proved problematic.

The whistling wind had drawn the family from their beds into a huddle around the battery-powered television set after midnight. Sheets of rain gave the big sliding glass doors the look of an aquarium wall. And then suddenly, as Reed stared through the glass, the abstract swirl of wet and wind and the winking reflection of the candlelight in the room behind her coalesced into the shape of a colossal oak, split in two with a cracking sound louder than thunder. Then the giant pines began to snap like popcorn kernels in hot oil, toppling here and there but, miraculously, not on any of the cars. The pine stand already decimated by what later was determined to be a tornado, the southwest wall began to shudder and audibly groan, threatening to spill books and bric-a-brac and a collection of stringed musical instruments from the built-in cedar shelving. The boys threw themselves against the wall until the others could maneuver a massive cypress dining table and two fifteen-foot benches into position as buttresses.

Near dawn, as suddenly as the storm had struck, it gave way to an eerie calm, and the family sensed Katrina's eye was passing. A quick hike about the property revealed that they were trapped. Fallen trees were everywhere, including giants, ten or twelve feet in girth, that now lay across the driveway, and Andria, for lack of dialysis, was beginning to bloat. It was Whitman who discovered a spot at the far end of the property where nothing but brush and a wire fence lay between the four-wheel drive Honda and a dirt road that did not seem hopelessly clogged with broken trees. Wire cutters—and silent apologies for the vandalism—dispatched the fence, and they were off, on a search for a dialysis center. The roads to the nearest one, twenty miles to the south in Picayune, were completely shut down. And so they drove toward Hattiesburg, thirty-five miles to the north—no power. Another four hospitals later, they reached Jackson, and Andria received her treatment, three hours of it, anyway; the needs of other patients were too great for her to get the usual four.

By dusk, they were back in Poplarville, which greeted them with a bit of a surprise: The driveway had been cleared all the way to the house by a neighborly farmer, a white man named Sambo Gentry, who had not only bulldozed and chainsawed clear passage to the house, he had refused their offer to pay for his help. The family was astonished. This was Mississippi, after all. Indeed, it was Poplarville, the setting, in the 1960s, for the last of the state's full-dress lynchings. Two days earlier, as Katrina bore down and her family fled toward the very heart of the state that had been most violently reluctant to leave segregation behind, Reed had taken note of an anniversary that chilled her: the murder of Emmett Till, the young man from Chicago who on August 28, 1954, was murdered in Money, Mississippi, for whistling—if indeed he did—at a white woman.

Gentry bolstered Reed's faith in humankind's basic decency. That faith would shortly be tested again. It was nearly midnight. They had digested their dinners and the news—more alarming by the hour—that New Orleans was filling with water. The older women had settled down to sleep when someone still restless enough to keep a vigil spotted the beam of a flashlight dancing through the woods leading up to the house. Wordlessly, the two oldest men slipped out a side door, Whitman with a rifle, Alex with a bow and arrows he had found in the house. Let others confront the white stranger. The two men with weapons would sneak around to his flank, just in case he needed to be stomped.

The situation resolved itself without incident. The stranger, come to check out storm damage at his own place, was disabused of his readiest assumption—that squatters from New Orleans had invaded an empty cottage and made it their temporary home. The names of Reed's absent hosts were invoked, mutual acquaintance established, and a huge divide was bridged. Alex and Whitman set down their weapons, and Reed headed back to bed, more mindful than she might have been of how easily a minor misunderstanding could have spun out into tragedy. She could envision the white man dead on the ground—more fodder for the ravenous press: Poplarville homeowner slain by black refugees from New Orleans. And, of course, if he had been armed, the blood soaking into the pine straw might have been from one of her own. Wednesday morning, they packed the cars and, nursing half-empty tanks in a world without gas, caravanned to Baton Rouge, where friends had agreed to take them in.

WITHIN THE WEEK, THE STATE CAPITAL WAS OVERWHELMED BY THE REFUGEE IN-flux. Street traffic slowed to a crawl, and real estate prices shot skyward as the Poydras Street professional class bet that the sleepy state capital and university town was poised to displace a shattered New Orleans as the business and financial hub of southeast Louisiana. New Orleans law firms and brokerages snapped up empty office space, and soon it was impossible to walk into Baton Rouge's glistening new Whole Foods Market without seeing familiar faces from the realms of New Orleans's civic and commercial life. Reunions were hearty and often tearful as old acquaintances hugged beside the cheese case—and then fell away from each other laughing at the stereotype they fulfilled: Where else but at a monument to gourmandise like Whole Foods would New Orleanians run into each other?

FOR MANY EVACUEES THE SOCIALIZING WAS LESS VOLUNTARY AND ONLY MORE intense. Shelters sprang up in scores of churches where the only partition separating one refugee's bedroom from the next was the back of the pew they were sleeping on. Larger shelters, such as the one in Southern University's sports arena, started out as barrackslike dormitories, with cots in grids so uniformly trim that you needed to count rows and tiers to find your own. But this soon gave way to more idiosyncratic arrangements. Families and friends began to cluster their beds, adults on the outside, kids in the middle. As FEMA tapped into the mighty resources of the U.S. Treasury and funds began to reach the evacuees, the money was made manifest in the further customizing of barracks bedding with throws and stuffed animals, bolsters and duvets. Intact families were the lucky ones. For a horrified minority, the trauma of evacuation had been made infinitely worse by losing a child along the way. Some five thousand children were reported missing in the storm's aftermath. Most would turn up in the custody of friends or relatives, but sometimes the connection would not be made for weeks. The most difficult to reunite were the forty-five young children found roaming the shelters un-accompanied by any adult whatsoever.

The federal largesse took various forms. After a botched effort to dis-tribute debit cards to evacuees, FEMA began simply cutting checks to any-one who had been uprooted by the storm. An initial $2,000 would turn up in the mail within a few days of registering online or placing a call—the on-hold time fell to less than half an hour if the call was placed after two AM. And then, in another burst of welcome if indiscriminate compassion, FEMA weighed in with a second check for $2,300. Unsolicited, it anticipated rental costs that might have followed the initial displacement—or might not, since many an evacuee was able to double up with friends or relations. Other kinds of aid were promised, depending on need. Some were actually delivered, though the most basic demand of all—for the temporary travel trailers that could be set up in the driveway of a flooded home or at least in some prox-imity to it, would be largely unmet.

If shelters were an introduction to the lower depths for people who had been accustomed to more in life, the evacuation was for others an exposure to the ways of the rich. Courtesy of a connection arranged by a school trustee, a young teacher and his family of four found themselves ensconced in one of the wealthiest households in Baton Rouge, a place from which the menfolk strapped on sidearms one morning and headed down to New Or-leans as though heading off on safari. They had somehow arranged passes that got them around the state police. Neil Nicholson, a pregnant teenager, otherwise destined for New Orleans's ample ranks of high school dropouts, was taken in by the family of an obstetrician in Decatur, Georgia, and after the delivery was soon back in a local high school while a nanny looked after her baby boy, Cody. Nicholson had been invited to stay on in Decatur at least through the end of the school year in June.

Inevitably, some evacuees began to wear out their welcome. Two broth-ers from the Uptown area arrived in Crested Butte, Colorado, of all places, to a reception committee, free use of a condo, and the opportunity to mow lawns at the munificent rate of close to twenty dollars an hour. But though the town's generosity remained unstinting, it was not long before muttering could be heard about the brothers' tendency to drive right down the middle of the town's main drag, windows open, hip-hop blaring. It was not that

Crested Butte had never seen young black men, it was just that it usually happened on TV. The brothers got comfortable enough to stay an extra month, but in due course were convinced to head back to New Orleans—in a used car the town generously provided as an inducement to hit the road.

Some refugees were never going to go back, and no one could be more surprised by their delight in new surroundings than the refugees themselves. New Orleans had been not only home but for many the only place they had ever been. Demographers spoke of the nativity rate, the proportion of residents who remained where they were born, and at 77 percent, Louisiana's rate was the second highest in the fifty states, after Pennsylvania. Nativity could be called a measure of the state's appeal, but it also reflected Louisiana's provincialism. Before Katrina made them nomads, many Louisianans had viewed the outside world with suspicion, if not dread. But in Houston, for example, as in Omaha and Seattle, these same New Orleanians were encountering vigorous economies for the first time, and the opportunity to land decent work—something that had been in short supply back home. Moreover, those with kids were struck immediately and forcefully by how much better the schools tended to be outside of New Orleans.

There were the inevitable tensions that came with being outsiders in a strange place. On the other hand, a certain cachet attached to refugee status, at least in smaller towns and especially among the young, and that was an offsetting emolument. Not all that the New Orleanians brought with them was well received, of course. By year's end, Houston officials were complaining that evacuees figured either as victims or suspects in a spate of twenty-three murders, or 20 percent of the city's total since Katrina.

The Baton Rouge area sustained the largest influx of evacuees who remained in the state. But twice as many people fled to Texas, 137,000 compared to the 60,000 displaced within Louisiana's borders. And another hundred thousand New Orleanians were scattered more widely, a diaspora that some pundits suggested would continue the dispersal of Southern regional culture and folkways that had begun with the great midcentury trek north from The Delta to Chicago and Detroit and New York. In an age of mass media, New Orleans's musical message was already out there. But there was no underrating the deepening impact of club acts, even second- and third-tier club acts, suddenly available on a continuing if not permanent basis in places like Omaha and St. Louis and Seattle. People in these places would have known to turn out for a Dr. John date or a concert by the Neville Brothers, but they might have had a hard time understanding how New Orleanians on both sides of the color line could have elevated a funky update of the old-time brass band sound to the top of hip's heap.

KATY RECKDAHL, LITTLE HECTOR, AND THE BABY'S DADDY, MERV CAMPBELL, the Treme Brass Band trumpeter, had fetched up in Arizona. Touro Hospital had not flooded, but with so much of the city underwater, Hector and his parents were still stuck there two days after Katrina. The power had gone out within hours of the storm. The water service failed Wednesday, and Reckdahl woke up in a panic-stricken maternity ward to rumors among the new mothers that their babies had been airlifted out of the city overnight. A stampede to the nursery proved the rumor false, but at eleven AM, a different sense of urgency set in with the announcement that all patients healthy enough to leave the hospital had about five minutes to do so. Reckdahl knew all about the Superdome, so a doctor's offer to take her and the baby over there occasioned nothing like gratitude or a sense of relief. Campbell, who had been on a walk through the hospital when the announcement to clear out was made, found Reckdahl sobbing in the corridor. She had a sister in Tempe; if only they could get to Arizona, a place that beckoned with special allure just then, sisters aside, for being as dry and dusty as New Orleans was wet and rotting.

A kindly nurse drove the family to the Baton Rouge airport, and by six PM they were boarding a plane to Phoenix, by way of Atlanta—a three-day-old baby in one hand, a satchel of maternity ward freebies and a garbage bag of clothes in the others. "We looked like we had just gotten out of jail," Reckdahl recalled. In Atlanta, Delta generously upgraded them to first class for the leg of the trip to Arizona, and so the family just recently incarcerated in a flooded city gratefully hauled their blue plastic bags to the front of the plane, more mindful than ever that it had been a while since any of the three of them had seen soap and water.

Freebie Pampers were one thing, but Campbell didn't even have his trumpet. That problem was rectified by a rich fan after local media in Arizona picked up on the story of the "storm baby" and his horn-blower dad. When Valley Presbyterian decided to "adopt" the refugees and chipped in with the down payment on a car and six months' rent in a furnished apartment, Campbell tracked down other members of the Treme Brass Band. He found his tuba player, Jeffrey Hills, a musician also known to audiences at Preservation Hall, in Mount Olive, Mississippi. Hills, his wife, and their three kids had waded from the flooded Lafitte housing project to the convention center before escaping the city. Valley Presbyterian sent money for bus tickets and upon their arrival, a few days later, gave the Hills a down payment on a car and six months' rent in a Scottsdale apartment. In short order, eight members of the Treme Brass Band were reunited in Arizona, the late arrivals financed by the Jazz in AZ foundation, with free rent through the end of the year. Soon they were the latest addition to the Phoenix club scene—a source of anxiety to fans back in New Orleans, who feared the Treme Brass Band and so many others like it might never come home.

Music was only one New Orleans export. Others—the celebrated style of cooking, the crafting of carnival masks, the speech rhythms and idioms, and all the rest—were commodities that required the hand delivery now offered by evacuees stepping off planes and buses, sometimes in places they had never heard of. In the case of Utah, the refugees were arriving in a place dominated by a religion that until recently had actively—and successfully—discouraged black settlement. African Americans were such a rarity, though now far more graciously received, that the newcomers reported to friends back home that they drew stares on the street. To allay tensions during the flights to strange places, FEMA sometimes chose not to reveal where the planes were landing until they had arrived, a strategy that was found to have only worsened stress levels among the passengers.

Texas, of course, was a place everyone had heard of. For a time, Houston's Astrodome was a replica of the Superdome, albeit a more orderly, sanitary, and better-nourished version, with a population that rose above twenty thousand. The early arrivals got there on their own steam, followed by a lull and then the onslaught of those evacuated belatedly by FEMA from the Dome and the convention center. One young man provoked a spasm of media attention by arriving at the wheel of a jam-packed school bus he had busted out of a locked yard in the Algiers section of New Orleans. Media, though clearly infatuated, framed the saga as an ethical conundrum: Was he a hero or a thief? Hollywood saw profit either way and handed the young man a movie deal. Months passed and media had mostly forgotten about the incident when New Orleans police came to their own conclusion and busted him back in Algiers on a crack-dealing charge unrelated to the drama of the hijacked bus.

Houston was the heart of the diaspora and bore its brunt, but then Houston had been nourishing itself on other disaster-struck cities at least since the ghastly Hurricane of 1900 destroyed Galveston. After that cataclysm—its six-thousand-plus death toll has never been exceeded by a U.S. hurricane— Houston promptly dredged its ship channel deep enough to handle oceangoing vessels from the Gulf, and in short order, Galveston's more vulnerable port was a shriveled relic of its former glory and Houston was on the way to regional dominance. But Houston gave as good as it got: a big, rich city able to absorb tens of thousands immediately and maybe even provide them with jobs and other inducements to make the stay permanent.

TWELVE

———— ⚜ ————

A Rockets Jersey and a Picture of Jesus

B Y THURSDAY NIGHT, BUSES FROM NEW ORLEANS WERE WRAPPED AROUND
Reliance Center, the complex that includes the Astrodome—scores of
buses, forty or fifty at a time, disgorging shell-shocked New Orleanians,
many of them in clothing they had worn for five days. Adding to the bustle
and mayhem was an influx of gawkers and do-gooders and just plain folks.
Texans had seen news reports of the influx and had yielded to the irrepress-
ible impulse to visit a spot where history and TV seemed to converge. A lot
of them brought along drinks and food—Texas chili, soda pop, chips—and
were dishing it up to the refugees out of coolers in the backs of their pick-
ups.

One among the thousands of evacuees peering into this thicket of late-
night activity from the window of an idling coach was an eighteen-year-old
named Alvin Crockett. After eight hours aboard a tour bus with no toilet,
Crockett was ready to bail out, drawn as much by the allure of this big new
city as repelled by the stench—there was no other word for it—of his clothing and that of fellow passengers. "I hadn't taken a shower in four days, and

neither had most of them." As far as family went, Crockett—a friendly, open-faced young man with a careful coif of pipe-cleaner-thin dreadlocks— had reached Houston alone. His father was dead (drug overdose) and his mother had been in and out of the hospital dealing with her own demons, he said. His two brothers and three sisters were all older and on their own—as Crockett had been, after dropping out of O. Perry Walker High, Mayor Nagin's alma mater, in his junior year. "Things overcame me," Crockett said of his decision to quit school. He had grown up in the Fischer public housing project. As a dropout, he lived for a time on the street, sleeping in cars, smoking pot—nothing too heavy. As Katrina bore down, he moved in with an uncle who, on Tuesday, was airlifted out of the city because of a heart condition. Crockett found a blue Rubbermaid storage bin in the apartment, just big enough to hold his earthly effects, and drifted down the block to a friend's place, a young woman with a couple of kids.

Two days later, after waiting three hours in the rain on an Interstate 10 on-ramp, they were loaded onto an evacuation bus headed for . . . who knew where? Who cared? Soaking wet, Crockett settled back into the warmth of the seat and was swept by a sense of relief that he doubted he would ever forget. Out of gratitude and just to while away the time, he pulled out a sketch pad and drew a picture of Jesus. But eight hours later, enough was enough. He had to get out of there. No matter that the driver was saying that anyone who stepped off the bus would not be permitted back aboard and might not be admitted to the Astrodome. What the hell. From the clamor in the street, Crockett had picked up that they weren't admitting any more people to the Astrodome anyway. The buses were reaching the front gates only to be waved on to some other shelter. Crockett pulled down the blue plastic storage bin and walked to the front of the bus. The driver reminded him that this was it, *sayonara,* and opened the door for him. Alvin Crockett stepped out onto the streets of Houston, homeless once again.

He wandered around awhile, savoring the hubbub, trying to convince himself he had options. Stephan, one of his brothers, was in Las Vegas. Maybe Stephan would take him in. But Las Vegas was a long way off and Crockett was hungry, tired, starting to lose heart. He set down his storage bin and was using it as a seat when one of the reporters working the scene for the local ABC-TV affiliate came up to him. Would he mind doing a little interview, just a few words to say who he was and what it was like to find himself in Houston after all he had been through. Crockett said okay, and all of a sudden he was bathed in light brighter than day, and the camera was rolling. He talked about this and that and held up the Jesus sketch he had done on the bus. The lights were still on, but the TV guy had wound down the interview and was looking for the next one, when a white man walked over to Crockett and said, "Are you Alvin?" Alvin said yes, whereupon this total stranger gave him a hug and said: "You're coming with me."

Clayton McKinnis, a thirty-five-year-old financial services rep for MetLife, had not set out in search of Alvin Crockett. He and his wife, Cindy, had been watching Channel 13 in their apartment directly across the street from the Reliance Center when the news came on, and the top story had been the buses and the tumult right there in the street below—the traffic jam Cindy had bucked on her way home from work as a Chico's branch manager. Frankly, McKinnis had been kind of nervous about having all these people from New Orleans in the street below and his wife not home from work. More than nervous, he was, as he recalled the moment, angry and fearful: "Angry because my wife was being delayed from coming home after working a ten-hour shift at her store, and fearful because, for all I knew, the reports of shootings, rape, looting, et cetera, that were being posted on all the airwaves were true, and those were the type of people who were being bused to Houston, directly across the street from our apartment."

But when she got home and they could settle back and watch the news, he began to relax. And when the Channel 13 crew stuck their camera in the face of an elderly woman and the grandson she was looking after, and the woman said they had nowhere to go, "It broke our hearts," Clayton would recall. The same impulse to do something—anything—the same impulse that had prompted good ol' boys with pickup trucks and tubs of chili to materialize along curbsides near the bus drop-off, sent Clayton out into the streets to look for that grandmother and the little boy and offer them a place to stay for the night—"to find us some company," as he put it.

There was more to this than sociability. Cindy and Clayton McKinnis were churchgoers: Second Baptist. Moreover, as members of a "care team" in service to the needy, they were adherents of a ministry that believed, as Clayton put it, "that everything we have been given belongs to God, and we are simply stewards of his blessings." With stewardship came a responsibility to see that blessings were used in a manner that brought glory to God. It was a matter, as Second Baptist's pastor, Ed Young, was accustomed to say, of "putting hands and feet to our faith."

"There's someone who can't be much of a threat," McKinnis would remember thinking to himself as Cindy drew his attention to the elderly woman and the seven-year-old boy. She fell to readying the extra bedroom, pulling out an air mattress, while McKinnis put his shoes back on. But in the time it took him to round up a friend in the building and reach the streets, the grandmother and her charge were spoken for. McKinnis had been within six feet of her when relatives emerged from the crowd and ABC viewers were treated to a tearful family reunion on camera. McKinnis and his friend milled around anyway, "watching history unfold before our eyes." When he called his wife by cell phone to tell her what had happened and that he'd be back in a few minutes, she mentioned this cute kid they were interviewing on TV. "He's holding a picture of Jesus that he drew, he's wearing a Houston Rockets jersey, and he's got dreads. . . . See if you can find him, Clayton."

It wasn't hard. McKinnis strode over to where the TV lights were still glowing, and there was the kid in the Rockets jersey. Under normal circumstances, Alvin Crockett might have thought twice about taking shelter with complete strangers in a city he had never seen before. And in a million years, Clayton and Cindy McKinnis might never have taken in a streetwise New Orleans teenager with dreadlocks and a funky stink to him. But these were not normal circumstances. The plan was to feed the boy, give him a hot shower, let him get some sleep, and send him on his way. But in the morning, as the McKinnises got ready for work, Crockett asked if they knew how he could go about volunteering at the Astrodome. That touched them, and the boy's stay was extended for another day. Three months later, enrolled again in high school—Lee High School—and an active member of Second Baptist Church, he was still living with them, though tensions, some predictable, some less so, had begun to mount.

"HOUSTON" BECAME SHORTHAND FOR THE EAST TEXAS PART OF THE NEW ORleans diaspora, but in fact Houston—even before the Astrodome was emptied out, after some three weeks as a shelter—got lots of help from across the region. Smaller Texas towns and cities also stepped up or, somewhat more reluctantly, found that New Orleanians had holed up in their motels and shelters and needed to be tended to. One such burg was Webster, about twenty miles south of the Astrodome. Webster had a population of two hundred at the turn of the twentieth century, and as late as 1958, when it was incorporated, it had a grand total of five businesses. And then, overnight, the space age arrived and Webster's prospects were suddenly sky-high.

In 1961, the sprawling gantries and hangars of NASA's space center began to poke up above the coastal plain, and in due course, the unrelievedly flat Harris County landscape, especially along Webster's main drag, NASA Road 1, was chockablock with the mundane exuberance of highway commercialism: the waffle houses, the Chinese buffet restaurants, the check-cashing and remittance services, fingernail parlors, Motels 6 and Super 8, ad infinitum, as far as the eye could see. And nestled in among the fast-food joints and winking neon and backlit plastic signage were Webster's collection of vast and anonymous apartment complexes: Clear Lake Springs, Baystone, Harbor Tree, and so on, home to some eight hundred service-sector families whose real homes were elsewhere—Mexico, as often as not, or El Salvador or, in Katrina's aftermath, New Orleans.

Webster was a natural for the New Orleanians, given the Red Cross shelters that sprang up there within a week or two of Katrina's landfall. But there were other draws, among them its itinerant and fluid population, the low-rent apartments that housed them, and a school system that, in addition to educating the children of the prosperous professional families drawn to the aeronautical industries, had developed a subspecialty in educating the children of the families who had fetched up in Webster to trim their lawns and hedges and vacuum their pools and detail their cars.

For the younger kids in Clear Lake Springs, a typical low-rent complex of 262 units on NASA Road, the walk to school passed through a gap in the fence at the rear of the development, then went down a short blacktop path to 300 Pennsylvania Avenue, site of McWhirter Elementary. Among other attractions, McWhirter was one of a few schools in the district that offered a bilingual program, mostly for Spanish-speaking kids, in kindergarten and first grade. McWhirter had gained added resources by becoming a laboratory school for teachers training at the University of Houston's Clear Lake campus, a maneuver that shrank the number of students per teacher from twenty-two to fifteen. And there were other benefits for at-risk kids, New Orleanians among them, except that saying "at risk" was a no-no at McWhirter. Instead they were called children "of promise"—a shade of difference, perhaps, but a clue that the Clear Creek Independent School System, to give the jurisdiction's full handle, was three hundred fifty miles from New Orleans in more ways than one.

McWhirter took its mission seriously and executed aggressively. Rather than waiting around to see who turned up for a school year that had already begun, Cindy Stamps, the coordinator of federal programs for the Clear Creek district and, as luck would have it, a former principal of McWhirter, had someone check in daily with the shelters to make sure every child of school age was on greased skids leading directly to a schoolhouse door. And when the kids and their rattled parents showed up, McWhirter didn't wrap them in red tape and junk them at curbside. No birth certificate? No problema—all that was required of parents was a photo ID. Stamps also agreed not to get hung up on missing immunization records. And with Lori Broughton, her successor as McWhirter's principal, Stamps set up a parents room with coffee, newspapers, and sofas to serve as a one-stop shop for tackling the newcomers' needs—a source of delight and astonishment after exposure to the sclerotic and hostile New Orleans public schools bureaucracy. Stamps also arranged for a mobile health van to visit the district each week, and got it based at McWhirter. "I take care of my own by taking care of everyone else," she said with a sly wink.

In the first weeks after the storm, about a thousand New Orleans kids flooded Clear Creek district schools, a number that fell by half over three months. By December about 10 percent of McWhirter's six-hundred-eighty-student enrollment were still Katrina evacuees, an influx that had required adding four classrooms. The shock for parents was how accommodating a school system could be. The shock for McWhirter was how far behind so many of the new pupils were. Fern Hanslik had never seen anything like it in all her years teaching second grade. Take little Maurice, for example, one of the kids from New Orleans. He didn't lack ability. Hanslik knew that from testing him. But as he entered second grade, essentially he was operating at the pre-K level. "When you showed him a puppy, he didn't know the concept of a baby dog. He did not know his alphabet. Most kids his age can sit about ten minutes," Hanslik had found. "He couldn't sit at all. It was like he had no concept of classroom behavior."

Even with the testing, Hanslik might have wondered if undiagnosed developmental problems would reveal themselves in Maurice's case. But no. Maurice was strong in math. Reading was the real problem. "He told me when he arrived that he couldn't read. I said okay, but if you leave here and you can't read, that's my fault, and I won't let it happen," Hanslik said. To that end, she began downloading books for Maurice and making a gift of them, each one signed: "To Maurice from Mrs. Hanslik." She also asked his parents to sit down with Maurice and read with him. Half an hour of it every night, no matter how tired his mother might be from hassling with her four kids or her job as a waitress at Ryan's, or his father from his work cleaning houses. "Do they do it? Yes they do," Hanslik said.

There were other marked departures for the New Orleans kids. Toilet paper in the restrooms, for one thing, and toilets that actually worked. School was no longer a daylong struggle to hold it in, for fear of visiting restrooms that were not only filthy but, at many New Orleans schools, hangouts for loiterers, toughs, and juvenile drug dealers. The corridors at McWhirter were actually quiet and orderly, not free-for-alls cruised by incorrigibles while teachers locked themselves in classrooms with more docile students, as was true in New Orleans, starting in middle school if not earlier. By Christmastime, Maurice was catching up with classmates in other subject areas besides math. At a rudimentary level, he was even reading. "When a kid learns to read, their eyes change from flat to sparkly. It's a miracle," said Hanslik, who noticed that a lot of the New Orleans kids wouldn't make eye contact with her when they first arrived. "It was like they did not see themselves as equals."

It did not surprise her to discover that Maurice's parents were themselves barely literate. Among many of the New Orleanians, illiteracy and the low incomes it all but guaranteed were a legacy passed on from generation to generation. McWhirter's first taste of it had been encounters with parents who could not fill out the simple forms to register their children, a problem that was addressed by assigning extra staff to assist them. Katina Henderson, an African American social worker at McWhirter, was so appalled for her people that she broke down crying at the thought of the illiterate parents and the failing children she had to help with their forms. "I just don't understand how this happened," she said, dabbing at her eyes. But actually she had a theory: In New Orleans, she discovered, kids weren't pushed to keep up with their age group, they were simply held back—"retained" in the jargon of the day—and parents settled for that, even seemed to take comfort in it. Henderson found that many of the parents were afraid of the school system, because of their own lack of education. "New Orleans cradled that," Henderson said.

The astonishing thing to Hanslik as well as Henderson was that little Maurice, the seven-year-old with the pre-K classroom skills, had been considered a good student back in the New Orleans public school system. McWhirter was prepared to bend over backward to educate the New Orleans kids, but it wasn't about to cradle them. When Nadora Dregory's five-year-old stopped turning up for school, McWhirter found out why. The little girl had fallen and broken a wrist. With the bone set, McWhirter could see no reason to prolong her absence. Her mother was reluctant, at first. Henderson kept after her, and soon enough the girl was back in class. A month or two later, Dregory would cite the school's persistence as a reason why she was so glad she had enrolled her daughter there.

"They say that if a student has just one decent teacher, you carry that with you," Hanslik mused over coffee in the faculty lounge one afternoon in early December. "One teacher can do it. I can't think of a nicer way to put it, but the teachers here, we wonder, 'What went on down there? What were they doing with those kids? What were you doing with your time?' It's an awful thing to say, but it's almost as if Katrina was a blessing."

DYNEL BIENEMY, ANOTHER NEWLY ARRIVED MCWHIRTER PARENT, COULD UNderstand that sentiment, but she could not bring herself to embrace it. Not fully. Not at first. Katrina had been a horror, through and through. It came back to her in bits and snatches and always would: the sense of relief she had felt—the words to the Johnny Nash classic, "I can see clearly now," swelling in her head—as the winds slackened after Katrina's initial strike. And then the wall of water that had swept over her home, well downriver in the St.

Bernard Parish hamlet of Violet. The horror of discovering that the ticklish feeling around her ankles was snakes, as she propped herself up on the roof after she and her fiancé and two of her sons cut their way out of the attic. The perch was made no easier by the elderly Down syndrome patient, the ward she was paid to care for, strapped to her back in a papoose she had made from a quilt to keep him from plunging off the roof. Later, after they were carried by boat to a ferry landing and then waited two days for evacuation, this forty-one-year-old nursing assistant had repaired a neighbor's disintegrating and infected colostomy port with duct tape and a garbage-can liner rinsed with water skimmed from a canal.

Dynel Bienemy, in short, was a woman of much perseverance and many talents, but they had been insufficient to the task of dealing with the schools' bureaucracy in southeast Louisiana. Lyndall, a learning-disabled ten-year-old, had been comprehensively assessed for the first time in his life at McWhirter. This was a boy who could neither walk nor talk when he was three, and yet, as he grew to a hulking ten-year-old, his mother had never been able to get the school system to address his problems. Instead he had been "retained," again and again. One look at Lyndall, who could easily pass for fifteen, had convinced McWhirter of the folly of placing him in the third grade. He was ten, he would be a fifth-grader and then be provided with a curriculum and tutoring tailored to his considerable needs.

About two-thirds of McWhirter kids were low-income, and most of them were Latino. Mostly African Americans, the New Orleans kids were immediately identifiable and somewhat exotic. Outside the classroom, a woman named Glenda Rice was the glue that held many of them together. She was the program coordinator for an outfit called Communities in Schools (CIS), a national nonprofit that had set up shop at nine schools within the Clear Creek district, McWhirter being one of them. (CIS had also been a presence in New Orleans.) In essence, Rice hooked up newly arrived low-income families with the services they needed. Someone had a toothache? Rice would scrounge for a dentist willing to pull the tooth for free. Blankets? She'd track down a donor. She leaned a lot on a women's group called ALBA that was good for a pair of quality tennis shoes and two or three outfits per needy child. At the sight of a likely prospect, Rice would whip out a tape and measure the child.

"I walk around the school and look," Rice said. "I'll casually ask a new kid, 'You got a coat?' " She got a school in a rich Clear Creek neighborhood to do a coat drive and came up with sixty. Book bags? Rice got Home Depot to kick in four hundred. She was also known for her signature "birthday boxes," soup-to-nuts party kits that contained candles, cake mix, party favors, and the like.

Rice was also good at thinking well outside the birthday box. One afternoon she was visited in her office by a New Orleanian named Yavana Johnson. Johnson had dropped off her kids at school, except for the baby in her arms. As much as anything she just needed to reminisce. She needed to talk about what it was like growing up in a city that seemed no longer to exist: the New Orleans of Mardi Gras parades and the Gumbo Man, who peddled his wares block by block from a vat in the back of a step van, and Mr. Bingle, the snowman whose annual apparition on the exterior wall of the big Maison Blanche department store on Canal Street (before the building became a hotel in the Ritz chain) signaled the onset of the Christmas season as surely as Advent calendars and Aaron Neville singing "O Holy Night" at St. Mark's Church. Johnson spoke of sweet potato pie and a snowball stand called Hanson's in her old neighborhood, just off Magazine Street, the long, pleasantly cluttered mix of residential and low-key commercial blocks that stretched the length of Uptown. Hanson's ice-shaving machine had looked even older than the old man who slurped the cones of shaved ice with flavored syrups in bright colors. The family recipes her grandmother had bequeathed Johnson had been lost in the storm and so had the pictures of her grandfather in his army uniform and the pictures of New Orleans in the 1950s—gone for good, the pictures and maybe the city itself.

"I was raised at Coliseum and Magazine," Johnson told Rice. "My grandmother made a quilt of all our old clothes. You'd look at the quilt and you'd say, 'That was the dress Grandmother made for me when I was four.' It told the story of our family. You knew why she chose each piece of material." Friends of Johnson had gone back for a look around and had told her New Orleans was like a ghost town. "The spirit of the city has died," she said.

Johnson's hair was tinted blue and piled high on her head. Her hoop earrings had blue beads worked into them to match her hair. She wore sneakers and pedal pushers—and so it came as no great surprise to Rice to learn that Johnson, a woman of fashion, had dreamed of becoming a beautician. Rice urged her to pursue her dream and found a beauty school not only prepared to admit Johnson but to offer her a $4,000 scholarship. Johnson held back. She would need day care. Rice hit the phone again and lined up day care. Johnson began to realize she might have a future in Webster, a town where it was hard to get Camellia brand dried beans and Zatarain's dirty rice, but a decent place, all things considered.

OF COURSE FERN HANSLIK HAD BEEN TOO SWEEPING IN HER CONDEMNATION OF New Orleans teachers, and she knew it. There were exceptions, even if they proved the rule, and one of them was right there at McWhirter. On the Saturday before Katrina made landfall, Stephanie Wyman threw her two little boys into the car, along with the family cat and three days' worth of clothes, and headed to a friend's house in Houston. Her husband had to stay put. Lt. Rob Wyman was the public affairs officer for the twenty-six-state eighth coast guard district, the one that included Louisiana. Within a few days, it seemed like every time his wife wanted a look at him, she only had to tune the TV to CNN and there he'd be. The really bad news he delivered personally by phone: Their house on Tonti Street, in the part of New Orleans called Mid-City, had flooded badly. She would need a lot more than three days' worth of clothes. She would need a job and an apartment. The Houston area meant more to Wyman than an old friend's home. A tall, good-looking woman with a heart-shaped face that made her look even younger than her twenty-something years, Wyman had taught in the Clear Creek system before Rob was posted to New Orleans. Now back in Texas, she went online to check out any openings, and a friend who was a principal in the system sent out an e-mail to other principals. McWhirter's Lori Broughton responded with an offer, and Wyman was hired as a fourth-grade math and science teacher.

In Wyman, McWhirter was getting one of New Orleans's best, a star teacher. After that first stint in the Clear Creek district, she had been recruited by the New Teacher Project, a nonprofit seeking to inject talented educators into the New Orleans school system. Her classroom work caught the attention of Tony Amato, the latest in a parade of nine superintendents and interim replacements who had attempted to guide the foundering system in the previous decade. Amato asked her to be co-principal of a boldly experimental school that he had been convinced to set up in underused parts of the Superdome, starting in the 2005–06 school year. The vision of a school piggybacked on a public facility like that was the brainchild of Steven Bingler, the New Orleans architect whose evacuation toward Texas from the French Quarter with his wife, Linda Usdin, and two daughters, had been interrupted by the fender bender and air bag deployment the day before Katrina.

Bingler had designed a number of similarly unusual schools, including one on the premises of the Henry Ford Museum in Greenfield, Michigan. Bill Gates was interested in funding the experimental Superdome school. Alas, it was not to be. After little more than a year on the job, Amato had been fired after failing to fend off the onrushing insolvency of a school system that effectively had been looted for decades by corrupt politicians, bureaucrats, and faculty. With Amato's ouster, any chance of immediately implementing the Dome School appeared doomed, except perhaps in Bingler's mind, and Wyman found herself out of a job.

She reported to work for her first day at McWhirter on September sixteenth. "The New Orleans kids were arriving as I was arriving," she said. Things went well, both for Wyman and for the five New Orleans kids in her class. "It was wild when they came; everyone welcomed them with open arms. What they didn't have, we provided for them. I can honestly say that no one had a problem adjusting."

It was a matter of no small consequence to New Orleans whether the likes of Stephanie Wyman would ever return to the city, whether her own adjustment to life in exile would prove all too satisfactory. With the cream of the city's academic, medical, and lawyerly elite easing into temporary arrangements at universities and hospitals and firms across the nation, there was a real and present danger that the brain drain would become permanent. At least as regards Wyman, it didn't look good. "I have never really processed this," she said in a reflective moment three months after her move back to Webster, "but prior to the storm, I had decided I didn't want to raise my kids in New Orleans. It is racially unbalanced and socioeconomically even more unbalanced. There are too many missed opportunities for too many children. Why do I have to have my kids go to a magnet school?" she said, referring to the small constellation of New Orleans public schools with selective admissions—among them, improbably, a top-flight arts-and-music program and one of the finest high schools in the nation.

"I would love to live in New Orleans," she added, glancing down at the number that had just appeared on her silenced cell phone. "The culture is fabulous. But for my kids, I'm not willing to." By coincidence, the call— Wyman could return it later on—was from Bingler, still avid to make the Dome School happen. And from his vantage on a blue-ribbon committee that New Orleans mayor Ray Nagin had set up to guide the city's recovery, Bingler was optimistic again that he might be able to bring it off. Indeed Bingler saw opportunity in disaster, the possibility, at least, that the school system's flood-ravaged physical plant might actually be a groundwork for radical innovation. After all, the demolition work preliminary to new con- struction had already been partially accomplished by Katrina. "He is trying to get me back to New Orleans," Wyman said. She said it casually, flattered to find herself courted by the school system where she had worked. But as she set the phone aside, a worried look had passed over her face.

THIRTEEN

Reversal of Fortune

IT WAS THE COMPARISONS WITH RUDY GIULIANI THAT REALLY GALLED RAY Nagin. The mayor of New Orleans had done his share of howling over the airwaves during that first hellish week in New Orleans. And, in the privacy of the place in Dallas he had rented as a refuge for his family—no, he had not treacherously bought it; *The Times-Picayune* had to correct an erroneous report to that effect—Nagin had howled some more at what he saw and heard played back at him on TV. When would they get off that Giuliani schtick! The New York mayor had revived a flagging reputation and achieved hero status in the aftermath of 9/11. But 9/11 had been totally different, in Nagin's view, a much more manageable disaster, however much worse the death toll. Emergency workers and Giuliani himself were able to retire to comfortable accommodations each night and then taxi to ground zero the next morning, refreshed. Katrina had devastated an entire city, including Nagin's own home, a spacious and modernistic place among other ample homes, torn by wind and water. From a small island in Bayou St.

John, they gazed back over well-manicured lawns and waterfront patios at the broad expanse of City Park's miles-long eastern flank.

Haggard, unshaven, unbathed until that blessed shower aboard Air Force One, Nagin presided over New Orleans from the windowless suite in the Hyatt Regency as the city fell to looters, floods, and fire. A week passed before he was able to get out of the city for the brief reunion with his family in Dallas. The nonstop TV news had been the first chance to assess the city's public image—and his own.

Reversals of fortune are rarely so diametric. Not a week before Katrina, Ray Nagin had had the Trump announcement to ballyhoo, and who could blame him. Say what you would about the developer's taste, New Orleans hadn't smelled a deal as big as that since casino gambling was legalized a decade earlier. And with a reelection campaign just months ahead, Nagin could point to the high-class condo tower Trump was promising to build as the capstone of a four-year effort to tackle corruption and make New Orleans a more attractive place to do business. Nagin's numbers looked good. No serious opposition had emerged. Six days later, the city was underwater, and Nagin was howling for help.

His salty tirade over the airwaves hadn't hurt. Wild exaggerations about epidemic rape and murder had been a mayoral embarrassment, however, and within weeks Nagin had discharged the man who had fed him too many of them, police superintendent Eddie Compass. (An uncharacteristic silence overtook the cashiered cop. It was broken twice: first by news that Mrs. Compass had been delivered of Marlon, the baby she was carrying when rushed by police cruiser to Baton Rouge immediately after the storm. Then came word that Compass had found work, as head of a guard service set up by local hoteliers.)

NAGIN HAD BEEN AN INTERESTING ADDITION TO NEW ORLEANS POLITICS WHEN first elected four years earlier, above all because he seemed to have no particular feel for it. He had run against corruption in a city that counted graft as one of its few growth industries. Without a political machine or even much street presence—a usually critical component of an Election Day triumph in New Orleans—Nagin had cultivated media and gotten his message out over the heads of the political power brokers. For the first several months of his administration, he governed that way as well, without bartering for support. He opened city hall doors to police raids and the purge of a municipal bureaucracy long suspected of quid pro quo shenanigans in the awarding of permits and licenses. And Nagin seemed to have no taste for the patronage games that had so clearly poisoned New Orleans as a place to do business.

The public perception was that he had brusquely cold-shouldered the crowd of political hangers-on accustomed to government handouts: no-work contracts, unneeded studies of this or that, and the set-asides whereby minority firms were attached to contracts principally executed by another firm, at added cost to the public. Marc Morial, the previous mayor, had indulged heavily in this kind of politics, portraying himself as a Robin Hood implementing a historic wealth transfer from the old white outfits to a new generation of minority-owned firms. Inevitably, the foes Nagin had pushed away from the trough grew resentful. Among them were prominent pastors fond of government grants for the social services operated by their churches. They started calling him an Uncle Tom, a white man in black skin, a tool of the white establishment, and so forth.

In the heat of the name-calling, one measure of Nagin's political naïveté was his failure to point out—perhaps even to realize—that in fact his administration had a better track record than Morial's. As the press discovered in exploring the issue, he had let more contracts to more minority firms than his predecessor—in part because Morial threw so much work to a select few cronies that there wasn't as much to go around. With that in mind, and mulling whatever promises they had won from the mayor in closed-door sessions to calm the waters, the pastors settled back into their limousines or lesser sedans and returned to their churches, leaving Nagin with what looked like a pretty clear path to reelection.

But a Trump deal would have been the clincher, a Big Apple vote of confidence in the Big Easy, a city not exactly brimming with faith in its own economic prowess. In New Orleans, Trump had seemed to see not so much a local market as a destination: an exotic local culture that the organization judged potentially attractive to the cosmopolitan rich, to men and women who wouldn't consider acquiring a second—or third or fourth or fifth—home in a city like, say, Atlanta, but who might be beguiled by New Orleans, with its international reputation for cultural sophistication, good times, and one of America's last, fully intact regional cultures. Globalization—the easy flow of capital around the world—had made New Orleans both a bargain and, for holding out against the cultural homogenization that was globalization's dark side, also a place with special appeal to the very people who were benefiting so handsomely from these same engines of global commerce. In any case, it would be nice to see construction cranes against the skyline, evidence that even New Orleans seemed to be catching at least the tailwinds of the real estate rocket that had boosted values—and morale—in cities otherwise unimpressed by the sluggish Bush economy.

But for the gauche and sprawling Harrah's casino built ten years earlier, a Trump condo complex would be the first major new construction in the downtown area since the flurry of office towers that shot skyward in the 1970s. As his car pulled into the city hall garage on the Sunday before the hurricane, Nagin could see those towers: Energy Plaza, the Amoco and Texaco buildings, the old LL&E tower, as folks still called it even now that Louisiana Land & Exploration had sold out, the Pan American building, and Shell—with fifty-one floors, the tallest of them all. God, those had been heady times—a frenzy of construction, a veritable Riyadh of construction. OPEC had goosed the price of oil all the way into the thirties, and you hardly needed to be a member of the Club of Rome to suppose that it was just going to go on up from there.

Instead, New Orleans had been treated to the oil crash of the mid-1980s, followed by the worst depression to hit a major American city since the 1930s. A decade later, with oil still in the tank, the city had begun a faltering economic revival predicated more than ever on tourism and the convention business. Legalized casinos (successors to the illegal ones that had flourished forever in Louisiana, and quite openly in the 1950s and '60s) were seen as a way to supercharge the city's appeal to visitors. Instead, politicians played games with the permitting process in exchange for whatever consideration they could exact from the casino companies—and even before Governor Edwin Edwards and his son were jailed for extortion, Mississippi's Gulf Coast casinos had stolen a march on the city and drained business that New Orleans had expected easily to attract.

But now here came Trump, his son anyway, and not Trump alone. Judah Hertz had taken a huge position, snapping up a preponderance of the city's class A office space and loudly announcing that he was in the market for more. Did they know something the natives didn't? Or was it only a matter of time before they glommed onto the truth about a crime- and poverty-ridden city famously inhospitable to business investment, and began to back out. If ever they needed an excuse to do so, Katrina provided it. After Katrina, what business would ever take New Orleans seriously? What Saudi satrap or New York investment banker with a big enough wad would ever again consider a city of looters and deserter cops that had torn itself to pieces on national TV?

"The national media did us a job," Nagin said, leaning back in his chair in New Orleans seven weeks after the storm, and reflecting on the disastrous PR he had witnessed on television in Dallas. He pondered the regrettable way his and Compass's overstatements had fed the supremely negative impressions beamed around the world. "Huge conventions that used to come here without blinking an eye aren't coming back," he conceded. It was October, a Thursday afternoon, and it found Nagin intermittently optimistic and daunted, angry and philosophical. Except on trips to Washington for appearances before Congress and visits with the president, of which there were several, he had more or less entirely abandoned the business attire he had worn for the past fifteen years. The new, more urgent Nagin, the Nagin of catastrophe and recovery, favored open collars and casual slacks, even jeans. They played well against his folksy charm and lanky good looks, topped by the shiniest shaved head in New Orleans public life, shinier even than Pete Fountain's, the city's most famous clarinetist.

IN THE DAYS OF DRIFT AND PETULANCE THAT FOLLOWED THE STORM, IT WAS EASY to forget that New Orleans's city charter vested fairly hefty powers in the mayor—far more power than a fractious city council ever seemed to muster. That is, unless it was a matter of zoning variances, and the customer who sought to overturn the planning commission had given generously to the incumbent council member's campaign. But as Nagin mused on the ruin of New Orleans and the city's prospects for recovery, he was, in effect, a mayor without much of a government to command. Days earlier, he had laid off most of the city's workforce, twenty-four hundred people, including virtually all office clerks and functionaries, the grease that kept bureaucracy moving. The layoffs were a horrible moment for Nagin but not a difficult decision. He was rapidly running out of money to meet payroll. And there was always the chance that drastic, even suicidal, gestures by local government would pluck at the heartstrings of federal officials, Bush among them, and that the money would be rushed to the scene of their greatest disgrace.

Two weeks after his Air Force One meeting with Nagin and Blanco, the president and his handlers had returned to the very heart of the French Quarter for what was clearly intended to be the definitive speech on Katrina, a chance to regain control of the storm's politically destructive momentum, perhaps even recapture the acclaim that had been his after the rousing 9/11 speech before Congress, the finest of Bush's career. "There is no way to imagine America without New Orleans," he declared that Thursday night against the backdrop of St. Louis Cathedral bathed in a dramatic bluish light, "and this great city will rise again." To that end, Bush had pledged billions and declared a war on poverty, reminiscent of LBJ at his most spendthrift. But then . . . nothing. The portion of the money that wasn't bottled up in Congress came with strings attached. Under provisions of the Stafford Act, which governed emergency response, Nagin could use some of the appropriation for overtime, but not for the base pay of the people who might have earned that overtime. And so the job cuts had been announced, and then, after a heart-stopping pause of a few days, during which it seemed impossible some way around this drastic surgery wouldn't be found, the cuts had been executed. Repercussions would be widespread, and some of them unpredictable.

How, for example, to collect desperately needed sales tax revenue now that the tax department had been gutted? Or this: The city charter required timely notice of any hearing on a request for a zoning change, for a conditional use permit, or for the waiver of normal building regulations. These deviations were the very air breathed by the city's real estate developers—also, alas, a traditional choke hold for the dispensing of political favors and the collection of bribes, or, more politely, campaign contributions. But now the planning commission staff had been cut from twenty-four to eight. Only two of them remained in land use, the division that screened zoning petitions, the most abundant item on the agenda at the planning commission's biweekly meetings. Compounding the problem, the mail room in the basement of city hall had flooded during the storm, and now there was no one around to re-open it, no one to fire off the notices that by law went to neighbors in the blocks surrounding any proposed variance, be it the opening of a day care center in a private residence or a request for permission to tear down a low-rise city block and build a high-rise Trump condominium.

That mail deliveries were problematic was another concern—there was an acute shortage of carriers. The devil is in the details, and so it was no small thing for the planning commission to learn at its early November meeting that Nagin had agreed to provide them with postage stamps as an al-ternative to inoperable postage meters. Of course, whether anyone had actu-ally moved back onto the block to read the notices sent out by the planning commission was anybody's guess—this side of the dreaded lawsuits that would inevitably be fired off by residents claiming not to have received timely notification.

It would be months before even first-class mail service had been re-stored to any semblance of itself, months after that before subscription mag-azines and the like were among the pieces that carriers slipped through mail slots and onto front-hall floors in the inhabited parts of town. When, after several weeks, the first carriers were glimpsed afoot in city streets, their vis-its were at most once or twice a week, sometimes followed by a gap of an-other week or more before their reappearance. As the routes were regularized, there remained a great mystery: What had happened to all the mail—tens of millions of pieces—that had been sent during the time when the post was out of service altogether?

Change-of-address forms filed from out of town might redirect a tiny portion of the usual bills and letters to an evacuee's new home. Back in the city, announcements were made: Such and such a zip code could retrieve old mail at such and such a location—trailers set up in the parking lot behind the Superdome, post offices in unflooded parts of town—and the small proportion of city residents who had actually returned would stand in line expectantly with satchels in hand, sometimes for an hour or two. The satchels turned out to be ludicrously unnecessary. The wait might avail two pieces of mail, one of them a circular announcing a Labor Day weekend sale that had never taken place. And the rest? The weeks' worth of mail gone missing? "Houston," was the muttered incantation. A mountain of mail was said to be in Houston, as were a great many New Orleanians, though the mail would have to be sent back to New Orleans before they would ever see any of it, if any of it was ever to be seen.

Some areas of government remained immune to cuts, the Sewerage and Water Board, for example. And for the police department, the sharp reduction in both population and crime was a welcome solution to what had been an acute recruitment problem. For years, the NOPD had struggled to bring its ranks within sight of an allocated patrol strength of seventeen hundred officers, rarely reaching the sixteen-hundred-officer threshold as recruits were offset by retirements and the expulsion of corrupt officers. In Katrina's aftermath, the nose count came closer to fourteen hundred, allowing for desertions and those who were under administrative review for looting. And even that looked like a generous staffing level in a city that was somewhere between half and a quarter the size it had been before the storm.

As mayor of New Orleans, Nagin retained the power to set an agenda and stick to it, to exhort his shattered city to begin pulling on the same oar. The radio tirade had been a piece of it, the angry demand that Bush and Blanco "get off [their] asses" and bring aid to the city. Nagin spoke for hundreds of thousands in that moment, and he spoke with a passion that was infectious if not particularly effective. Nagin's next resort to the bully pulpit, in the third week after Katrina, was to announce early success in getting power and water back to at least some of the city's unflooded neighborhoods—the French Quarter, the central business district, Algiers, and parts of Uptown—and to schedule their phased-in repopulation. "I'm tired of hearing these helicopters," he declared. "I want to hear some jazz." The announcement breathed with confidence; it showed that progress was being made—months earlier than envisioned in the first dismal recovery schedules. And in phasing in the reopening of neighborhoods, the mayor seemed to be signaling that he was willing to exercise intelligent discretion. If parts of the city were habitable, parts were not, he seemed to realize. The only problem was that the bold, welcome decision was easily assailed. It had been made in isolation, without consulting FEMA's new man in charge, and, as it happened, coast guard vice admiral Thad Allen was not in favor of the plan and had no hesitation about saying so. In fact, he thought it was reckless and irresponsible to complicate the work of emergency responders by suddenly putting a lot of local residents underfoot, and with two months of hurricane season still to go.

Nagin dug in his heels. Yes, the muck into which he dug them, that ghostly whitish gray ooze covering so much of the city, was of uncertain toxicity and was likely to become an airborne presence that would carry even into unflooded neighborhoods. Yes, there were no hospitals, at a time when big-city residents with limited experience as lumberjacks would be firing up chainsaws and attempting to clear fallen trees off their property. Yes, they would be up on rooftops, trying to patch ripped shingling, until they fell off rooftops and needed to be patched themselves—but where, with so many hospitals out of service? Yes, there were no working streetlights or traffic signals in a city where emergency crews had grown accustomed to blowing through major intersections and defying one-way signs. Yes, New Orleans had been hit by a bad hurricane, but in Nagin's view, and many shared this view, the citizenry as well as the city would be better off if people got back to their accustomed haunts. To linger in Dallas or Little Rock was to risk setting down roots.

Fortunately for the mayoral ego, the impasse was resolved in the vice admiral's favor by a third-party arbitrator: Hurricane Rita. The pending storm provided Nagin with the cover he needed to postpone "repopulation." Indeed, there was reason to wonder if there would be a landscape left to repopulate as Rita swelled suddenly off the Florida coast and by Wednesday, September twenty-first, had become a Category 5 cyclone of the greatest intensity ever recorded. A second hundred-year storm in a month? It seemed almost inconceivable, and yet once again evacuation warnings were being issued to the dazed and storm-wearied people of New Orleans, the few who were left. Windows were being boarded up, and this time a fleet of buses was assembled on high ground to whisk survivors to safety, if it came to that.

With the city's levee system in shambles, work crews rammed sheet piling into the very mouths of the drainage canals, a measure that would plug them against storm surge coming in from the lake, but at a price: If the city were hit with heavy rains, there would be no way to pump out the water until the canals were unplugged—a recipe for massive street flooding. Blessedly, the storm stayed to the south of the city and continued to slide west, eventually coming ashore that Saturday on the Texas-Louisiana line. "You want to see kids scared, you should have seen the kids from New Orleans when they heard that another storm was coming and that they'd have to move again," said Stephanie Wyman, the young New Orleans teacher working with evacuated children in the Houston suburbs.

It was as if Rita had chased the Louisianans to the very place where they had fled to escape Katrina three weeks earlier. The storm scared Houston into a mass evacuation, a catastrophically bungled exercise in gridlock and highway death. Two dozen Houston nursing home residents would perish aboard a bus when their oxygen tanks exploded on a choked highway that turned the usual three-and-a-half-hour drive north toward Dallas into a twenty-four-hour nightmare. And for the first time in a long time, New Orleanians looking back over their state's ordeal had reason to think that in evacuating a million people ahead of Katrina maybe it had got at least one thing right. Texas governor Rick Perry tried to suggest otherwise, making the best of a botched evacuation with the observation that being stuck in traffic for fifteen hours "sure beats being plucked off the roof by a helicopter."

Rita veered east at the last minute, leaving Houston to sweep up broken glass, ripped roofing, and downed trees, while the storm's full fury was visited, once again, on Louisiana, this time the Lake Charles area. With the storm at Category 3 strength upon landfall, the Calcasieu Parish seat endured heavy flooding while fishing hamlets and beachfront resorts to the south, along the so-called Cajun Riviera, were wiped from the map. In New Orleans, the plugged outfall canals held fast, inspiring the crude, makeshift strategy that would be offered by the army corps in the coming hurricane season until it could come up with a more elegant fix. But the Ninth Ward was again underwater, thanks to storm surge sweeping through the sieve that was the Industrial Canal, and pumping resumed all over again.

Two days after Rita expired in a welter of flailing winds and surging water, Nagin reactivated his stalled repopulation plan. "With Hurricane Rita behind us, the task at hand is to bring New Orleans back," Nagin proclaimed. But in a concession to Vice Admiral Allen, if not to reality, Nagin urged caution: "We want people to return and help us rebuild the city. However, we want everyone to assess the risks and make an informed decision about reentry plans," Nagin said. The first phase of the reentry would be sharply limited. Residents of the unflooded communities across the river in Algiers could return, and business owners in the French Quarter, the central business district, and Uptown could do the same. And by six in the evening, anyone participating in the return had better be out of the city again, or at least under cover. The curfew remained in place until eight AM, freeing itchy-fingered patrols to assume that anyone at large was probably a looter. Even during the day, returnees were under orders to carry identification at all times and not to stray from the zip code in which they lived or did business—draconian injunctions that were not strictly enforced.

The city's official announcement that the door was ajar for at least a tentative return came in a brochure with a list of daunting warnings in richly varied typography. Among items on a list of seventeen advisories:

- There is very little access to medical services at this time. We are not prepared to handle critical care patients. **You should have tetanus shots before you enter the city.**

- Federal authorities suggest you limit your exposure to airborne mold and wear gloves, masks, and other protective materials to protect yourself. You must supply your own protective equipment.

- The sewage system has been compromised. With the exception of Algiers, you are advised not to drink, bathe, or wash your hands in water from your tap. WE RECOMMEND THE USE OF BOTTLED WATER UNTIL FURTHER NOTICE. BRING A

SUFFICIENT SUPPLY OF BOTTLED WATER FOR DRINK-
ING, BATHING, AND PERSONAL USE. You may flush toilets.

- The traffic lights are out throughout the city. ALL INTERSEC-
TIONS ARE FOUR-WAY STOPS and the speed limit is 30 mph
regardless of the posted speed limit. You are required to follow
all street directions. Proceed with extreme caution.

- Standing water and soil may be seriously contaminated; avoid
contact. If you come in contact with dirt or water, you should
wash with antibacterial soap and bottled water as soon as possible.

- AVOID CARBON MONOXIDE POISONING. Do not connect
electrical generators to the electrical panel or an outlet in your
business or home.

- Natural gas customers: DO NOT ATTEMPT TO TURN GAS
ON YOURSELF.

- YOUR HOME OR BUSINESS MAY NOT BE STRUC-
TURALLY SOUND; ENTER AT YOUR OWN RISK. Use extra
care when navigating upper floors and attic space.

The word "navigating" had a certain unintended charm. Nonetheless,
these reminders of recent inundation and the toxic residues clinging to every
once-waterlogged surface were not enough to dissuade the stouthearted.
Many of them had slipped back into the city on their own schedules and
were already pulling rotted wallboard and carpeting out to the curb as the
first step in gutting their properties right down to the joists and rafters and
then dousing the mold with bleach. And the mold, whether toxic or merely
revolting, was everywhere. Red, black, green—within days of the flooding
and only more luxuriantly after the waters receded, huge blooms of it ran
like wallpaper from floor to ceiling. Mold infiltrated every cabinet, refrigerator, and bookbinding. Upholstered furniture that hadn't become sodden
needed to be discarded anyway, and soon the streets of some neighborhoods
were lined with reeking, fly-specked fixtures and furnishings.

Curbside refrigerators became unforgettable icons of the city's distress, not just because of their abundance and the ungodly stench that rose from them, but because they lent themselves so handily to the posting of graffiti: "Do not open. Tom Benson inside"—a reference to the owner of the Saints, the city's NFL football team; Benson was already making noises about turning traitor and moving the team away from New Orleans. Other inscriptions, some referencing Benson, others playing on Katrina's gender, ranged from the obscene to the scatological. And some were even clever.

Indeed, in the absence of many modes of communication, graffiti, whether on refrigerators or traditional locations, became a more important part of the dialogue that is at the heart of any urban culture. Chris Rose, a newspaper columnist with a gimlet eye for the irresistible inanities of life in New Orleans, noticed how some of the graffiti amounted to a running commentary. "Don't try," the owner of a rug shop warned looters within a day of Katrina's strike on the city. And the crude lettering on the plywood covering his display windows backed up the warning with particulars: "I am sleeping inside with a big dog, an ugly woman, two shotguns, and a claw hammer."

"Claw hammer, nice touch," Rose said to himself. By week's end, the graffiti had been updated: "Still here. Woman left. Cooking a pot of dog gumbo." By the end of the month, the warning had been further revised to salute early returnees: "Welcome back, y'all. Grin and bear it."

As retreating floodwaters and his work schedule allowed, Mark Schleifstein ventured back down to New Orleans from the paper's temporary digs in Baton Rouge to check out his house, which stood in one of the most deeply flooded parts of Lakeview. He returned with a droll report. "I only had a foot of water," he deadpanned. A pause. ". . . on the second floor." He was not exaggerating.

WELL INTO OCTOBER, WORD REACHED TRINA PETERS AT THE HOUSES SHE AND her mother had rented in Reserve that even the Lower Ninth had finally been removed from quarantine. But residents would be permitted only a quick visit called a "look and leave," the mayor decreed. Such visits would be under police escort, partly to prevent looting, if anything remained to be looted, partly because many structures were so badly damaged they were in danger of collapse and must not be entered. Peters and her kin presented themselves at the checkpoint at St. Claude and Poland avenues on the very first day of these grim homecomings.

Patrina, her mother and father, Damond, Keia, an uncle, a couple of friends—there were enough of them to require two cars. And as they rounded the corner onto Lamanche, they scanned the block for a first glimpse of their beloved camelback. It was easy enough to spot their front-yard fence, through the row of flood-battered cars that had washed up against it. And there was the old metal lawn swing, the two-seater where many of them had whiled away a summer's night. But the sight of it did not occasion whoops of affectionate recollection. Indeed, no one in the group was capable of speech or any other sound as they lifted their eyes toward the pile of splintered joists and weatherboard that had once been their house. As the waters had retreated, the first floor had pancaked, shattering the concrete foundation sill and leaving only the peak of the long narrow roof just a few feet above ground level. To the rear, the second-floor camelback squatted over the flattened floor beneath it, like the fo'c'sle on a sinking ship. It was immediately clear that providence had been with Peters and her daughter when they leapt to the roof of the floating house that had knocked against theirs. A smaller, newer structure, it remained intact, still lodged against the pecan tree that Peters remembered from childhood.

If there was solace on that otherwise blood-draining trip to the Lower Ninth, it was the sight of the family church, Battleground Baptist, a lone sentinel, still standing in a sea of flotsam. Her faith had seen Trina back to sobriety after the seven lost years she'd passed amid the smoke and laughter that followed her decision to break with an abstemious family and "do things Trina's way for a while." She credited Battleground Baptist and also that other man of God in the family, her cousin the Reverend Freddie McFadden, pastor of St. Claude Avenue Baptist Church. And she credited his brother James with guiding Damond into the culture of the Mardi Gras Indians. Menfolk in the family had been Indians, a rich tradition in which neighborhoods gave rise to "tribes" or "gangs"—the Ninth Ward Flaming Arrows, in their case. And on special occasions they had taken to the streets in wildly feathered costumes of their own design and crafting. It was a tradition said to have begun in homage to the Native Americans who gave shelter to runaway slaves hiding deep in the swamps. No sooner had the latter-day Indians

massed in full regalia than the men would rip apart that year's costumes, sal-
vage the beads and feathers, and begin to make the next. It was a tradition
that Damond had fully embraced, and his stitchwork had been coming along
nicely, everyone agreed. Once a week, every week before the storm, he had
gone to his uncle James's house just down the street to join in with a dozen
men working on their costumes.

Could any of that be saved? Peters wondered. Weeping, wordlessly the
family piled back into the cars and headed upriver to the temporary home
that looked suddenly much more permanent, Reserve.

BY THE TIME THE COAST WAS CLEAR, MOST PEOPLE COMPELLED TO MOVE BACK
into the neighborhoods that allowed or overlooked the reentry were doing so
on their own initiative and their own schedule. And Nagin had moved on to
his next major exercise of mayoral authority, empaneling a committee of
worthies to bring expertise and guidance to the terrible questions con-
fronting the city.

What to do? How to rebuild? The clunkiness of its title did not in any
sense diminish the stature of key members of the Bring New Orleans Back
Commission (BNOB). Wynton Marsalis might not have lived in his hometown for years, but as a musician in his own right and as head of the jazz or-
chestra at Lincoln Center, he was, since Louis Armstrong's death, the
planet's most important living embodiment of the city's musical tradition.
Joe Canizaro was another high-profile choice, a rich banker and avid Republican who could get the president on the phone. The racial balance of
bankers was righted by the appointment of Alden McDonald, the top of the
Creole social heap and the president of Liberty Bank.

Jimmy Reiss was another appointee with real clout: a millionaire businessman who had taken charge of the city transit system for Nagin and had
chased out the management team headed by former mayor Marc Morial's
uncle, a man then under indictment on federal corruption charges. (Months
earlier his wife had pleaded guilty to charges associated with bribing a
school official for a piece of the insurance business.) There was a certain
amount of political chutzpah in appointing Reiss. Remarks quoted in *The
Wall Street Journal* in the first days after Katrina passed were construed—

misconstrued, Reiss insisted—to mean that he thought the city would benefit from a little demographic tweaking. Fewer poor people would mean fewer
criminals, he suggested, a comment that was seized upon as evidence of
racial bias. City council president Oliver Thomas was on the BNOB committee, another African American, as were a variety of less well-known civic
leaders. And one of the committee's first moves was to accept an offer from
the Urban Land Institute, a prestigious city planning group, to come up with
recommendations for the city that New Orleans needed to become in the
post-Katrina world.

Inevitably there was grousing, even before the commission began for-
mulating its recommendations. Some black critics saw the BNOB as too
white, too suburban. Okay, Marsalis was aboard, a marquee name of international stature, but when had he last puckered up for a New Orleans street parade? Whites saw the committee as redundant, given that Blanco had created
a state-level Louisiana Recovery Authority peopled with worthies of similar
stripe. Her chairman was Norman Francis, in his fourth decade as president
of Xavier University. The vice chairman was Walter Isaacson, a New Orleans native who had gone on to glory in New York as editor of *Time* magazine. After a stint running CNN, Isaacson was now in charge of the Aspen
Institute and its worldwide network of seminars and conferences.

The proliferation of blue-ribbon panels was verging on the ludicrous
when the city council announced plans for its own rebuilding commission, a
doubly redundant idea that was withdrawn amid shouting and laughter. An
impasse between Nagin's and Blanco's committees was avoided, but not for
good, when each commission arranged to seat a member of the other, and it
was agreed—Nagin's group didn't have much choice in the matter—that the
city commission's work, once completed, would be passed on to the LRA.
Thus, at least on paper, the LRA would be the state's voice in dealings with
Don Powell, the Texas banker Bush had named as his coordinator of the Gulf
Coast recovery effort. But over time, perhaps the biggest question about
Nagin's panel was whether, ahead of elections scheduled for the coming
winter, he would have the political courage to adopt any of the recommendations the BNOB came up with, or to wait respectfully until they had com-
pleted their work, before rolling out some of his own.

The answer to the latter possibility was quickly provided.

No sooner had Nagin set up his panel and charged the group to complete its initial set of recommendations by year's end, than he jumped the gun. Again without much consultation, none at all with the city council, Nagin called the media before his rostrum to declare that what post-Katrina New Orleans needed to jump-start its economy and assure solid, perhaps even frenzied, growth was an expansion of casino gambling in the downtown area. A big expansion. A measure that would allow any hotel over a certain size to open a casino. What it would do to the huge Harrah's New Orleans casino at the foot of Canal Street was anybody's guess, including Nagin's, because he had not sounded out the state's biggest taxpayer before making his move. Harrah's shelled out $60 million in annual taxes under a contract that guaranteed its right to operate the only land-based casino in the city, a monopoly that would be broken under Nagin's plan—whether to Harrah's delight, because the tax burden would have to be lifted, or dismay, over the added competition, remained to be determined.

A plan calculated to touch off a gold rush in New Orleans instead triggered howls of disgust from enough important people to prompt Nagin to run for cover. Some dismissed his "out-of-the-box" idea, as he called it, as hopelessly trite—and entirely unworthy of the great city it proposed to save. Another criticism was the somewhat shopworn argument that gambling would be the death of the city's more diversified tourism infrastructure, the same argument that had been used against casino gambling when it was legalized a decade earlier. Instead, the huge casino at the foot of Canal Street had been in and out of bankruptcy, and the city's riverboat casinos, once four in number, had dwindled to one; and it too had been threatening to steam off in search of a better market, even before Katrina.

Meanwhile, tourists had continued to throng Bourbon Street and the city's museums and clubs and fine-dining establishments and to sign up for tours of riverfront plantations, alligator-infested swamps, and every other item on the city's considerable menu of attractions. Casinos hadn't gobbled up New Orleans's tourism. Tourism had nibbled on the casino industry and spat it out, and Nagin could not but scoff at the bluenoses, so het up about a few more casinos in a state where cockfighting was still legal and half the church halls functioned at least one night a week as bingo parlors. "I just think our character and our culture is too strong for any one thing to defeat it," he said. The other tangent taken by Nagin's critics was that there was no consistency of vision, no guiding theme, no steady hand on the tiller. Having rolled out his big idea—evidently without doing enough of the political groundwork that might have made it fly—Nagin looked ready to drop it, and in short order he did, almost as an aside when asked about the casino plan during an appearance before Congress.

In the absence of better-honed ideas or evidence of much leadership at all, former fans of the mayor, some of them once quite adoring, began to turn on him. An extreme case was Doug Brinkley, the popular historian who had recently been lured to Tulane from the University of New Orleans, where he had been the late Stephen Ambrose's handpicked heir as head of the Eisenhower Center. Brinkley, while culturally adventurous—he had managed to affiliate himself with Hunter Thompson and the Jack Kerouac estate—was no wild-eyed political radical, and yet he condemned Nagin's post-Katrina performance as nothing short of "criminal." Weepy moments in the teeth of the storm and an overlong wallow in the luxury of the Air Force One shower were construed by Brinkley as evidence that the mayor was coming unhinged. Other defectors from the mayor's camp, among them Clancy Dubos, owner and editor of a local weekly, took a more restrained view and decided that Nagin's collection of strengths and weaknesses was simply the wrong mix to lead the city through a time of unexampled crisis.

AS HE REFLECTED BACK ON HIS POST-KATRINA LEADERSHIP ONE AFTERNOON IN October, Nagin conceded that his big idea was a bomb. "But my big frustration is this," he said, "I'm not hearing anybody else come up with anything! I just hear a lot of people remembering 'when I used to get beignets at Café du Monde.' "

It seemed possible that the mayor wasn't listening very hard.

FOURTEEN

In Search of Common Ground

MALIK RAHIM HAD NEVER LACKED CONVICTION. IT SAW HIM THROUGH days of rage as defense minister of the local Black Panther chapter during a bloody standoff in the Desire public housing project back in the 1970s. It led him to renounce his given name, Donald Guyton, as he embraced, and then backed away from, an adherence to Islam that sustained him for many years. And so, when a neighbor came by Rahim's house on the Friday after Katrina to say that white vigilantes had begun roaming the streets of the unflooded Algiers district, there was little likelihood Rahim would ask what else was new. The vigilantes had hassled the neighbor— "jammed him," as he put it—demanding to know where he lived and where he was going. Carless, after punching a hole in his gas tank so a son could fuel up a borrowed truck and escape the city with his wife and kids, Rahim hopped onto his bicycle. Sure enough, street barricades had been set up by the rambunctious gunmen—middle-class guys, some of whom Rahim knew. Packing pistols and assault rifles and evidently energized by the opportunity to brandish them, they were intent on making sure looting did not spread their way.

It was not the ideal moment to be a black man with dreadlocks that fell well below his shoulders, but at least they were gray. Rahim, a temporarily unemployed fifty-eight-year-old with seven kids, twenty-six grandchildren, and a great-grandson so new he was still wet behind the ears, confronted the men. "Who deputized you to do this?" he wanted to know. "Who gave you the power?" As they were beginning to square off, a cop pulled up. "These guys are acting like vigilantes," Rahim complained. The cop affirmed their right to protect their neighborhood. "We all have a right?" Malik asked. The cop repeated himself: "They have a right," he said, in Rahim's recollection of the moment.

Rahim's political career had not ended with the demise of the Black Panthers nor with a five-year prison sentence for armed robbery that he had served in California during a long-past phase of his life. Since returning to his hometown, he had dabbled in local politics a few years back, with an unsuccessful run for city council on the Green Party ticket. But if you had told Rahim—or the men he confronted—that within weeks he would be in charge of a multimillion-dollar relief operation that was drawing volunteers from all over the United States and donations from all over the world, he would have had reason to turn his large, gray head and give you a skeptical stare.

Katrina was a convulsion in many lives and in many ways. And inevitably the most widespread reaction, even among people who had not been much favored by the old order, was to yearn for restoration. Never had étouffée tasted so good, even the faked version evacuees found at the New Orleans–style cookeries in Texas; never had the memory of a brass band's jubilant wail been so powerfully evocative. But advocates of social and political change, many of them more temperate in their views than Rahim, others angrier and less flexible, saw in the destruction of New Orleans the opportunity for a new beginning—and they were not inclined to sit around waiting for Ray Nagin. For some, the vision was of moving forward into the deeper past, to a time when New Orleans had been a majority white city, a richer city, a safer city, and blacks had known their place. From his days with the Panthers and his continuing allegiance to the Green Party, Rahim was in the very different orbit of people, dreamers and doers alike, who welcomed the collapse of a political and economic establishment that they described with phrases like "systemic racism" and "internalized oppression." Some of that language had been developed in the antiracism workshops conducted by the homegrown People's Institute for Survival and Beyond, both in New Orleans and all over the United States. Rahim had participated in those workshops, and was a longtime friend of the institute's director, Ron Chisom.

With the hurricane in the offing, Rahim had defied Nagin's evacuation order and stayed on with the woman then in his life, Sharon Johnson, in the one-story bungalow he had come home to from California in order to nurse his mother in her final years. He stayed in the city because he had always ridden out hurricanes, and he stayed because, as he would say in hindsight, "I saw a necessity." The necessity arose from his perception, an accurate one, that the city had made no plans to evacuate people who could not get out on their own. At a pre-storm meeting with some twenty people from the neighborhood who were staying behind, Rahim convinced the group that they needed also to stay in touch. He stockpiled life jackets and then made a bunker out of his kitchen, reinforcing the ceiling with upright two-by-fours in case the roof fell in. With Algiers emptied of all but perhaps a fifth of its fifty-five thousand residents, Rahim scouted his neighborhood for empty two-story houses that might be taken over and occupied in a pinch. He laid in food for four or five days. In other words, Rahim could say ironically, looking back on his disaster planning, "We were ill-prepared. Next time I would have food for thirty days."

But if Rahim was ill-prepared, he was also lucky to live in a part of town that, with this hurricane, anyway, did not flood. Late Monday, Rahim was raking up twigs and preparing to patch his roof when one of his brothers called to tell him New Orleans was underwater. Rahim was incredulous. "I'm laughing at him; I couldn't believe it." But on a stroll up onto the massive levees for a look back across the river at New Orleans's east bank, Rahim cocked his ear and swore he could hear the sounds of people crying for help. On Tuesday, the son who needed gas rolled up with a tale of woe. He and his wife and their three young kids had waded to a two-story house and bivouacked there with twenty-one other refugees before despairing of rescue and walking six miles to the Superdome. They arrived ahead of the flooding in that part of town but in time to see that the Dome was untenable. After helping them to his tank of gas and seeing them on their way out of town, Rahim began to wonder if he shouldn't have gone with them.

That same day the governor had announced that troops were arriving at last, with weapons "locked and loaded," which Rahim, and not Rahim alone, took to be a shoot-to-kill order endorsed as well by Mayor Nagin, a man he loathed. Rahim would claim in coming days to have seen at least one bullet-riddled black corpse. But there was more obvious evidence of the way the city was fracturing along racial lines. On Friday, as Rahim attempted to cross into Jefferson Parish, he was—like the group of refugees who had tried to walk across the river to Gretna—cut off. White friends arriving from Texas with guns of their own to protect Rahim were able to slip into Algiers despite checkpoints and the curfew. That same day, a black doctor, trying to enter Algiers armed only with medicines, was turned away. Young blacks in the neighborhood were starting to get antsy to do something about the white vigilantes cruising by in their pickup trucks. "Don't even think about fighting them," Rahim warned. "You won't win."

IF THERE WAS A SINGLE PEBBLE THAT PRECIPITATED THE AVALANCHE THAT WAS about to reorder Malik Rahim's world, it was the jingle of his telephone late Thursday night, three days after Katrina. Sharon Johnson picked it up—it was a caller on in years, to judge from the sound of her voice—and handed the phone to Rahim. Mary Ratcliff was the editor of a small San Francisco weekly, the *Bay View*, pitched to African American readers. She and her husband, Willie, had gotten to know Rahim during his California years. He had led a fight they'd supported against the Hope VI program, through which federal housing administrators were encouraging demolition of old-style housing projects and their replacement with . . . Well, that was the problem, as Rahim saw it. In New Orleans as in San Francisco, the housing projects were never fully replaced, and a lot of residents found themselves uprooted from familiar communities and with no place to go. Ratcliff had not called to talk about Hope VI, of course. Desperate for more news about Katrina than she was finding on the Web, she'd flipped through an old address book and come across a number for Rahim. TV was reporting that the 504 area code was down, but she dialed the number anyway. The only reason she got through was because Rahim had yet to join the cell phone revolution—couldn't really stand them: numbers too small to read, features you didn't need. Cell phone service was kaput. Some landlines were still working, Rahim's among them.

"So much of this doesn't add up," Ratcliff said to Rahim, once they got past the surprise of being in touch for the first time in quite a while. "All we're hearing on the news is that the rescue effort is being pulled back because of gangs and terrible danger. People there have boats. Why aren't they rescuing people who need help?" Rahim began to talk, and then he began to vent, and seated at her computer, Ratcliff quietly opened a Word document and began to type as fast as she could. Which was very fast.

"This is criminal," Rahim began. "From what you're hearing, the people trapped in New Orleans are nothing but looters. We're told we should be more neighborly. But nobody talked about being neighborly until after the people who could afford to leave left. . . . There are gangs of white vigilantes near here, riding around in pickup trucks, all of them armed. . . . There were enough school buses that could have evacuated twenty thousand people easily, but they just let them be flooded. My son watched forty buses go underwater—they just wouldn't move them, afraid they'd be stolen. . . . People whose homes and families were not destroyed went into the city right away with boats to bring survivors out, but law enforcement told them they weren't needed. . . . I'm in the Algiers neighborhood. . . . The water is good. Our parks and schools could easily hold forty thousand people, and they're not using any of it. This is criminal. These people are dying for no other reason than the lack of organization."

As Rahim wound down, Ratcliff asked how people could help: "Everything is needed," he said, "but we're still too disorganized. I'm asking people to go ahead and gather donations and relief supplies but to hold on to them for a few days until we have a way to put them to good use."

Rahim's message had clicked. Even before she posted it on her paper's website, Ratcliff e-mailed "This is criminal," as the screed came to be called, to a select list of thirty activists. "They sucked it up," just as she had, Ratcliff said, and sent it on to their own friends and connections, thus beginning an algebraic pattern of dissemination that shortly seemed to have reached the U.S. activist community in its entirety. Within days, Rahim had been interviewed on KPFA, the nonprofit Pacifica station in the Bay Area, and then by Amy Goodman on National Public Radio. And there things might have stalled, a flash in the pan, another overnight media darling to be just as quickly forgotten, except that Rahim's message brought focus to an insurgent yearning among a whole slew of folks—mostly young, many of them white—appalled by Katrina and looking for some way to get involved. It would remain to be seen if good intentions could be translated into useful service.

On Friday, the day after Ratcliff posted "This is criminal," a registered nurse and herbalist named Maureen "Mo" O'Brian up in Dillon, Montana, got an e-mail from a woman she knew only as Bork, someone she had met in Boston in 2004 during protests against the backdrop of the Democratic Party convention. Bork's message: She was driving down to New Orleans from Washington, D.C., with a truckload of medicines. O'Brian asked if there was anything she could do to help. Bork said, sure: Round up some medics. O'Brian had just started a new job in Dillon. That would have to wait. "I got off the phone and said, 'Shit. I'm going to New Orleans.'"

O'Brian called a trio of young community health people she had worked with in Boston and then again that summer at the Republican Convention in New York. She reached Roger Benham and Noah Morris in Washington and they agreed to go. Then she called Scott Mechanic, at twenty years old, the youngest of the three, in Philadelphia. Roger and Noah are going, she told him. Are you? Mechanic played the question back to her: "Am I?"

Within a day, Mechanic had hooked up with the others in Washington and they were on their way to New Orleans in Bork's truck full of medicine. Bork, for all the medical supplies she had rounded up, did not see herself as a health professional. She worked with a radical housing organization called Mayday that also advocated on behalf of homeless people. And the young men were not doctors or nurses; their skill levels were about those of emergency medical technicians. They could give shots, clean and bandage wounds, perform CPR. Mechanic earned his living as a caterer. But like Morris and Benham, he thought of himself as a political activist by profession. He volunteered as an organizer against sexual assault and lived with like-minded squatters in a building they had taken over. At any opportunity he was quick to swap his caterer's apron for a scrub shirt and work as a "street medic," ministering to the health needs of demonstrators and the like.

It was only en route, as they ran into other young people caravanning to New Orleans, that they heard about Malik Rahim's efforts to get something going in Algiers. That had a certain appeal, but it seemed prudent to check in first with a better-established relief operation across Lake Pontchartrain from New Orleans called Camp Covington. Veterans for Peace had set it up with financial help from the documentary filmmaker Michael Moore. On Tuesday, eight days after Katrina, the group from D.C. headed into the quarantined city, bullshitting their way past military checkpoints by saying they were envoys from a major relief organization. One blowout later—and the happy coincidence of it occurring beside an unguarded tire store with exactly the product they needed—they reached the Algiers address someone had given them. Sharon Johnson answered their knock. The relief operation did not yet even have a name, but two European videographers had picked up on the media buzz and were interviewing Rahim as the three young white boys arrived. Rahim directed them and the van of medicines down the street to an abandoned storefront mosque, Masjid Bilal, a place where he had worshipped during his days of fealty to Islam.

"It smelled like rot everywhere," Mechanic said, recalling the sickly sweet smell of putrefying refrigerator food that would waft over the electricity-less city for weeks to come. "But we had what we needed to begin." Step one was to empty the refrigerator at the mosque. In deference to the sacred Muslim space, Rahim had required that they put tarps on the floor. Then they set out their supplies: gauze, hydrogen peroxide, blood pressure cuffs, vitamins, herbal supplements, insulin, and so on. They spray-painted a sign on the mosque's exterior wall: "First Aid." The grand opening was Thursday, a week to the day after Malik's late-night chat with Mary Ratcliff. Rahim's cadre of volunteers had been given a name: Common Ground. Now all they needed were patients.

Among the first visitors was a local woman, known as Mama Souma, and her two daughters. Souma was in her sixties, her daughters in their forties, and their home doubled as a local African American cultural center, a scene of community-level performances and exhibitions. Mama Souma told the medics to follow her as she made her rounds of the community, the small portion of it that hadn't evacuated, or that had trickled back to a dry part of town in the storm's aftermath. She'd introduce them. "It was like knock-knock-knock—no one would answer," Mechanic recalled. "Knock-knock-knock again—no answer. Finally, 'It's Mama Souma!' Then someone would come to the door."

Another approach, of interest to Rahim because it might allay racial tension as much as build a patient base, was to send one or another of the young white men out into the streets on a bicycle, his skill set advertised by the stethoscope around his neck. If the bicyclist saw someone sitting on a porch, he'd stop and say something. Need water? And he'd mention the clinic, which soon was alive with customers, some seeking tetanus shots or insulin, some fresh back from cross-river rescue missions and with cuts and scrapes made much worse by exposure to the toxic swill washing over the city. But most arrived simply with the chronic conditions that come with poverty: asthma, diabetes, hypertension. "We had come here to do emergency medicine, but it was not what was needed," Mechanic discovered. "People had had inadequate care. The concept of an annual physical was nonexistent."

The sight of the young white medics had the hoped-for effect on the vigilantes who had been spoiling for a confrontation with looters. "Word got out not to mess with these young guys," said Rahim, who as the weeks went on would take flak from critics concerned that his largely white volunteer force was an affront to black self-empowerment. Rahim was not one to let ideology get in the way of pragmatism. White skin had its privileges, all parties to the discussion could agree. It also had its uses, Rahim discovered. As far as he was concerned, the street medics had come just in time. If a nervous black trigger finger had led to the death of a white vigilante, Rahim was convinced that the African American community still hanging on in Algiers would have been slaughtered in retaliation. "Scott, Noah, Roger—they are my heroes," Malik would say, looking back on the crisis that had given rise to Common Ground. "They stopped the whole city from exploding."

As the military began fanning out on regular patrols from bases they had set up upon arrival the weekend after the storm, inevitably the clinic caught their attention. And so it was that the close-cropped young men of the Eighty-second Airborne and the Louisiana National Guard encountered the very different army arriving to work with Rahim. Mechanic saw wisdom in limiting conversation with inquiring GIs to health care, but Bork was the let-it-all-hang-out type, quick to identify herself as a lesbian anarchist and put her work in the larger political context in which she saw herself operating. Mechanic and the other men cringed silently the first time they heard her get into it: "We're like, 'No, no, Bork. Too much information.' "

On his first visit, the talker among the soldiers casing the joint repeated Bork's account of herself as if uncertain he had heard it right: "So you're the anarchists in the mosque brought in by the ex–Black Panther giving free health care?" A pause. "Cool, that's great."

And the soldiers had roared off in their Humvee, leaving Mechanic, Bork, Benham, and Morris to wonder if, on their next visit, the army would arrive with plywood and padlocks to shut down the unlicensed health clinic in a city that had just reiterated a mandatory evacuation order. In fact, as additional volunteers flocked to Common Ground, the army would prove to be an ally, above all against the police, a source of continuing harassment, most of it petty. There was the case of the volunteer arrested for double-parking, and the twenty squad cars that wailed to a stop in front of Rahim's bungalow in pursuit of a volunteer suspected of stealing an ice chest. From Rahim's perspective, the greater sins of the city government were omissions: an utter lack of support for the clinic and what he was trying to do; a refusal to act on a request for park space, for example, in which newly arriving volunteers could set up tents.

And almost overnight, to Rahim's amazement, the new arrivals had become an onslaught. Six days after the clinic opened, some forty out-of-state activists were camped out in and around Rahim's home. By year's end, a total of one hundred seventy volunteers would have rotated through the clinic, including three dozen locals. Some were licensed doctors, both local and then out-of-state, after Governor Blanco eased licensure rules on an emergency basis. Common Ground's first-aid station had become a full-service medical clinic, still a cash-free operation dependent on in-kind donations and volunteers. Some practitioners drawn to it were versed in new-age medical arts less familiar to a low-income black community. Mo O'Brian, the registered nurse and herbalist who had recruited Mechanic, Benham, and Morris to join Bork for the trek to New Orleans, had arrived herself after a five-day drive from Montana. Noah Morris had been the first familiar face at a clinic that by early October was treating over a hundred drop-ins a day. "You wanna see patients?" he asked, and O'Brian, too exhausted from her drive to say no, put on a scrub top and set to work. She would stay on into the new year, as would her street medics and many others. O'Brian was joined by massage therapists and acupuncturists, and soon it was not uncommon to see a row of a dozen or more patients, their ears bristling with needles. To accommodate the influx, the clinic recycled a trove of red plastic chairs that, according to legend, FEMA had dumpstered after using them only briefly at the convention center.

The clinic also spawned a program—the Latino Health Outreach Project—to contact migrant workers in motels and at assembly points where they gathered to make themselves available as day laborers. Storm-chasers, who swept into New Orleans on Katrina's tailwinds, they had come from all over—Texas, Mexico, Central America, some with papers, many without—to gut and re-roof houses, shovel debris, wash dishes, empty latrines, and in hundreds of other ways make themselves essential to the recovery effort. In one of his clumsier public pronouncements, Mayor Nagin in October told a FEMA-sponsored business forum about his concern that New Orleans might soon be "overrun by Mexicans," a lapse into racism and xenophobia decried in the press as unacceptable from the mayor of a city that preened itself on its multicultural diversity.

Things could be tough enough for the Latino workers without the big guy picking on them. Their conversations buzzed with stories of bosses who routinely stiffed them for dollars an hour and frequently full days in a week, when they went to collect their pay. Often undocumented and frequently with limited facility in English, they could do little about these abuses—which, of course, was exactly why unscrupulous bosses seized the opportunity to rip them off in the first place.

To assist those bold or desperate enough among the Latino workers to fight back, Common Ground collaborated with legal aid groups—including a Loyola law school clinic and affiliates of another group of movement lawyers called the Advancement Project. The health clinic also made house calls to look in on workers injured on the job. On a random Friday, one of the injured workers was a stocky thirty-seven-year-old Honduran, Javier

Aguilar, with a cast on one arm and a red baseball cap covering his thick black hair. Two years earlier, Aguilar had paid a coyote $5,000 to escort him on foot, by car, and then on the swim across the Rio Grande by which a *mojado* made his way to Texas. Working jobs in the states and remitting money to his wife back in Comayagua seemed the only hope to continue feeding their five children. Sensing opportunity in disaster, he had reached New Orleans in October. Steady work for a company with contracts to clean out schools and hospitals gave way to day labor when the clean-up company, C&B, left town. Aguilar was working for a roofing company when he fell off a ladder and broke his arm. After a five-hour wait in the emergency room of a private Uptown hospital, he was given an X ray, and a doctor slapped a cast on the damaged arm, evidently without properly setting the fracture. Days later, and assailed by shooting pains that had only worsened, Aguilar found his way by word of mouth to Common Ground and their advocacy program for Latinos.

In the pre-storm era, Aguilar could have sought treatment at Charity. But the once mighty poor-folks hospital had been reduced to a MASH unit called "Spirit of Charity" that was operating out of tented emergency rooms inside the convention center. Instead Aguilar was referred on to Charity's counterpart in Baton Rouge, Huey P. Long Hospital, the nearest facility that would deal with an uninsured patient not arriving on an emergency basis. The New Orleans hospital had badly botched the broken arm. After four hours of surgery at Huey Long, and the installation of a plate and two pins, Aguilar was sent home to begin a three-month convalescence, a devastating financial blow for his family that Common Ground hoped to alleviate by going after the roofing contractor for whom the Honduran had been working when he was injured.

COMMON GROUND WAS NOT OPERATING ITS MULTIFACETED SOCIAL SERVICE PROgrams in a vacuum. An outfit called the People's Hurricane Relief Fund and Oversight Coalition mounted an effort that intersected collaboratively with Common Ground on several projects, including the gutting of flood-damaged houses. While Common Ground was a magnet for an out-of-town, largely white army of young people interested in social action, the People's Hurricane Relief Fund was dominated by local people of color with an agenda centered on network building and demanding a voice for those displaced by the storm. Then there were the enormous efforts of more traditional agencies, the Red Cross and the Salvation Army. Acorn, a grassroots collaborative, mustered hundreds of volunteers to help flood victims gut their houses and start over. At street-level, the conspiracy-minded congressional witness who called herself "Mama D" had drawn more favorable attention to a feeding program she'd set up across the river in Treme, an African American community directly across Rampart Street from the French Quarter and with architecture nearly as antique. Habitat for Humanity would commit to building housing for a community of musicians, a multimillion-dollar investment in the city's comeback. A group of Uptown women of means began a petition drive and lobbying campaign to force the state legislature to bring the balkanized and patronage-ridden system of levee districts under consolidated and professional management. Another equally well-heeled group, Women of the Storm, would prove effective in lobbying Congress first to visit New Orleans and see the damage firsthand, then to cough up the appropriations that would begin to alleviate it.

Faith-based groups were critically important throughout the disaster zone, nowhere more so than in the community centered around Mary Queen of Vietnam Church, on the far eastern fringes of New Orleans East. Under a dynamic young priest, the Reverend Nguyen The Vien, the community, which had the good fortune to be located on a slight rise in an otherwise devastated floodplain, reverted to a collectivist approach to life that older members of the congregation remembered from Asia. Father Vien had been thirteen in 1975 when he joined the refugee exodus ahead of the fall of Saigon. After completing his education at Notre Dame and Catholic University, he had taken charge of Mary Queen of Vietnam just two years before Katrina struck, and had promptly established himself as a leader among the six thousand Vietnamese in eastern New Orleans. He had weathered the storm in the rectory with about ten parishioners. Another one hundred survived Katrina in the school behind the church. They took the storm in stride, Nguyen said. "They have been through many years of wars. . . . None of my people were terrified," he said. And with steadfast resolve, they had installed showers at the church, which doubled as a dormitory and feeding station as the people dispersed by the storm set to work gutting houses, caring for their children and elderly, and reclaiming their world.

BUT IN WAYS THAT SURPRISED NO ONE MORE THAN HIM, RAHIM'S EFFORT BE-came emblematic of post-Katrina activism. He could be called a brilliant or-ganizer, or the right man in the right place—which soon was everyplace, including trips to Cornell University, to San Francisco, even to Europe, as the philanthropic community seized upon him as a handy focus of their de-sire to do something for the hurricane-stricken city. And immediately, Com-mon Ground's range of options mushroomed. The health clinic had been partnered from the beginning with a nonmedical Common Ground dispen-sary of army rations, water, disposable diapers, and other basic supplies. Un-bidden, two members of Veterans for Peace had arrived with a load of supplies. "It's for y'all," they told Rahim, who first had mistaken the white men in the truck for vigilantes.

The trip to Cornell yielded four hundred personal hygiene kits assem-bled by students, some of whom came down as volunteers. A second clinic was established, along with a tree-cutting service and a program for gutting houses and tarping roofs. In addition to the advocacy center for Latinos, lawyers affiliated with Common Ground joined forces with the People's Hurricane Relief Fund to make certain that red-tagged houses—those deemed irreparable—were not bulldozed without their owners being noti-fied. Common Ground also birthed a toxin-testing service complemented by a garden for the cultivation of red worms, sunflowers, and other plants and critters that remove toxic chemicals from contaminated soil, a substance abundant in post-Katrina New Orleans. Meg Perry was a stalwart volunteer with the toxin-testing program, an elfin young woman from Maine whose death in a traffic accident in early December gave her something like eternal life in the lore and legends of Common Ground. It infuriated Rahim to see her described as "a drifter" in media reports of her death.

By year's end, the collective could claim to have served thirty-five thou-sand Orleans Parish residents—eight thousand of them through the clinics—

and to have handed out uncounted millions in donated goods through distribution centers that had spread from Orleans, where there were two to three other parishes. One donation was targeted at Rahim personally: a cell phone, courtesy of filmmaker Michael Moore—a stripped-down model with big numbers and none of the gewgaws that had bedeviled Rahim's earlier effort to join the communications revolution. Rahim was too important to Common Ground and—with a travel schedule that kept him out of town more than half of each month—too nomadic to be tethered to a landline.

"No one could have told me I'd be the head of an organization like this. I've been blessed beyond my wildest dreams," Rahim said, reflecting in late January over the most tumultuous four months in New Orleans's history, and his own. The clinic, which had moved across the street as the mosque recovered its congregants, was looking for ways to become a permanent part of the post-Katrina landscape, not the temporary response it had been thought of at its inception—a new model for delivering medical services in a city of uninsured, low-income people afflicted with all the scourges such a condition breeds.

But personal acclaim and organizational success had not sweetened the old organizer. What infuriated Rahim was that Common Ground had even been necessary. "No one had to leave this area because of the flood," he said. "A hundred thousand people could have been absorbed by towns along the west bank—Gretna, Algiers, Westwego, Bridge City, Waggaman. They didn't flood and there was enough space in those places. They wouldn't take in people from the east bank because most of them was niggers. They wanted to make it the nation's problem, and they did. They spread us to the winds."

FIFTEEN

If They Can Rebuild Beirut

O NE HOUSE HAD A MARINE CORPS BANNER SUSPENDED FROM THE EAVES; the one next to it on Dauphine Street flew the Jolly Roger—a juxtaposition of emblems that said little about the allegiances of New Orleanians except to suggest their variety. The proud ex-marine, Tony Bower, was the more improbable denizen of the Bywater district—a low-income bohemia that in recent years had caught gentrification's wave. Unsung artists, layabouts, bottom-feeding real estate speculators, waiters working on novels or computer graphics, dreamers, drug dealers, had begun to move in among the welfare families and working poor, mostly black and Hispanic, who had in their time displaced the blue-collar white ethnics who abandoned Bywater and most of New Orleans after the schools were integrated in the 1960s.

With so many economic indicators pointing south—indeed, perhaps because of it—New Orleans's ascendancy as a counterculture mecca was a timely asset. As San Francisco had lost ground to Seattle, and in turn Seattle had come to seem stale, New Orleans in the early part of the new millennium had hit stride again with a vigor reminiscent of its bohemian glory days in the 1920s and the 1960s. Young people and not-so-young people had begun pouring in from all over the country to take advantage of one of the last places in the United States where it was still possible to rent an apartment without a trust fund and to find a day job—waiter, croupier, sidewalk sketch artist—that really did allow time for nights devoted to love, wine, rock, and finishing the great American screenplay. There was a plucky resourcefulness to these latter-day hipsters, and when it came to jump-starting New Orleans after the flood and evacuation, it would well serve the neighborhoods that had accommodated them.

Bywater, home to Charmaine Neville, among others, ran downriver from faubourg Marigny to the Industrial Canal, the Rubicon that divided the Ninth Ward into its upper and lower parts. Beyond the Lower Ninth, where Trina Peters had nearly died, lay Arabi and Chalmette, white working-class burgs that had as little to do with New Orleans as possible. In the other direction, on the upriver side of Marigny, and perhaps two miles from the heart of Bywater, was the ne plus ultra of New Orleans tourism and inner-city chic, the French Quarter. The real estate speculators dreamed that one day Bywater would be more like the French Quarter, or at least more like Marigny, which had gentrified more vigorously in recent years. Artists, drawn to Bywater's cheap rents and funky ambience, would rue that day. But the gent with the pirate flag hanging off his house was a bit much for either camp. Indeed, Tony Bower, the ex-marine, hadn't spoken to his neighbor, Robert Zas, in about a year and a half.

Zas, a taut, wiry forty-two-year-old, had fallen from grace with the good people of Bywater not over the flag—which he saw as an assertion of rugged independence and also as a deterrent to burglars—but over an incident in early 2004 that was subject to diverse interpretations. At first blush, the situation was simple to explain: Narcs had raided Zas's house—whereupon Zas had done what any sensible New Orleanian might do under similar circumstances; he called the police. How else to make sure these alleged agents of the law were not impostors? Posses claiming to be narcs had raided other houses in the Bywater area not long before Zas's place was hit, and folks claimed personal property had been taken, not all of it drugs. This was New Orleans, after all, a city in which more than a few of the men and women hired to chase criminals had long since forgotten which side they were playing on. It only stood to reason that criminals might try to pass themselves off as cops, might even be assisted in that charade by the owners of government-issue blue serge and badges. Whatever was really going on, pursuant to Zas's phone call, NOPD squad cars had arrived, sirens screaming, but it was Zas and his mother who got bundled into a cruiser and taken downtown, not any of the narcs. After interrogation, Zas was let go—innocent in the eyes of the law. In the eyes of his neighbors, he looked more like trouble, and the marine and his wife were not alone in giving him the cold shoulder.

Zas really didn't need neighbors. He thought of himself as kind of a loner, as the pirate flag seemed to suggest. Besides, he had his mother and his grandmother to care for, right across Dauphine in adjacent houses. The two buildings were a sort of compound with a central courtyard and a slip to park in. Zas had his trusty Jack Russell terrier, Terra. And he had steady work as an audiovisual tech, much of it tied to the convention business.

The women were a job in themselves: Basque immigrants with not a lot of proficiency in English. (Zas was born in Madrid, but had lived in New Orleans since infancy.) And the grandmother was bedridden and on oxygen. Those might have been reasons to get out of town ahead of Katrina. They also were logistical challenges that contributed to Zas's decision to sit tight and ride out the storm. They had food and water, and on his omnipresent Blackberry, Zas could flick back and forth between music and Internet news even after the electricity failed.

By Thursday, three days after the storm, he didn't need the Blackberry to know the situation was deteriorating fast. A huge riverfront warehouse about ten blocks away had gone up in flames, torched by looters, as best as anyone could tell, and the fireboats and helicopters had been unable to put the fire out. More immediately at hand, rescue boats had begun dumping the bedraggled and sometimes dying residents of the disastrously flooded Lower Ninth onto Poland Street two blocks away. From Poland, the Bywater street that ran along the Industrial Canal, those capable of walking had begun the long trek to the Superdome or the convention center, taking what they needed where they could find it, and some with an eye out for additional opportunities, Zas feared as he watched the survivors straggling down Dauphine.

The floods that had swept away so much of New Orleans also seemed to have stripped Zas of his customary inhibitions and tendency to isolate himself socially. That same Thursday he found himself scrawling a notice in chalk on the wall of Sugar Park Tavern, a pizza joint and watering hole at the center of life and commerce in that part of Bywater. Steve Polier and Shannon Stith, the couple from Brooklyn who ran the place, had evacuated, or the tavern might have been the meeting hall. Instead, in another major social realignment brought on by the crisis, the ex-marine got over himself and actually spoke to his next-door neighbor. Bower, now a dispatcher for a New Orleans taxi fleet, had been willing to concede that Zas's community meeting was a good idea. In fact, Bower's wife, Vicky, chimed in, they could have it at their place.

About forty people showed up, and one of the ideas they kicked around was implemented immediately: setting out fifty-five-gallon drums on street corners and building bonfires in them, both to provide illumination in the pitch-black electricity-less night, and also to signal to the forces of chaos that Bywater, at least this little corner of it, had its shit together. It was further resolved that Jimmy's Food Store, the beer, milk, and cigarette shop right across France Street from Sugar Park Tavern, should be protected against looters—if only because the assembled residents might need to loot it themselves when their own supplies ran down. For the time being it was their larder and storehouse and should not be touched, all agreed.

It was a promising start and also, as became suddenly much clearer the following morning, Friday, a last hurrah. Overnight the last vestiges of civic order had disintegrated. Zas woke to find neighbors who had hung tough the night before now making hurried plans to get out of the city. Tony and Vicky Bower were among them, and as for any lingering bad blood between them and Zas, bygones were now bygones. "Dude, I don't know what you plan to do, but thank you for what you have done so far," Bower said as he took leave of Zas and the neighborhood they both had called home. With that, he pressed a single-shot .22 rifle into Zas's hands—"You'll need it."

The notion of husbanding the corner store inventory a little longer had also lost favor overnight. Neighbors were preparing to break in when cousins of the owner, Ray Khalaileh, drove up. Zas offered to try to protect the place, but he told the cousins they probably needed to make a decision: either dispense the food or prepare to see the store looted. The cousins took off to look for Khalaileh, and when they didn't return, Zas knew it was just a matter of time before the store was picked clean. If it had to happen, better the process should be orderly, he decided. To that end, he approached four young men milling about in obvious anticipation of being among the first inside. "Dude, we have a dilemma," he said to the alpha male in the group. "This store is going down. I'm not going to say go in and rob, but you can help me make sure it doesn't get out of hand."

One of the men darted home, a distance of a few blocks, and returned with an AK-47, which he brandished as a mute warning that things had better not get too crazy. A bystander produced a crowbar, and moments later the wood barked as the lock was pried off and the doors swung open.

At first, anyway, the looting was orderly. People mostly followed Zas's injunction to take only what they needed. When a young woman snatched a bag of phone cards, he reminded her that she'd have to get them authorized before she could use them, and she sheepishly put them back.

At one point a cop drove up, a cop who remembered Zas from the narcotics raid and his interrogation downtown. "How's it going, Robert?" Under the circumstances, being on a first-name basis with the police was not exactly a boon, but the cop was cool. "You gotta do what you gotta do," he said, sizing up the looting operation before driving off.

In due course, the looting was less systematic, and then all of a sudden there wasn't a blessed thing left. Ray Khalaileh would be stoic about it when he finally got back to his shop four weeks later and started putting the pieces of his business life back together. Unhappy with his carrier, he had canceled insurance on the store not many weeks prior to the hurricane and was still shopping for a replacement policy when Katrina hit. "I just took the loss," he would say of this misfortune. A Palestinian Arab who had grown up in Jerusalem and Ramallah, Khalaileh knew about the vicissitudes of life, and this was just one more of them, a serious blow but no worse than the decimation of the three thousand square foot home in Chalmette he had provided for his extended family, or the damage to the four rental apartments he had acquired since moving to New Orleans in 1991, fresh out of a Jerusalem high school.

As Katrina and the looters knocked over his modest holdings, Khalaileh, thirty-five, was holed up in the Chalmette High School gym. He had been sipping tea at home on Monday morning when his wife's scream alerted him to the suddenly rising water all around their house and, soon, inside it. He and her brother had swum out into the floodwaters to round up any boats not already requisitioned. After putting his wife, Linda, and their younger kids in a passing outboard heading to higher ground—wherever that might prove to be—the men had gone door-to-door in a smaller craft, rescuing those trapped inside. Exhausted, Khalaileh had staggered into the gymnasium as dusk fell over Chalmette, uncertain what had become of Linda, their kids, and her father—and there she was. "She starts to cry," Khalaileh says, in faintly accented English. "She is looking at me and I am looking at her. She says, 'What are we going to do?'" Conditions in the gym—now crowded with more than a thousand of his fellow Chalmetians—weren't much of an improvement on the Superdome, from what Khalaileh would later hear. "People are coming in with broken bones, people are dying. No air-conditioning." Those were first impressions. On further reflection, Khalaileh decided against eating any of the limited food the shelter was supplying, partly because he could not trust its safety, partly because the thought of having to relieve himself in the already Augean bathrooms was more than he could bear. He subsisted on water and sticks of beef jerky for four days before the family was able to walk to the Chalmette ferry landing and get aboard a bus that took them to Baton Rouge.

Back on an all-but-deserted Dauphine Street, Zas, like other holdouts, had gone into survivalist mode, and maybe he had gone just a bit wiggy as well. In the storm's aftermath, he had looped razor wire around the two-house compound occupied by his mother and his ailing grandmother. This, he had decided, was his "first perimeter," a designation he extended to the space behind the adjacent Sugar Park Tavern, which he also rimmed with wire. The entire block was his "second perimeter," he decided, and so he secured every point of access—every driveway and doorway and back alley—with plastic tie straps, the type used for wristband name tags in hospitals. He knew better than to think the flimsy plastic was impenetrable. As with the bonfires, now extinguished, the idea was to signal occupancy, and in a world providing many opportunities for pillage, he hoped it might be just enough to cue the bad guys to try somewhere else.

Bywater was not alone in having a Robert Zas to haunt its mostly empty streets. Self-appointed sentinels—Malik Rahim for one—remained behind in other unflooded neighborhoods. Twenty-five blocks upriver from Zas's lookout, a nightclub operator named Kenny Claiborne declared himself "Radio Marigny" and blasted generator-powered music from speakers on his porch on Chartres Street to fill the void in a neighborhood too empty without it. There was Clarence Rodriguez, who, against considerable odds, hung on in the Ninth Ward and, after the waters receded, found a contentment that soothed his sometimes troubled soul, while he also kept an eye out for looters. At the far end of the city, in Uptown's most fashionable district, a silk-stocking lawyer named Ashton O'Dwyer took up a sentinel's post on his vast front porch, bantered with passing journalists, and plotted the lawsuit for countless billions that he planned to bring against the army corps on behalf of the citizens of New Orleans. His neighbor Jimmy Reiss, who would shortly be named to the mayor's BNOB Commission, preferred more traditional protection: a posse of well-armed men in black, agents of an Israeli security company that he brought in by helicopter and paid handsomely— $200 an hour was the going rate—to guard his very fine home.

Meanwhile back in Bywater, Zas for no money at all checked his plastic ties to see if anyone had busted past one. At night, he patrolled the rooftops along his mother's side of Dauphine, using the backyard pecan tree, which had fallen onto her roof, as a ladder, one he scaled with his gun in one hand and Terra, the Jack Russell terrier, in the other. For reasons that might seem to have had more emotional than practical value, he began secreting little stashes of .22 pellets here and there along the roofline.

By day, Zas passed the hours sitting on the front stoop—stoop-sitting being a venerable New Orleans pastime usually pursued without the prominent display of a rifle. Down the street, the young man with the AK-47 did the same thing. Police challenged neither man's right to bear arms, though elsewhere in a city, falling to looters, at Nagin's behest the NOPD began confiscating every weapon they could find—an indifference to the Second Amendment that was met with howls from the National Rifle Asssociation and a successful lawsuit. "You wanted people to see you with rifles," Zas would explain, particularly the people still trickling up off the Poland Avenue beachhead, where the rescue boats had dumped them, hungry people, angry people, people who had lost any illusion that the governments of New

Orleans or Louisiana or the United States of America were going to look after them or were even capable of it. The first throngs had been barefoot, as often as not. Then they started walking by in crisp new shoes from the store Patrina Peters had seen looted, and Zas knew they had learned to look after themselves.

The greater danger, Zas sensed, might be coming in the other direction: gangs of looters moving downriver from the central business district and the richer residential areas—the French Quarter and Marigny. Then inspiration struck. Zas was sitting on the stoop with Terra at his side one evening a few days into his vigil when he became mindful of the sound of other dogs barking, some near, some farther away, a backdrop to life in New Orleans too familiar to pay much heed. But under the exigencies of the moment, unfamiliar thoughts were coming to Zas, including this one, as he recalled it: "Holy shit! Here's a way to make my perimeter even larger."

Using food that various self-appointed animal rescue teams had begun leaving behind on sorties around and about New Orleans, Zas created six feeding stations at intersections in the area. Each morning, he replenished the food supply, whistling Andy Griffith's "Mayberry" theme song as he made his rounds. ("Humor was my way of staying sane.") At night, he put out water only, so the strays would be hungry and hanging around come morning. He figured he was feeding two packs of dogs, maybe a dozen in all. The canine alarm system worked excellently when it came to announcing a stranger in the area, and Zas had no doubt that it also scared off interlopers he never laid eyes on.

"It was almost easier then," Zas would say, reflecting back on a period in his life when survival was the only item on the agenda. "There was a certain simplicity. You just went day by day. I did things you couldn't pay me to do now, like stringing the razor wire. It was just 'Keep going.' " By early October a lot more of his neighbors had returned, and so too had the intricacies of urban life. "Now before I go to sleep, I think of all the problems, all the complications," Zas said.

At least he had his home, more than could be said of Ray Khalaileh, the neighborhood grocer. Khalaileh and his wife and kids had been in Baton Rouge four weeks when they got word that the electricity had come back on in the store. With Shariff, their twelve-year-old, and Nadena, the nine-year-old, in school in Baton Rouge, it would have made more sense for Khalaileh to go back down to New Orleans alone and get things started, but Linda would not hear of it. The house next to the store, a place they usually rented out, was vacant. They could live there. No electricity? They could run an extension cord from the store to power up the refrigerator and a couple of lights. That's all they really needed. The kids could commute to Chalmette for school. New Orleans might have canceled classes for a year, but Chalmette had at least a vestige of their system up and running, a single school—kindergarten through senior high—that they had managed to open not with help from FEMA but in defiance of the agency's funding priorities and red tape.

It took Khalaileh three weeks just to clean the store out. Across France Street, the owners of Sugar Park Tavern, Polier and Stith, were going through the same ordeal. They had evacuated to north Louisiana ahead of the storm, with three dogs penned in the bed of their pickup behind chicken wire, and a cat in the front seat so nervous that she had peed copiously and repeatedly onto Polier's jeans, raising a rash on his legs well before they reached Minden. After three days there, they had ventured on to Florida, and then for a time they took shelter with Polier's kin in New York. Upon finally venturing back to New Orleans in October, their first glimpse of the Ninth Ward was across a barricade manned by soldiers who forbade them to pass. They cruised Elysian Fields Avenue until they spotted an unguarded intersection and plunged through it, eventually working their way to Dauphine at France.

Their challenges were immediate and spectacularly disgusting. As poor timing would have it, on the Friday before the storm, Sugar Park Tavern had taken delivery of a big order of pizza toppings, including ten five-pound tubes of ground beef. With no electricity, the refrigerator had quickly reached parity with the 90-degree temperatures outside. More than a month later, the tavern's walls were crusted with maggot shells, and the meat tubes gave off a gag-triggering stench that was beyond ungodly. Gloved, booted, and masked, Stith and Polier eased the beef tubes into garbage bags, where they exploded anyway and then, mysteriously, underwent a chemical reaction that, by Polier's estimate, pushed the temperature of the biohazardous toppings above 100 degrees. Perhaps it had also accelerated processes of genetic mutation. The slop seethed with maggots the size of palmetto bugs, maggots as big as this, Polier said, pinching his index finger below the first joint. And it was their color that made the gargantuan insects truly bizarre: a translucent blue on the back and pale white on their bellies. "I'd never seen anything like it in my life," Polier said.

Now what to do with the stuff? Stith located a dumpster behind the Pentagon's emptied-out Naval Support Activity base on Poland at the river, a multi-story office complex that ran the better part of two blocks. The tavern owners drove the bags over in their pickup and tossed them in. Appropriating other folks' refuse systems was, of necessity, a practice as widespread during Katrina's aftermath as appropriating unbought food and clothing. Stith and Polier's only deviation from the norm established after the storm was in not simply wheeling the whole refrigerator out to the curb and leaving it there, one of the hundreds of thousands that stood around for weeks, reeking pungently, until they were picked up by crews under contract to FEMA and hauled to compacting centers where they were crushed, and then to landfills for burial.

The stepson of a professor, Polier had read somewhere that taverns in the era of the American Revolution were more than grog shops. Mail was delivered there; indeed colonial towns could not get a charter if they didn't have a tavern to serve as the political hub and communications center, Polier said. That was kind of Sugar Park Tavern's role in post-Katrina Bywater, as it had been for the pizza joint Stith and Polier operated in Brooklyn's Williamsburg section before they became sickened by the yuppie invasion and, disenchanted with New York, fell in love with New Orleans. In addition to revitalizing their bar and pizza business, Stith and Polier fired up sidewalk grills and served free chicken and burgers to the neighborhood as it began repopulating.

By mid-October, Ray Khalaileh's corner grocery was back up and running as well, though not with much help from his landlord and certainly with none from the city or the feds or the local utility—which had declared bankruptcy before Katrina's winds had even died down. Entergy New Orleans now treated much of the city to rolling blackouts as it nursed along an infrastructure it seemed reluctant to repair without first finding out if the feds would cover the cost. On his own initiative and at his own expense, Khalaileh had put a tarp on the roof, replaced sodden ceiling tiles, and bought a new freezer. "I was not waiting for anyone to help me. I wasn't worried about the cost. My business is my life, and if I didn't do these things, I wouldn't make it," Khalaileh said.

The landlord, when he finally checked in, had other ideas. He told the grocer he would need to vacate the building for three or four months while damage was repaired, damage that in some cases had long preceded the storm, Khalaileh pointed out. It would be discourteous to suggest that Khalaileh's landlord, like so many others, had decided to attend to years of deferred maintenance now that he saw an insurance settlement to lay it off on. And then there were all those FEMA grants and Small Business Administration loans floating around. "I say to the landlord, 'Why now? You will get your rent. This is my life. You can't cut my roots.' " The landlord said he doubted Khalaileh could make it with so much of the community gone. Then, as if to make sure, he jacked up the rent.

In fact, Khalaileh's first few months back were a bonanza like he'd never seen. With the chain supermarkets on St. Claude Avenue and down toward Chalmette still out of commission, his store was hopping. "Every day more and more people come in," Khalaileh could report in mid-November as he took delivery of another vanload of goods from two brothers, also Palestinians, who operated a wholesale business out of Gretna, across the river. "They call it the barber shop. They come to talk," he said of his steady customers. Khalaileh figured the business would trail back to normal levels once a few other stores got back on their feet, but that was all right too. He had survived.

And the city? "If people rebuilt Beirut after the war, why can't we rebuild New Orleans?" he said, grabbing a case of canned soups from the stack of boxes left by the delivery van. "It's a big deal, but you do it. If your house catches on fire, you rebuild it."

SIXTEEN

Crunch Time

Y OU GOT TO THE HOME DEPOT AROUND DAWN, SIX AM AT THE LATEST, IF
you were going to have any chance of getting supplies to your crew
and a day's work out of them. By eight, the lines by the contractor pickup
bays would be hours long. Gregory Richardson, the real estate investor who
had swum from his flooded home in eastern New Orleans after two nights in
the attic, was the type to be there at six. He was in a struggle to avoid becoming a statistic. Eight thousand small businesses had failed in Louisiana after
Katrina, the bulk of them in New Orleans. And Richardson's every instinct
told him there would be many more going under as soon as the mortgage
companies ended their posthurricane grace period and started cracking
down again on monthly payments. The banks had been decent with him so
far, but it was practically a full-time job just dealing with them. He left it to
his wife. A medical records keeper by trade, she was good at it, and many a
night she sat up with him these days toiling over the books. There could be
screwups. The bigger banks were almost like city hall. She had worked
something out with a creditor on one of the fourplexes—he had six of them,

plus another two dozen rental units scattered all over town—and the next day, someone had shown up with foreclosure papers. They had straightened that out, but it was nerve-racking, to say the least. His truck loaded with a day's supply of subflooring, a set of kitchen cabinets, and a batch of PVC pipe, Richardson pulled away from the loading dock and headed back into town, the sun just rising.

For every Ray Khalaileh or Gregory Richardson struggling to bring a business back onto its feet, there were several businesses that had already failed. Catering services that had been dependent on the now decimated convention business. Fish- and shrimp-packing sheds along a coast with no fishermen. Those were among the thousands Katrina destroyed. Others, like undergrowth suddenly exposed to sunlight by a forest fire, had flourished after the hurricane, few as luxuriantly as Home Depot.

Richardson had not stayed long in Atlanta, after the ordeal of the convention center and the bus ride to what turned out to be Arkansas. He had to get back to New Orleans, and by mid-September he was dodging cops and curfews to keep tabs on his holdings. Counting the family home, he and his mortgage holders owned forty-nine residential units. Fourteen of them were in the ravaged Lower Ninth and were mostly beyond salvaging. Another twenty-four, the six fourplexes, were in Mid-City, an area of older homes off Canal Street between downtown and the newer neighborhoods out by the lake. The rest of Richardson's properties were scattered about Uptown and New Orleans East. Every one of them was hit by flooding to varying depths, but by Richardson's appraisal, all of them were structurally intact, with the exception of one Ninth Ward unit, which had been red-tagged by the city for demolition. And every one of them had flood insurance, Richardson could report—except one. It happened to be on Flood Street.

Richardson had a certain affection for his hometown, but not so much that he didn't give serious thought to just walking away from New Orleans with all its problems. That he couldn't, at least not without wiping himself out financially, was one reason why academics spoke of the "resilience" of cities, even catastrophically damaged cities. There was a stabilizing inertia in real estate investment that, in Richardson's case, required him to rebuild what he could of his holdings before he even knew fully what holdings he still had. But for all the chatter about hastening the reconstruction of New

Orleans, from Richardson's perspective, both the government and the insurance industry were proving to be more impediments than allies. It made him suspicious. The foot-dragging at so many different levels savored of a policy decision to discourage repopulation of the city. Why? "Maybe to have more land to do what they want with," said Richardson, echoing a theory nearly as widespread as the notion that the levees had been deliberately breached.

An initial snag was that for a couple of months Richardson could not even gut some of his flooded Uptown properties because they were under lease and still furnished with his former tenants' possessions. No matter that the household effects were hopelessly mucked up and the tenants were indicating no desire to return. State officials, fearing a wave of heavy-handed evictions by landlords eager to boost rents on still habitable apartments and houses, had imposed a moratorium that was not lifted until late October.

The more ominous problem was insurance. Richardson's claims would reach above $1.5 million, but by year's end, the adjusters had settled only a handful of them, sometimes for infuriatingly small amounts—$3,000 in the case of some units that had been flooded heavily. Pending settlements on the rest, he found himself in a race for his financial life. He needed to get rental units repaired and back on the market before the banks declared an end to deferred mortgage payments and came after him.

A licensed contractor, he had managed to hang on to a full-time crew of ten men good for all aspects of rehabbing. But getting the work done was just the beginning. Then there was the business of getting it certified. Before Katrina, the city had eight inspectors; afterward, six. Yet it was after New Year's before the mayor's staff relented and agreed to let licensed contractors begin to certify a backlog of repair work that was a multiple of what inspectors would normally have looked at in a year. Prior to that, Richardson had been obliged to sit around for weeks with wiring and plumbing exposed for review by city inspectors who never seemed to show up. Only then could he slap the wallboard in place and think about renting the unit—assuming it had power. Other parishes hadn't been nearly so persnickety about requiring a government inspection, and from what he could tell, the out-of-town insurance settlements were coming through a lot faster too. As a result, repair work outside the city had progressed that much more rapidly—further evidence to Richardson that New Orleans was tacitly discouraging the revival of some neighborhoods, no matter how often Nagin denied it.

Richardson's beef wasn't with FEMA. Unlike so many thousands of people for whom dealings with the federal bureaucracy were a continuing nightmare, Richardson had smoothly collected the FEMA checks totalling $4,300 that he and his family were entitled to for being displaced by the storm. He had even—amazing to tell—managed to get FEMA to deliver a trailer to one of the Mid-City properties, a place for him to live. In theory, anyway. The trailer arrived before Thanksgiving. But Easter had come and gone and still Richardson could not get the city to inspect the electrical hookup and let juice start flowing to the temporary house.

For all the snafus, Richardson was cautiously optimistic that he could put most of his property back in commerce. Not the holdings in the Lower Ninth. That was a long-term proposition. He'd just have to see. The key was having his own crew. They could generally do a rehab for 50 to 60 percent of what the insurance companies were prepared to settle on him—if only the checks would arrive before the banks started repo proceedings and the whole house of cards collapsed. "I'm entitled to that," Richardson said, masking his anger and his anxiety in reasonable tones. "I paid my insurance every month." The banks signaled an initial willingness to be lenient. Richardson had to wonder how long it would last.

As the wait lengthened and the insurers stalled, Richardson jobbed his crew out to other landlords who were trying to repair their holdings. It added a revenue stream to his business operations, but there was a risk: defections, as other contractors desperate for help tried to lure his men away with higher pay. It was a labor market gone crazy. The $5,000 signing bonuses paid by fast-food joints in need of burger flippers was one famous symptom. Skilled laborers were hauling down two and three times what they had made in August, and the more enterprising among them were going off on their own, to set themselves up as independent contractors. Starting small, just as Richardson had. So far, his men had stayed loyal, knowing him for a decent boss, as contractors went, and that the feeding frenzy currently roiling the construction trades wouldn't last forever.

Richardson had no doubt that there was a market for his rental units, possibly an even better one than before the storm. People wanted to come back to New Orleans, if only they could. Richardson needed to look no further than his own extended family for proof. Flooded out of their homes, his relatives called every week to ask for updates on life in the city and to see if any of his units were available.

As for his own home, the house in the Lake Barrington subdivision that had flooded to the rafters, Richardson wasn't quite sure what lay ahead. Inspectors had assessed the damage at 53 percent of the total value of the house, pushing Richardson over the 50 percent mark that was the legal difference between a salvageable house and one that had been totaled. Under federal rules, a house that had been totaled needed to be either abandoned outright or raised above the "base flood elevation" (BFE)—wherever that turned out to be. FEMA was still reworking its floodplain maps and wasn't expected to have them ready until spring—which further condemned owners such as Richardson to a costly and frustrating limbo. Not that Richardson had much doubt about the Lake Barrington place. At four feet below sea level, his house surely stood below the BFE. And raising a house was a pricey proposition, especially a house like his, built on a slab. The federal flood insurance program would kick in an extra $30,000 in settling with homeowners willing to raise their homes above the flood level; raising a slab-built house would cost two or three times as much.

But there was a game being played with the 50 percent rule, and some of Richardson's neighbors were already getting good at it. Because if you went down to city hall and argued that the damage really wasn't quite as extensive as all that, building permits were being issued anyway and your property would be "grandfathered in" under the old floodplain maps. Damage estimates were hardly an exact science. The city, at federal expense, had brought in one of FEMA's favorite contractors, the Shaw Group, to do the assessments. Shaw had hastily mustered seventy inspectors, some of whom—a pizza deliveryman? a pet groomer?—had stirred outrage when their credentials were exposed. Shaw had culled the bad hires and stood by their assessments. But city hall saw wiggle room and, everyone assumed, political expediency.

When Richardson heard that a neighbor with a similar house, similarly situated and similarly damaged, had scored a permit to rebuild, he was excited to think he might soon be back in the Lake Barrington place. Surely a difference of 3 percent on his damage estimate was negotiable, and in due course Richardson would prevail. In fact, city officials candidly admitted that they had issued thousands of permits, in some cases to properties that had been declared 57 percent damaged. FEMA, however, was already catching on to city hall's permitting game. And the danger was this: Jurisdictions that were substantially out of compliance with floodplain realities could be summarily dropped from the federal flood insurance program. Insurance was already looking to get expensive in New Orleans. Indeed, some private carriers were threatening to walk away from the state. But if the federal program was also off-limits, that would truly sound a death knell for landlords like Gregory Richardson. Not only would they be fools to risk their own money, no bank or mortgage company would be willing to back them.

As for Richardson's properties in the Lower Ninth, those were at the bottom of his priority list. It was his hunch that eventually the whole area would be condemned and owners would be offered a buyout. Up to 60 percent of the properties' equity was one figure that was built into a bill by Congressman Baker, from Baton Rouge. The measure failed in December, but there was talk of trying to revive it. The bill proposed that the state determine what properties were worth before Katrina—no simple task—and then reimburse owners and mortgage holders the 60 percent. It was a bigger gift to the congressman's many friends in the banking industry than to homeowners, given the way most mortgages were structured to pay off interest faster than principal. But at least it would be something, enough for low-income families to start over, though perhaps not in New Orleans, where a housing crunch was already driving up prices. There was another reason why Richardson was attending to his more viable properties first. The decimated Lower Ninth was a landscape of deep personal pain for him. Not only was it where he had grown up, it was the place where Katrina had killed his father.

He could remember that last phone call, the old guy bravely insisting that he'd be all right. That someone needed to stay on and look after the place. And after all, it was where they'd ridden out Betsy. What could be worse than Betsy? And then there had been the gruesome aftermath: Richardson's return to the neighborhood immediately after getting back to New Orleans, and the discovery of an X marking the family house, and the inscription "1D" in the bottom quadrant of the X, code for one dead inside. All right, there had been the living to attend to. Richardson could bring himself to understand that the indignity in leaving his father's remains to rot in the house was a matter of priorities. Soldiers and civilian rescue teams were combing the Lower Ninth for survivors. Corpses could wait. And at least he had been warned. Other people, in rich neighborhoods and poor ones, had come home from evacuation and stumbled upon the putrefying remains of a family member who had never been reported dead. But this is what really stuck in Richardson's craw: All these months later, what possible justification was there for the refusal to release the body for a decent burial?

His father's remains had been identified by DNA sampling in mid-November. That was progress. With the Louisiana death toll standing at 1,057, authorities had identified 881 bodies by then, but well more than 500 of them were still in the morgue, some because they continued to defy identification, too many because the parish coroners simply hadn't completed the paperwork. February would roll around and Richardson still hadn't secured release of his father's remains. He had called repeatedly, and every time he called, he was referred to another FEMA bureaucrat. In Baton Rouge? In Washington? Richardson had heard that some of the phone work was being handled by call services overseas, like telemarketers hawking magazine subscriptions. "They could be anywhere," Richardson said. "You don't know who you're talking with or where they are."

Richardson tried to avoid the Lower Ninth when he could. "It's agony for me to go past his house," Richardson said. But for his mother, who had evacuated with Richardson's wife to Atlanta and stayed on there, it was excruciation of another kind. She needed to hear prayers said over her husband's remains, a memorial service. Something that would bring closure. She just needed to know that her lifelong companion was at peace.

RICHARDSON'S PROBLEMS WITH HIS INSURERS WERE TYPICAL. INSURED LOSSES from Katrina ran to an estimated $40 billion. But acknowledging that burden—indeed, seeking government relief from some of it—was not the same thing as prompt settlement. With the new year months old, many claims would still be pending.

Selling insurance had always been about convincing people to protect themselves from a dreaded event that probably wouldn't happen. Everybody

understood that. What you were buying was peace of mind. One of the bitter lessons of Katrina was that when it came time to collect, insurance was
also about convincing people that actually the dreaded event still hadn't happened. Katrina wasn't a hurricane, it was a flood, the private insurance companies argued. Homeowner policies did not apply to floods. Wind damage?
Yes. Rain damage? Maybe. Flood damage? No. That's what FEMA's federal
flood insurance program was for. In an age that had made a mantra of privatization, the private insurers were trying to lay off the storm's costs on the
public. With good friends in Washington and battalions of skilled lawyers on
the corporate pad, there was every reason to assume the insurers would succeed.

The problem was that while almost everyone routinely carried homeowner policies (a.k.a. fire insurance), flood insurance was both less common
and less generous. It was required only in areas identified as flood-prone,
and even there it was often canceled as a nuisance expense once the mortgage was paid off and a banker was no longer around to insist on it. (In areas
not deemed flood-prone, bankers and mortgage companies would themselves routinely argue against carrying it. It was one of those moments—and
there weren't many—when the financial officer could posture as the home
buyer's friend, her ally in finding ways to pare down the monthly note. And
besides, that left more money to spend on the mortgage itself, the part that
yielded interest.) The added problem for those who actually carried flood insurance was that settlements generally topped out at $250,000 per house-
hold, less than the replacement cost of many homes, often far less.

Patrina Peters's experience with flood insurance was frustrating in a different way. Before the storm—just before the storm, as it turned out—she'd
estimated that her house in the Lower Ninth Ward would have brought about
$95,000 on the open market, and so it made sense when the flood insurance
people said she and her parents should raise their coverage above the
$88,000 they were carrying. They complied on August nineteenth, paying an
extra premium that boosted the coverage to $148,000. Peters had no doubt
the insurers would declare the house a total loss, and was looking forward to
the check for $148,000, when the adjuster read her the fine print. The new
policy had to be in effect for thirty days for her to collect on it, not the mere
ten days that had elapsed when Katrina struck. FEMA cut a check for

$88,000. It was only worse with her private insurer. The catastrophic damage had been caused by flooding. Peters couldn't dispute that. But she knew full well that some of the damage had been caused by the hurricane-force winds. After all, she had been out on the roof to see the shingling rip off. State Farm agreed to cover $5,000 in damages, minus a $3,200 deductible Peters had arranged, to keep payments low. Keia had bought a car four days before the hurricane, three days shy of the week the policy had to be in effect before she could collect on it.

Many New Orleanians who had dutifully shelled out for "comprehensive" homeowners insurance over the years discovered in their moment of greatest need that they were not comprehensively insured. In the absence of federal flood insurance, they had no insurance at all. None. Desperation inspired sometimes imaginative legal strategies, none of them very promising. One was to concede that, okay, floods had caused most of the damage—who could deny it?—but a hurricane, a cataclysm of wind and rain, had caused the flood. Not to mention the human element—the faulty engineering—that worsened the flooding so horribly when the levees failed.

The industry held its ground. In fact, it stretched the logic of its argument even thinner, infuriating no constituency more than the shoreline residents along the Mississippi coast. Not only was the industry exempt from flood damage, the insurers argued, they were also under no obligation to pay for houses wrecked by storm surge. The collapse of a levee was an unusual event. The worst engineering failure in U.S. history did not happen every time tropical weather reached the coast, not even every time it reached New Orleans. But storm surge of whatever intensity was as integral a part of a hurricane landfall as high winds and rain. And differentiating a surge from a flood was more than mere semantics. What had happened in New Orleans was, by any definition, a flood. The water rose, sometimes with catastrophic speed, sometimes not, and then it sat there, working its joist-warping, mold-nourishing will for weeks on end. The thirty-foot wave that surged up out of the Gulf of Mexico and fell heavily on mile after mile of coastal housing, slid back into the sea almost as quickly. It was water. It was cataclysmically destructive. Did that make it a flood? And who was to say, in that exact moment when rafters split apart, the roof flew onto the neighbors' lawn, and the weatherboard fell in a heap like pickup sticks, that it was the surge or an accompanying microburst of wind-driven rain that was the prime agent of a home's decimation?

Mississippi attorney general Jim Hood, a Democrat, proceeded to sue the insurers. But Mississippi Republicans, chief among them Governor Haley Barbour, decided informally among themselves that negotiation would be the better strategy. For one thing, insurance companies had always been good friends to Republicans at the state level and in Congress. For another, Barbour warned, the insurers carried a grenade in their collective back pocket: the threat of simply walking away from states that proved insufficiently devoted to the corporate bottom line. The truce between Republicans and the insurance companies held into December, when one vigorously Republican resident of the waterfront despaired of exacting a settlement from his insurer, State Farm—by all accounts one of the more responsive companies operating in the disaster zone. U.S. senator Trent Lott had been knocked down a peg or two—and stripped of his role as majority leader—after a birthday salute to a fellow Southern senator, Strom Thurmond, bespoke just a tad too much nostalgia for Thurmond's glory days as an archsegregationist. But Lott remained a giant among Mississippi Republicans, and his defection from the detente was an ominous one for the industry, only more so given that Lott's lawyer was his brother-in-law, Dickie Scruggs, the plaintiff's attorney who had secured national fame and enormous fees by rampaging against the tobacco industry.

Lott's strategy was to argue that the heap of flotsam on the Pascagoula waterfront that he had once called his home—only a portion of his loss covered by flood insurance—was at least as much the result of hurricane gales as of the surge. "Today I have joined in a lawsuit against my longtime insurance company," Lott said in a prepared statement, "because it will not honor my policy, nor those of thousands of other south Mississippians, for coverage against wind damage due to Hurricane Katrina. There is no credible argument that there was no wind damage to my home in Pascagoula."

And just in case anyone thought Lott was simply pandering to his political constituents, announcement of the suit was followed within a day by the avowal that he might not seek reelection. His urgent and pressing need, Lott conceded, was to make more money than he could as a senator. The Pascagoula house, with $400,000 in losses that State Farm refused to cover, had amounted to half his net worth, Lott said. There was another factor behind an ardent Republican's ruminations on political retirement, Lott let on. The Bush administration's response to Katrina, he said, had been so inept, "I'm almost embarrassed." In due course, Lott demonstrated that the specter of his immediate retirement was an empty threat. But the lawsuit lumbered on, and it would not be the only campaign for post-Katrina redress waged in the courts.

SEVENTEEN

———— ⚜ ————

Sue the Bastards

THE CHANGE OF SEASONS WAS MARKED DIFFERENTLY IN NEW ORLEANS
that fall. Deciduous trees, stripped of every last leaf in the hurricane,
burst forth with a second growth of green instead of turning brown or yellow. A dead cat that over the course of the summer had settled slowly into the
parking lot pavement where she expired, was now one with it, a faint pattern
of tiger markings partially concealed beneath the corner of a dumpster. The
dumpster, the size of a railroad car, had been hauled onto the lot behind the
Municipal Auditorium, a traditional scene of graduation ceremonies and
fancy Mardi Gras balls one block north of the French Quarter, to receive the
wastes of relief workers and police encamped there in a generator-powered
village of tents and trailers. While the cat had merged with the pavement,
during that same summer, a leaky outdoor faucet had ceaselessly spattered
water onto the concrete sills around the edge of the auditorium. The washers
must have finally been replaced, because the faucet had stopped leaking, but
an identical sound continued to be provided by dried leaves skittering over
those same sills ahead of an equally dry autumn wind.

It was about this time—late November, early December—that New Orleans reached what one had to hope was the very darkest hour before the city's long, slow resurrection might begin, if indeed it was ever to begin. The initial outpouring of affectionate support for the nation's Cradle of Soul had given way to distractions, if not indifference. House Speaker Dennis Hastert, the Illinois Republican, had retreated—crawfished, as Louisianans might put it—from his notorious observation that maybe taxpayers had no business shoring up a city as precarious and unworthy as New Orleans. But others had taken up where he left off, if more discreetly. They questioned whether Louisiana was capable of honest stewardship of the billions recovery would require. And Bush, the president who had appropriated Jackson Square as a backdrop to declare before television cameras and all the world that "there is no way to imagine America without New Orleans," also seemed unable to imagine how on earth he was going to extricate himself from the failing war effort in Iraq—rightly an obsession, but one that seemed to have eclipsed all other considerations. In any event, the money had yet to reach the Gulf Coast. The levees remained largely unimproved amid signals from the army corps that simply restoring them to pre-Katrina strength was likely to be a scramble before the onset of the hurricane season, six months away, and a Category 5 defense would take years.

Walter Isaacson, the journalist and Aspen Institute leader named vice chair of Governor Blanco's blue-ribbon Louisiana Recovery Authority, had gone public with the view that the Bush administration was bungling the recovery as completely as it had the immediate relief operation in the first weeks after the storm. "It's like when FEMA wasn't that creative, and the water was rising and people were stranded," Isaacson told a reporter. "Once again people are being stranded and businesses are starting to die."

The New York Times seemed to best capture the mood of despondency with an editorial that ran in the Sunday paper of December eleventh: "We are about to lose New Orleans," the editorial began. "Whether it is a conscious plan to let the city rot until no one is willing to move back or honest paralysis over difficult questions, the moment is upon us when a major American city will die, leaving nothing but a few shells for tourists to visit like a museum.

". . . At this moment, the reconstruction is a rudderless ship," the *Times* went on to say. "There is no effective leadership that we can identify. How many people could even name the president's liaison for the reconstruction effort, Donald Powell?"

The *Times* put the price tag for protection against a Category 5 hurricane at $32 billion—"a lot of money," the editorial acknowledged, while noting that it was little more than 1 percent of the federal budget and a tenth of the money spent on "the war on terror," Iraq and Afghanistan included.

The editorial saved its harshest insinuations for the end:

"Maybe America does not want to rebuild New Orleans. Maybe we have decided that the deficits are too large and the money too scarce, and that it is better just to look the other way until the city withers and disappears. If that is truly the case, then it is incumbent on President Bush and Congress to admit it, and organize a real plan to help the dislocated residents resettle into new homes. The communities that opened their hearts to the Katrina refugees need to know that their short-term act of charity has turned into a permanent commitment.

"If the rest of the nation has decided it is too expensive to give the people of New Orleans a chance at renewal, we have to tell them so. We must tell them we spent our rainy-day fund on a costly stalemate in Iraq, that we gave it away in tax cuts for wealthy families and shareholders. We must tell them America is too broke and too weak to rebuild one of its great cities.

"Our nation would then look like a feeble giant indeed. But whether we admit it or not, this is our choice to make. We decide whether New Orleans lives or dies."

Maybe the message got through. Four days after the premonitory requiem for New Orleans on the *Times*'s editorial page, through its nuncio Don Powell, the Bush administration threw in an extra $1.5 billion, doubling the president's earlier commitment for levee repair. The money, Powell said, would bring the levees within a couple of years to the strength they were supposed to have had before Katrina: enough to stand up to a fast moving Category 3 storm. To that end, pumps would be placed at the lakefront mouths of the drainage canals, first on an interim basis and then permanently once the sheet piling plugging the canal mouths had been replaced with gates. Where necessary, levees might eventually be armored with rock and concrete, reducing the chances of their simply washing away again. A small part of the money—$250 million—would be dedicated to coastal restoration. Levees that had subsided would be brought back up to their proper heights, and the whole system would be probed to determine if other parts of the chain now constituted the weak link that would be the next to fail. Category 5 protection? Maybe, maybe not. Four million dollars were dedicated to a study of what, if anything, should be done beyond the measures already announced.

Whether intentionally or by default, the delay worked to Bush's advantage. By waiting awhile, he had been able to deliver less. A month, two months earlier, New Orleans had been rock-solid on only one thing: the need for Category 5 levees. Bush had asked Louisiana to speak with one voice, and the Category 5 storm protection was at the top of every commission's agenda. Every politician had spoken of it as the first principle of the one true faith. Without Category 5 storm protection, the city could not be revived. What business investor would settle for less?

But the intervening period of limbo—the fear that perhaps New Orleans had been forgotten altogether or that its past sins were so egregious as to cost it any sympathy among the Republicans in Congress—had wrought a sea change. The Bush plan masqueraded as a grand and generous allocation, when on inspection it was a rejiggering of funds already appropriated. Even the usually skeptical men and women of the media were temporarily beguiled. The clamor for Category 5 protection had been subdued by a stalling tactic. There would be a study, perhaps even a resolution to build a system able to resist big storms. But it would have to be funded incrementally over the years, by Congresses less and less able to remember the horrors that, just months after Katrina, many on the Hill already found less than compelling.

It was a jujitsu approach to leadership, a matter of feints and dodges. You could call it deference to future decision-makers, or you could call it buck-passing. But the effect was the same, and it was reminiscent of nothing so much as the daisy chain of shrugged responsibilities that had seen the corps use Water Board soil borings to build a system whose integrity was left to the levee board's grass-cutting crews and a roomful of political hacks eating crab cakes on the public's dime.

It was in this climate of gathering despair that thoughts began to turn from supplication to confiscation. If the feds weren't going to bail out

Louisiana and its largest city, then maybe it was time for Louisiana to re-mind the feds just what was at stake here. One suggestion was to slap a con-fiscatory tax on the substantial portion of the nation's petroleum imports and gasoline refining that passed through the state. Gas at five dollars a gallon would have a focusing effect on the national debate, it was argued, and meanwhile, the revenues could be used to build our own goddamn levee sys-tem—a good one this time, no thanks to the corps. Wouldn't a tax like that simply make the refining industry want to pack up and leave Louisiana? Of course it would, proponents acknowledged. But where were the refiners going to go? And how fast did they think they could get there? Not many states were as open to them as Louisiana. And the permitting process for constructing a new refinery could take a decade.

Then there was plan B: Sue the bastards.

There were a lot of reasons why practically no big businesses were headquartered in New Orleans, and one of them was that a big business ab-solutely devoted to New Orleans was the plaintiff's bar and the liability lawyers who fed off it. They came in all sizes, of course, the preponderance being ambulance chasers looking to squeeze an extra few bucks out of an in-surance company if they could establish that their client had been in excru-ciating pain ever since she endured invisible injuries when an errant cab rear-ended her. (A semi dispatched by one of the big national trucking com-panies was a more promising defendant, but a cabby would do, provided he was covered and that his carrier was more or less solvent.)

But there were big players at the plaintiff's bar in New Orleans too—the tobacco lawyers, the chemical leak lawyers, the asbestos lawyers—and few of them came bigger than John Cummings. Indeed, everything about Cum-mings was a little bigger than life, excepting, perhaps, his physical stature, that of a compact, white-bearded Irishman. His family was big—eight kids; his real estate holdings, including the three thousand acres in eastern New Orleans, albeit much of it rather soggy, made him, he believed, the largest property owner in the city. The truck in which he escaped to Birmingham ahead of Katrina with his son Sean's entourage was a colossus, a Ford 350. And then there had been the settlements over the years, big ones for big calamities: the 1986 fire at the Dupont Plaza in San Juan, Puerto Rico; the

1988 explosion at the Shell Oil refinery upriver from New Orleans at Norco; and his piece of the biggest of them all, the tobacco litigation.

And so it was no mere empty threat when Cummings stood up in the city council chamber on the first day of December, three months after Katrina, and in a stem-winding harangue vowed to sue the sumbitches on behalf of the people of New Orleans and their duly elected representatives, many of whom were visibly elated by the show Cummings put on.

The sumbitches, in this instance, were the Army Corps of Engineers, not least because they had the deepest pockets around, and notwithstanding the absolute immunity the corps enjoyed from just the sort of lawsuit Cummings seemed to be threatening.

Cummings knew the law and he knew its history. The immunity granted the corps dated to the 1927 flood, a watershed event in a number of different ways. This was the flood that had inspired the civic elite of New Orleans to blow up the levee at Poydras Plantation, some fifteen miles downriver, an arrogant and probably unnecessary act that lowered the pressure on the city's levee system—and permanently raised the blood pressure of participants in all future dealings between New Orleans and St. Bernard Parish, which flooded, devastatingly. The 1927 catastrophe was also the flood, to credit John Barry's account of it in *Rising Tide,* that permanently sundered the faith Delta blacks had once placed in the region's patrician landowners, paving the way for the great migration to Chicago and Detroit and New York, and, ultimately, kindling the civil rights movement. Whatever it did for black-white relations, without any doubt the flood opened a new chapter in the annals of the army corps. Flood control, the nation had come to realize, was too important to entrust to local landowners and the sharecroppers they dragooned, sometimes at gunpoint, to sandbag levees during times of high water. After 1927, the corps would build the levees, sometimes on an accelerated schedule, and inevitably mistakes would be made. Hence the immunity—absolute and unqualified—given the corps against any suits for damages having to do with water.

Cummings's research showed that in some two hundred cases that tested that immunity, the only time the corps lost was after it dynamited an ice floe to restore river traffic, and the ice damaged a vessel. The court ruled that ice was not water, but then ice was not an issue in New Orleans and never would be. If a levee failed due to incompetence, the corps was protected. If negligence lay behind the failure—same thing. And as far as Cummings could tell from researching the legislation that put the corps in the levee-building business, these immunities weren't just ex post facto defenses contrived by clever lawyers. They were exactly what Congress had intended all along: a legally bulletproof corps.

So where was the chink in the corps' legal armor? Cummings believed it lay in finding not negligence or incompetence but criminality at the heart of the corps' fiasco in New Orleans. "Immunity is never granted for criminal acts, and so it occurred to me that what we must do is amend that statute so it's clear it doesn't apply to a criminal act," Cummings said, in a rumination on legal strategies the day after his city council speech. "And if we can, then we will be able to compensate all our citizens."

Cummings, as he spoke, was fresh back from a ride in a helicopter he had chartered to lift him up over his vast holdings in eastern New Orleans. He had returned with a grim assessment: "not a tree left standing," the trees in question being pulp wood, but once his, in almost limitless abundance. The far greater blow, financially, was that Katrina had almost certainly put the kibosh on any push farther to the east in the New Orleans development game. There had been a time when Cummings's acreage had seemed certain to be the next wave of the great housing boom that swept eastern New Orleans in the 1960s and 1970s. But the wave had come the other way, a tidal surge that had rolled in from Lake Borgne and continued west until it met the only counterforce that could tame it: the equally destructive wall of water spilling out of the city's navigation and drainage canals.

Cummings's office bespoke both his love of old New Orleans and his sense of affinity for people whose principal experience of that old-time city had been oppression, the city's black population. The walls of the room were lined with tomes, from the deep green carpet right up to a ceiling high enough to require an oak staircase on casters. But the top of a two-sided cabinet of books in the center of the room provided a surface on which Cummings displayed a collection of freestanding figures of black nightclub musicians: a crooning Big Mama, a puff-cheeked trumpeter, and so on. Sharing shelf space with the musical octet was a slightly larger statue of a thin man of indeterminate color in wire-rimmed glasses: Gandhi? Doc Cheatham? A visitor was left to wonder, and then forgot to ask, as Cummings snapped out of his reverie and returned to the subject at hand.

For an act to be deemed criminal, it is not necessary that you be arrested or indicted or convicted, Cummings said. It is enough to convince a jury and let them make the determination that something criminal has occurred. And Cummings had every confidence in his ability to convince a jury of most anything at all.

Where did the criminality lie?

"If your supervisors are asleep—they simply don't supervise the installation of the sheet pilings—that's incompetence or gross negligence," Cummings said. "But when they certify that the sheet piling is twenty-three feet long and it's really seventeen feet long, that's a crime," he said. Cummings was picking up on the allegations from LSU hurricane specialist Ivor van Heerden that, in a few days, would be challenged dramatically when an army corps crane pulled sheet pilings from the area of the Seventeenth Street Canal breach.

The corps might try to deflect attention from its engineering failure to the inconsistencies in the soils, to subsidence and to rotting stumps and animal carcasses—"egrets and alligator tails," as Cummings put it—but he wasn't buying. The root of the catastrophe, he contended, lay in a willful decision to ignore known risks and warnings.

"I have reason to believe that a communication was made between the Orleans levee board and the corps at the time this design was presented," Cummings said, harking back to the Pittman suit and its revelation that the flood walls were not lining up properly. "And the corps was told it was defective; the corps was told that if you build it, it could cause great harm." But the corps went ahead and built those flood walls anyway.

And because the Pittman communications were exchanged by post, there's mail fraud, Cummings said. And Jim Letten, the federal prosecutor, is exploring whether there might not be racketeering involved, in which case the damages are trebled, Cummings added.

And what might those damages be?

Cummings started with the deaths, whatever that still-fluid number would turn out to be. For purposes of discussion, round it down to a thousand, Cummings suggested. At $1 million apiece, there's a billion. And business interruption? That has to be another $2 billion. Insured property damage is said to be between $34 billion and $50 billion, which might seem to be money off the table—unless the insurers went under, as Cummings thought they well might, and they too became parties to a suit against a corps by then stripped of its immunity.

Like any good plaintiff's lawyer, Cummings also was mindful of the emotional damages. "What's it worth when you have to evacuate a city of 475,000? As a direct result of flooding, my daughter and her husband have relocated to Bethesda. What about my loss? Every Sunday, I had been building a playhouse for her children, my grandchildren—two-story, cedar, with a rubber ceiling fan. The water picked it up and floated it off its foundations. What's it worth to take my grandchildren away from me? With your Visa card, that may be priceless. With a civil case, it's not," he quipped. By now, Cummings was up to $40 billion in his casual tabulation of possible damages, $120 billion if racketeering was proved.

Of course, Cummings's approach was not the only legal avenue open to the tort lawyers. Joe Bruno, a bit further down the profession's food chain, had already filed a class action lawsuit seeking damages based on fraud: The corps had promised a levee system able to withstand a certain level of hurricane violence—Category-3-force winds and surges—and clearly hadn't delivered. Another Bruno lawsuit targeted the insurers. The policies may exclude flooding due to storm surge, rising tides, and acts of God, Bruno said, but this was a man-made flood. The insurers should pay and so should the man—or men—who made the flood: the army corps. Danny Becnel had hit on the idea of suing the Murphy Oil refinery in Chalmette. Murphy's tank had ruptured, precipitating the ugliest oil spill ever seen by Clean Harbors, the Maine-based toxic waste handler hired to clean it up.

Cummings was scornful of those variant legal approaches, particularly the class actions, and assumed those cases would be dismissed. But at times it seemed as though he lacked faith in his own strategy and that it might be as much saber rattling to scare the feds into promised appropriations as a serious bid for a jury award. Asked directly, Cummings did not deny or confirm that analysis. Instead he started talking about a different outcome, one in which the case was presented on the city's behalf in the Court of Federal

Claims, in Washington. If the court affirmed the city's claim, then it could be referred to Congress for settlement. This was the course of action Cummings had recommended to the city council. "I can get out of the Court of Claims in two years," he said, "while it would take eight years to litigate."

"I'm convinced that we lost everything because of this crime, and it just hurts me to think that our citizens are being victimized again, actually slandered by people in Congress saying we are corrupt—as if Congress wasn't corrupt!" Cummings noted with some satisfaction that a Republican congressman who had just copped a guilty plea in a bribery case was among those who had assailed Louisiana as too corrupt to be entrusted with vast sums of recovery money.

Another of the tort lawyers getting active could be called uniquely knowledgeable about at least one of the defendants he was targeting, the Orleans levee board, because Bob Harvey had once been its president. That a former president of the Orleans levee board lived within a block of one of New Orleans's now notorious drainage canals might have been seen as a vote of unshakable confidence in the city's flood-protection system. Or you could have surmised that, like most New Orleanians, Harvey never gave a moment's thought to the possibility that these fixtures of the urban landscape could fail catastrophically. Either way, you'd have been wrong. Harvey certainly did not expect the levees to fail, or he would not have reared his seven children in a city below sea level. But he knew full well that they could. Indeed, his tenure as president of the board had coincided with the lashing that Hurricane Andrew gave Louisiana in 1992, after the hurricane's much more serious assault on south Florida. Even a worn-out Andrew had torn holes in a couple of Orleans levees, breaches quickly stanched by sandbaggers that Harvey dispatched after running the one-hundred-thirty-nine-mile levee system in a helicopter borrowed from an oilman.

And so there had come a moment in the mid-1990s, shortly before the end of his four years as levee board president, when Harvey's dismay over yet another cut in federal funding for New Orleans flood protection had inspired him to buy an inflatable rubber boat—with two oars and a big old pump to blow it up with. It was partly symbolic, of course—a joke by a man given to raucous laughter and with a well-developed sense of the absurd, *une geste,* as the Cajuns might say, and as a part of Governor Edwin Edwards's inner circle, Harvey had hung around Cajuns much of his political life. The rubber boat, which found its way into Harvey's attic and languished there for a decade, unopened, uninflated, also bespoke exasperation.

Bob Harvey was no babe in the political woods. In the aftermath of Katrina, there were those who would look back on his years at the levee board helm as the epitome of an era in which the board distracted itself with all manner of patronage-rich sidelines—a casino, a yacht harbor, a money-losing airport, a resort hotel, a scheme to rim the city with fiber-optic cable—sidelines that either had little to do with flood protection, or directly compromised it. Of course, Harvey saw things differently, and only more adamantly in hindsight.

The levee board was not just about cutting grass and opening and closing floodgates along the lake and the river ahead of a storm, he would have you know. With only half the tax millage other levee boards were empowered to collect, the Orleans Levee District, to use the organization's proper title, was in the business of raising revenue. Had to be. No way around it. In fact, back in the 1920s, in approving ambitious levee board plans to landfill the swampy Lake Pontchartrain waterfront and develop parks, marinas, and upscale housing, the state legislature had mandated that the board provide recreational opportunities to the citizenry of New Orleans. For years the levee board had been able to count on a flow of oil and gas revenue from the vast Bohemia tract, a holding on the east bank of Plaquemines Parish, downriver from New Orleans, that had been taken over as a spillway. Now even that was drying up, a financial shortfall compounded by a $23 million judgment against the board from a rising tide of lawsuits brought by the families whose property had been seized in order to put the tract together. "If you had the money, then you could focus solely on flood protection," Harvey said in offering a blanket explanation of the board's entrepreneurial misadventures.

In late December, Harvey, flooded out of his own home and holed up in a daughter's house across the line in Jefferson Parish, was nursing a bad cold. A TV set flickered in the wall cabinet across from the chair where he sat, but Harvey had muted the volume. A more urgent focus of attention was scattered across the floor at the far end of the living room: legal file boxes crammed with minutes and memoranda and letters and newspaper clippings from his levee board years. The scattered file boxes attested to Harvey's renewed fascination with that chapter in his life, especially now that catastrophe had inspired him to sue the agency he once led.

Of course many of Harvey's burdens as levee board president were inherited. So were many of his opportunities. But the casino boat was his idea, one that he had every confidence would please his patron, Governor Edwards, an inveterate gambler. Harvey had donated generously to Edwards's campaign when the silver-tongued and legendarily crooked Cajun came out of semi-retirement in 1991 to trounce ex–Ku Klux Klansman David Duke once and for all and reclaim the governor's mansion—his last hurrah before incarceration in a federal penitentiary for shaking down would-be casino operators trying to secure licenses in Louisiana.

"Go ahead, Bob. You're the levee board president." That, as Harvey recalled the moment, had been Edwards's way of signaling his satisfaction with the idea of putting a floating casino at South Shore Harbor, the money-losing yacht basin the levee board had built on the lakefront when the oil business was booming and yachtsmen were more abundant in south Louisiana.

A decade later, Harvey's pencil-thin mustache had gone from jet to gray, but even with the head cold that December night, he had the restless energy of a man nowhere near sixty-four. The tassel loafers bespoke a regard for lawyerly decorum; otherwise Harvey had dressed down for an evening with his buddy Bob d'Hemecourt, another Edwards crony: faded jeans, a V-necked T-shirt. D'Hemecourt was equally casual, his own civvies offset by the limousine-size Lexus (black) out at the curb.

Not many days prior, Harvey and d'Hemecourt had paid a prison visit to Edwards, and as they swapped stories and reaffirmed their shared faith in the utter idiocy of the federal response to Katrina, there was something almost touching in the fealty of these two stalwarts to a fallen leader. Edwards, they were certain, would have handled this mess a helluvalot better than Kathy Blanco or Nagin or any of that lot, to say nothing of the unspeakable Michael Brown. "Edwin would have been on the phone with Bush from day one. 'I'm gonna say it once and I'm not calling you back, George. You get some goddamn soldiers down here today.' " And if that didn't work, he'd have choked off river traffic until the price of gas in Iowa was twelve dollars a gallon, d'Hemecourt said, warming to the fantasy. Would they have sent marshals down here to break it up? You bet they would have, but it would have caught people's attention. "They treat us like a third world country, maybe it's time we started acting like one," d'Hemecourt brayed, to howls of laughter from his buddy Bob Harvey.

The rewards of the game had come late for Harvey. Indeed, he had not even gotten a chance to play until, at forty-seven, he'd finished a fifteen-year off-again, on-again bout with night school, secured a law license, and hung out a shingle. The millions had come swiftly from glorified ambulance chasing and a series of classier tort cases that included a $4 million settlement for survivors of an oil field roustabout killed in an offshore rig explosion. Framed replicas of several six-figure settlement checks adorned the walls of Harvey's office, until it went under in Katrina flooding. Belated or not, the money felt good. The son of an alcoholic, Harvey had scrounged to feed a couple of wives and those seven kids in a series of dead end jobs that ranged from shoe salesman to medical clinic manager. Suddenly, with a wave of Edwards's wand, he was a power broker. A power broker with a rubber boat in his attic.

MONDAY HAD COME AND GONE, AND KATRINA WITH IT, INFLICTING NO APPARent damage on the Harvey family manse on Bellaire Drive, fast by the New Orleans Country Club and the Seventeenth Street Canal. On Tuesday, after a stroll through the neighborhood now littered with fallen branches, Harvey and the son who stayed with him to ride out the storm had eaten a full meal and fallen asleep in front of the television. Harvey woke with a start. His hand, the one dangling off the sofa, was underwater. After an interlude of pandemonium spent rushing valuables upstairs, Harvey remembered the boat, unopened after all these years, but its seams reassuringly tight. Father and son had soon set out across the drowned city, astonished by the sight of cemetery crypts, their doors burst open in the flooding, and above all by the silence: the slurp of their oars, the occasional cry for help in the distance, but other than that, nothing, not even a breeze. Nor a cop, fireman, or soldier. Where, for that matter, were the levee board personnel, Harvey would come to wonder.

"In a hurricane, the levee board is like police and the fire department,"

Harvey said. "They're first responders. They should never, ever leave their posts. If they have to drown, they just have to drown. That's their job: to protect the lives and property of the people of New Orleans. I have yet to hear where the levee board was on August twenty-ninth at nine-thirty in the morning, when the breaches happened. No one has said. I hear they were in Baton Rouge. I've heard all the equipment was taken out of the field yard and sent off somewhere. And where were the crews, the levee board workers—they've got three hundred of them. No one has addressed that."

Harvey had a point. Many levee board personnel had evacuated, leaving the rest in dire need of such assistance as could be provided by their colleagues from Jefferson Parish and eventually the army corps. But with the Baton Rouge reference, Harvey's real point was to have some fun at the expense of his successor as levee board president, a businessman named Jim Huey. In legal terms it probably didn't matter whether Huey had passed the storm in Baton Rouge, Buenos Aires, or with his finger stuck in a widening canal breach. But he had been heavily sanctioned in the court of public opinion after press reports revealed that Katrina had provided him with opportunities to enrich his family.

His wife's cousin, a Baton Rouge attorney named Carmouche, who already benefited from a lucrative consulting contract with the board, was now nominally the board's landlord as well, to the tune of an extra $5,000 a month for letting the board call a portion of his office its temporary headquarters. And Carmouche's son had been cut in on a juicy deal with a Florida firm hired to salvage or otherwise remove damaged yachts from levee board harbors. To top it off, without notifying his colleagues on the levee board, Huey had cut himself a check for $98,000 after suddenly deciding that he was owed for five years' worth of work over and above the stipend that levee board members collect to cover expenses. Huey had been shamed into giving that sum back and, as Harvey relished his successor's misfortunes, a federal probe was under way.

All that was small potatoes compared with the steak and truffles Harvey was aiming for with his lawsuit, a class action worth potentially billions in damages. The suit Harvey contemplated was no mere political statement. Harvey intended to win, and he thought he had found a way around the immunity Congress had granted the army corps. That would be by ignoring the corps altogether and concentrating on the levee board. It might seem to have put Harvey in the odd position of suing himself, given that his tenure as board president had coincided with construction of some of the very flood walls that had failed. Not so. The criminal negligence Harvey believed he had identified was much more recent, in his view. It had occurred on the very day of Katrina's glancing blow.

Knowing, as it should have, that engineers had warned about irregularities in the soils that made the Seventeenth Street Canal flood walls difficult to align, the board had a responsibility, one that had been breached just as surely as the levees themselves, Harvey argued. Either the board should have condemned the endangered residential neighborhoods as floodplain and compensated owners for properties seized or, at minimum, they should have alerted residents to the impending danger. The same obligation was only greater when the levee first began to fail—a mere twenty-foot gap, as Harvey understood it, that widened into the catastrophic two-hundred-foot breach over many hours. And the further responsibility of the board would have been to immediately stanch that breach, or at least try to. "I'd have driven trucks into that breach," Harvey said, bringing to mind a Dutch ship captain who did indeed stanch a collapsing dike by ramming his vessel into it, during the disastrous 1953 flood in the Netherlands. "Fill it up with anything you got, and you don't waste time," Harvey added.

"Where was the levee board and their three hundred workers and their sixty pieces of heavy equipment and their three-thousand-pound sandbags? That's what you use to plug a breach. Where were they? In Baton Rouge, enriching Jim Huey's relatives! I mean, that is the comedy of this whole thing: Water is rushing into the city of New Orleans by the trillions of gallons and they're in Baton Rouge at his wife's cousin's! I'm sorry. To me, it's criminal. It sucks and it's criminal, and I wouldn't have any problem, if I was sitting up there on the bench, saying its criminal."

Jim Huey, of course, had gone public with a different take on the matter before his lawyers suggested silence might be the better strategy. He had insisted that his wife's cousin had performed yeoman service on the levee board's behalf. And the ninety-eight grand? Huey said he hadn't even cashed the check before media exposure inspired him to public-spiritedness and the decision to give back the money.

Huey was not the only focus of Harvey's scorn. "Here, take a look at this." Harvey rifled through his file boxes and tossed a thick sheaf of papers onto the sofa: the minutes of a levee board meeting during Harvey's tenure in the early 1990s. A Colonel Diffley of the army corps had appeared before the board to lambaste the performance of the board's chief levee-design consultant, a politically wired operative who had been on the pad as long as any then current members could remember. Not only was the flood-wall work laggardly enough to have cost the board $5 million in deferred appropriations that year, it was incompetent—a menace to the people of New Orleans. The corps, Diffley said, had never seen anything quite like it. The board, at Harvey's prompting, proceeded at that same meeting to strip the consultant of his levee work. "But look at this." Harvey now flopped another set of minutes onto the sofa. The Huey era had begun and the disgraced engineer was back in the board's good graces. Once again he was supervising flood-protection work—and once again he had fallen behind schedule.

Not that construction delays were unusual; they were chronic. Within a decade of Hurricane Betsy, the completion date for the upgraded flood defense that Congress had mandated for New Orleans had already been pushed back thirteen years. Incredibly, one section of flood-wall work, on the Orleans Avenue Canal, would still be unfinished as Katrina struck, eight years after Harvey stepped down.

There was more to the corps' grousing than dissatisfaction with one design firm's performance. At heart was a strategic disagreement over how best to fight flooding. The corps' engineers—and common sense supported them, Harvey would contend—believed that the best solution was to put flood-gates at the lakefront mouths of the drainage canals: take the battle to the enemy—the lake—rather than letting it penetrate miles into the city before pumping stations tried to turn it around. Storm surge would batter the gates and sweep on down the shoreline, but with any luck it would be barred from turning drainage canals into water cannons aimed at the heart of the city.

In the mid-1980s, with the height of the whole levee system being raised in reaction to inadequacies laid bare by Betsy, the army corps had fought hard and unsuccessfully for what was called "frontal protection"—lakefront gates. The levee board, in its wisdom, had fought harder and very successfully for flood walls that would line the levees—"parallel protection," in industry jargon. The corps might have thought it had an open-and-shut case. The gates made sense not only hydrologically; at $20 million, they were a third the cost of raising miles of levees and topping them with flood walls. The rub was maintenance, a responsibility that would devolve to the levee board, as did all aspects of the New Orleans levee system once the corps had completed construction of a given component. And this worried the levee board. Levee maintenance, at least as practiced in New Orleans, was a matter of keeping the grass cut, breaches stanched, and obvious erosion shored up—familiar, unthreatening tasks already routine along the drainage canal embankments. The gates might be a trickier proposition. Indeed, and to the corps' great embarrassment back in 1987, with a busload of city and levee board officials on hand for a demonstration at the corps' Vicksburg, Mississippi, hydrology lab, a prototype gate had malfunctioned, requiring that it be redesigned.

But what really needed to be redesigned, from the levee board's point of view, was its statutory relationship with the corps. The oil crash had put a crimp in the local tax base. Revenue streams from the waterfront amenities the board had built for high rollers—the airport, the yacht basin, and the like—had also suffered, making the board more dependent than ever on the 70 percent of hurricane-protection costs that the corps generally picked up. But drainage canals were not part of hurricane protection, at least they were not meant to be if gates were properly placed at the lakefront. Drainage canals, as the name implied, had more to do with storm sewerage. Under this interpretation, the board would have had to pay for the drainage-canal improvements by itself. Moreover, the corps warned, to properly raise the drainage canal levees—broadening their earthen bases rather than simply slapping concrete flood walls on their crests—would have meant condemning some of the residential lots that butted against the toe of the levees and sometimes rode right up onto them. That too would have been a levee board expense—and also costly in political terms, once the elected officials who appointed the levee board members heard from the outraged owners whose properties would be condemned.

The corps' expertise was engineering. There was no arguing with that. But the levee board had a trump card of its own: political savvy. Here the mighty corps was seriously outmatched. The levee board lobbyists struck late on an October night as the 1990 version of the annual Water Resources Bill underwent its final nips and tucks in a congressional conference committee meant to resolve differences between the House and Senate versions. Climaxing a well-coordinated campaign, the levee board lobbyists inserted sixteen words, seemingly bland and unassuming language that in fact rewrote the history of New Orleans: "The conferees direct the corps to treat the [drainage] canals as part of the overall hurricane project."

Not only would the corps have to abandon waterfront floodgates and opt for flood walls, they would have to pay for the lion's share of the second-rate system they were condemned to build. It got worse. Consistent with the patronage-happy political culture of Louisiana, the corps would find itself obliged to partner with design and construction firms that the board hired, a cost that the board could write off against the 30 percent share of levee construction costs, whether the firms knew what they were doing or not. Simply integrating their work with the corps' designs made for higher costs—and then, inevitably, there was that portion of the work that was amateurish and had to be redone. The corps, while pretending to partner with the levee board, was in fact in a grudge match with a patronage machine better skilled at pumping out contracts for politically connected firms than at keeping the city pumped dry.

How had it come to this? How had the corps and the levee board—both once world renowned for expertise in levee construction—acquiesced in such a gathering fiasco?

Sheer corruption was a part of it. Harvey would contend he had been witness to contractors kicking back substantial amounts of money to their patrons on the levee board and the legislative committees that regulated it. How much did it cost a contractor to keep a place at the trough? "Let me put it this way," Harvey said, wrapping up a story about a fund-raising gala at which he saw a levee board contractor slide a stuffed envelope into a state senator's coat pocket. "If there were dollar bills in that envelope, which I doubt, then your senator just pocketed about $200. If they were hundreds? Well, you do the math." Of course Edwin Edwards's levee board guy was bound to attract his own share of skepticism. The Metropolitan Crime Commission, a nonprofit New Orleans watchdog group, accused him of padding the payroll with cronies of his own, and Harvey acknowledged that after he resigned in 1995, the FBI poked around in the records from his tenure as levee board chief. "They didn't find anything," he said.

But there was a malaise that cut deeper than quid pro quo corruption, in Harvey's view: apathy. "It had been so long since we got touched by a hurricane that we started to get complacent," Harvey said. "A lack of initiative, a lack of enthusiasm, on the part of the leadership of the levee board and then of our legislators, and of our country and Congress." This was, of course, the wisdom of hindsight, and, in hindsight, Harvey could also see his own place in the pattern of inertia. From his Bellaire Drive mansion, he would stroll over to the Seventeenth Street Canal. He'd see the trees and thick brush that had been allowed to grow up on the Orleans side, and the banks properly mown on the Jefferson side. "It depressed me," he said, but evidently depression didn't constitute a cure for the problem. Apathy—the blown deadlines, the lost federal appropriations, the deferred maintenance—might seem to have run crosswise to the sheer venality that animated so much of New Orleans politics, the politics of backslapping and stuffed envelopes. But in fact they were sides of the same coin: an indifference to the public well-being that turned government work into a jobs program for people who couldn't make it in the private sector or couldn't be bothered to try.

Harvey's effort had been focused more on revenue generation than flood protection, but with mixed results. After successfully luring the casino boat, many of his entrepreneurial ventures with levee board money came up craps. A plan to put movie studios on levee board property bombed. Creation of a resort hotel on a man-made island went nowhere, as did the fiber-optic scheme. That last defeat still galled him—and no doubt as well the Edwards cronies who had been offered an exclusive no-bid fifty-year contract on what would have been one of the biggest deals in levee board history. The fiber-optic cable was envisioned primarily as a utility that would attract rate-paying businesses. But it would have doubled as a flood-alert system, Harvey said. "If I had had that in place for Katrina, there would have been no flood in the city of New Orleans, because sensors would have picked up on the weakening of the levee and reported the first drop of water. . . . And it was such a clean deal, with no outlay of money." When even army corps money started to get choked off by Congress, Harvey bought himself a rubber boat, resigned from the levee board, and rededicated himself full-time to his law practice.

As it did for every other New Orleanian who survived the storm, Katrina intensified Bob Harvey's interest in flood protection, and he was delighted by the corps' announcement that it was abandoning twenty years of "parallel protection" to put gates at the mouth of the drainage canals. But certainty that the corps was right twenty years ago had not made Bob Harvey completely confident that they were on top of the levee repairs needed before the onset of the 2006 hurricane season, even the paltry Category 3 flood barriers they had committed to rebuilding. Hell, Harvey had come up with a way to build Category 5 protection by June first—and at a fraction of the cost, maybe $300 million, he estimated. At a social function a few nights before Christmas, Harvey had run into Biff Burk, one of the city's abler engineers, and Harvey had tried out his idea on him.

"Everybody is moving toward complexity," Harvey said, summoning to mind the call for giant gates at the mouth of Lake Pontchartrain and elaborate schemes to rebuild coastal marshes over decades to come. "I'm looking for simplicity," he said. Simplicity wasn't necessarily very pretty.

"What have we got: seventeen miles of drainage canal levees? Seventeen times 5,280 feet—call it 90,000 linear feet of levees? Okay, my answer to that is, you get a thicker sheet pile; you drive it deeper—seventy, eighty feet, capped at the top with maybe thirty feet exposed. There's the I-wall and inverted T-wall, but we don't have time for all that crap. We've got to drive pilings! Why isn't the corps out there right now driving pilings? One pile driver can drive a hundred linear feet of sheet pile in a day, down to good solid earth that will hold it—seventy, eighty feet deep. Then you multiply. That's three thousand feet in thirty days; eighteen thousand feet in the six months until hurricane season. So what do you need? Five pile drivers, ninety thousand feet. Use ten drivers and you finish in half the time: March."

Bob Harvey at full cry: "It's a nightmare, so somebody ought to be driving sheet piling. Then you can spend five or ten years building up the levee behind it, doing what you want to do. Put the floodgates in. But you better get us some protection by June first. By the time they go in there and do their inspections and find the weak spots, they could be driving piles. I would have the most aggressive construction project going in the world. You wouldn't believe what I would be doing out there."

Aesthetics? So what if the millionaires along the lakefront don't like staring at rusty thirty-foot sections of corrugated steel. "Paint 'em purple," Harvey yelled.

Not surprisingly, Harvey had paid attention to what was politically the most volatile part of the post-Katrina debate on flood protection: the gathering momentum to consolidate levee boards, turning the old political fiefdoms into one professional flood-protection board to wrestle mano a mano with the corps. Harvey was skeptical of the consolidation idea as it had been broached to him: a mighty amalgamation of levee boards in which every parish had two votes. That, in his judgment, was a prescription for paralysis. But a state-level board? By all means: "Each parish goes up there and says, 'We pay x dollars in taxes, we want x dollars in protection.' And if the department doesn't give it to you, you go to the state legislature."

Harvey gave his nose another blow, then settled back into his chair, silent for a moment as he thought back over the chain of events that, in his view, had led to Katrina. "But if you want to kill the Orleans levee board," he said, almost as an afterthought, "that might not be such a bad idea."

EIGHTEEN

A Comparable Catastrophe

T HE SUICIDES WERE PREDICTABLE BUT STILL SHOCKING. THERE HAD BEEN warnings from the psychiatric community that this sort of thing lay ahead. As surely as mold followed floodwater into the houses, where it sat for weeks, despair would follow disaster, once the initial pandemonium had subsided and people could take stock of circumstances that were beyond anything life had prepared them to cope with. A prominent Uptown physician—a father, a husband, a success in his profession—hanged himself in his attic in mid-November. Maybe his very attainments were what unhinged him, friends speculated. Accomplishments that might have instilled confidence in another man had seemed impossible to replicate in what remained of his lifetime, a tower that could not be climbed twice.

Filmmaker Stevenson Palfi, best remembered for a documentary on the legendary pianist Professor Longhair, also was numbered among the suicides. In his case, there could be no replication of a life's work. It was all gone: films, canisters, negatives, videos, notes, cameras—reduced to sludge by the inundation of his home and work space. The police suicides, both of them, had been as startling as any of these deaths because the men were young and because their work had brought them so regularly into contact with death and chaos. The official explanation—that they had been undone by a terrible sense of betrayal as other officers mutinied and became loot-ers—seemed elegiac, a veil draped over the more personal foibles and disap-pointments that lurk at the heart of every suicide, but it made sense. Cops, after all, were men and women deeply attracted to order, if not the law. And in the spectacle of a police force run amok, some of its officers would have seen the underpinnings of the city itself knocked asunder. The cops had killed themselves almost immediately, as though bringing to bear the hair-trigger instincts that would have served them well in an encounter with an armed desperado. More typically the suicides were the end point in a longer process of reflection and gathering doubt.

And of course the suicides were the extreme cases. The more wide-spread affliction was a generalized depression that settled over the city as weeks passed, losses mounted, and little in the way of leadership or decisive-ness of any kind seemed to manifest itself, least of all in Washington, toward which all eyes had turned. The mass layoffs at city hall had been impera-tive—there was simply no money to meet payroll. But there had been an air of unreality about them. Could a city government simply cease to exist? Surely Congress or FEMA would come crashing through with a bailout. But Congress hadn't, and unemployment checks were proving no substitute even for the paltry salaries afforded the clerks and inspectors and assorted mae-stros of the rubber stamp who had peopled the city bureaucracy.

With Charity and University hospitals shut down and the medical schools that fed off them—Tulane and LSU—dispersed to other cities, every day brought news of another high-powered doctor or lawyer who had found reason to call a place of temporary evacuation his or her new home for good. University's Dr. Lynn Harrison, for one, had moved to the Northeast, where he quickly found opportunities as both a practitioner and a professor at the University of Massachusetts. He and his wife decided to keep the French Quarter apartment they had bought as an investment and used as a pied-à-terre on weekends. Perhaps someday there would be opportunities to return to; Harrison guessed two or three years. But a man in his sixties didn't have time to play waiting games. He would return to New Orleans as often as he could, but as a tourist in a town that no longer had enough of them.

The splintered bungalows of the Lower Ninth Ward had a visual impact that drew countless television crews and, in due course, the buses and stretch limos engaged in the hospitality industry's latest wrinkle—"disaster tourism," though eventually the Lower Ninth would rise up in disgust and ban the voyeurs. Overexposure had a numbing effect. The houses knocked apart where they had once stood, or budged out into the streets and sagging on a collapsed corner sill, as though kneeling in defeat, had become trite, like the images in the first days of the post-Katrina floods of people dangling from helicopter hoists or of shotgun houses with standing water to their rafters. To connoisseurs of this sort of thing, the much stranger testament to the city's devastation was not the wrecked housing of the down and out. Poverty and catastrophe were old friends. It was the mile upon mile of middle-class housing—silent, uninhabited, unilluminated even months after the storm. The fecal-brown perfectly horizontal flood line somewhere between the doorstep and the eaves bore mute testimony to what had gone so terribly wrong for these middle-class householders, black, white, Hispanic, and Asian.

Stranger still were the abandoned flood-lined mansions along Northline Avenue, a Valhalla of haut bourgeois pretense and display fast by the Metairie Country Club. Some of the houses had been gutted by owners willing to try again, or at least concerned enough about the family exchequer to want to maximize a diminished sales price before dumping the place. But others of these marble and cypress and brick mausoleums—the ones with no signs of damage other than the telling flood line—had been thrown onto the market without so much as a nostalgic last visit from the evacuated burghers who had once called them home, a neighbor said. There was an angry undertone to it—a signal of contempt for a jurisdiction that would allow this sort of thing to happen. It was also a way to assert financial indifference. Life would go on, it's just that it would go on elsewhere: in Houston, perhaps, or New York, or among the horses on the ample acreage a prudent patriarch had assembled across the lake in Folsom or up near Natchez or Vicksburg. Who really needed New Orleans, after all? It had always tested one's patience.

Now agents and executors could be engaged to extract whatever value remained, and what couldn't be extracted was always useful as a write-off come tax time.

In this climate of paralysis and abandonment and worsening despair, it had seemed like an excellent idea to get the hell out of New Orleans for a while and ponder the example of other places that had undergone comparable devastation. They spanned history and the globe, from Atlantis—or whatever real city had inspired that ancient myth—to Pompeii. From Lisbon, after the terrible earthquake of 1755, to San Francisco in 1906. There was Galveston, to draw an analogy closer to New Orleans, a Gulf shipping and financial center (like New Orleans) when it was ravaged by the Hurricane of 1900, the deadliest storm in American history. There was Grand Forks, straddling the Red River on the border between North Dakota and Minnesota, inundated by flooding in 1997 that, like the flooding in New Orleans, had lingered for weeks with appalling consequences.

But Grand Forks was a small town, compared to New Orleans. And Galveston—the Galveston of the historic storm—was a long-ago town. To understand the contemporary prospects for recovery in a city comparable to New Orleans both in size and in the scope of its devastation, a visit to Kobe, Japan, suggested itself. Among other points of appeal just then, Kobe was a city about as far from New Orleans as it was possible to go.

ON A FRIGID JANUARY MORNING IN 1995, AT 5:46 AM TO BE EXACT ABOUT IT— and the survivors always were—Kobe had been jolted awake by the shuddering of the Hanshin-Awaji fault, an event of ten seconds' duration that almost instantly claimed 6,401 lives and reduced vast swaths of a great port city to rubble. About eighty thousand housing units were destroyed—a figure roughly identical to New Orleans's losses—if not by the quake then by the fires that swept through the picturesque older parts of town, precisely those parts of town that had survived Allied bombing. Including all of the outlying Hyogo prefecture, 2,600,000 households were without electricity and a little less than half that number had no water. Refugees in need of shelter numbered above three hundred thousand, and in due course—but not quickly enough—many were holed up in the Japanese equivalent of FEMA trailers: essentially oversize versions of the metal boxes used in containerized shipping. Many were doomed to live there for years.

And yet a decade later, it was possible to stand across from Kobe's city hall and see no clue that the building's fifth floor had pancaked suddenly that morning in 1995 and become the fourth floor; that hulking office towers along Flower Road had broken ranks and lurched out into the street; that the massive concrete and steel columns under the elevated Hanshin Expressway had keeled over like duckpins; and hundreds of yards of the superhighway had crashed onto the surface level roadways below. A decade later, Kobe's web of bullet and commuter trains once again threaded the city seamlessly to Ashiya and Osaka and Tokyo, on a track that in the quake's aftermath had coiled like concertina wire over rail beds that had been blasted sideways or trestles that had been knocked down.

By some measures the recovery was incomplete. The port was still shy a fifth of its former trade volume, and there were scattered parts of town—blue-collar Nagata chief among them—that had not regained their former density. But in the last few years, Kobe had finally exceeded its pre-quake population, and to judge from the city's new spine of glistening apartment and office towers, the capital class had decided that, whatever its seismic faults, Kobe was a good bet for investment, at least at the higher ends of the market. The question was, what had it taken to bring about so robust a revival.

There was some comfort in the similarities with New Orleans: the trailers, and the criticism of the central government for not mustering them quickly enough. And, yes, even the looting that had broken out in Kobe. Though not on as epic a scale as what happened in New Orleans, it suggested that a city of saints was not the precondition for a miraculous comeback. There had also been a racial component to the postquake strife, in which Koreans—though a far smaller proportion of the population than African Americans in New Orleans—found themselves on guard against scapegoating and persecution. But from the perspective of the three-months mark following a catastrophe, there were some marked dissimilarities between Kobe and New Orleans, and they did not bode well for New Orleans.

Some of them were rooted in the loam of two very different cultures. A far more homogeneous society, Japan did not have to bridge the yawning economic gap that made New Orleans really two cities, a city of haves and have-nots, sometimes seeming to require disparate recovery strategies. And the ingrained deference of the Japanese, in dealings both with government and with one's peers, would mute—though not eliminate—discord when it came to planning and then imposing a recovery strategy.

A fundamental difference lay in the nature of the destruction. Katrina's devastating floods had affirmed the wisdom of the city's original settlement pattern. The oldest parts of the city survived because they stood on the ridges and natural levees that had been the city's only habitable turf in the era before pumps and flood walls. In Kobe, the Great Hanshin Disaster visited itself most ruinously on the old city, the parts that hadn't been bombed into oblivion during the war. The older city was also a wooden city—kindling for the postquake conflagration.

Another difference was education. Eighty-five percent of Kobe's school-houses were damaged, a figure roughly comparable to New Orleans's. But it did not occur to the Japanese to suspend school for weeks, let alone an entire year as New Orleans had first resolved to do. Fire had chased a throng of half-clad residents of Kobe's Nagata district from one schoolhouse to another before they finally found shelter in a third. Like the Superdome, the Nagara School quickly began to swim in its own sewage, and weeks would pass before orderly sanitation and feeding were established. And yet, within days of the quake—acknowledging that the main buildings were needed for shelter—school administrators had hauled trailers into the school yard and resumed classes. Not that New Orleans's school administrators needed to look all the way to Japan to feel ashamed. Just over the line in devastated St. Bernard Parish, school officials did not bother to wait for assistance promised from the terminally constipated FEMA bureaucracy. Instead, within weeks of the storm, they had run up the requisite millions in bills— God only knew how they'd pay them—to convert what was left of Chalmette High into a K–12 school open to every student in the parish.

Above all, the salient difference between Kobe and New Orleans was leadership. The mayor of Kobe was uniquely well suited for the disaster that befell his administration, having begun his career in the city planning department as a bombed-out Kobe rebuilt after World War II. Within an hour of the 1995 quake, Kazutoshi Sasayama had stepped into a car driven by the vice mayor, his right-hand man and political heir apparent, and as they picked their way through rubble-clogged streets en route to city hall, began inventorying the damage. Upon arrival, he summoned the city's best architects and planners and set them to work around the clock, crafting a blueprint for reconstruction consistent with a long-moldering master plan that was meant to guide long-term development. New Orleans had a master plan as well and had been working on an update for years. It would be ignored as civic leaders in and out of office instead fell to squabbles and posturing that seemed tailored more to the election season ahead than to the hurricane season that had put New Orleans's very future in doubt. Tough decisions were needed, but tough decisions, by definition, carried a political price. The irony would be this: Eventually the lack of decisiveness at New Orleans City Hall would become as galling to flood victims trying to plot their future as any of the plans timid politicians floated and then disowned at the first sound of grumbling.

The contrast with Sasayama couldn't have been more striking. "Forty-five minutes of direct observation gave him enough information to start in on the whole thing," said Haruo Hayashi, a Kyoto University professor with expertise in earthquake mitigation. From the damage he had witnessed firsthand, Sasayama was able to extrapolate the full scope of the catastrophe, adjusting the master plan accordingly. High on his agenda was a desire to fireproof the old neighborhoods by widening and straightening streets, the Kobe equivalent of New Orleans's need to raise buildings and reengineer itself with the threat of floods and wind shear in mind. For Kobe, it meant replacing the collapsed wooden housing with structures made of concrete. It also meant creating open squares and parks central to each community, places equipped with reliable water supplies, both for human consumption and as firebreaks, should it come to that again. More open space meant less buildable space. And so the plans called for construction of apartment towers that rose above the skyline of the old city.

One of Sasayama's first and most aggressive steps in rebuilding Kobe had been, paradoxically, to impose a moratorium on rebuilding anything at all. The goal was straightforward enough: to prevent Kobe from following in the footsteps of post–World War II Tokyo and winding up with endless miles of shantytowns shaped only by urgent need, limited resources, and no central planning whatsoever. The same concerns had been behind the moratorium recommended by Nagin's blue-ribbon commission, but not until months had passed and many a permit had been issued, some of them to property owners already at work restoring houses in parts of town that the same blue-ribbon panel deemed too flood-prone to be safe for resettlement. And then Nagin had vetoed the moratorium idea anyway.

Not that Kobe's recovery had been all sweetness and light. Sophisticated members of the Kobe intelligentsia, Hayashi among them, understood what Sasayama was up to and took heart in his tough stance as an early sign that Kobe was going to come back better. But the grassroots political repercussions were toxic. People displaced from their homes by the quake, a chorus joined by those dislocated by the reconstruction that followed, accused the government of exploiting the disaster to ram through a redesign of Kobe that residents might have opposed—were they not scattered far from home. Critics dubbed the government planners *"kajibadorobo,"* a Japanese term that translates roughly as "thieves at the scene of a fire." New Orleanians, straining for a political metaphor, might have called them looters.

The vice mayor was undone by the intense hostility, which also took the form of lawsuits to stop city hall. He committed suicide on the first anniversary of the quake. Sasayama rode out the firestorm and two years later was rewarded for the recovery's slowly emerging promise with an overwhelming reelection margin.

Ten years later, it was interesting to talk to men like Ikuhiro Kusuba and Sadaharu Ueno to get a perspective on what it had been like to live through a successful recovery. One rich and one poor, both had lost their homes to the Great Hanshin Disaster, either immediately or in the reconstruction that followed. Both had fought actively against the mayor and his planners, turning up as representatives of their neighborhood association—a *machizukuri*—to picket in front of Kobe's city hall. Both were now at home in the city's redeveloped Rokkomichi district, albeit in diverse accommodations reflecting their different stations in life.

A worker in a metals processing plant, Ueno had owned his home but, like many Japanese, not the land underneath it, and being denied permission to rebuild had seemed to strip him of his only material asset of real worth. Kusuba owned a company that manufactured electronic components—and also a three-story house and the land under it. Ueno had been jolted awake quickly enough by the quake to remember an old saying: "When the earthquake strikes, cover yourself with a cushion." The available cushion was the matrimonial futon that Ueno pulled over himself and his wife, saving their lives. Help came three hours later, a brigade of neighborhood volunteers, but too late for Ueno's eighty-six-year-old mother. Like many elderly Japanese, she had slept on the ground floor rather than risk the steps to a sleeping loft, and had died in the rubble. Ueno and his wife lived in their car for a day or two until they could get to a daughter's place in Osaka. Within several weeks, they were able to secure temporary housing in one of the glorified shipping crates that Ueno's employer had set up for his workers at the processing plant.

It was their home for five years and far from Rokkomichi. But through their community association, Ueno stayed in touch with old neighbors, among them Kusuba, whose home had not collapsed but which was targeted for demolition as part of the neighborhood's redesign. In due course, the community association, like others throughout Kobe, would demand and get a role in the process that transformed the neighborhood from a warren of one- and two-story houses vulnerable to both quakes and fire, into a cluster of high-rise towers. The towers surrounded a small well-tended park and playground popular with skateboarding adolescents, small children, and their mothers. Ironically, the park was one of the features of the redevelopment plan that for a time had been a lightning rod for community opposition, every square foot of it seemingly stolen from the old low-rise neighborhood remembered only more fondly now that it had been reduced to rubble and ash.

The New Orleans analogy seemed unavoidable: nascent plans—horrifying to residents in their path—that would turn the deepest, most flood-vulnerable parts of New Orleans to parkland. The areas were manifestly dangerous for residential use, proponents of the conversion argued; and aside from its appeal as a recreational amenity, the green space would sop up rain and floodwater, rather like a giant retention pond. The cruder imperative behind such thinking was economic. Projections showed New Orleans's population base rebounding to only half its pre-Katrina level within five years. A shrunken tax base would make it simply impossible to sustain the infrastructure of schools and police and sewerage and transit that had served a city of a half million. Some areas needed to be retired, temporarily, if not forever. Why not those that had proved most vulnerable to storm surge and flooding?

Grand Forks had removed housing from areas to make floodplains after their disaster. The same idea had been recommended after Katrina. New Orleans was angrily resistant to the idea, but Kobe had been too. "People complain that it's not the way it used to be," commented Robert Olshansky, a University of Illinois disaster expert, who was strolling the Rokkomichi park in late November 2005 on one of several visits he made to Japan to study the recovery. "But the way it used to be was perfectly designed to collapse and burn in an earthquake."

Over a cup of tea ten years after the quake, Eiji Tarumi, who was head of Kobe's housing department during the quake, was willing to concede—as he never could have prior to his retirement from Japan's caste-like civil service—that a greater effort should have been made to include community members in decisions that shaped Kobe's recovery strategy. But in defense of the way things were done, Tarumi made an interesting point: Prior to the disaster, government planners had always operated in a thirty-year time frame, he said. From that perspective, it had never been necessary to factor current residents into the equation because, in all likelihood, they would be dead or dispersed by the time the thirty-year plans came to fruition through the more gradual processes of a city's growth and evolution. The earthquake response required different thinking, Tarumi had come to realize. Neighborhoods were not just about bricks and mortar and money. Their vigor and resilience hinged on flesh-and-blood people, people like Ueno and Kusuba—however irritating it had been to see them and their neighbors waving placards in the faces of Tarumi's staff as the bureaucrats had arrived at work.

There were limits, however, to Tarumi's apostasy. He would make no apologies for the goals of the planning process, however indelicately achieved: a mix of earthquake-proof and fireproof towers and low-rise structures that would replace rickety traditional housing all across Kobe, one hundred ten thousand units of new public and private housing, all told. Not only was haste necessary to secure funding from the central government, Tarumi had seen himself in a race against the dangerous hodgepodge that would result if homeowners simply rebuilt what they had lost, with gaping holes in the urban fabric left by those who chose not to return. Kobe needed a guiding vision for its future, to mitigate both future seismic damage and the equally costly blight that Tarumi feared would set in if planning principles were ignored. The alternative was chaos and further degradation as already-traumatized communities came back partially or not at all.

"This is an important lesson for you," Tarumi said quietly.

Some of Ueno's neighbors gave up on Rokkomichi and moved away for good before the elaborate $840 million cluster of towers could be implemented through a mix of public and private financing—one of three such high-rise residential developments that changed the face of Kobe. But by riding herd on the government as a member of the *machizukuri,* and by refusing to relinquish his rights as a stakeholder in the community—albeit the lowly rights of a mere tenant—Ueno eventually secured compensation in the form of a rent-subsidized two-bedroom apartment on the fifth floor of one of the new towers. It was a decent place, but not as big as the house destroyed in the earthquake, and the five-year subsidy was beginning to expire as Kobe, seven months before Katrina struck New Orleans, completed tenth-anniversary observances of the Great Hanshin Disaster. After that, the Uenos were on their own. "I'm happy here," said Ueno, seventy-six and long since retired.

Kusuba had reason to be happier still. He and his wife had come out of the Rokkomichi overhaul not with subsidized rent but with title to a penthouse condo commanding a panoramic thirteenth-floor view over Kobe's waterfront—their due, the government had agreed, for the house and land taken from them to make way for the redevelopment they had first opposed.

Kusuba's only regret: a rebounding Kobe meant many strangers in the rebuilt community—not all of them quick to grab a broom and spend a

weekend afternoon in the collective effort through which survivors com-
memorated their ordeal and the political strategies that had seen them
through it.

CHARLIE SCAWTHORN, AN AMERICAN DISASTER EXPERT, HAD THE GREAT GOOD
fortune, professionally speaking, to be present for the Great Hanshin Disaster. In one of seismology's neater coincidences, Scawthorn had just arrived
in Osaka for an annual conference of worldwide earthquake experts, when
he was jarred from a jet-lag-induced slumber that winter morning in 1995.
Participants immediately scrapped the conference agenda and threw themselves into the business of appraising the damage and otherwise studying the
quake.

Kobe had been in Scawthorn's mind ever since, only more so since he
had landed a professorship at Kyoto University. In January 2006, fresh back
from surveying the catastrophic seismic destruction recently visited upon
Pakistan, at the cost of eighty thousand lives, he toured New Orleans and the
Mississippi coast. Scawthorn was something of a fatalist. City's were resilient creatures, he could agree, but their long-term survivability after a disaster was contingent on economics and the prevailing political ethos, he had
come to believe. So what were New Orleans's ineradicable claims on the
global economy? Well, tourism, certainly, and what was left of the offshore
oil fields. But perhaps the reason why there would long need to be a New Orleans of some size was its importance as the Mississippi River's southern-
most port and the web of rail and barge links that converged there. The
thought of it beguiled Scawthorn, that railroads could figure so importantly
in a city's prospects: "A nineteenth-century industry may turn out to be the
key to twenty-first-century survival," he mused.

But that still left a spectrum of possible outcomes, Scawthorn cautioned. By his account, they ranged from full-blown revival of New Orleans
as a major population center to the shrunken vestige of the pre-storm city
that would be sufficient to service French Quarter tourism and handle the
rail and river traffic. "Disaster," said Scawthorn, coining an instant adage,
"can be a perturbation or a catalyst for whatever was going to happen anyway."

• • •

FOR NOBUAKI OZAKI, THE KOBE QUAKE HAD ANNOUNCED ITSELF WITH THE shattering of a whiskey glass he had set upon the bookshelf by his futon after a bedtime nip the night before. The twenty-eight-condo complex in which he and his wife had lived with their three sons seemed to have survived the terrible shuddering that coursed through Nagata, but he yelled out to his family to watch for broken glass as they stirred in the predawn dark. Safe behind concrete walls from the fires that raged in Nagata's wooden districts, they would camp out in their apartment for months before city services were fully restored, cooking with bottled gas and flushing their toilets by hauling buckets of water from the bay.

Ten years later, Ozaki was in the Miami airport en route to Vancouver in his capacity as a surveyor and auditor with a major maritime company, when the TV news showed pictures of Governor Blanco ordering a mandatory evacuation of metropolitan New Orleans. When he reached his wife by phone, she was already packing to flee the brick ranch house in Metairie that had been their home for the past three years. They would survive Katrina as they had survived the Kobe quake, at once lucky in their limited losses—the Metairie house was a rental and took on only about a foot and a half of water—and freakishly unlucky to have been caught up in two of the greatest disasters of the postwar era.

It would be a year, their landlord told them, before the house would be habitable again. Meanwhile, the Ozakis had replaced their rotted furniture and clothing and rented a place across the river in Gretna. They had come to like the New Orleans area and had no intention of leaving before Ozaki, a lithe, young-looking fifty-six-year-old, reached retirement and he and Mrs. Ozaki moved back to the house they still owned—in Kobe. "The last earthquake in Kobe before the one in 1995 was a hundred years ago; the chances are small that Kobe will have another soon," Ozaki said, flicking a bit of lint from the well-pressed chinos he had topped with a striped open-collar shirt and a baseball cap bearing the insignia of his employer, ClassNK. "Chances are much greater that there will be another hurricane in New Orleans." But the Ozakis had no hesitation about staying on a few more years. After all, to choose another city might be to visit disaster upon that one too.

NINETEEN

Visions of a City Reborn

THERE WAS A RETRO FEEL TO THE TITLE OF THE MAYOR'S RECOVERY PANEL, the Bring New Orleans Back Commission. But then New Orleans— with its stunning trove of historic architecture and the traditional jazz legacy that infused even contemporary, streetwise musical styles—was a retro kind of place. (Even the levee system had proved to be as quaint and funky as a row of shotgun doubles along a backstreet bayou.) Could the city be brought back? Should the city be brought back? Its charms were never more powerful than when recollected from the distance imposed on evacuees, whether they found themselves in Baton Rouge or Anchorage—yes, one contingent was set down in Alaska. But erasure of the city's physical landscape also set many people to dreaming of ways to redraw New Orleans, a matter of turning catastrophe into an opportunity, not just for personal profit but also for the betterment of what was, after all, a deeply troubled town even before Katrina.

That was how Steven Bingler saw things. And he was just one of many professionals—Bingler was an architect, but also a community planner—

who threw themselves into the task not of bringing New Orleans back but of driving it forward into a better future than had seemed likely before the storm.

Bingler could coordinate the activities of Concordia, his architecture firm, from almost anywhere, thanks to cell phones and the Internet, a development that foretold the day when big cities might not have the gravitational pull over professional classes that, for now anyway, was one of New Orleans's best hopes for recovery. The first staff meeting had been a conference call on Tuesday, the day after the hurricane. Bingler was then still in Houston, recovering from the fender bender (replete with air bag deployment) that had marred his escape from New Orleans on Sunday with his wife, Linda Usdin, and two young daughters. His colleagues were scattered—Arkansas, Cincinnati, South Carolina. Staff had lost their homes, and the firm's newest hire would shortly resign to follow her husband to another city where he could pursue graduate studies no longer available in New Orleans. But, personal news attended to, it was business as usual, almost all of it for out-of-town clients unaffected by Katrina.

Houston had been a stopover for a family that had decided to turn dislocation into an adventure, not because they were homeless—the French Quarter hadn't flooded—but because there was no knowing how long Anya's and Josephine's schools would be shut down, and education was not something either of their parents took lightly. From Houston, they had moved on to Atlanta, and when Atlanta didn't quite cut it, they decided to try New York. And here things started to click. A friend in the entertainment world was able to tip them off to a free apartment, and in short order, the New Orleanians and their pet cocker spaniel, Ruby, were rattling around in a cavernous and elegant condo on the Upper West Side. It would be theirs, gratis, until the end of the year, when the woman who owned it—the ex-wife of a Hollywood film legend—returned from an out-of-town sojourn of many months' duration. When the Ford Foundation offered Usdin a job as a consultant on various of their Katrina initiatives, and a couple of good private schools—Columbia Prep for Anya, Trevor Day School for Josephine—agreed to waive tuitions and admit the girls, it wasn't Ellis Island, but there was no doubt that New York had remembered how to make refugees feel at home.

As much as Katrina tore lives apart, it sometimes pieced them back together in unexpected and interesting ways. Bingler was at the New York end of what soon became a long-distance commute to and from New Orleans, when the phone rang one afternoon and the caller announced himself as Wynton Marsalis. Bingler knew the man by reputation: the most accomplished member of New Orleans's first family of jazz, the head of the Lincoln Center jazz program, the most important trumpeter to have emerged from New Orleans since Louis Armstrong. What Bingler wanted to know was how Marsalis knew him.

BINGLER: How did you get my name?
MARSALIS: I've been knowing about your work for a long time.

It should not have come as a surprise. Bingler's approach to organizing communities around multipurpose schoolhouses—schoolhouses that doubled as community centers and town libraries and museums and senior centers and the like—had been written up in *The Wall Street Journal* and in *Time*. In the wider world of schoolhouse architecture, he was known nationally. He just didn't have much of it to show for himself in New Orleans, and there was a reason why: Bingler had refused to abide by the pay-to-play rules of government contracting in New Orleans. He didn't curry political favor with campaign contributions or bribes of any other sort, and so, until recently, when his growing national reputation made him harder to ignore, he hadn't been on the list of local architects who got all the work. His big New Orleans jobs—one being conversion of Jax Brewery from a riverfront beer factory to a French Quarter retail and restaurant complex—had mostly been for private developers. The biggest public sector job he had tackled—transformation of the old Desire housing project into rent-subsidized townhouses—came his way only after the federal government had taken over the city's derelict public housing agency and purged its staff of political hacks and hangers-on.

Bingler had seen the greatest promise for his particular approach under the dynamic but ill-fated tenure of Tony Amato as superintendent of New Orleans's schools. But then Amato had been shown the door during the death spiral that preceded what amounted to a state takeover of the school system.

The dysfunctional Orleans Parish School Board was effectively shunted aside and a private management team brought in from New York to run things. And so Bingler had gone about his business—building schools and conducting community planning sessions in cities far from the town he called home.

What Marsalis had in mind was not a new building from Bingler but his participation on Ray Nagin's recovery panel. Marsalis was only the most famous of the Bring New Orleans Back Commission's seventeen-member mix of politicians, business executives, and high-powered professional people, and he wanted Bingler to join him on the subcommittee that would address ways to recover and enhance the city's cultural assets. "Music is an important part of the New Orleans cultural scene," Marsalis said, stating the obvious, "and so is architecture. I would like you to represent planning and architecture."

In fact, the divisions of labor weren't so tidy, and the first few meetings of the subcommittee were fraught with anger and frustration verging on meltdown. The source of enmity was a group of ten or so street artists who started showing up as observers. Their suspicions were predictable: Who were these suits who presumed to speak for New Orleans culture? Were they interested in anything other than the symphony and the big museums? Why were there no mimes and tuba players and jugglers among them when so much of New Orleans culture happened in the streets?

A woman named Barbara Lacen Keller stood up and glowered at the committee members. "I'm here representing marching bands. I represent the Social Aid and Pleasure Clubs," she said, referring to venerable organizations responsible for most of the city's "second-line" parades, the high-stepping, umbrella-toting groups associated with jazz funerals and neighborhood street festivals. "We're not on anybody's radar screen," Lacen Keller said accusingly. In a moment of inspiration, Marsalis's co-chair, Cesar Burgos, a businessman and lawyer, parried her anger with an invitation: "Then why don't you join the committee," he said. Nonplussed, Lacen Keller said, well, just maybe she would.

"You bring a group of creative people together—be careful. You get creative ideas," Bingler discovered. "Sometimes these ideas are completely out of reach or not responsible or make no sense. But some of them work."

One idea that got walked around the block at least a few times before it was junked came from Blaine Kern, a craftsman who had prospered in a line of work with a distinctive New Orleans twist: the multimillion-dollar business of making the elaborate floats that haul bead-tossing masquers through carnival-choked streets. Kern's proposal was that New Orleans throw an "interim" Mardi Gras as a way of signaling the city's revival. (That it would also throw a little something into Mr. Kern's coffers could not be held against the proposal.) E-mails began to fly thick and furious, pro and con, and eventually a consensus was reached in opposition to the idea. Some questioned the appropriateness of putting energy into anything so frivolous as Mardi Gras at a time when many people were still grieving and homeless. That concern would arise again—to no effect—when the city announced it was forging ahead with plans for the real Mardi Gras that reaches its culmination on the day before Ash Wednesday. The stronger argument against an interim— some called it a fake—Mardi Gras was that it would compete with the real thing and maybe suck some of the life out of it.

Bingler soon found himself teamed up with committee member Steve Pettus, a partner with the Brennan family, the dominant force in the city's high-end restaurant business. Their mission was to contact all two hundred sixty cultural nonprofits in the city, from historic homes to the opera, and not neglecting social aid and pleasure clubs. Via the Internet, the organizations were asked to inventory damages they had sustained in the storm and to estimate what it would take to put them back on their feet. The aggregate returns spoke both of the economic importance of the cultural sector and of Katrina's impact on it. More than eleven thousand people working on both commercial and nonprofit sides of the culture business had lost their jobs, Bingler and Pettus determined. Total employment had plunged below five thousand. Seventy-five percent of the cultural institutions remained closed three months after the storm. Uninsured damage to the sector exceeded $80 million. The number of musicians in the city—an ingredient essential to the cultural experience of residents and tourists alike—had fallen from more than two thousand to fewer than two hundred fifty. And Lacen Keller's constituency—the social aid and pleasure clubs, the Mardi Gras Indian tribes, and the second-line organizations—had incurred losses due to damaged instruments, costumes, and the like that were pegged at $3 million.

Subcommittee members flew into town for some of the meetings, or interrupted more personal efforts at business and professional recovery to attend. Bingler was struck by the esprit de corps. For some of the meetings, once the dust had settled politically and members were able to get down to work, Bingler tuned in by conference call, occasionally from Marsalis's apartment overlooking the Hudson River at West Sixty-sixth Street. And it was in that same apartment that the two of them polished the report of the cultural subcommittee. The report, as forwarded to the mayor, did not skimp on costs. All told, the committee called for an expenditure of $647.6 million over the coming three years—a lot of money by New Orleans standards, but a mere 1 percent of the Katrina recovery dollars then promised by the feds, they hastened to point out. There was money for museums and the philharmonic, of course; there was also money for Mardi Gras Indian tribes who had lost cherished costumes, but the big sums were for marketing and other investments that promised a return on the dollar as well as direct support for New Orleans's most distinctive commodity: its culture. To ask, of course, was no guarantee the requisition would actually be honored. Nagin would eventually cut the recommendation in half and require that it be meted out in $100 million increments contingent on matching funds raised through philanthropic donations—assuming the state officials in charge of federal block grants agreed to fund it at all.

The cultural report was one of seven that the BNOB subcommittees would generate on themes that included economic development, schools, health care, and the like. The machinations of the subcommittee on land use would be much the most contentious and closely watched, and over the course of meetings on the issues it raised, the temperature of the discussion would rise alarmingly. But the BNOB had no monopoly on big-picture revamping of post-Katrina New Orleans.

Tulane University, the city's largest employer, had suffered some $180 million in damage to the rear portions of its Uptown campus, but Scott Cowen, Tulane's president, had plunged forward, using the hurricane as an excuse to drastically reshape both faculty and curriculum in ways that had tempted him before Katrina made the changes mandatory. And when alumni squawked about his most controversial decision, substantially slashing the offerings in engineering, Cowen stood his ground. Only first-rate programs would survive his budgetary axe, he said. Katrina had left him no choice.

The business world also saw opportunity amid chaos. Restaurants adjusted their menus and raised or lowered prices to reflect a market sharply changed by the abundance of relief workers and the absence of many traditional customers. Bourbon Street strip clubs had never done better, given the suddenly disproportionate number of men in the city, some of them soldiers, some of them roofers, debris haulers, and other storm chasers, many of them lonely for women left behind in other towns. For Fredy Omar, a popular Latino crooner from Honduras, Katrina's huge influx of migrant laborers from Mexico and Central America made for his first-ever gig as a Bourbon Street house band—welcome relief after years of scattered bookings around town and on the road. Eventually, his more permanent fan base would lure him back to Café Brasil in the Marigny.

BY EARLY DECEMBER, FROM HIS LOUNGE CHAIR IN THE CHIC AND CAVERNOUS lobby of the International House, Sean Cummings could watch the comings and goings at a hotel in recovery mode, and nurse his own dreams of a city transformed. The beautiful, the talented, and the merely ambitious eased the day's burdens at the hotel bar, then drifted by to schmooze with the proprietor. He was clad in his signature outfit: worn denims, glasses pushed up onto his scalp to tame an unruly head of dark hair, and a black leather jacket almost exactly the color of the razor stubble that Cummings somehow seemed to keep perpetually and precisely two days old. Here was Greg Meffert, one of the more mercurial members of the Nagin administration, to crow about his coup announced the day before, that New Orleans was about to become the first city in the nation entirely under the penumbra of wireless Internet access. The arrangement had not been achieved without retribution from vendors of rival communication services, Meffert admitted. Overnight, it seemed, BellSouth, the phone company, had rescinded its offer to let police and emergency management services permanently take over the building in eastern New Orleans that had become a temporary outpost for first responders during the storm.

Meffert shuffled off, leaving Cummings to mull a coup of his own. That same day, and without fanfare or even a public announcement, he and his father had acquired a prime parcel of land a few blocks away on St. Charles Avenue. It was currently a parking lot, but a parking lot with a capital *L* location: right next to the chichi Intercontinental Hotel, one of Cummings's more serious rivals for the custom of the hip-oisie—the visiting film and TV people, the investors from New York and Los Angeles sniffing for opportunity in the city's ruin. With the parking lot zoned for sky's-the-limit commercial redevelopment, Cummings's ambition for the site was succinct: a four-hundred-foot $50 million apartment tower that would be, very simply, "the most beautiful high-rise in New Orleans." No. Cummings corrected himself. It was not enough that it be the most beautiful high-rise in New Orleans. That was too easy. The New Orleans of an earlier era had been studded with beautiful buildings, including, Cummings would argue, the one he was sitting in. But the architectural heritage of more recent years was, in his view, derivative. Banal. Drawings for the Trump tower still planned on nearby Poydras Street (but contingent on tax breaks that Cummings doubted even Trump would be able to wring from the city) were "really quite ugly," he contended, a facsimile of buildings already abundant in Houston and Chicago. "I would hope the Donald would revisit that part of *The Art of the Deal*," Cummings sniped.

Was Cummings proposing to begin work immediately on his St. Charles Avenue high-rise? More likely in two years, unless post-Katrina tax incentives or low-interest loan programs proved irresistible—and the 50 percent depreciation allowed in the first year under the so-called Gulf Opportunity Zone was maybe just that. Allow two years for construction, and the tower could be ready for occupancy in 2009 or 2010, Cummings speculated, his taut fingers prodding and shaping the air as he talked.

And then suddenly Cummings's feistiness and ebullience seemed to desert him, and he fell silent. When he came out of his reverie, it was to acknowledge that maybe it was insane to be banking on a comeback. Maybe New Orleans—all too evidently a leaderless city just then and of rapidly diminishing interest to Congress—really was staring into the abyss. In the past week alone, eighty-seven Uptown mansions had come on the market, he said. Eighty-seven rich lawyers and CPAs and doctors and what-not: gone. Eighty-seven of the very people who kept alive the boutique hotels and fancy restaurants that made New Orleans a tourist draw. He mentioned Mike Brunet, a physician so distinguished that Tulane had built a center for orthopedics around him. Gone to Charlottesville and with no plans to return.

The losses of wealth and home equity and intellectual capital, they are incalculable—massive, Cummings said. As he spoke, the population of New Orleans was reliably estimated to have fallen from four hundred seventy thousand before the storm to somewhere in the neighborhood of seventy-five thousand—with an additional seventy-five thousand commuting into the city to work. Tim Ryan, the University of New Orleans chancellor known for sometimes rosy economic-impact studies, was projecting a rebound to about two hundred fifty thousand within a few years. Fifty years earlier, the city's population had peaked above six hundred thousand. "The demand side of the equation is really very scary to me," Cummings said quietly.

Cummings had considered bailing out. He could not deny it. Los Angeles was a city that spoke to him. Indeed, he had spent much of the autumn there after leaving his father and others in their entourage in Birmingham. They had driven all night, checking in around dawn at the Tutweiler, an aging grand dame of a hotel already amply supplied with evacuees. Cummings was backing his Porsche out of the parking lot when he all but ran down Trent Lott, the Mississippi senator rendered homeless by the licking Katrina had dealt the Pascagoula waterfront. And no sooner had Cummings thought better of turning the Mississippi senator into a bumper sticker on his Porsche than he spotted a New Orleans attorney named Janet Howard, the head of a nonprofit government watchdog agency called the Bureau of Governmental Research. It so happened that Howard had applied the considerable prestige of the BGR to a broadside attack on a riverfront hotel development deal that Cummings had overhauled after Mayor Nagin named him head of the New Orleans Building Corporation. His mission: identifying underused city property that could be redeveloped. Howard's group had not accused Cummings of self-dealing or hanky-panky in plans to convert the city's World Trade Center to a hotel. But from the public's point of view, the BGR had decided, the deal stank. It was too generous to the political hangers-on who had managed to attach themselves to the building back when the Morial administration first began maneuvering to take it private.

Cummings consumed a goodly number of drinks with Howard at the Tutweiler bar that night and came away pleased that they had buried the hatchet, and not in each other's brows. But that was enough of Birmingham.

The next morning Cummings had checked his Porsche at the Birmingham airport's long-term lot and hopped on a plane. It took him to Dallas. He had a sister living there, and it was in Dallas, on CNN, that he watched fires and looting begin to consume the city where he and his father had invested so much of their lives and their money. One fire particularly obsessed the camera crews, partly because they could angle in on it very advantageously from the hotel across Poydras Street where many of them were staying, partly because, in the densest part of the downtown area and with water service knocked out, there was reason to wonder if it might not spread to other buildings near at hand. Cummings's attention to the building was easier to explain. His father owned it: a collection of residential units operated as a time share, with a Subway sandwich shop as the ground-floor tenant. Another fire, larger and harder to photograph, had broken out a mile or so downriver. The TV people were calling it a warehouse in the Bywater district. Sean Cummings owned a warehouse in the Bywater district, one that he had spent the summer planning to convert to an apartment complex. It would have been the largest commitment of private capital to the Bywater area since the blue-collar neighborhood had begun attracting the first wave of artists and musicians a decade earlier. After several hours, Cummings was able to satisfy himself that the burning warehouse was not his. Rather harrowingly close to his, as it happened, but not the same building.

Cummings had flown on to Los Angeles and rented a house in Malibu. For the next forty-five days or so it would be his home, a chance to catch up with people who had gone into the movie business after their years together at Brown, but basically, a chance to think. There was much about New Orleans that he missed—the revelry, the creativity. In fact, as he stared at the Pacific surf and contemplated his options, merriment was under way at his place on Esplanade Avenue, the French Quarter mansion he had purchased from movie actor Nicholas Cage after the collapse of Cage's brief marriage to Elvis Presley's daughter, Lisa Marie. A friend had asked if CNN could use it for a stress-relieving blowout for the crews working Katrina. Word of a thoroughly successful bacchanal trickled back to Malibu. That was nice, but

Cummings could not entirely resist thoughts of just kissing off New Orleans. A collapsed levee system was kind of the last straw on top of the corruption, the failed schools, and all the rest of the slow-motion debacle that had characterized governance of the most interesting city in America for at least as long as Cummings had been alive. Of course, cashing out assumed there was something left of the family real estate empire to sell.

A friend with FOX News had been able to move about the city on her press pass and report back to Cummings that the International House, in any case, looked okay. A more incisive and rather less encouraging report on the hotel was delivered by its chief engineer, a member of a volunteer fire department in the nearby suburb of Harahan who was in and out of the city as part of the relief effort. The problem, unseen by the FOX newshound, was this: a blown transformer critical to the delivery of electrical service in the downtown area had cracked the underground vault that housed it, and water had begun streaming into the hotel's basement. The phone system was destroyed as were its administrative offices, its laundry—the list went on. Moisture and generally fetid conditions had also fouled more than half of the hotel's one hundred forty rooms. "In New Orleans, if you shut off power for thirty or forty days, it turns into a petri dish, no matter what," Cummings discovered. Damages eventually would be assessed at $5 million, of which $1 million was an uninsured loss. Cummings, by his own account, operated one-third of 1 percent of the hotel rooms in New Orleans. By extrapolation, he could speculate that the downtown hotel industry and its insurers had taken a $1.5 billion hit.

Get his father to sue the utility company for its role in the losses? Entergy had made sure there was not much point in that. The water moccasins were only just starting to bask on sunbaked shingles of flooded houses when the utility saw fit to put its New Orleans division into bankruptcy. A half year after Katrina, Entergy New Orleans would still be moaning for a federal bailout against losses that had climbed above $700 million—a burden that would double customer rates unless subsidized, the utility warned.

Opening windows and bleaching moldy joists and plaster might be part of the process of rehabilitating a lakefront bungalow. A hotelier needed big-time help. A day after he shook hands with a local construction contractor, two tractor trailers operated by an "industrial hygienist" out of Beaumont,

Texas, pulled up alongside the International House, and a two-hundred-man crew set to work at a cost of $260,000 a day. Ten weeks and $3 million later, the International House was back in business. Sort of.

The flooded circuitry and moldy walls had given way to another problem: staffing. Cummings had tracked down and continued to pay International House employees in full for the first two months after Katrina—as did many other sizable employers, though not all of them. By November, a core group of thirty-five either had returned to the hotel's service or were extended on salary to the end of the year while school-age kids completed the semester in cities far from New Orleans. One employee had died in the flooding, or so pathologists determined after linking a DNA swab taken from his baby daughter to one of the hundreds of unidentified corpses in the giant morgue set up at St. Gabriel, near Baton Rouge. The hotels.com website had solicited donations on behalf of the International House and other damaged lodgings in New Orleans. Cummings had decided to use his share of the money to seed a scholarship fund for the baby girl.

By November, the hotel was open again, but a dozen or so rooms were needed to house staffers who had lost their homes, further weakening the revenue potential—not that it was all that high. Cummings's marketing people had just come up with an appalling statistic: Before the storm, 1.1 million conventioneers were booked into New Orleans for 2006. Post-storm confirmations stood at one hundred twenty thousand—a 90 percent collapse of business in a year that, before the storm, had shown every sign of being the best the International House had seen since Cummings opened it in 1998.

Cummings had also been hit with a more personal and deeply infuriating loss. In his absence, sometime between Katrina and Rita, the Esplanade Avenue mansion had been looted, and he had a pretty good hunch who had done it. Just prior to the storm, he had allowed police onto the property, a detail tasked with providing security for high-profile visitors to the city, some of whom came by the house for receptions. In a chummy way, Cummings had shown the cops some of his own treasures and the informal security measures he took to protect them: a valuable painting by the local primitivist Clementine Hunter that he slid behind a stack of lesser works when he was away; some rare shots of Audrey Hepburn. That sort of thing. And sure enough, those were precisely what had been taken, along with a TV set and some random electronics.

But there is no profit in pessimism, nor much point to it at all when the blonde is as good-looking as the one who drifted across the lobby and just then, bending over the back of his chair, wrapped her arms around Cummings's head. Indeed, disruption is fraught with opportunities, Cummings suggested, referring to the storm and his business, not the blonde. As she drifted away, he was off again, his hands sculpting the air as he expanded on his vision of a city transformed by disaster: a "boutique city," smaller, classier, more sophisticated—"a city not just built around drinking."

A Santa Fe? "That's what Walter would tell you," Cummings said, making reference to homeboy Walter Isaacson, vice chair of Blanco's Louisiana Recovery Authority. "Walter sees Santa Fe. But we're bigger than Santa Fe, more cosmopolitan. I see something more like Seattle."

Getting there, Cummings said, required that New Orleans recover its commitment to excellence, a commodity he felt was in short supply even before the storm laid bare the utter incompetence of the levee keepers. New Orleans built the first apartment building, the first opera house, he said. It came up with the pump that drained the swamps and made it possible for the Dutch to drain the Netherlands; it came up with the Higgins boat, the landing craft that Eisenhower said was the one indispensable component of the Allied victory at Normandy. "Imagine a New Orleans with decent schools and without all the crime."

Cummings pulled himself up short, a tad embarrassed by his boosterism. Hoping for an infusion of genius was one thing. Solving the New Orleans crime problem? Now, that would really be something. "Look, I'm just a simple Buddhist real estate developer with a boutique hotel in a boutique city," said Cummings, whose dabblings in Eastern religion were informal at best. Just then another habitué of the International House bar blew air kisses his way and sashayed over to see if they would be reciprocated. "And sometimes I wonder if I'm not just Sisyphus pushing a rock."

SAUNDRA REED WAS NOT THE SORT OF PERSON TO SPEND MUCH TIME IN THE BAR of the International House or, for that matter, in the high-end restaurants where young professionals might settle in for dinner after a few nips of Sean Cummings's spirits. But it was ominous for New Orleans that by Thanksgiving, the likes of Reed had begun to feel comfortable in Baton Rouge, her more permanent refuge after the eye of Katrina followed her and her family to the fragile cottage in the woods of Poplarville, Mississippi. It had taken a while, but after scouring the classifieds for something she could afford in a suddenly escalating real estate market, Reed and her mother had been steered by a friend into a $750-a-month rental in north Baton Rouge, a 1960s ranch, close to Airline Highway but with a big backyard. "In some kind of weird way, it is becoming home," Reed had to admit.

And this despite commitments back in New Orleans that required her to commute one day a week to her job as a community organizer in Central City—a poor but promising neighborhood that had the potential to become a laboratory for New Orleans's revival, activists and their allies in the funding world seemed to think. Indeed, the prospects for Central City's transformation had never looked better, Reed thought. And her faith was shared by Steven Bingler and Linda Usdin, the husband and wife team who had loaned her their Poplarville cottage. From New York and on visits to New Orleans, the couple had stayed in touch with Reed—he as architect and community planner, she through her liaison work with foundations that had taken a special interest in Central City.

Central City's main drag, Oretha Castle Haley Boulevard, had been black New Orleans's principal shopping district in the decades when Jim Crow walked tall in the South, and the broad thoroughfare lined with department stores was known as Dryades Street. With the integration of Canal Street, then the city's premier shopping area, blacks had bailed out on the Jewish merchants who'd sold to them on Dryades, and the big old department stores collapsed, one after another, even Handelman's with its atrium of a ground floor circled by tiered mezzanines. Dryades was a ghost town by the time proponents of urban revival took an interest in the area and renamed the street for Ms. Haley, a 1950s civil rights activist. The much-delayed reconstruction of the Dryades Street YMCA after a suspicious fire was a step along the road to revival. Another was conversion of one of the old department stores into a mixed-income condo complex over an Afrocentric exhibition, performance, and meeting space called the Ashé Cultural Center. But the area was poorly served by grocers, chain restaurants, or businesses of any other kind, and many of its buildings were abandoned.

For a time, about the only action on O. C. Haley besides Ashé and the Y had been a shelter for homeless men alongside the elevated expressway that cut off Central City from the rest of downtown New Orleans. Then, early in 2005, a community credit union had established itself on the boulevard, an event heralded as much for what it said about the area's brightening prospects as for the convenience it provided neighborhood residents, Saundra Reed among them.

Reed's house on Baronne Street had survived Katrina. Sort of. The windows had blown out. Some of the siding and gutters had been torn away, and so had part of the roof, which meant rain had soaked some interior walls and ceilings. But at least it hadn't flooded. Indeed, most of Central City had stayed above water, further proof that the city's older districts, black or white, tended to be better situated than the areas that had been settled after the war. Before Katrina, Reed would have told you the house was insured for $100,000, more than enough to cover what she estimated would be $25,000 in repairs to the roof and the siding.

But Travelers saw it otherwise, once she managed to hook up with their adjuster, no small task in itself. "What these adjusters do, they call on Tuesday and say they want you to be at your house on Wednesday. There is no understanding that people are in different parts of the world." In Reed's case, Baton Rouge. "You can't call me in the afternoon and say come the next day," she said. "I have a job and a child on dialysis."

More disappointments lay ahead. Reed felt the damaged roof and walls should be replaced. The insurer would offer only a patch job. Moreover, because the damage was hurricane related, some clause in the policy stipulated a higher deductible, more like $5,000 than the $1,500 Reed thought she was in for. "In the end, I got about $1,000," she said—scarcely enough to refloat some Sheetrock, let alone replace a roof and windows.

And so Reed resigned herself to continuing the commute from Baton Rouge, while trying to figure out what to do about her mortgage, now that the bank was ending the three-month grace period that many lenders had offered storm victims.

The good news was her work. Reed did her community organizing in part through board membership on an urban renewal nonprofit called the Central City Renaissance Alliance. CCRA was one of numerous grassroots organizations that had popped up in low-income neighborhoods all over New Orleans in the past several years as some of the big foundations—Ford had chipped in with the grant that put CCRA on its feet—got active in the city, addressing problems of race and poverty that much of the rest of America would profess to discover during live coverage of Katrina's aftermath. CCRA prided itself on representing the "first black zip code" to get up and running after the storm, and with six of eleven members back in touch and appearing for regular meetings, the board was charging ahead with plans for an aggressive post-Katrina neighborhood revival.

As far as Reed and fellow board members were concerned, CCRA was precisely the sort of neighborhood association that the mayor's Bring New Orleans Back Commission said it wanted to see start up all across the city to guide the recovery. And in case the BNOB disagreed, Reed had an ace in her hand. She actually knew the mayor; she had Nagin's e-mail address and phone number and was not above shooting him a message on his Blackberry from time to time. As often as not, he'd fire right back, reaffirming a relationship that had been forged three years prior, when he'd picked her at random out of a crowd of people at a meeting at city hall and demanded to know what she thought of the ideas for a community planning project that architect Steven Bingler was asking the city to fund. "I have people offering me ideas about organizing neighborhoods all the time," Nagin said as the whole room turned to look at Reed. "Why is this better, worse, different? What do you like or dislike about what Mr. Bingler is saying?"

Reed had come back at the mayor with a streetwise answer in support of Bingler's consensus-building approach and his local roots: "Carpetbaggers come and go," she told the mayor. "Before you know it, they're gone and the message has changed." Whether he liked the message, Nagin liked Reed. He began to tap her as an ally and sounding board in his own dealings with Central City. Reed accepted his overtures: "It had been about ninety days since he took office. What else do you say to a new mayor?"

In short order, Reed and a committee of about a hundred Central City residents were working with Bingler's firm, Concordia, a year-long process to develop the vision they presented to city hall in December 2004. It called for building on the area's Afro-Caribbean cultural infrastructure both as an educational resource and as a tourism magnet that would create additional jobs. Ten months later, Katrina had scattered the committee to the winds, but the core ideas seemed more germane than ever.

The early weeks of reactivating the Central City Renaissance Alliance post-Katrina had mostly involved "pressing the flesh," Reed said. "You see someone on the street, and it's 'Hey, girl, where you been?' It is a personal rejoining." A major meeting on Central City's future seemed like the logical next step, a way to signal—to the BNOB as well as to the community—that CCRA was back and not to be ignored. They leafleted the neighborhood and got a friendly newspaper deliveryman to slide a circular in with *The Times-Picayune* he was tossing onto residents' doorsteps.

As a run-up to that gathering, in late January CCRA had a hand in a related event, conference, colloquium—call it what you will; organizers called it "Making It Happen." Centered at Ashé, it spilled down Oretha Castle Haley Boulevard and into various storefronts for roundtable discussions. Central City was the backdrop, but community groups from all over the city turned out to meet with an equally varied gamut of experts and visionaries. Big foundations were present—Ford, Nathan Cummings, Robert Wood Johnson, among them—as were MIT, Outward Bound, and Mel King, the professor and civil rights leader. King hooked up with representatives from two historically black universities in New Orleans, Dillard and Xavier, and by the end of the weekend they had decided to raise money for a summer program for schoolchildren. A representative of the Henry Ford Academy, the school of four hundred students that Bingler built within the premises of Greenfield, Michigan's Henry Ford Museum, hooked up with Ron Forman, head of the Audubon Institute and its expansive collection of nature exhibits, including a zoo, an aquarium, an insectarium, and a center for breeding endangered species. In at first idle conversations, they stumbled on the idea of setting up a Ford Academy at the zoo and the aquarium, and began plotting ways to make that happen. And so on and so forth, through a weekend that included a presentation by futurist David Thornburg. Oh, yes, and plenty of food—jambalaya, red beans and rice, fried chicken—all the good stuff that was so hard to get outside New Orleans, cooked right, that is.

(Reed's first principle of community organizing: "If you feed them, they will come.")

The second meeting, to herald CCRA's return and assess the community's recovery, was at the rebuilt Dryades Street YMCA. Reed's experience of that meeting was one of sheer "jubilation." Residents were coming back to Central City, from what she could tell. "Even when the conversation got conflicted, when the passion and anger were evident, I was all atwitter inside," Reed would recall. "It was all the energy. It was like something is really going on and people feel empowered to get something done. A helplessness and hopelessness invaded us after Katrina. Now people seemed to feel like they wanted to go right back in and start fighting again."

The highlight of a Friday night kickoff dinner at the Ashé Center to-do was a speech by Reed's pastor, the diminutive (little more than five feet tall) and extraordinarily dynamic Reverend Dwight Webster, whose Christian Unity Church sprawled through a collection of buildings, including a bowling alley and a dance hall. The church had, in a quick fifteen years, become a center of community-minded Christianity in New Orleans.

Reed, resplendent in billowy blue slacks and a pink top, her graying hair drawn back from her forehead in braids, got to introduce the dashiki-clad pastor, the godfather of her children. And when the evening's formalities had been attended to, local musicians took to the stage—a way to say thank you to the many presenters who had come from considerable distances on their own nickel, a chance as well to immerse them a little more fully in the culture of a strange and beautiful city. As the music sang out, inevitably some of the locals fell into a high-stepping second line. In a trice, one contingent of them had hopped up onto the stage and were strutting and shimmying for all they were worth, Reed among them, a big, broad-hipped woman moving like a hurricane across that stage, a woman come home to a city she would never leave.

———— ⚜ ————

TWENTY

Blue Tarps in a Chocolate City

IT HELPED NOT AT ALL THAT IN LATE SEPTEMBER, WITH INPUT FROM EVERY LOB-byist within hailing distance, Louisiana's U.S. senators, Mary Landrieu and David Vitter—Landrieu a Democrat and Vitter a Republican—had sub-mitted a $250 billion spending request to Congress, a "hurricane recovery" wish list so packed with pork that it oinked. The list included $23 million for a sugar cane processing plant and $8 million for alligator husbandry—plus more relevant targets of federal largesse, such as storm-damaged hospitals and transit systems, but in amounts that would have made the Pentagon blush: $50 billion for housing grants; $5 billion to give to financial compa-nies to cover six months of mortgage relief; $7 billion for what was called evacuation and energy supply routes, on top of $5 billion for highways—as if the state had not just been appropriated $3.1 billion for highways in an omnibus transportation bill. The request also specified $2.5 billion for elec-tric utilities and $748 million for a new lock on the Industrial Canal, a decades-old project widely regarded as a boondoggle.

By contrast, Mississippi in late September had already begun working more artfully to tailor its list to storm-related losses and then to stitch the spending requests into appropriations that targeted the relevant concern, be it transportation or medical needs.

The ridicule from commentators in and out of Congress was harsh; Landrieu and Vitter backed away from their wish list, hastening to say it was just that, an inventory of long-term needs. They didn't expect every request to be funded. Good thing. Many, it seemed clear, would not be.

It wasn't just Republicans or conservative media who jumped on Landrieu and Vitter. "Like looters who seize six televisions when their homes have room only for two, the Louisiana legislators are out to grab more federal cash than they could possibly spend usefully," *The Washington Post* editorialized. Taxpayers for Common Sense weighed in more succinctly: " 'Brazen' doesn't begin to describe it."

Vitter and Landrieu's approach wasn't criminal. No one accused them of lining their pockets, but it was in stride with a system of loose spending— "The Louisiana Way"—that for generations had fostered thievery as well as waste.

Even without the $250 billion request, Louisiana's reputation for political corruption would have hung over every nickel of recovery money Washington saw fit to dispense. And this rankled more than a little, at a time when Republican corruption was in the headlines and every day brought new revelations of stunning overspending and financial mismanagement by FEMA. But what could you do? The Republicans were in control in Washington, and Washington had the money.

It did not help Louisiana's cause that former governor Edwards was in federal prison for shaking down casino interests. It did not help that the school system in Orleans Parish had collapsed in the previous year, requiring takeover by a management team, and the discovery of millions of dollars in payroll fraud stretching back years. It did not help that over the summer former New Orleans mayor Marc Morial's uncle Glenn Haydel had been indicted on charges of swiping hundreds of thousands of dollars from the city transit agency he had once run, and that the feds had already collected a guilty plea from his wife for paying bribes in exchange for school system insurance contracts. Nor did it pass unnoticed in Washington that just weeks before Katrina, the FBI had raided the home of U.S. congressman Bill Jefferson and come away with a wad of cash that had turned up in Jefferson's freezer. It did not help that some few months after Katrina, Jefferson's brother-in-law, Judge Alan Green, would be sentenced to four years in prison for wire fraud in connection with payouts received from a bail bondsman doing business with his court. It didn't help that the region had generated some three thousand applications for financial assistance from FEMA to bury hurricane casualties, when in fact the death toll was a third that number.

It helped, but only a little, that Tom DeLay, the Texas Republican, had lost his job as majority leader and was facing trial for money laundering and ties to convicted influence peddler Jack Abramoff, the lobbyist.

But what really galled Louisiana about Washington's hypervigilance over a famously corrupt state was not so much the calumny as the evident hypocrisy. Because even by local standards, the padding built into FEMA's contracting practices was a scandal. Worse yet, a lot of the money wasn't going into local pockets.

FEMA was paying more (about $70,000 a pop) to move rickety little travel trailers into a demonstrably dangerous hurricane zone than the cost of an innovative hurricane-proof house—the so-called Katrina Cottage (price: $67,000) that a gaggle of housing firms were eager to start building en masse. FEMA cited the Stafford Act and said it limited the agency to funding only temporary housing, just as it had made funds available only for overtime, to be earned in municipalities that no longer had the wherewithal to pay straight time. In the same crazy spirit, FEMA was paying favored contractors as much to tack down blue plastic tarps as it would have cost to permanently reshingle the same damaged roof. Or, looked at through the other end of the telescope, the contractors actually performing debris removal services in the streets were getting a dollar for every cubic yard they scooped up, while middlemen sucked twenty times as much from FEMA's teat—for doing little or nothing.

The huge price inflation stemmed from the way contracts were tiered, or "nested," a practice that seemed calculated less with efficiency in mind than with the desire to stroke the well-connected industry giants who served as primary contractors. In one example dredged up by *Times-Picayune* reporters Gordon Russell and James Varney, the Shaw Group was collecting

$175 "a square"—roofer lingo for a one-hundred-square-foot swatch—for tarping roofs. Shaw subcontracted the job to A-1 Construction for $75 a square, which in turn paid Wescon Construction $30. Wescon then lined up the small-fry contractors, the ones willing to accept $2 a square, the going rate even in a tight market like post-Katrina New Orleans. Shaw's contention was that its superior management skills and cash reserves were critical to the success of an emergency operation mounted on the fly. A roofing salesman who spoke to Varney and Russell had another term for the $100 that Shaw pocketed for every $2 paid to the men on the roof. "Gouging, pure and simple," the salesman called it.

A February report from the Department of Homeland Security's inspector general would reveal a vastly broader array of waste and fraud in the way FEMA managed the taxpayer billions at its disposal. Abuses ranged from payments to evacuees for beachfront condos and $400-a-night New York hotel rooms, to the services of tattoo artists and a massage parlor that had been raided for prostitution. In addition, FEMA had rolled over for millions in fraudulent or duplicate claims without checking to see that the claimant had offered a vacant lot or a nonexistent address as his or her residence.

In defending the nested contracts, FEMA cited the need for personnel oversight, financial credit, and insurance costs as the reason why, on an emergency basis, it had turned to the army corps and, through the corps, had handed no-bid contracts to the big contractors. It was Iraq all over again. Indeed, as the House report on Katrina would note, 80 percent of the $1.5 billion that FEMA shelled out in the initial wave of post-Katrina work went to "sole-source" contractors. But a Louisiana state lawmaker who also landed a debris-removal contract offered an additional insight. FEMA forced local governments to play along because FEMA had agreed to cover the costs only if FEMA and its favored contractors did the work. If a city wanted its own workers to clean the streets or wanted to deal directly with the private contractors actually scooping debris into dump trucks, FEMA would only pay 90 percent of the costs, and maybe none too quickly. Reimbursement for the local share would have to be sought after the fact.

When the corps yielded to growing outrage and, eight weeks after Katrina, sought competitive bids from minority-owned companies, prices fell by half: $1,000 per tarped roof, compared to the $3,000 to $3,500 charged by the big companies that had already pocketed $300 million on an emergency basis.

"FEMA went to the corps because FEMA doesn't know anything about debris cleanup," said Troy Hebert, the state representative with the debris contract. "But the corps doesn't know a thing about debris cleanup either. So they turned to the big major corporations they already know, the guys that follow the corps around all the time."

In some cases, the middlemen that the big corporations turned to didn't even own the equipment that would have qualified them to do tarping or hauling themselves. It was a pure pass-along, with a generous cut for the middlemen.

Plaquemines Parish president Benny Rousselle saw enough of it to sicken him. "They say they don't want to send money to Louisiana because of our reputation," Rousselle said. "I would ask them to take a look in the mirror. If they think this is a legitimate expense of federal money, they ought to be ashamed of themselves."

The move toward privatization and the outsourcing of government functions had been billed as a way to imbue government with some of the dynamism and flexibility of business. Instead, it was as if businesses had been infected with the lethargy and bloat of the worst government bureaucracies—and by Mike Brown's own account, the Department of Homeland Security was indeed one of the worst. But not all the sins of the stalled recovery could be laid at FEMA's door.

The Reverend Nguyen The Vien had been ebullient in late October as his congregation streamed back and Mary Queen of Vietnam Church began to see service not only as a place of worship but as a public bath, a dormitory, a feeding station—an all-purpose center for a community in recovery. As a calf roasted on a turning spit in preparation of the group's evening meal, one of Nguyen's congregants spoke with pride of the challenges he had faced since returning to eastern New Orleans after evacuating with his ailing mother to Tallahassee and then Dallas. "My mom calls and asks to come back," said Tho Nguyen, part of a ten-man work crew that was going from house to house to assist with gutting and reconstruction. "I still say no. It is very hard living here. No water. No electric. She wants to see the house.

She told me not to throw any of it out. But I had to. There is a beautiful picture of my daddy on the curb."

But with generators to power fans and a freezer, and with two eight-hundred-gallon tanks rigged up to flush toilets, civilization was returning to Mary Queen of Vietnam. All that was needed were trailers. By the third week in October, FEMA had delivered two thirty-two-footers, and Father Vien, as his congregants called him, had installed them on a twenty-six-acre lot the church owned across the street. FEMA was promising a hundred more within two weeks. "We will go ahead and roll trailers out there as a little community for them," said Stephen DeBlasio, FEMA's trailer czar in Louisiana. "We're moving forward. We're in the assessment phase right now." But it would take more than good intentions to get results. Months later, Nguyen and his congregation were still waiting—but not for FEMA.

For a time, it had been expedient among New Orleans politicians to crow loudly about the need for temporary housing and to berate FEMA for not delivering trailers as promised. FEMA provided, as usual, a fat target. Nguyen's early success was unusual. For months, flooded-out homeowners desperate to put a trailer in the driveway and begin rebuilding could not seem to catch the attention of anyone in the federal bureaucracy able to make it happen. Meanwhile, many an office worker long since back home would pick up the phone and field an unsolicited call from a FEMA representative inquiring as to whether a trailer could be delivered to her residence. In the French Quarter? Well, no, not really. And where would you put it if I asked for one? Jackson Square?

All of a sudden, in mid-December the trailers were available in bulk at staging areas in Arkansas and Mississippi—thirty-one thousand of them, according to FEMA officials. But where to put them? The mayor, invoking an emergency power, had claimed the right to set them up in city parks and playgrounds. Which would be fine with the city council—provided the park or playground wasn't in the member's district. The trailers, once so angrily in demand, were now about as popular with politicians as plans to drop a rendering plant or a nuclear reactor into a leafy subdivision. When the city council passed an ordinance requiring that members be given the right to approve—that is, reject—any and all temporary housing installations in their districts, Nagin vetoed it as hopelessly impractical, only to see his veto overturned at the council's next meeting, on December fifteenth.

The council members explained their opposition imaginatively, but no one who heard their bleatings, whether grateful for the rhetoric or repulsed by it, had any doubt what was really going on. As surely as the majority of the displaced had been black and poor, so too would be those still in need of government housing—only more so now that there had been time enough for the more self-reliant to put something together back home or give up on New Orleans altogether and start new lives in Houston or Chicago or Atlanta. Of course it was not possible to confess honestly to qualms about moving clusters of low-income blacks into the neighborhoods that had not flooded. One council member, a white, spoke plangently of the importance of leaving our parks and playgrounds free for recreation by happy, healthy children. Another white council member countered the insinuation that her opposition was racist by arguing that what she really was up to was guaranteeing that whatever trailers went into her district would be for first responders. And many first responders were black, so don't go calling her racist. A black councilwoman was as noisy as any of her colleagues in running off a trailer encampment planned in Annunciation Square. But then, her district included the affluent, largely white Garden District.

There was nothing about this little orgy of race and class bias that would have been unfamiliar in hundreds of American communities, but it was unbecoming, to say the least, in a city that had been calling itself the Soul of America while pleading for sympathy, a federal bailout—and lots of trailers. The Reverend Nguyen The Vien and his dreams of a hundred-unit trailer park for his congregants in eastern New Orleans was a collateral casualty. The Asian community might lack clout, but that was incidental to the cross fire between the city's principal racial antagonists. While Nagin and the council feuded, the paperwork that would have authorized delivery of the trailers sat on the mayor's desk, awaiting the mayor's signature, Nguyen had been told. "I don't like to use the race angle," he told a TV reporter who'd found the community making a bonfire of shipping pallets outside their tents on a frigid night the week before Christmas. "But sometimes you have to wonder."

Whether because of FEMA's failings, Nagin's, or the city council's, incredibly Nguyen's congregation would still be in tents or patched-up houses well into the new year. But as a political free-for-all, the trailer flap had subsided with a come-to-Jesus meeting convened by Governor Blanco. Appalled by the message that New Orleans was sending to potential benefactors in Congress, she strongly advised city officials to get their act together. Shortly, sizable tracts of land suitable for trailers were identified within the domain of the federally operated city housing projects, which had been almost entirely emptied by Katrina. In a further concession, Nagin agreed to consult with the relevant city council member before any trailer camps were set up in his or her district. When a list of trailer sites approved by Nagin continued to draw political heat, Nagin waffled again, accusing FEMA of an egregious indifference to the people of New Orleans in actually installing trailers at sites he approved. Shrewd analysts of such imbroglios will have guessed that, by then, the upcoming mayoral election was looming larger.

Whatever goodwill had accrued to Nagin for first seeming to stand up to Council pettiness on the trailer issue was quickly squandered in what would remain, one hoped, the unsurpassed outbreak of a loose-lipped mayor's chronic case of foot-in-mouth disease: The Chocolate City Speech. Early symptoms of the outbreak were familiar to Nagin watchers. A blacker accent would come over him during such moments, typically moments of communion with African American voters, the present occasion being a Martin Luther King Jr. Day oration before a dispirited crowd of about seventy-five. He began normally enough, imagining himself in a conversation with the fallen civil rights leader, and many of Dr. King's ideas, as imagined by Nagin, were reasonable ones: that black leaders should stop tearing each other down in public; that the federal government should have come more swiftly to the aid of the evacuees who were trapped in the Superdome; that the young black men shooting at each other in cold blood must stop. In sum, that "we're not taking care of ourselves. We're not taking care of our women. And we're not taking care of our children when you have a community where 70 percent of its children are being born to one parent."

Maybe Nagin thought he had gone too far down a path that Bill Cosby had been treading lately. Maybe he felt he had to curry favor with the audience he had just gently scolded. The speech might better have been over, Nagin would come to agree, when he lapsed into a riff that was replayed endlessly on network and cable news services around the nation: "It's time for us to rebuild a New Orleans, the one that should be a chocolate New Orleans," Nagin said. That line having failed to generate a responsive chorus of amens—or much response at all from Nagin's audience—the mayor plunged on, his hand gestures becoming faintly stiff-fingered in the hip-hop style, and the rhythm of the performance beginning to borrow more heavily from the pulpit. "And I don't care what people are saying Uptown or wherever they are. This city will be chocolate at the end of the day"—a pause and still no hallelujah chorus. "This city will be a majority African American city. It's the way God wants it to be." And then the coup de grâce, a folksy double negative: "You can't have New Orleans no other way."

The racism, of course, was disturbing to vanilla New Orleans, a group not limited to Uptown whites. But Nagin went on, taking prisoners from other camps: "And as we think about rebuilding New Orleans, surely God is mad at America," he intoned. "He's sending hurricane after hurricane after hurricane, and it's destroying and putting stress on this country. Surely he's not approving of us being in Iraq under false pretenses." The invocation of the deity as an explanation of disaster was bizarre, a rhetorical strategy more familiar in the rantings of the far right. It was also a jab at the foreign policy of a war-time president whose favor the mayor of a disaster-struck city was better advised to cultivate rather assiduously. The uproar was tumultuous, if short-lived, with black and white voices blending before news cameras in a chorus of dismay. Nagin's mimicry of the Bible-thumper's style had been oafish—a "goofball" of a speech, civil rights attorney Tracie Washington called it. Business interests groaned and set to work heading off a threatened wave of convention cancellations. Politicians lamented that this was not remotely helpful at a time when the city was begging Congress for a federal bailout of epic scale. And within a day, Nagin was publicly apologizing to anyone who had taken offense. It would take the upcoming election to know whether he had inflicted lasting damage on himself, and that was still three months off, time enough for plenty of additional distractions to boil up out of the cauldron of city politics.

TWENTY-ONE

Shrink-Proof City

MR. JOE CANIZARO, I DON'T KNOW YOU, BUT I HATE YOU."
Those words, hurled at a bank president and millionaire developer by a gardener from eastern New Orleans, marked a nadir, one had to
hope, in the fractious politics of New Orleans's post-Katrina recovery. The
comment, in a packed hotel conference room, augured the effective collapse
of the months-long BNOB planning process at what was supposed to be the
moment of its consummation: the release in mid-January of the report com-
piled by the subcommittee on land use, Joe Canizaro's subcommittee. It
might have been called the footprint subcommittee—"footprint" having become shorthand for a batch of considerations having to do with the size and
shape of the future city, all of them humming with overtones of race and
class.

On a pro bono basis, the footprint committee had retained the services
of the Urban Land Institute (ULI), a city planning consortium from Washington, D.C., for which, not by coincidence, Canizaro had served as board
chairman and that he had used in other business maneuvers that required

community acquiescence. In consultation with planning and disaster experts across the nation, ULI had quickly come to the conclusion that there were parts of New Orleans that really shouldn't be rebuilt, at least not for a good long while, not until the city regained its economic footing and recovered more of its population base than was expected back any time soon.

In its simplest iteration, the argument in favor of a reduced footprint was advanced on grounds of public safety: It was simply dangerous, indeed fool-hardy, to rush right back out into the parts of the city that had proved most vulnerable to flooding. It would be a decade or more before a Category 5 flood defense could shield eastern New Orleans from the violence of a surging gulf. But the safety issue was underlain by a more complex consideration: Until New Orleans regained sufficient population density, it could not afford to scatter infrastructure investments and services to the farthest reaches of the floodplain, the experts warned. The argument for public safety was easy to make. A flood line up near the eaves of a house in eastern New Orleans spoke with unambiguous eloquence. But the economic argument against repopulating the entire city leaned on speculative judgments about New Orleans's future that were susceptible both to dispute and to accusations of racial bias. How could you be sure population densities were going to be insufficient? And might that not be a self-fulfilling prophecy, calculated to keep blacks from returning to New Orleans? Might that not be Mr. Canizaro's way of assembling large tracts of land on the cheap for massive redevelopment?

The only problem with the recommended retrenchment was this: By the time Nagin had convoked his committee and the ULI had been given time to do even a preliminary report, those same parts of New Orleans—or at least a few scattered neighborhoods within them—were already being rebuilt. "I gut my house already," a diminutive, round-faced member of the Mary Queen of Vietnam congregation said when asked what had brought her to a land-use committee meeting way back in November. "Now they tell me I can't live there? No way they can tell me that." Her pastor, Father Vien, put it this way, and there was no answering him: "We cannot leave this area; we have buried our dead here."

The explosive urgency of the issue was apparent in the throng of hundreds who turned out for the November meeting when ULI reps had first laid out their recommendations. The crowd represented a cross section of the city. Former mayor Sidney Barthelemy was there as was socialite and civic activist Anne Milling, wife of the Whitney Bank president, King Milling. So too were the working poor, black, white, Hispanic, as well as the somber few dozen souls from the Vietnamese church congregation, a group of war refugees not inclined to let a patch of rough weather and a few feet of standing water separate them from hard-won homesteads.

In truth, ULI was not telling anyone where they could or could not live. The reps were tactful. They wanted to make clear their research did not culminate in go/no-go decisions. They did not presume to tell the commission that the city would be foolish to rebuild eastern New Orleans, or the deeper abysses of Lakeview and the Lower Ninth Ward, however strongly the reps might believe it. Instead they had come up with the concept of "neighborhood investment zones." On the color-coded map that ULI projected onto the wall of the Sheraton's Napoleon Room, the deep purple wash was meant to indicate not areas that should be off-limits because every house in them had flooded up to the eaves, but rather areas that should be "closely studied" before "investment" was made. And rather than rank them on a scale of one (don't bother) to ten (rebuild if you dare), the operative concept was "sequencing"—as in which areas should be "closely studied" first, and last. The decision-making, ULI reassured the crowd, would be up to the commission, which hastened to say that it would be deferring to the city, which, by extension, meant the good people of New Orleans—a daisy chain of buckpassing-in-the-name-of-democracy that threatened to leave New Orleans residents right where they had been all along: below sea level and, now and again, underwater.

As ULI went on with its presentation, it was not hard, through the haze of rhetorical feints and dodges, to see the outlines of a sensible—if politically improbable—plan for mitigating future disasters. The "buyout" word dared to speak its name, and Joe Canizaro, who used it, jumped in with more specifics: Homeowners in areas where "close study" ultimately suggested that it would be folly to rebuild would be bought out "at pre-Katrina prices," he said, with shares going to the owner and the mortgage holder proportional to their equity. This assumed of course that Washington would kick in billions sufficient to the task, but Canizaro had friends in high places, and from what he was hearing, the money might be there. Homeowners who accepted relocation to safer parts of town would be guaranteed the value and rates of their pre-Katrina mortgage to buy or build anew. In short, everyone would be "made whole," Canizaro promised, to scattered applause from some quarters of the room and hisses from others.

The problem that would come with failure to do the redevelopment systematically—concentrating efforts in the most viable areas and restraining it where "close study" seemed warranted—was "the jack-o'-lantern syndrome," the ULI warned. The jack-o'-lantern syndrome—so named because of the gap-toothed look of neighborhoods reviving unevenly—would kick in if you had scattered rebuilding amid widespread abandonment, as might be expected in eastern New Orleans if the doughty Vietnamese were to cobble their houses back together but everyone else on the block were to decide that Houston felt pretty good, and choose to stay there.

Alden McDonald did not like what he was hearing, and as the committee's most eminent black executive, he was going to take a few minutes to say why. His concerns were twofold, and they were rightly centered on the east. (He acknowledged his "bias," as he called it: His home was in the east, and so was his business, Liberty Bank—a black-owned and -oriented institution—of which he was president.)

In particular, McDonald was concerned that all this talk of floodplains, and ULI's implication that certain parts of town were untenable, was dirty linen that really should not be aired in public. What if insurance underwriters got wind of this nay-saying? "We're looking to repopulate the city and this is sending the wrong signal," McDonald said, to a surge of applause. Addressing Ray Nagin, who had arrived late, McDonald went on: "I think we need to be careful, Mr. Mayor, about how we publish this stuff, because it's causing people to look at relocating."

As if a purple wash on a map showing areas of the city most vulnerable to flooding would be news to people who had seen their refrigerators float out the door and their kin and neighbors drown in their attics. Or as if, Canizaro reminded his colleague, the insurance industry wasn't hard at work on its own flood-risk assessments. "Insurers are going to get their own maps, Alden." Canizaro went on: The ULI maps were not about compassion for flood victims or their dreams of rebuilding. "They show facts"—the depths to which the city flooded. But the flooding, McDonald retorted, was the result of a break in the levee, not a hurricane. Levees break, Alden. It was time to move on, but McDonald had a parting shot: "I'm concerned that the outside world not take these maps as gospel."

Ah, the outside world. McDonald's offhand remark seemed to summarize three hundred years in the history of a city that had always seen itself as separate and, for better or worse, as somehow secret from the rest of America. It was the instinct that had nurtured a musical and culinary culture as different as the flora and fauna of the Galápagos is from the continental mainland of South America. And, of course, it had also contributed to the sense—an aspect of New Orleans that McDonald deplored as heartily as anyone in the room—that the city was somehow outside the law, that the pettifoggery of its political class would elude detection, as indeed for many years it had.

It fell to Oliver Thomas, a populist in a baseball cap among men and women in suits, to play peacemaker. The baseball cap was a ploy, Thomas's way of reminding folk of his humble origins, that he had grown up in the Lower Ninth Ward. But he was an at-large member of the city council, and also its president—a respected politician widely assumed to have an eye on the mayor's office if the stars ever came into proper alignment.

Thomas began by seeming to reject the ULI analysis. "Look, the jack-o'-lantern effect is nothing new," he said. "There's always been a jack-o'-lantern—for thirty years people have been living with abandoned houses down the block." But that said, he was willing to throw ULI a rose. "There are some realities we have to deal with," he agreed. Indeed, he wanted to embrace reality. And his assumption was that other homeowners were waiting on the same blunt assessment in order to plot their next move: "If certain parts of the city aren't going to be rebuilt, let me know!"

It was time for Nagin to begin to wind down the formalities and turn the mikes over to the people on the floor. He saw fit to remind the city that the committee and its retention of ULI was his idea, that the goal was an unvarnished view by national experts of what was best, but that it was then up to New Orleans to "kick the tires" of the ULI report "and decide what works for us." And if that wasn't enough to vitiate whatever political momentum might have begun to flow toward the idea of a seriously reengineered city,

Nagin had another sop to champions of the status quo: "It is our intention to rebuild all of New Orleans," he said, pausing a moment and then repeating the applause line, "all of New Orleans." Our intention now is to make sure that we do that "smartly," Nagin added, in a lurch back toward the principles embodied in ULI's thinking.

Yes, but when will people know what "smartly" means, Thomas piped up. In the words of Dr. King: "How long?"

The afternoon's rhetorical last word fell to a man who had remained silent through the proceedings to that point: Jimmy Reiss, the millionaire businessman whose quoted comments about reengineering the city's demographics as well as its levees had provoked a retreat to his Uptown mansion and then to a lodge in Aspen and a vow to have no further contact with the jackals of the media. His comments on this occasion were pitched directly to evacuees still lingering in far-flung cities. "I'd like people to understand the situation now," Reiss began in a basso monotone that bespoke utter conviction and also a certain impatience, not just with political pandering but maybe with the planning process itself. "Not in ten or twenty years, but now," he reiterated. What New Orleans had as of the moment in which he spoke, Reiss said, was this and only this: a pledge by the army corps to reconstruct the levee system to pre-Katrina specs by next June. Beyond that, the army corps had committed to spending $8 million on a two-year study of the feasibility of building a strengthened levee system. "A study. Two years. Period," Reiss said. He had a reminder for a city once again eager to throw itself into the loving embrace of the great god army corps: "The levees were not overtopped," Reiss intoned flatly. "They were undercut; they failed."

"So what have you got? Today?" Reiss thundered. And then he answered his own question: If you think the levees we had, properly built, will not fail, "then you should feel safe about coming back." And if you don't . . .

Reiss's point was not about the safety of the levee system. Levees always fail eventually, as even the Dutch, the world leaders in flood protection, had discovered and planned for. Reiss wanted to put responsibility for their futures on the people clamoring to be hypnotized back into the happy delusion that everything was going to be all right. That Big Daddy was going to fix the levees. That New Orleans would be just like before. And that everyone could exercise "the right to return," a catchphrase that was rapidly gaining the force of a mantra.

No matter what it did, the city wouldn't be able to guarantee perfect safety for flood zone residents. It couldn't even rig its building codes and flood elevation maps to make life in a floodplain affordable, Reiss cautioned. "Whether a homeowner can get insurance is up to the market," he said, raising the specter of a jump in rates that could well eclipse taxes and perhaps even mortgages as the biggest annual slice of a homeowner's budget.

The implications of what he was saying were worrisome, but it was hard not to admire the bravura of Reiss's tightrope walk. The crack-of-doom edge in his voice could be read two ways at once: as an importuning of stay-away evacuees and wallflower businesses to get over themselves, get back to New Orleans, and get to work. Now. But it could also be called a jeremiad against ever being so foolish as to think of New Orleans—parts of it, anyway—as a safe place to live and prosper. And either way, it was clear that if people were going to accuse him of insensitivity to the special needs of the New Orleans underclass, well, that was their problem.

TWO MONTHS AFTER THAT FIRST MEETING, THE FOOTPRINT COMMITTEE ASSEMbled to officially release its final report, and the tensions had not abated one whit. Harvey Bender, the man who stood up to declare his hatred of Mr. Canizaro, was followed by others offering not just anathemas but threats of armed resistance. "If you come to take our property, you better come ready," Ninth Ward resident Rodney Craft warned when it was time for public comment and he had snaked his way to the front of a long line waiting for the microphone.

Canizaro was a rarity on the New Orleans scene, not because he was a right-wing Republican in a Democratic town—there were others—but because his politics did not preclude an active and sometimes quite effective role in civic affairs.

With the ULI as his cat's-paw, several years earlier he had initiated an elaborate planning process to build community support for a huge apartment complex that, once complete, was seen by his critics as the destruction of the very neighborhoods the ULI had maneuvered into yielding to Canizaro's plans. He had built the downtown area's premier retail, office, and hotel complex, Canal Place. And he had made himself and two partners, a jeweler and a liquor distributor, very much richer by snapping up a seventy-two-acre riverfront tract from the Missouri Pacific Railroad for a paltry $11 million and then unloading it in pieces to private and public entities, including the Ernest N. Morial Convention Center, for a nifty gross profit in the range of 700 percent.

In recent years, Canizaro's most extravagant investment may well have been his home, a beaux arts palace in old Metairie replete with a private chapel. The cost? Upward of $12 million if you counted the $1 million mansion Canizaro bought as a teardown to make room for it—complaints of his neighbors notwithstanding—and not counting whatever it took to refurbish the place after Katrina flushed a goodly sea of sewage and floodwater across its glorious acres of alabaster. It was there, in the private chapel, that Canizaro had nourished a deeply mystical Catholicism. It had taken him to Medjugorje, where children communed with a recurring apparition of the Virgin and where Canizaro had stared into the sun, somehow without permanently damaging his eyes, until he'd seen an image of the Eucharist. Meanwhile, he kept his name in good odor in Republican circles as one of the party's heaviest donors. The president took his calls; Karl Rove was a pal. Indeed, colleagues who had joined in the task of rebuilding southeast Louisiana would grow tired of Canizaro's name-dropping, his repeated declaration of what he believed to be Rove's view on a given subject, and the implicit assumption—often a good one—that this was the view that would prevail at the White House.

Fully five hundred people gathered for the PowerPoint presentation that disintegrated into name-calling that Wednesday morning in January. And though the really ugly remarks from the general public would follow the razzle-dazzle of the footprint committee's rollout, the room coursed from the start with the tensions that would shortly erupt.

Which was sad, if only because it cost the audience the properly upbeat and dreamy mood in which the presentation, for what it was worth, was best savored. The New Orleans envisioned by Wallace Roberts & Todd, the national planning company engaged by the commission to follow up on ULI's broad-brush advisory report, was a city reimagined. The historic districts were largely spared by the planners, as they had been by the floods. But where the waters had been deepest, the blueprint called for reversion to green space, an archipelago of parks and retention ponds linked by pedestrian malls and bicycle paths. A light-rail web—at a cost of more than $4 billion—would weave the whole city together and over the longer term lace it to Baton Rouge and the Mississippi Gulf Coast. The in-town railroad embankments would double as secondary levees to control flooding, should the heavily reinforced levees envisioned as New Orleans's perimeter defense be overtopped.

Redevelopment, in the form of consolidated residential and retail shopping complexes, in the New Urbanist mode, was to be clustered within walking distance of the transit stops and built to withstand storms and flooding. Drainage canals would be channeled through massive subterranean conduits and covered over, both to fortify them against breaching and to create yet more parkland. And for industry—all those manufacturers and service sector firms that would be lured by tax incentives to a city they had long shunned—the plan designated "infill" areas in the parts of town least appropriate for residential revival. The huge swath of land that had once been home to the notorious Florida and Desire public housing projects was one of them. Infill was also the prescription for recovery in the northern portion of the Lower Ninth Ward.

The vision carried the whiff of both the pipe and of midnight oil, heady expansiveness and last-minute changes wrought with near-term political calculations in mind. In the few days since a draft of the plan had been leaked to *The Times-Picayune,* the time frame for proving a neighborhood's prospective viability, once set at three years, had been reduced to four months. By May—May twentieth, to be precise—to become eligible for full revival and the gamut of city services that had once been taken for granted, each of thirteen planning districts would need to complete an assessment process and establish that a sufficient number of former residents had come back or planned to. A 50 percent return rate was the number bandied about as the threshold for officially sanctioned near-term revival, though the report did not specify a number. Districts that fell short of the mark would be bulldozed, their residents offered buyouts and various options for relocation under the supervision of an outfit to be called the Crescent City Recovery Corporation, another last-minute addition to the plan that very likely would delay, perhaps even scuttle, its implementation. Because empowering the recovery corporation would require a referendum to change the city charter, as would another of the plan's recommendations, that the city council be stripped of the power to reverse or revise decisions on land use approved by the city planning commission—a long-standing practice that had been an open invitation to graft and favoritism.

Even without these infringements on specific powers it had long abused, the city council was adamant in its opposition to the BNOB plan. A month earlier, the council had embraced a resolution that would effectively gut the committee's report, if not urban planning itself. City services would be distributed evenly throughout New Orleans, the council had decreed; no reduction of the city's footprint would be tolerated.

In a huddle just before the land use committee's presentation, the council reasserted its refusal to countenance any talk of retrenchment. Council member Cynthia Willard-Lewis, whose district, New Orleans East, was now a vast ghost town of abandoned housing interrupted here and there by tiny clusters of revival, emerged from the meeting to tell the press that the council had come out with a "strong and forceful declaration of the right of everyone to return." There it was again, that "right to return," buzzwords that, however well meaning, had a magical way of aborting further thought about just what those vested with that right would be returning to.

As politics, it worked fine, because of the way a right to return meshed with the widespread, if unsupported, suspicion that the big shots on the mayor's commission—Canizaro in particular—were really just there to scout for private opportunities and make "land grabs." Invoked as part of a planning exercise, the right to return gained added force by effectively polarizing the process along racial lines; the implication was that construction of a safer city would entail the abridgement of hard-won civil rights. Black New Orleanians were acutely sensitive to the way history and racism had conspired to place them in the city's most vulnerable landscapes—the last to be settled, and the first to be flooded. The irony was that by invoking the right of every resident to return to properties that had proved so dangerous, the politicians pandering to these constituents were condemning them to the same fate all over again.

Canizaro had struck a cautionary note, grounded, as might be expected of a banker, in a straightforward calculation of homeowner self-interest: "I hope that the people in this community, when they make their investments, make sure that they're going to have neighbors and they're going to have services provided," he said. "The city may not be able to provide services if they're stuck out there by themselves," Canizaro cautioned.

Likewise true to form, the mayor wanted it both ways. He had taken delivery of Canizaro's plan—his to tweak before passing it on to the state-level Louisiana Recovery Authority—but not without revealing that he was uncomfortable with the very essence of it, the possibility that the footprint should be shrunk if the city were to survive. Even the temporary moratorium on building permits, recommended as breathing room until the four-month district-planning process could be completed, was more than a politician facing a reelection fight could countenance. He would not be able to support a moratorium, Nagin declared.

Mel Lagarde, a health company executive who had assumed a leadership role in commission activities, was appalled by the way "political foolishness," as he called it, had overtaken what he saw as a city struggling for its very life. "The size of the problem always dictates the size of the decision," he said, "and there's no way you're going to be able to finesse a decision around a problem of this magnitude that everyone's going to be comfortable with." Leadership, were the political sector capable of it, would reveal itself in the courage to make enemies, Lagarde was saying—an observation that brought Kobe's mayor to mind.

As the meeting broke up, Canizaro brushed off an aide trying to restrain him, and followed his denouncer, Harvey Bender, out into the hall. The banker buttonholed the gardener, assuring him that Canizaro interests had no secret financial stake in the committee's plan. And he urged Bender to participate in the planning process, or what was left of it.

Another two months would pass before Nagin formally digested the various subcommittee reports and released his recommendation for the city's future, and even then the plan would require planning commission review and city council approval. Much of the plan survived the mayor's scrutiny, including proposals to replace the elected school board with an appointed board for the next five years, and to replace the city's seven elected assessors with one trained professional. But while concerned about the dangers of re-populating the areas hardest hit by flooding, in particular the Lower Ninth Ward and parts of eastern New Orleans, the mayor could not bring himself to say that any part of the city would be cordoned off. "I have confidence that our citizens can decide intelligently for themselves where they want to re-build, once presented with the facts." It could be called a radical deference to democracy and the marketplace, or a massive default of leadership at a time of great trial. It might take years to find out which.

TWENTY-TWO

———— ⚜ ————

Safe Enough for Cows

I VOR VAN HEERDEN WAS NOT ONE TO GO DOWN WITHOUT A FIGHT: "THE FACT that the corps found some sheet piling sunk to minus seventeen does not negate the fact that we had catastrophic structural failures of the levees in fifty-eight locations around New Orleans," he snapped, when told about the corps' exercise in damage control that chilly morning at the site of the Seventeenth Street Canal breach. Mark Schleifstein had reached him the next day, as van Heerden returned from a tour of Holland and the planet's finest flood defense. The piling pull was a comeuppance, but van Heerden was not about to concede that his sonar readings were wrong—not yet, anyway. Neither was he willing to reveal exactly where he'd found the abbreviated pilings, except to say that they were some two hundred feet south of the breach. The army corps made a point of asking, but then conceded that even if they knew just which pilings to pull, the area was beyond the cofferdam that had been built around the breached area to allow for its repair. Pulling pilings outside the dammed-off area would trigger flooding. "The sooner the Corps of Engineers accepts responsibility, the sooner we can move forward," van

Heerden said, and with that, both sides retreated to their respective corners to wait for the inevitable next round.

"It's easy to tip Ivor's crew over, because they're shooting fast and frequently and they all have wild hair," Ray Seed said only half in jest during one of his and Bob Bea's many visits to New Orleans, this one in early January. Point men in the National Science Foundation's probe of the levee failures, the two Berkeley engineers were also under the gun and concerned not to be "tipped over" themselves, not by the corps or anyone else. Their goal was to finish the NSF report on the levee failures before the corps released its own final conclusions, their hunch being that whoever got done first would effectively frame the debate.

Seed and Bea could not be accused of having wild hair. Bea, in his late sixties, had no hair at all, the wand of fashion (a razor) having combined with the indignities of advanced middle age to leave only a snow white mustache and eyebrows north of his neck. The shaved head gave him a raffish, slightly bohemian look that was underscored by his jeans and black shirt. By contrast, Seed, with a cropped salt-and-pepper beard and equally conventional grooming up top, could have passed for an insurance salesman. But the minute either one of them opened his mouth, which both did frequently and for considerable lengths of time, sometimes stepping on each other's lines, it was clear that these were men of extraordinary intelligence. Seed, by then in his forties, favored a rapid-fire delivery worthy of an auctioneer but in a deadpan monotone that he wielded to amusing effect. Bea was given to expostulation, accompanied by aggressive gestures. And not the least remarkable thing about Bea's performance was the contrast between the extreme precision of his mind and the brute force of his thick-fingered ham-size hands waving around his head.

Bob and Ray: They brought to mind the 1950s comedy team of the same name, except that the showbiz duo were given to a laconic Yankee style of speech while these guys spieled. They were well paired in many respects. Seed brought world-class geotechnical expertise to the table. Bea could fluently converse in that same language but also specialized in the human dimension: the institutional structures and maladies that made for success or failure in the administration of large-scale engineering projects.

If Seed, the leader of the NSF team, was the consummate academic, Bea had the more diversified work history. Seed was the son of the man who had once occupied the very chair in which his son was now ensconced as a tenured professor at Cal Berkeley, home to one of the nation's top civil engineering departments. It was the place where Ray Seed had done his undergraduate and graduate work, and but for the few years when he'd taught down the peninsula at Stanford, it was the place where he would almost certainly spend the rest of his working life.

Bea too had followed in the footsteps of his father, but only for a while. The elder Bea had gone from West Point to the place where many of the nation's finest engineers once made their careers: the army corps. After college in Florida, the younger Bea had lasted four years in the army corps before bailing into the private sector. For Seed, the New Orleans catastrophe was an intellectual challenge intensified by his sense that something had gone very wrong in American engineering as practiced by the once almighty army corps. Bea combined those motives with a more personal connection to New Orleans. He was living there in 1965 when Betsy hit, working for Shell as the giant offshore oil drilling platforms came on line. Betsy had flooded him out of the house he'd owned near the lakefront levee in eastern New Orleans. He slept under his office desk for a month, eating three meals a day from vending machines. Forty years later, he still did consulting work on pipelines and offshore drilling platforms, his Crescent City heritage memorialized in the Dixie beer bottle filled with Mardi Gras beads that he kept on his desk at Berkeley.

Remembering his New Orleans connection, former students who were scattered around the Gulf had been in touch with Bea over the Internet as Katrina struck. He didn't reach Louisiana until early October, but his and Seed's sleuthing was already well under way by then, much of it a paper chase through documentation the corps had to be coaxed to give up. The NSF team was confident that eventually the foot-dragging would stop and they'd get at the documents they wanted. Seed: "The corps is maniacally careful about keeping its smoking guns on file."

Sheet piling depths had not yet become an issue when the engineers first reached Louisiana, but Bea knew, through the early revelations by van Heerden and others, that the soils beneath the flood walls were suspect. Within minutes of arriving at the Seventeenth Street Canal breach in the first week of October, Bea was pretty sure that he could verify van Heerden's hunch and add some insights of his own. The first clues to the catastrophe were the clumps of rotting vegetation—call it peat or humus—that had been washed right out of the collapsing levee into the backyards of adjacent houses, dark and gnarly substances mixed in with the lighter sands. And then Bea's attention was captured by a toppled oak tree, the one that had been rooted at the levee's landward toe. The old tree's root ball, twenty feet in diameter, had been like a giant cork, Bea concluded. When the tree went over in high winds, the cork was popped; water could begin flowing into crevices the roots had occupied, and soon the water had found an escape route from the canal. In short order, the whole wall of the levee had skidded sideways, revealing the lozenge-shaped pockets of peat that never should have been tolerated in the first place by levee engineers, at least not without sinking sheet piling considerably deeper than the army corps had seen fit to do.

Bea's tree thesis had suffered a temporary setback. While a toppled oak was clearly visible below one of the breaches in the London Avenue Canal, no tree was in sight at the second London breach. A pre-Katrina photograph Bea stumbled upon restored his faith in the tree theory. It showed a towering oak in the exact center of that second breach. Evidently the force of the water had washed it right off-site. Of course, knowing what had happened still left open the more challenging question: Why? What process of incompetence or corruption—or both—had led to a levee built with peat and shallow sheet pilings? How had a sizable tree been able to grow up so close to the levee, when maintenance rules forbade even brush?

Bea and Seed were less interested in who was to blame than in the processes, both scientific and institutional, that underlay the failure. What sequence of misjudgment and miscalculation had led to the levee breaks? As Ivor van Heerden realized as well, any deeper understanding of the catastrophe's human agency would require an exact grip on the mechanics of the failure, a matter of close and levelheaded analysis.

But to call Bea and Seed dispassionate scholars in pursuit of pure science would be to misapprehend the intensely political nature of disaster mitigation in general, and flood control in particular. These were competitive men actively involved in the issues of the day, not armchair intellectuals.

Bea had been tapped as part of the team hired by NASA to analyze the Columbia shuttle disaster a couple of years earlier. When Katrina hit the Gulf Coast, Seed was a consultant with the California Department of Water Resources in an increasingly tense struggle to avert a catastrophic levee break in northern California, one that could flood the 738,000 acres of the Sacramento–San Joaquin delta, much of it below sea level, and—the costlier part of the failure—poison the supply of freshwater on which the state's giant agriculture industry depended. Katrina was both a tragedy and a professional opportunity. But it would quickly become a personal crusade as well—fraught with the possibilities for embarrassment, even humiliation, that come when your enemy is the federal government and billions are at stake.

Which explains why, after burning through an initial $29,000 fronted by the NSF to cover the costs of their pro bono investigation, rather than suspending the probe, Bea and Seed found themselves using their wives' credit cards to finance the research. Eventually, in late autumn, university and foundation support kicked in and the pot of available funds rose to about $200,000, Seed said. Enough to keep the men in plane tickets and coffee, but a pittance compared to the $18 million the corps had at its disposal to understand the levee failures—or to obscure the corps' culpability, as some scientists feared they would try to do with the information they gathered. "You can make a problem so damned opaque, normal people can't understand it," Bea said. "Then you're at the disposal of the experts."

The soft-spoken van Heerden was the mad dog among the various engineers probing the levee failures, the one willing to make the angriest assumptions about the corps' culpability and to ask the nasty questions, as he had in publicly questioning the sheet piling depths. Not that members of the NSF team were shrinking violets. David Rogers, a geotechnical engineer at the University of Missouri's Rolla campus, did not hesitate to say that there was something odd about the way the corps' Seventeenth Street Canal factor of safety—a complex calculation of variables that stand between an engineered construct, such as a levee, and its point of failure—had come in at exactly the minimum allowed. "From the outside, that's suspicious," Rogers said, as the NSF team tried to get their hands on the paper trail that would make them insiders. "If you come across something like this, you say maybe the answers they want to get are driving the analysis, not the analysis driving the answers."

And Seed himself testified before the Senate committee investigating Katrina that there may have been "some conscious human error involved" in the levee failures—decisions to save a buck by building the levees lower and weaker than specified, or by using less expensive fill around the flood walls. "There may have been some malfeasance," he said, using a word that could only thrill the plaintiff's bar.

The problem, as Bea saw it, was this: "No one is doing hurricane protection levees; they're building river levees. The factor of safety dates back to the 1940s, when they were protecting cows."

But van Heerden remained the lightning rod for the corps' rebuttals. Bea and Seed watched and learned, taking careful note of just what kinds of evidence the corps seemed to be gathering to defend itself, and wondering all the while if van Heerden hadn't been set up by the corps on the occasion of the sheet piling pull. Seed had been present that day. It wasn't because he had had much doubt about the outcome. Though the corps had been claiming all along that it couldn't find the "as builts" for Seventeenth Street—the final documentation of the engineering process that recorded what actually went into the ground—Seed had decided it might well have been a ruse to hold off the press and scientists like him, who were demanding to see the paperwork. No, Seed assumed the pilings at that particular spot would prove to be the length specified in the design memoranda—or the corps wouldn't have been pulling them so publicly. The whole media production struck him as too slick, too contrived.

What interested Seed, an amateur psychologist as well as a scientist, was reading the looks on the faces of the corpsmen present for the occasion. To see who knew all along how this was going to turn out, or tried to pretend that they didn't. What Seed saw did nothing to dissuade him from the belief that at least some of the corpsmen in charge of the event knew precisely what they were going to find that day as cameras hummed and clicked. Van Heerden would later discover Seed's hunch was on target, that the sonar analyst who had been hired to interpret his and the army corps' sheet piling readings had made a mistake in concluding that the pilings were so short.

But the analyst had reported that error to only one of his two clients, far and away the bigger one—the army corps. Van Heerden was left in the dark to face a temporarily discrediting embarrassment.

From close examination of the Orleans design memoranda and other documents, to Bea and Seed it was as obvious as a toppled tree that the corps, for all its claims to excellence, had fallen well out of step with engineering's cutting edge as early as the mid-1980s. It was not enough to observe that the design work associated with the flood wall projects was deeply flawed, the soils too peaty, the pilings too short—if not as short as the flawed sonar readings had suggested. That was obvious: The damn things had failed! More telling to the NSF team, and more ominous because of what it said about the vast reaches of the Orleans flood barrier that hadn't failed— yet—was that the underlying science, the site analysis, had been as quaint as the construction had been goofy.

The advent of computers had allowed engineering to move to what was called a "finite-element model" for examining systems of stresses and resistance, such as a levee under siege by rising water. This model had forced the engineering world in the mid-1980s to abandon some hoary assumptions. One of them was that levees failed along horizontal planes, as a heavier and heavier load of water pushed against the earthen rampart and whatever reinforcements (sheet piling, typically) might be inside it. In fact, as finite-element modeling showed, the patterns of stress and eventual failure were arcs or rings, as a result, in part, of the levee wall being sloped. The water pushed down as well as sideward before the levee gave way. The difference was of more than merely academic interest. It meant the designs needed to call for significantly deeper sheet piling, lest the downward thrust arc below the iron reinforcement.

"It's like I'm going through a time warp, but I'm going through it backward," Bea said after reviewing analytical practices he deemed Neanderthal. "These are paintings on the walls of a cave in France."

Ironically, some of the finest finite-element modeling was being done by the Army Corps of Engineers itself, in its Waterways Experimental Station (WES), at Vicksburg. This was the corps' brain trust, its carton of eggheads, a vestige of the days when the corps, at every level of operation, routinely creamed off the best young engineers from that year's crop of university graduates and put them to work, sometimes for a lifetime, as the corps had Bea's father. But while private sector engineers working for the oil industry had long since moved to the finite-element approach to structural analysis, the good work by WES wasn't reaching army corps engineers in the field. The billions at stake in constructing offshore platforms and making sure they didn't leak or topple in a storm had compelled Shell to adopt state-of-the-art science. The price of the levees—mere millions—was determined by how deep you drove your sheet piling, assuming you chose not to include human lives in your cost-benefit analysis.

Computer science wasn't the only development that was leaving the corps in the dust. The 1980s saw the rise of the neoconservative wave that crashed over a half century of liberal hegemony in Congress and the White House. Aggrandized government programs were out; privatization was in—both in the name of good old-fashioned cost-cutting and because an ever-expanding public sector was seen ideologically as a threat to individual liberties, not to mention the after-tax net of corporations and the rich. Where money could be saved, it would be. For the Reagan administration, cutting money from defense programs was folly. Indeed, they would demonstrate a willingness to sink trillions into the unproven Star Wars antimissile shield. But to pay for lavishness on that scale, it seemed best to pinch other parts of the Pentagon appropriation, and one of the most vulnerable line items was the army corps. For one thing, much of its work scarcely seemed military at all—in any case, not in ways that redounded to the advantage of weapons manufacturers or seemed likely to hasten the collapse of the Soviet Union.

The trimming continued under the second president Bush—and especially in the army corps district that included Louisiana. The district's budget was slashed from $147 million in 2001 to $82 million in 2005, and Bush had proposed a further cut, to $56 million, for 2006. The corps did not help its cause by coming under fire in recent decades for some massively expensive and ill-conceived projects: the Tombigbee waterway, for example, in northern Alabama; the failed Teton Dam, for another. Environmentalists were hardly the darlings of the Reagan era, but they had been unwitting co-conspirators with Reagan in tenderizing the corps for a blow from the budgetary axe that Republican Congresses would continue to wield right through the 1990s.

In Louisiana, the leveeing of the Mississippi River—one of the corps' major projects of the twentieth century—was clearly implicated in the destruction of coastal wetlands now starved of their infusion of river sediment during annual flooding. Not to forget the corps' Mississippi River Gulf Outlet, at minimum a shipping shortcut that did not even remotely repay its unexpectedly high costs, not if you factored in the devastating impact on marshlands and estuaries in which more crab, fish, and fur-bearing animals had once thrived than in any other place in North America. And of course, if you factored in Mr. Go's role as a hurricane highway, it wasn't just a costly mistake, it was deadly. After Hurricane Betsy, the corps had begun talking about putting a flood barrier at the mouth of Lake Pontchartrain—an idea that would, after Katrina, suddenly seem like the highest sort of wisdom. But environmentalists sued to stop the project, something that foes threw back in their faces after Katrina. But that was the wisdom of hindsight. What Bea and Seed knew was that the corps was on the defensive and in retreat as it set about the business of shoring up New Orleans's flood defenses in the mid-1980s. The brain drain into private industry coincided with a hefty increase in the corps' responsibilities as the fight against coastal erosion began.

It was not long before even the cutting-edge Waterways Experimental Station had been axed, though the corps would eventually realize it could not limp along without some sort of high-level research arm. WES was brought back, but under a new name: the Engineer Research and Development Center, or ERDC (pronounced "urdik"). As far as Bob Bea could tell, the name change was nothing more than a fig leaf to spare the corps and congressional cost-cutters the embarrassment of having completely reversed themselves. ERDC was in charge of the corps' self-review of the levee failures after Katrina.

But once again, there seemed to be a disconnect between the corps' brain trust and corpsmen on the ground. When they were out at the Seventeenth Street Canal during that first visit to New Orleans in early October, Bea and Seed were appalled by what they saw. The corps, hastening to more permanently plug the breach, as all New Orleans hoped they would, had subsequently dumped fill over the sandbags and boulders that had been dropped into the crevasse in the desperate hours when the city was still flooding. Unfortunately, the fill the corps had used was mixed with sand and silt, which made it hydrologically unstable. Sinkholes had already developed in the fill. Seed grabbed a goodly length of pipe from the debris alongside the failed levee and poked the pipe into one of the holes. He couldn't reach the bottom. Any doubt that these holes had penetrated all the way to the central core of a levee already stripped of its flood wall was eliminated by the underground gurgling sound that was clearly audible, even with heavy equipment rumbling in the near distance. The whole patch was about to fail in a way that once again would make much of New Orleans a part of Lake Pontchartrain.

Seed notified a honcho with the ERDC: Paul Mlakar, senior research scientist in charge of the corps' probe of the levee failures. Seed respected Mlakar and assumed the matter would be immediately attended to. It was, but not well. On the next day, a Wednesday, Seed and Bea returned to the site to find that the crest of the patched area had been topped with a thick layer of stones ranging in size from six to twenty-four inches in diameter, and a row of large sandbags had been placed along the water's edge. The whole arrangement reminded Seed of nothing so much as flower pots along a garden wall, and could be presumed to be about as effective in stanching the sinkholes that were eating into the levee and sucking in water below the surface of the canal. As much as could be said for the corps' emergency work since Monday was that it made the problem harder to see.

A day later, Seed paid a third visit to the site and found that the cosmetic—or was it better called camouflage?—work had been brought to a level of perfection that was positively spiffy. The corps had dumped another load of silty gravel onto the patch and had bulldozed it tidily. So dire was the threat posed by another levee failure, and so clueless was the response of the corpsmen at ground level, that the NSF team argued among themselves about whether professional ethics required them to camp out in sleeping bags at the site, both to draw attention to the problem and to be present to sound an alarm if the sinkholes suddenly and dramatically deepened and the levee threatened to give way. Proponents of passing their last night in hotels prevailed.

In a memo fired off the following Tuesday, recapping his observations at the breach and urging the corps to take the sinkholes seriously, Seed lapsed into the form of bland technobabble that is, as he put it, "the sound of an engineer yelling." Of the carefully bladed second load of silty gravel he wrote:

"This succeeded in hiding any and all evidence of the evolving underlying erosive distress, and in obstructing any hope of monitoring internal erosive distress until it develops considerably further." He went on in the same vein, the gravity of the problem he was warning about making his understatement of it almost comical: "It had become apparent by this stage, based on the local District's responses to our formal notifications, that the urgency of the emergency response operations may have precluded application of the level of geotechnical oversight that would otherwise have been ideal."

Yes, a second inundation of New Orleans (perhaps a third for those parts of town that had been hit by Rita as well) would have been less than "ideal." In a return memorandum, four days later, Mlakar assured Seed that the situation was well in hand and that, with or without anyone camping out by the breach, the corps was prepared to alert the public if another levee failure appeared imminent and evacuation was advised.

Early in the next week, on October seventeenth, the corps issued a memorandum addressed both to the NSF team and to the group from the American Society of Civil Engineers (ASCE), who were working in tandem with Mlakar and ERDC. The memo was at once chilling and reassuring. The issues addressed by the teams—the ASCE had also spotted a problem: tension cracks along the landward side of the Seventeenth Street Canal levee—were being addressed, the corps said. But the federal engineers, the men and women responsible for dams and levees and much more across the breadth of the nation, seemed almost to plead for sympathy.

"The USACE [army corps] is stretched right now and has its hands full, but there cannot possibly be a more urgent task than keeping this from failing again," the memo said, adding this caveat: "The USACE has been required to reduce its geotechnical expertise in recent years." The theme—which could have come from the mouth of as harsh a critic as Bob Bea—was reiterated: The problems of levee stability that Bea and Seed were warning about "are difficult issues that require expertise in geotechnics not typically available in emergency task teams," the memo read.

THE BREACHES IN THE INDUSTRIAL CANAL AND IN THE TWO DRAINAGE CANALS along London Avenue and Seventeenth Street were only the best-known levee failures. The drainage canals had flooded residential neighborhoods—some of them high-income neighborhoods that hadn't gone under even during Hurricane Betsy. The breaches also gained notoriety by being within easier reach of media crews working the story. But like van Heerden, Bea and Seed repeatedly toured breaches along the entire run of the levee system, sometimes by air, sometimes by car or boat, and some of what they saw was even more disturbing because of what it said about the overall integrity of the region's flood defense.

Bea may once have worked for big oil, an industry accused of precipitating the collapse of Louisiana's marshlands by lancing them with canals during the drilling boom in the early part of the last century. But no one was more convinced than he of the importance of restoring those marshes as a buffer against onrushing hurricanes and storm surge. And if his own faith had ever wavered, it was reinforced by what he saw when he got to the levees along Lake Borgne, the brackish body of water connected to Lake Pontchartrain by the narrow passage known as the Rigolets. Bea thought of two curving bays in Lake Borgne as "cheeks"—one to the northeast and the other to the southwest. Both were leveed against the storm surge that had blown through the Rigolets and on into Lake Pontchartrain in the hours before Katrina's eye crossed that same area. The northeast cheek backed up against intact marshland; there was even a stand of old cypress, the relic of a time when the whole area was forested. The southwest cheek hadn't fared so well.

Decades earlier, the Mississippi River Gulf Outlet had been hacked through the marshes adjacent to the lake's shoreline, triggering rapid erosion as intrusive salt water killed the grasses, and ship wake uprooted whatever vegetation might otherwise have survived. In some areas along that side, the levees had collapsed altogether during Katrina, miles of them at a stretch, and Bea suspected the failure had occurred even before the storm surge reached them. Where levees still stood, their crests were gouged—"crenellated" was the word he used—by the water that had streamed over them. To Bea, they looked like the walls of an old castle. Stepping out of the boat, he reached down and picked up a handful of the soil used to create the levees. The sand and shells told him all he needed to know. The chewed-up levees had been created of muck scooped up on-site and heaped to the designated height. A more durable levee would have been made from a stickier mix of clay and loam. On the other side of the failed levees lay open water where the marsh had once been—open water choked, that is, by flotsam and up-rooted trees.

Then Bea traveled over to the northeast side of the lake, the cheek that had been spared the environmental insult of the Gulf Outlet. Not only had vegetation survived, so too had a small fishing village situated not behind the levee but right out there on the batture, as Louisianans called the land be-tween the toe of a levee and the water's edge. Many structures in the village had been damaged by wind, but several houses remained intact, and one of them, a yellow house with white trim raised on pilings twenty feet high, ap-peared to be occupied. As he drew near, interested in examining the under-pinnings of so robust a building, Bea was startled to see an elderly woman sitting in a rocking chair on the front porch, high above the debris-strewn waterfront. He asked her how she had managed to survive the storm. She had a six-word rejoinder that Bea could only regret was not the army corps' motto: "We build to exceed all standards" the old woman said, her rocking uninterrupted by Bea's inquiries.

IVOR VAN HEERDEN HAD WON A MAJOR VICTORY IN PROVING EARLY IN THE GAME that the Seventeenth Street and London Avenue flood walls had not been overtopped by water, as the corps wanted to believe. The levees had failed even before water reached the heights the walls were meant to contain and, in some cases, after it had begun to ebb. But the Industrial Canal levees, like those along the Gulf Outlet at Lake Borgne, had indeed been overtopped. On inspection, it was clear to both the NSF and Team Louisiana that as the water spilled over, it had washed away the soils in which the Industrial Canal flood walls were planted. The walls' collapse under those circumstances was ut-terly predictable, and the preventive measure couldn't have been simpler, Bea concluded. Concrete splash pads running down the levee from the base of the flood wall would have stopped the erosion like a piece of slate below the downspout on a suburbanite's green lawn. And the cost? Bea estimated informally that it would have jacked up the price of the flood wall project about 1 percent.

FAILURES ARE THEIR TEXTBOOKS, BUT FORENSIC ENGINEERS ALSO LEARN FROM the resilience of structures that survive. And so it was with some fascination that Bea toured the Orleans Avenue Canal, the only one of the three drainage canals that had not been breached. Might it offer clues that would be valuable in reconstructing the levees that hadn't made it?

If Bob Bea was given to outrage over all that he was learning about the fiasco created by his alma mater, the army corps, his sometimes morbid sense of humor could not be entirely extinguished. Levees along the other two drainage canals were coarse and workmanlike, but for some reason—pressure from a politician living in the area?—the designers of the Orleans Avenue flood walls had seen fit to adorn them with statuary and bas-reliefs. Concrete funerary urns stood above joints in the wall sections, connected by concrete swags looping from one to the next. "We built you a goddamn mortuary," Bea snorted. His exploration of the mysterious robustness of the Orleans Avenue Canal did not take long. Bea's first stop was also his last: the massive pump station that sluiced water into the canal, powering it in the direction of the lake, several miles to the north. Bea was startled to be shown the engines and to learn that they were originals, Baldwin Wood pumps installed in 1913. But they had worked, said the operator. On duty the night Katrina struck, he had seen water streaming through the brick walls of the station, exposing the crew to the risk of electrocution before the power failed.

After swapping storm stories in the proper post-Katrina manner, Bea got around to the purpose of his visit: figuring out why these levees hadn't failed. "Bob, that's easy," the man said. "The water never gets high in the canal." And why was that? "Go outside and take a look." Bea walked out of the station and looked toward the lake. What he saw floored him. The flood wall simply ended about three hundred feet shy of the pump station. The walls hadn't been knocked down by the raging water. They had never been built, and so the surge rushing in from the lake had spilled out into the streets before reaching the pump station that was supposed to turn it around and push it back out of the city. Here was a way to guarantee that an army corps flood barrier wouldn't fail, Bea thought ruefully: Don't finish it.

——— ✤ ———

TWENTY-THREE

Children with Bad Timing

THE WHITE HOUSE HAD DEMANDED ALL ALONG THAT LOUISIANA DEVELOP a single set of priorities and a single board or agency that could speak for the state with a single voice—a reasonable enough request, it might have seemed, and one that Louisiana would be quick to honor, given the billions of dollars riding on the administration's pleasure. Not so. Even before Don Powell was named federal coordinator and began ending his e-mails with the mantra "One voice, one commission," there were enough official voices holding forth on urgent themes to form a choir, and not a particularly melodious one. The competing noisemakers ranged from levee boards to the mayor's commission to the Louisiana Recovery Authority that Governor Blanco had set up. Tuning out the cacophony, Powell turned his good ear to the LRA and left it to Blanco's panel to tame the levee boards and deal with whatever good ideas—or political imbroglios—Nagin's group coughed up.

But even when unanimity on aspects of Louisiana's agenda had been achieved, Washington could get squirrelly. A Category 5 storm defense had been at the top of every list, and yet by year's end, Washington had committed only to studying the possibility of building a modern flood-control system. When the congressional delegation from Louisiana threw itself behind the Baker Bill—as a framework within which to rebuild, and in some cases relocate, flooded neighborhoods—the White House balked, and a measure that had seemed headed for passage expired with the congressional session that ended with the new year. Well, it would be tweaked and taken up in the next Congress, the Louisiana delegation reassured itself and the folks back home, not yet fully aware how deeply the Bush camp despised the measure. For one thing, it set up a federal bureaucracy to do what the Bush credo held that markets would do better. An underlying problem seemed to be that the bill, essentially a mechanism for compensating homeowners for their losses, was too even-handed. The Bush people wanted to draw a punishing distinction between homeowners who had or hadn't carried flood insurance. If you lived in a floodplain and didn't participate in the federal insurance program, then you deserved your losses. If you lived outside the flood zones, well, maybe that entitled you to some consideration.

Louisiana was outraged. The levee system that had failed was federal. For that matter, so were the floodplain maps that had proved completely unreliable as those levees collapsed and almost the entire city filled with water. But the administration held its ground. The biggest problem was that the bill's cost structure was potentially open-ended. The numbers were all wrong. By late January, it was clear that the Baker Bill was on life support, but its author and Governor Blanco still clung to hope that they could keep Bush's people from yanking the plug. At a press conference, the Louisianans laid out some numbers of their own. The state's housing costs were not infinite, but parity with Mississippi would require $12 billion in community development block grants, not the $8 billion then on the table. And as for those out of the floodplain who'd lost their houses anyway, well, there were twenty thousand of them. More to the point, Blanco and Baker declared that they would not even take the ribbon off a federal package that had nothing for the uninsured. The impasse looked to be intractable.

By coincidence, that same day, LRA vice chair Walter Isaacson settled down to lunch in the West Wing with Al Hubbard, Bush's closest economic adviser. Strictly speaking, it wasn't an LRA lunch. Isaacson's range of interests as head of the Aspen Institute gave him plenty of other things to talk about with Hubbard. But when Karl Rove ambled by, the political fortunes of the Baker Bill cropped up in conversation, and it became suddenly very clear to Isaacson that the bill was well and truly dead. Rove would have nothing to do with it. All right. "Then what's the alternative?" Isaacson wanted to know. From the conversation that followed, Isaacson came away with the sense that money probably could be found to boost the per-household compensation to Mississippi levels. The disparity, with Blanco invoking it so regularly, had to be an embarrassment even to an administration that liked to reward its political allies, and Mississippi governor Haley Barbour was decidedly part of the "in" crowd. But if Louisiana wanted some kind of Baker Bill–style recovery corporation to pay off homeowners and then sell or hold their property for redevelopment, well, Louisiana should set that up at the state level. The administration liked to think it was in the business of paring down the federal bureaucracy, not adding to it.

Isaacson had high regard for Blanco. Let others call her indecisive. For Isaacson, the greatest value of having Blanco at the head of Louisiana government just then was that she was an honest politician—if that wasn't a contradiction in terms—and she was sufficiently aware of the gravity of the moment to be willing to look beyond purely partisan self-interest. As proof that she was not just playing politics in the tried and true fashion of the Louisiana way, Isaacson needed to look no further than her decision against peopling the LRA with cronies or representatives of special interests to whom she might have felt a need to pander. Isaacson, for one, had never met the woman, hadn't even spoken with her, when she called out of the blue and asked him to join. Her reasons for turning to Isaacson were straightforward enough: She wanted a Louisianan with clout in Washington, she said—and it wasn't clear whether John Breaux, the formidable ex-senator turned lobbyist would be available. And in approaching Xavier University president Norman Francis to chair the board, she had turned to a black Louisianan utterly beyond reproach. "Putting Norman Francis on the board made it clear that it was not going to be politics as usual," Isaacson said.

Some of the same thinking had shaped her approach to the legislative session. Rather than setting an agenda with maximum partisan appeal, she had been encouraged by the LRA to stick to key ideas that would be the clearest expression of post-Katrina reform: levee board consolidation, the streamlining of New Orleans's government, creation of a program for housing recovery. "Maybe it was bad advice," Isaacson would muse as the second emergency legislative session entered its final hours, with the key parts of the Blanco agenda still on the ropes, "but it was the correct thing to do, in my humble opinion."

Isaacson's opinions were not always humble ones, but they had propelled him to considerable success as a journalist and pundit, and now, at the Aspen Institute, made him something of an impresario in the world of men and women with big ideas. From early jobs as a reporter in New Orleans, he had gone on to *Time* magazine, where his major books on establishment figures ranging from Averell Harriman and his circle to Henry Kissinger had landed Isaacson the managing editorship at a tender age. Before taking charge of the Aspen Institute and its worldwide network of conferences and publications, Isaacson had served a stint as top dog at CNN.

One of his opinions that didn't fly far at all was a formula for compensating flood victims that Isaacson offered up to his colleagues on the LRA along with his advice, based on the West Wing lunch, that the Baker Bill was toast. Isaacson's formula, like Baker's, was based in part on homeowner equity, but the formula did not fully account for the fact that even 100 percent of that equity might leave the recipient without a nickel if the mortgage holder did not agree to waive its claim. "It was such a dumb idea, it challenged them to come up with something better," Isaacson said, "proving why I'm not a housing expert."

If Isaacson's hunch about the need to retool the buyout plan left any room for doubt, it was eliminated in a phone call Don Powell placed that Friday to LRA member Sean Reilly. The Baker Bill was dead; it was time to come up with something else. A Harvard-schooled lawyer and former two-term state legislator who ran Lamar Outdoor, the giant billboard and advertising company based in Baton Rouge, Reilly had emerged as a lead dog on the LRA. Indeed, with Andy Kopplin, the aide Blanco had tapped to take charge of the state's recovery, and Stephan Pryor, who had run the Lower Manhattan Development Corporation after 9/11, Reilly had helped draft the executive order that set up the recovery authority in the first weeks after the storm.

Over the weekend after Powell's discouraging call, Reilly worked up a white paper on the way to move beyond the impasse. On the following Friday, January twenty-seventh, at Powell's invitation, Reilly hopped a plane for Amarillo.

A casual if imposing man given to open-collar striped shirts and cowboy boots, Powell showed up at the airport in person to meet the supplicant from Louisiana. On the way back into town, he pointed out the tallest building against the Amarillo skyline. They could eat in the tower, he told Reilly, in the Amarillo Club, but there was the likelihood of repeated interruptions as local business and political honchos paid him court. "I'll have to talk to people," Powell cautioned. Instead they opted for the anonymity of a nondescript pasta joint with white paper tablecloths. Shove aside the napkin dispenser and the salt and pepper shakers and the paper tablecloth provided as good a surface as any for drafting Louisiana's future. In short order, it was crawling with numbers and calculations, cross-outs, and second stabs at a buyout plan the Bush people could agree to: how to penalize the uninsured residents of the floodplain without leaving them out of the buyout package altogether; how to structure governance of a state-operated housing trust, now that the White House had rejected the notion of a federal-level agency; what to do about repairing New Orleans's critical sewerage and water infrastructure; and how about Entergy, the bankrupt New Orleans utility? New York after 9/11 had been given enough money to bail out Con Ed, but somehow when it came to the far more heavily damaged New Orleans utility, the Bush people had remembered their neocon catechism and had come out against a government bailout for a private industry.

Toting up the state's immediate needs, Reilly's numbers came close to $7 billion—"way high," he would come to concede. Powell was offering to pay for pasta, not prime rib. As negotiations continued, the gap narrowed, sometimes because better data had been provided by the number crunchers backing the two men; in some instances because the men had, or shortly would, overcome polarizing policy differences. By the time they left the restaurant, they had not worked out every detail, but they were on the way, and the tablecloth—it seemed strangely indiscreet to Reilly to be simply leaving it behind like that—ranked right up there with the deed for the Louisiana Purchase as one of the formative documents in the history of the state.

The heart of the recovery plan that Reilly and Powell had roughed out was a "direct to homeowner" arrangement that would pay full value for a property at its pre-Katrina appraisal—no percentage-of-equity formulas in play—minus whatever flood insurance and FEMA payments had been collected.

Reilly was back on a plane for Baton Rouge within an hour or two of his lunch in Amarillo, but discussions among Kopplin, Reilly, and Powell's people continued in person and by conference call more or less nonstop for four days. Blanco was in Washington on the last day of January, to testify before the Senate panel probing Katrina and to hear Bush's State of the Union speech. The next day, she dropped in on Powell personally, and then briefed the state's congressional delegation on where things stood—or where she thought they stood. The following morning she picked up *The Washington Post* and had reason to wonder how she could have been so wrong. Not only had Powell defended the current level of federal outlay for the disaster in terms that suggested there would be no Mississippi-level enhancements, but, in a paean to free-market economics, he seemed to trash the very idea of government intrusion in the housing market.

"As a former chairman of the Federal Deposit Insurance Corp. and someone who spent 40 years in the banking sector," Powell wrote, "I do not believe making the government a broker and landlord for the region will ensure a healthy long-term recovery. Doing so—at a cost of up to $30 billion with an option to renew, and little chance of recouping those funds—would destroy free-market mechanisms."

Isaacson went ballistic, and in remarks that were picked up in *The New York Times* and later regretted, he said the Powell pronunciamento threw Bush's credibility into question. Blanco too was livid, though she would find other ways to express her disgust.

Given the invitation from the White House to attend the president's State of the Union speech, Blanco had arrived for the event cautiously optimistic that there might be something in it for Louisiana. Nagin had been invited as well and was in Washington, though he would skip the speech in favor of meetings with evacuees. The political class had been buzzing with hope that Bush would use the moment to announce a new initiative. Senator Landrieu placed her hopes in a dedicated revenue stream from offshore oil and gas royalties. Congressman Jefferson mentioned housing, perhaps an adjusted version of the stalled Baker Bill. Instead, what Blanco got from Bush was a glancing, substanceless reference to Katrina near the end of the speech, and a televised peck on the cheek as the president worked the crowd on his way out of the House. He had lavished $85 billion on the Gulf Coast, he said in the speech, a figure that, while impressive, was also deceptive. It included not just aid to Louisiana, Mississippi, Alabama, and Texas but operations costs of the federal bureaucracies that were administering that aid, FEMA and the army corps among them—"dysfunctional bureaucracies," Senator Mary Landrieu had snapped in decrying the decision to pump into them billions of what were meant to be Gulf Coast recovery funds. At $18.5 billion, the third largest item on the federal menu was the cost of payouts by the federal flood insurance program, a cost that was supposed to have been covered by premiums paid by the insured—except it wasn't. Like so much of the federal government just then, the program was drowning in red ink. As it turned out, only about half the $85 billion had actually been spent by the time Bush made his speech—"more than half," the White House contended; about a quarter, Powell suggested. No one seemed to know for sure.

Two days later, Blanco met privately at the White House with Powell, chief of staff Andy Card, and Isaacson's sometime lunch partner Al Hubbard. Powell's op-ed piece had done nothing to improve her mood. The problem wasn't that Blanco thought Powell was too political, though he had been a major fund-raiser for Bush; it was that he wasn't political enough. Beyond whatever life lessons he may have learned as a banker in Amarillo, Texas, Powell's vantage on wider horizons was his service as chairman with the Federal Deposit Insurance Corporation, and from what Blanco could tell, that lifted a banker above the fray rather than honing his instincts for real-world give-and-take, a view she would disown as Powell began to come through for Louisiana. "You shouldn't be out there fronting for the president," Blanco had not hesitated to tell him in a separate conversation before their meeting with the Bush staffers. "He's got plenty of people doing that for him. You need to be a mediator, between Louisiana and Washington. You tell us what the president's looking for; you tell him what we need. You shouldn't let yourself be squeezed like this." She let rip with a final salvo: "You're dealing with some evil politics up here."

At the White House, she unloaded some more, telling Card and Hubbard that from here on out it was hardball. And when they asked her why, she was blunt. " 'Being nice hasn't paid dividends,' I told them. 'Nice doesn't get results.' " She pointed out that she had not cast a single aspersion on the president personally and had no intention of starting, but thereafter, she warned, she was going to assume the White House was not acting in Louisiana's best interests, and she would do what she had to do to be sure those interests were at least acknowledged. "Don Powell went into meltdown," Blanco said, lapsing into a moment of mimicry. " 'Oh, Governor. That's really not the best way to do business. We need to talk numbers.' But you and I were talking numbers last night," she snapped back, "and you didn't tell me you had that op-ed piece coming out in the *Post* this morning."

Five days later, as she launched the special legislative session, not in the state house but with a speech at the New Orleans convention center, the scene of so much recent misery, the hardball player threw another curve, one that Bob Harvey and the Edwards crowd would have been proud of: Unless the federal government got serious about coastal restoration and flood protection, she warned, Louisiana would not consent to the annual auction of offshore oil and gas tracts in the coming year. Before the federal auction could take place, the EPA required the governor to sign a pro forma release confirming that the drilling envisioned in the auction would be consistent with the state's environmental well-being.

"I'm an oil and gas governor," Blanco would say in explaining her stance, but in good conscience she couldn't allow the drilling if degradation of Louisiana's coastal infrastructure would continue unchecked. It was a technicality, but Washington was big on technicalities, she had come to see. Could she get away with it? Blanco assumed the feds might find a way around her obstructionism, but the point would be made, and Americans might be reminded, those who weren't learning for the first time, that Louisiana was more than Mardi Gras and spicy food and lazy living along a bayou. It was among the nation's most important fisheries and yet one of only eight states that tolerated offshore drilling. What Blanco was really after was a share of the $5 billion in federal oil and gas royalties that, by her estimate, the feds collected annually on the outer continental shelf. The feds kicked back 50 percent of such royalties to inland oil and gas states, while

Louisiana got almost nothing. With even a portion of that money, Louisiana would have a dedicated revenue stream to cover the state's obligatory portion of the huge flood-protection projects that Blanco's trip to Holland had convinced her must be built.

Two could play this game, of course. Unless the southeast Louisiana levee boards were consolidated, a condition attached to the Gulf Coast recovery spending package by freshman congressman Bobby Jindal, the Republican that Blanco had beaten in the governor's race, required that Congress withhold $12 million that the army corps was counting on to continue studying a Category 5 flood-control system. That was a threat Blanco could put to her own uses in the fight for levee board consolidation. Twelve million dollars might not be all that much in the scheme of things, but in language the patronage crowd could readily understand, it made the federal priority distinctly clear. Consolidate the levee boards or kiss the money good-bye and with it orderly progress toward a stronger flood defense. Blanco was not hesitating to remind reporters and lawmakers of that at every opportunity as she pushed and prodded her agenda into the sausage-maker that was a legislative session.

It had become fashionable to dismiss Blanco as a disaster insufficient to the task of coping with a catastrophe. Republicans in Baton Rouge saw Louisiana's salvation in Jindal, a whiz kid bureaucrat at both the state and federal levels before his election to Congress. The Bush camp's attempted vilification of Blanco dated to the very week of the storm, and had seemed to demonstrate an urgent and focused need to shrug blame for the bungled relief effort. But the trashing of Kathleen Blanco sometimes seemed to arise from less coherent impulses and evaluations. In mid-November, *Time* magazine had declared her one of the three worst governors in the nation, a ranking that pivoted less on what she had actually done in the teeth of the crisis than on her seeming "dazed and confused" after working around the clock in a windowless command center for three days.

The designation savored less of serious journalism than an in-joke in a high school yearbook, aimed at a departed alumnus—Walter Isaacson, perhaps, now allied with Blanco as vice chairman of the LRA. But local media had fired off their shots as well, rescinding plaudits accorded Blanco during the first emergency legislative session for snatching at least one victory from

Katrina's jaws: the virtual state takeover of the atrocious Orleans Parish school system. It had been a notably deft and bloodless coup, long overdue. But the press, and Blanco's own team, wanted more, a bolder stroke that would show Washington that Louisiana was serious about political reform: consolidation of the balkanized and patronage-ridden system of district levee boards.

The Times-Picayune, a Jindal backer, took Blanco to task for not making that consolidation happen in the first emergency legislative session, in early November. A bill put forward by Republican state senator Walter Boasso, a burly container-shipping handler from devastated St. Bernard Parish, had failed, despite heavy lobbying by business interests. It would have consolidated some, but not all, levee districts in the New Orleans area. Blanco had focused more intently in the first legislative session on a successful bill that created something called the Louisiana Coastal Protection and Restoration Authority (CPRA). As far as she was concerned, the CPRA could speak cogently for Louisiana's flood-control needs whether district levee boards were consolidated or not. Boards that substituted patronage games for sensible flood-protection strategies would be subject to ready discipline by government's ultimate threat: The CPRA could simply choke off their funding.

In reviewing the successes and failures of that first emergency legislative session, the Blanco camp suggested that the enacted CPRA was, de facto, the consolidated levee board that the good Republican senator from St. Bernard Parish had tried and failed to achieve. But her critics were not assuaged. Their insinuation was that Blanco didn't have the courage to stand up to the patronage pigs, many of them Democrats, who had fattened themselves on levee board contracts over the years. She would explain in other terms her willingness to let the consolidation bill die that first time out: It was a bad bill, "no meat on the bone." And it surely was emaciated, compared to the fifty-page version that her staff helped Boasso put in the hopper for the second emergency legislative session three months later. It went further than Boasso's original bill, which had stopped short of amalgamating the parts of Jefferson Parish west of the Mississippi River into the consolidated district—a concession to political necessity that Blanco would come to appreciate the hard way.

And the revamped bill addressed bedeviling issues that had not been thought through in the bill that failed: how to handle debt run up by the separate districts; how to collect and apportion taxes, given their very different revenue structures; how to police the levees. Now that she had the bill she wanted, Blanco was prepared to fight doggedly for it. "Hydrology doesn't know political boundaries," she said. It would become a catchphrase in her rhetoric during the second legislative session, and when the anti-consolidation forces countered with the argument that separate drainage basins—there being basically two of them in the New Orleans area: one into Lake Pontchartrain and the other into Barataria Bay—required separate levee boards, she pointed out that the river, the mightiest flood threat of them all, cut across both. "Scientists are laughing at us," she said of parochialism's attempt to disguise itself as geographical insight.

Patronage games were a malignancy at the heart of levee board politics, in Blanco's view, which is one reason why the consolidation bill she backed proposed to strip the Orleans levee board of all its distractions: the private airport, the casino, the marinas, the tennis club—all that stuff. But patronage games were not the only basis for resistance to consolidation, she would concede. More honorably, the smaller districts feared losing clout to Orleans and Jefferson parishes. "We know there is an awful lack of trust; local communities fear their voices won't be heard," she said, which put the onus on her to explain that the whole idea behind a consolidated board was to make it also a professional board, comprising at least some engineers who actually knew something about flood control. There was an irony in this distrust that was not lost on Blanco. "Washington doesn't trust Louisiana with the money we need to recover; and we don't trust each other," Baton Rouge journalist Robert Travis Scott remarked as he headed off to cover the session's second day. Yes, Blanco could understand the anxieties of the smaller parishes, but her sympathy extended only so far. "Levee districts that feel left out now may feel left out even more if they don't support a consolidated board," she warned.

THERE HAD ALWAYS BEEN SOMETHING DECEPTIVE ABOUT BLANCO: A SURPRISE in the discovery, which might take awhile, that she carried a sharp political knife in the folds of her grandmotherly togs. This was no accidental governor. She lived and breathed politics, and as with most who are successful at the Great Game, there was a steeliness behind what, in her case, could seem like a soft touch. Blanco could also be credited with consistency, a calm and steady hand on the tiller. And after Ray Nagin's fits and starts, his embrace of a recovery committee whose key policies he would then disown—not to mention Aaron Broussard's sobbing and self-pity—steadiness was an attribute in short supply just then in Louisiana. Whether her hand on the tiller was steering Louisiana straight toward a reef would be for history—or the electorate—to decide.

But Katrina had changed Blanco—or, more exactly, her vilification by Bush and others had changed her. Her public demeanor remained unruffled, but as the new year dawned and it became clear that Washington had retreated from the spirit of the many bold promises Bush had made when Katrina was still a photo op, Blanco gave up on cajolery and a gentler style of Southern womanhood and declared war. She still foreswore personal attacks. Bush was, after all, the president of the United States. Even Nagin was spared excoriation. She was a politician; he was a politician. She knew what was going on: "You've got a mayor stuck in an election cycle at an unfortunate time," she said over a dinner of snapper and crabmeat at the governor's mansion after a long day in the trenches of the legislative session, "so he's reacting to every little thing, every smidgen of controversy."

Indeed, Nagin was facing a lengthening slate of opponents for a mayoral primary election that had been postponed by the storm from February to April. Earlier that very day, the powerful and richly financed husband of Nagin's own press secretary had thrown his hat into the ring. Once a bookkeeping functionary at city hall, Ron Forman had parlayed the successful upgrade of a sad-sack city zoo into stewardship of a collection of municipal attractions that included a world-class aquarium, a soon-to-open insectarium, and a research center for breeding endangered species. Lieutenant Governor Mitch Landrieu, the son of a former mayor and the brother of U.S. senator Mary Landrieu, was also tempted by the prospect of swapping his job for Nagin's.

Blanco was coy about the mayor's race, however much a Nagin trouncing might have delighted her. "A lot of my friends are getting into this race;

it looks like it's going to be a hot one," Blanco had said earlier that day to a TV reporter trying to goad her into a more partisan remark. Disaster traditionally had been cruel to incumbent politicians. Polling for the mayor's race was all but impossible, given an electorate scattered to fifty states, but Nagin had been a lightning rod for bitter recrimination from participants in a series of "town hall" meetings in cities—Atlanta, Houston, Memphis—with large evacuee populations that would be able to vote absentee. Blanco's numbers were also in the tank. A poll in late November suggested that only one in five Louisianans was definitely planning to vote for her, but the election was two years off. That gave Blanco time—and a sense that she had nothing left to lose gave her license—to rethink her strategies.

There were incongruities in the juxtaposed emblems of Governor Blanco's power: the 1930s art deco chic of her office on the fourth floor of the state house clashed with the Orwellian wall of closed-circuit television screens on which, without leaving her desk, she monitored legislative committee hearings on the floors below; there was the battered knapsack that this otherwise primly dressed grandmother tossed onto the backseat of her limousine and from which she proceeded to pull mascara and lipstick, making herself up as she was ferried on a too-tight schedule from a legislative luncheon to the studios of the state public television station for a round of remote interviews with journalists from far corners of the state; there was the elegance of the limousine itself, a black Lincoln, undercut jarringly by the butt of an assault rifle visible alongside the seat occupied by Blanco's driver, Chavis Verrett, a huge and cheerful man well schooled in deadly arts. Actually, Blanco was said to be no mean shot herself, after a lifetime of duck hunting. In recent years it had been one of the special things she did with her sons—just Blanco and her boys, a once- or twice-a-year outing in the Louisiana marshes, which, while they lasted, were among the continent's most important flyways for migratory birds.

Makeup in place, Blanco had a few minutes to leaf through paperwork her communications aide, Bob Mann, was handing back to her from the front seat. And then, instead of the next piece of paper, he was handing her his Blackberry and directing her attention to a couple of text messages. The bad news: the bill to streamline New Orleans city government had emerged from committee with three dozen amendments. Astonishingly, the levee

board consolidation measure seemed to have made it out of the senate committee unscathed—and this after the noon news on the dominant talk radio
station in New Orleans, WWL, had carried commentary to the effect that the
bill was dead on arrival. Of course, the session was young. There would be
plenty of opportunities to peck the levee board bill to death on the floor of
either legislative chamber, but still . . . "Wait, I want confirmation on this,"
Blanco said, as the aide proposed a phone call to WWL to set the record
straight. "Remember how they said the miners weren't dead?" She referred
to the dozen men killed weeks earlier in a West Virginia coal mine collapse,
which was initially reported to be nonfatal. In seconds, the aide had the committee chairman on the phone and the report was verified, but the decision
was made to nix a gloating call to WWL.

From the studios, it was back to the governor's office and then one crisis
after another requiring phone calls, sudden visits by the governor and her entourage to committee rooms for other bills that needed resuscitation, a meeting with the newly elected head of the state Democratic Party, a very heated
discussion by phone with an elected state official who had gone public with
a policy position out of sync with an aspect of the LRA agenda. Her voice
never rising above a purr, the governor listened to the man explain his lapse
by complaining that he had been left out of the loop. "You go popping off
like that, you're going to lose our trust," she warned.

The afternoon ended with a much more upbeat call: congratulations to
Walter Boasso for getting the levee board consolidation bill out of committee relatively unscathed. Boasso flattered the governor by asking what her
behind-the-scenes role was. Blanco wanted the moment to be all Walter's.
"The governor never said anything," she said, referring to herself in the third
person. "I didn't put a heavy on anybody. We're all in the same rowboat.
You're either on board or you're not."

Theories varied as to what made Blanco tick, what had driven this
housewife and mother so remorselessly to the pinnacle of power and what
kept her going seven days a week at a pace aides half her age could barely
match. Theories were available. One held that her drive and her fortitude
were a coping mechanism, a way of enduring the unendurable loss she had
suffered in the death of her son Benedict nine years earlier. Ben, then nineteen, had been working at an industrial site near Morgan City when a crane

malfunctioned and he was struck by a giant weight as his brother, Ray Jr., looked on. Then there was her deep Catholic faith and the austere childhood she had endured as the oldest of seven kids—a virtual mother to the younger ones—in a salesman's household with little scratch. Or was she just one tough politician in a state that makes them as tough as any other? Gravely insulted by a hurricane—make that two hurricanes—and by her president, maybe it was all about defying the pollsters and clawing her way back to the top. "It's no fun when you're out of power," she said at one point, apropos not of her own still considerable power but of an ousted official whose name had cropped up in dinner table conversation.

In a sense, humiliation had been liberating for Blanco. "I don't feel any more boundaries," she reflected over a cup of hot lemonade as the day finally began to wind down. "I have nothing to lose." But the loss was Louisiana's as well, as Blanco saw it. "They have wounded my capacity to be a governor," she said of the Bush smear campaign. She said it matter-of-factly, a doctor of politics diagnosing her own condition.

BUSH, WHEN QUIZZED BY MEDIA IN THE DAYS AFTER KATRINA, HAD BEEN UNable to come up with anything he felt he'd done wrong. Brown, after first blaming FEMA's failings on Blanco and Nagin, had recanted that view in early January and publicly accepted responsibility for the fiasco. Contrition did not last long. Coincident with Louisiana's second emergency legislative session, Brown had been called back to Washington by Maine senator Susan Collins's committee on Katrina. Now speaking as a private citizen, he donned a prophet's robes and insisted that he had been warning for years about how severely the Bush administration's obsession with terror was eviscerating FEMA. The new villain in the piece: his old boss Michael Chertoff, a man so indifferent to FEMA's needs and methods that Brown had gotten into the habit of calling the White House rather than dealing with the sclerotic DHS bureaucracy that Chertoff commanded.

Blanco's mea culpas were measured, if not grudging. Like any politician, she preferred to dress them as proposals for reform. There were some points she would not concede, no matter how vehemently the White House and its talking heads rebutted her. On reflection, she remained convinced that within two days of Katrina, she had thrown everything she had into the relief effort, every bus, soldier, and rescue boat that could be mustered or commandeered by Louisiana authorities. And she would continue to insist that the evacuation, overall, had been a triumph; for proof, one needed to look no further than Houston's performance ahead of Hurricane Rita.

That said, Blanco was embarrassed by her administration's failure to work out a plan for emptying the nursing homes and hospitals before Katrina—something that would be only more necessary in the coming storm season, given weakened levees. In her most recent appearance before the Senate committee, Blanco had also implored the panel to revamp the Stafford Act in ways that freed FEMA to make investments in permanent housing. For the exorbitant amounts of money being lavished on sweetheart deals with plugged-in fat cats in the trailer business, FEMA could have built "Katrina cottages" or refurbished apartments to accommodate the tens of thousands of Louisianans who still found themselves homeless five months after the hurricanes.

The shocking breakdown in emergency communications during the storm also needed to be addressed with interoperable gear (financed by the feds), Blanco felt, and, in a concession that she should have more quickly suspended licensure rules for out-of-state doctors, Blanco vowed before Congress that she would streamline emergency credentialing for law enforcement personnel as well. And then, of course, there was the overarching commitment to building a more efficient and professional state system of levee management—if only she or her legislative floor leaders had the tactical skills to overcome the local politicians who had fed so gluttonously and for so long at the patronage trough.

Those were key points on Blanco's official list of errors acknowledged and the reforms vowed. But more idiosyncratic lessons would jump out at her during her endless ruminations on Katrina. "We need to find a way to get the bus drivers' families to safety early on, so they can commit to doing their jobs without that distraction," Blanco said as the dinner table conversation circled back around to the proper role—if any—of government vehicles in a mandatory evacuation before a hurricane. And another thing: "I want to see all those big downtown buildings equipped with a rooftop helicopter pad," Blanco said. The proposal was borne of deep admiration for what she had seen pilots do in the emergency. On rooftops cluttered with the usual array of air-conditioning condensers and antennas and vents and ducts, a helicopter pilot would put just his front wheel down on the roof's edge, Blanco said, picking up a piece of the mansion's heavy silver flatware and touching the handle end of the fork to the edge of the mahogany table. And then he'd maneuver the helicopter horizontally until the midcraft door abutted the edge of the roof, she said, replicating that sideways motion with the fork. A soldier would stand with one foot in the copter and one on the roof, lifting each terrified evacuee over the narrow but vertiginous chasm plunging to the street below. "Those were the real heroes," Blanco said, almost to herself.

THE GOVERNOR OF LOUISIANA WAS TOO MUCH OF A POLITICIAN HERSELF TO NOT see the White House's maneuvering against her for what it was. Rove had been aboard when Air Force One touched down in New Orleans five days after Katrina. It was the only evidence Blanco needed, to know that Bush was not so consumed with concern for the dying and the dispossessed as to be oblivious to the political peril to which the hurricane had exposed his administration. And of course Republican Haley Barbour's Mississippi was going to be made whole while Louisiana, with a Democrat for governor, would be made to suffer.

One factor in her analysis of Bush's performance fell outside the domain of pure partisanship, however: the war in Iraq. And then there were the deficits, a related but separate issue. Blanco had been to Iraq to visit with the substantial deployment of Louisiana Guardsmen, and though she was there not long after the invasion and attendant aerial bombing, the recovery had already progressed nicely. "It looked better than it does here," she said. The federal budget was hemorrhaging money for Iraq, Blanco realized, at a time when deficits were already spinning out of control under an administration that refused to raise the revenue necessary to cover its costs. And then along comes Louisiana, hat in hand. "We are like children with bad timing," Blanco said, pushing herself away from the table and heading upstairs to make the sixteen phone calls that she had to return before she could even consider her husband's entreaty to just let it all go for a few hours and come to bed.

Four days after her call of congratulations to Walter Boasso, the levee consolidation bill ran into stiff resistance, and he pulled it back—triggering headlines to the effect that Blanco's entire agenda was going down in flames. In fact, Boasso's retreat, orchestrated by Blanco and her people, was tactical and, as would become clear, rather shrewd. But for the nonce, it triggered a round of catcalls, some even from her own floor leaders, that the governor wasn't working her agenda hard enough.

If Blanco had seemed at times distracted during the legislative session, there was a reason why. Baton Rouge was only one theatre in the war she was fighting. The LRA's behind-the-scenes dealings with Powell and the White House had continued unabated. On Sunday before the session's second and final week, Sean Reilly had flown up to Washington for yet another meeting with Powell, accompanied by Blanco aide Andy Kopplin, LRA co-chair Norman Francis, and Joe Canizaro, the banker with Nagin's Bring New Orleans Back Commission. By Tuesday, all differences had been worked out and Powell had pledged to support an additional appropriation of $4.2 billion.

Isaacson, who had been away over the weekend, would credit Nagin with a significant contribution at this juncture. Operating in a universe parallel to but not quite congruent with the state-level effort, the mayor had floated a plan earlier in the week that would have based compensation—if money could be found—on a formula that took depths of flooding into account. Eclipsed by the governor, Nagin had nonetheless rallied the support of adjacent parish leaders to Powell's new offer, and so it was that Aaron Broussard of Jefferson Parish, Benny Rousselle of Plaquemines, and St. Bernard's Junior Rodriguez were aboard the corporate jet that carried the Louisianans to Washington the next day. Isaacson "commandeered," as he put it, a Senate office room, and the group sat down for a final round of kumbaya with Powell and the state congressional delegation. There might be some final nips and tucks to the compensation formulas as the parishes worked out their differences. Powell seemed to understand that. But the plan had White House backing. Getting it through Congress would be another matter, very much contingent on whether Louisiana behaved itself and passed a levee board consolidation bill in the emergency legislative session set to expire that same week.

To impress the politicos with the gravity of the moment, Don Powell flew down to Baton Rouge and, with the governor at his side, took a seat on the dais as the amended levee bill came up for a final vote in the Louisiana house. For Powell, it was an opportunity to bask in his and the LRA's success in securing Bush's backing for the added $4.2 billion in block grants. But Powell's presence also served as a warning. With the eyes of the nation—and Congress—upon them, Louisiana's lawmakers had best not revert to type and reject levee board consolidation he warned. It would be taken as an expression of the state's hopeless entanglement in the clutches of cronyism and patronage politics, also as an open invitation for other state delegations in Congress to make a run at the money still not officially appropriated for Louisiana. And under Powell's watchful gaze, not to mention considerable pressure from business interests, state reps approved the measure almost unanimously. State senate approval on the session's final day was foreordained.

Blanco had not gotten everything she wanted. Legislation she had backed that would have set up an agency to manage the housing recovery made possible by the infusion of federal billions died and would have to be taken up in the regular legislative session coming in the spring. So would the measure to rid New Orleans of its extra assessors and sheriff and judges. Even the levee board bill represented a compromise, though one Blanco had been prepared for, despite the rhetoric with which she had sought the purest form of consolidation. The patchwork of districts had been reduced not to a single board but to two of them, one on either side of the river. Nonetheless, it was a measure that defied decades of the proud and arrant parochialism that had been the very essence of the state's political culture. Equally important, in merging the east bank levee districts in St. Bernard, Orleans, Jefferson, St. Tammany, and Tangipahoa parishes, the bill stripped Orleans of its patronage-ridden distractions: the airport, the marinas, and so forth.

There were ways to portray the outcome for Blanco as a glass half-empty, and the New Orleans paper found them by reminding readers of the session's earlier brush with disarray. But Blanco did not have to reach far to claim victory. "If consolidation of the New Orleans area levee boards was the only accomplishment, I would call the session a total success," she said. Boasso, the bill's sponsor, saw the moment as a watershed: "We're entering something new in the world of politics in Louisiana," he said. "The future of our state is going to depend on changes like this."

"It sends a . . . message to the people of southeast Louisiana to come home," said Ruthie Frierson, whose red jacket symbolized her membership in Citizens for 1 Greater New Orleans, an Uptown lobbying group dominated by bottle blondes of a certain age and generally prosperous circumstances—Frierson was a real estate agent. The group had amassed fifty-three thousand signatures on a petition and then had relentlessly trod the halls of the state house in support of the levee board consolidation. "The federal government can now feel assured that the billions of dollars we receive for levee projects will be held accountable by professional boards," Frierson added optimistically.

By coincidence, the session's final day was marked by two other milestones. The New Orleans convention center, for the first time since Katrina, was being used not as a seething shelter or temporary trauma center but for a trade show. About five hundred jewelry exhibitors drew fifteen thousand buyers. And after the orders had been placed and logged, those of a sporting inclination could walk down Convention Center Boulevard to Harrah's casino, which also reopened that evening, providing jobs for twelve hundred generally eager employees, or about half the pre-storm payroll.

Mardi Gras lay just ahead, a calculation in the casino's reopening. So too did the 2006 hurricane season for a city with weakened levees or, in some areas, still no levees at all. "You know something," lawyer John Cummings had said in a reflective moment some few weeks earlier, "another bad hurricane like Katrina, two in a row like that, and it's all over for this town. There won't be a comeback from another storm like that. And we could have one this year."

TWENTY-FOUR

———— ⚜ ————

Failure Is Not an Option

CONSOLIDATED LEVEE BOARDS WERE A FINE THING. NOW ALL THAT WAS needed were some levees. As the calendar page flipped and January became February, the official onset of the 2006 hurricane season was exactly one hundred twenty days away. Whippet-thin, his reddish orange hair cropped so close to his balding scalp you wondered why he didn't just take a razor and be done with it, Col. Lewis F. Setliff III began that last day of January as he began most days, with a four-thirty AM jog through dark streets. Very dark. Fully half the city streetlamps were still out, as were the traffic lights. But at least the debris piles had been mostly cleared away in the downtown area. If only something could be done about the wrecked cars. Casualties of the flood, their upholstery rotting, their sides and windows still coated in the weird whitish gray brine that had once coated houses, shrubs, trees, and everything else across the city's huge floodplain, the cars had been hauled under overpasses and long stretches of elevated expressways, giving the areas the look of ghost parking lots. Just why Mayor Nagin continued to dicker with contracts that should have removed them months earlier was one of the mysteries of municipal politics, but none of a military man's business.

It was a scattered existence for Setliff, the officer tapped by the army corps to rebuild the area's horribly degraded levee system—a billion-dollar task even if it just meant mending the system that had failed, and so far that's all Congress had authorized. Tuesday: New Orleans; Wednesday: Destin, Florida. A talk with corps brass meant a trip to Washington. Research specific to the levee reconstruction project was funneled, like the continent's mightiest river, through Vicksburg, Mississippi, the corps' regional command post and the location of the world's most sophisticated flood-control laboratories. Setliff's home just then was St. Louis, where the long-suffering Mrs. Setliff was decorating her seventh residence in ten years. She had joined her husband in New Orleans for Christmas. Well, Christmas in a flood-ravaged city might not have been everyone's idea of a holiday dream come true, but at least they were together—not something that had happened with much regularity during another of Setliff's recent missions, the fifteen months he'd spent commanding combat engineers in Iraq. On Christmas Day, he took Lizabeth out to see the Seventeenth Street Canal breach. Unexpectedly, the place was mobbed; disaster tourism had picked up with the holidays, and, to the disgust of residents trying to resurrect their homes, Bellaire Drive was a parade of crawling cars and gawking pedestrians. Setliff ordered the site sealed. There were liability issues to consider as well as common decency.

Bringing Lizabeth to New Orleans for a firsthand look at the devastation had recommended itself to Setliff as the best way for her to understand the challenge he faced and the ungodly amount of time he was going to have to devote to an almost impossible task. Except there would be no calling it impossible. Not even with one hundred sixty-nine miles of levee to repair, some sixty contracts to monitor, millions of cubic yards of soil to dig from borrow pits all over the Gulf South.

It was inconceivable that every aspect of this monumental undertaking would be finished by June first. It was likewise inconceivable that Colonel Setliff would publicly countenance the possibility of not finishing by June first. "Failure is not an option." That was one of his mantras. Another: "The strategy is part of the solution." That failure was not an option was easy enough to understand. Just how the strategy and the solution converged might take a little longer for the uninitiated to grasp.

His predawn jog completed, Setliff poked some sustenance—but not much—into his skeletal frame, and shortly was clomping in high-gloss black combat boots around the offices of Task Force Guardian, as the levee reconstruction mission was known. The corps had taken over two floors in the Federal Reserve Bank's heavily fortified redoubt off Poydras Street in New Orleans's central business district, and it was here that Setliff had based a staff of 183 that ranged from lawyers to engineers to graphic artists and communications specialists. He was an improbable warrior, if brawn and stolid thinking figured into your preconception of the breed. Setliff was as cerebral as he was scrawny. His drivers were accustomed to his paging silently through a sheaf of documents as he was bustled by SUV from one site inspection to the next and on through meetings and interviews and more meetings. His day rarely ended before eight or nine at night and often, as in the upcoming meeting in Destin with engineering firms eager for an army corps contract, went on far longer than that.

There was a time, well before Setliff's career began, when the army corps had truly commanded an army, and to order up a bridge or a levee or a dam was to stir that army to action. Budgetary constraints and the congressional yen to give constituent engineers and contractors a piece of the action had changed all that. Now the work was outsourced almost entirely, and the commander's role adjusted accordingly. Setliff was one of just three uniformed personnel among the 186 people on the Task Force Guardian payroll, not to mention the hundreds more private-sector employees working for some forty contractors. Even staring down the barrel of the June first deadline, the preponderance of civilians made the colonel less the lion tamer he might have been, with a horde of soldiers under his command, than a herder of alley cats.

Out of respect for the vestiges of the old order inherent in his camo duds and spit-and-polish boots, site supervisors hopped-to when Setliff arrived unannounced, but the crack of his whip was muffled. Because the initial round of contracts was designed on the fly and subject to continuing modifications, except in the case of the one to gate the plugged drainage canals, it

had been impossible to build in the monetary performance incentives that
sometimes inspire the private sector to extra effort. Setliff was instead reduced to cajolery and hand-holding. That might seem to have required more
psychology than engineering science of the West Point grad. But knowing
whose hand needed holding and when to give it a sharp squeeze required
weekly, even daily, monitoring of the contractors' performances, and that in
turn meant knowing the technical aspects of every challenge they faced.
Hence the constant flow of paperwork and the briefing from the colonel's
immediate underlings as his driver cut through floodgates and delivered him
to a scene of toppled flood walls or thrumming sheet pile hammers.

One stopover that morning was a site along the Industrial Canal where
water had surged over the flood wall that rose an extra few feet above the top
of the levee. As it had cascaded down the landward side of the flood wall, the
water had dashed and eroded the levee soils on which it fell. Elsewhere
along the Industrial Canal, that process—the engineers called it scouring—
was implicated in the outright collapse of the flood wall and the breach that
had devastated the Lower Ninth Ward. Setliff noted with satisfaction that
trenching had been completed preparatory to laying down a concrete splash
pad to catch the spillover—just the sort of thing Bob Bea said should have
been there all along, a simple improvement that would have saved a city. But
as Setliff's entourage prepared to leave the site, Setliff had a terse question:
"The trees?"

The inner banks of the canal were lined with them: good-size trees,
thirty and forty feet high, trees that clearly had been growing for years in
blatant violation of maintenance rules—corks in the levee wall just waiting
for a high wind or raging water to pop them. It was not Setliff's job to cri-
tique the performance of his good friends on the Orleans levee board, the
people responsible for maintenance after the corps built a levee. He was
there to make New Orleans flood-proof, insofar as time and money allowed.
The aide in charge of this particular section of levee rehabilitation hastened
to assure the colonel that the trees would be gone, and it was certain that if
they still stood there the next time the colonel made one of his biweekly visits, the tone of the discussion would be somewhat less mellow.

At another site along the Industrial Canal, fast by a cluster of shredded
warehouses and rusting derricks, the issue was not trees—there being little

likelihood that even a weed could crop up in such a moonscape—but sheet piling. Long H-shaped girders had arrived on schedule and had been hammered into the ground at an angle to the flood wall that they would soon support. It was a design that had proved far more stable than the I-shaped walls that had toppled on the Seventeenth Street and London Avenue canals as well as along the Industrial Canal. But the flat sheets that were meant to be driven some sixty feet into the ground as a barrier against seepage had yet to materialize, and the work was falling behind schedule. "We're fighting it, sir, to be honest with you," the subcontractor confessed.

At another site, the flat sheets had arrived; it was another type of sheeting, the H-piles, that were wanting. One contractor was going gangbusters with his flat sheets; another had managed to hammer less than a hundred linear feet of piling into the ground, during a two-week interval that should have seen three times as much progress. The problem was that the piles, which locked together like tongue-and-groove planks, were seizing up belowground and, in some cases, peeling apart as they were hammered. The contractor had brought on-site a crane with a heavier hammer, but it had proved to be too big for flat piles; it had a tendency to smash, not sink, them. The contractor was asking for a design modification—and an adjusted budget—that would permit him to use more rigid and more costly Z-shaped piles. The matter was to be attended to at an engineering review meeting later in the week.

Meanwhile, Setliff had a question: Had any thought been given to staffing the job twenty-four hours a day? In his mild-mannered way, Setliff had cracked a whip. Working around the clock was an option, but expensive for contractors, due to overtime and nighttime pay differentials. Setliff could strongly encourage it, though he did not feel comfortable demanding it. In this instance, the on-site supervisor seemed adroit at fending off the colonel. Of course he understood that going to twenty-four hours might become necessary, the supervisor said. They were considering it. "But the men, sir, don't feel it's safe to drive pile at night." And Setliff, who did not complete a site visit without asking about safety precautions, knew to back off—for the time being.

And if the contractor didn't solve his problems and get the job back on track? Setliff's options were limited. He could reduce the scope of the contractor's work and bring in "additional resources" to make up for the short-comings, Setliff said. At the least a mitigation strategy would be requested, one that would draw attention to the contractor's shortcomings and propose how to bring the site back up to speed. But Setliff shunned rule by terror. "We're out here to make our contractors successful," he said, adding that the corps had no intention of "infringing on their right to a reasonable profit."

For all the tension caused by the deadlines he—and the impending hurricane season—had imposed on Task Force Guardian, Setliff radiated a contagious calm. He was given to bland understatement of the extraordinary circumstances in which he found himself. "I have no problem getting up every morning coming to work," he said of the maniacal focus required in his every waking hour. "We can't let this happen again." Aides said dawn's jogger was generally still at work when they called it quits and slipped out of their offices in the Federal Reserve building late in the evening. Setliff credited others on the task force with similar zeal, so much so that he sometimes had to hose them down. "I tell them this is a marathon, not a sprint," Setliff said. "I worry about them working too much. I have to keep an eye on them." If that level of dedication was not universal among government bureaucrats, Setliff readily understood why Task Force Guardian personnel, the bulk of them local to the area, were an exception. "They live behind these levees themselves," he said.

The collegial spirit in which he worked did not extend much past the doors to the Federal Reserve. As the public face of Task Force Guardian, Setliff had grown accustomed to media interviews that shaded over into browbeatings. What did the colonel have to say of reports that the contractors were just scooping up sandy muck at the site of the failed Mr. Go levees and heaping it back into place—a recipe for certain failure. "It's simply not true," Setliff insisted before launching into an explanation of the way the sand, on-site, was being segregated out from the good sticky clays, which were then cured to make sure the moisture content was not too high.

Privately, Setliff could be mordant on the subject of the much-maligned Mississippi River Gulf Outlet, the shipping shortcut vilified by politicians and the press as a "hurricane highway" funneling water into the heart of the city. "If you have a two-hundred-seventy-mile-wide hurricane coming from east to west, when it reaches Gulf Outlet, that surge is not going to take a left turn and get funneled," said Setliff. The surge simply washed away everything in its path as it swept over St. Bernard Parish and into eastern New Orleans, he was convinced. "But this is New Orleans," Setliff added, with a wink, "they could have smart water."

How was it possible, a TV reporter with one of the big network news shows demanded, that the corps, five months after the biggest engineering failure in U.S. history, still could not say exactly what had gone wrong? And what was the point of building the levees to "pre-Katrina" strength when pre-Katrina had proved so catastrophically inadequate? And how could you not conclude that the corps-designed flood system was a fiasco, given that the levees collapsed in a storm that was barely at Category 3 strength when it passed over New Orleans?

The colonel's answers were honed through repetition. Levee failures were very complex processes and Setliff was not one to jump to conclusions before all the data were in, he would say—a thinly veiled reference to some of the corps' quick-to-jump detractors in the scientific community. As for re-creating the levees that failed: That's all Congress had authorized the corps to do. The answer to the third question depended on Setliff's mood. The so-called standard project hurricane, the hypothetical storm against which the corps measured the flood defenses it had begun building in the post-Betsy environment of the 1960s, '70s, and '80s, did not correlate exactly with the storm-size lingo that had come into general use. People spoke of the standard project hurricane, the storm the New Orleans levees were meant to survive, as roughly equivalent to a fast-moving Category 3 storm. But the categories related to wind speeds, while levees were damaged by surging water. Sometimes Setliff took a stab at it and tried to explain to the uninitiated how the intricacies of storm surge and wave action could be more destructive in certain Category 2 storms than they would be under Category 4 winds in a cyclone of smaller radius than Katrina. Other times Setliff just smiled and played the good ol' boy: "At the end of the day, it was just a real big storm."

Just how big, and exactly why it had proved so astonishingly destructive to New Orleans, was the province of the longhairs drawn from a spectrum of universities and research specialties under the aegis of the corps' Interagency Performance Evaluation Task Force, or IPET. To lead IPET, the corps had turned to Ed Link, who put in thirty-four years as head of the corps' brain trust, the Waterways Experimental Station, at Vicksburg, before settling into semi-retirement in 2002 as a professor at the University of Maryland. Yes, it was a question of the corps investigating itself, but IPET's work was under simultaneous peer review by a team assembled by the American Society of Civil Engineers. And of course the independent NSF team under Berkeley's Ray Seed was a competitive challenge sure to keep everyone on their toes.

Link was a folksy, avuncular man who during his decades in Vicksburg had kept his three kids busy by setting up a youth soccer league that had threaded small towns together throughout Mississippi. He was also a competitor with much more than an armchair interest in the outcome of the investigation he was overseeing. Human lives were at stake and so were scientific reputations, which is why he had had no trouble whatsoever in recruiting a cadre of engineers who saw themselves as every bit the rival of the Beas and the Seeds and the van Heerdens of the world.

The competition was not less than fierce, but Link flatly rejected the notion that van Heerden had been set up by the corps or anybody else when the sheet pilings pulled at the Seventeenth Street Canal threw the LSU team's sonar readings into question. "That's just crazy," Link expostulated during a conversation about IPET's probe of the levee failures. "There were more lawyers running around there than there are shrimp in Louisiana," Link quipped, harking back to the December morning when the pilings were pulled. "No way it could have been staged." But as Link went on with his story, it became clear that there was at least as much theatrics as deductive science behind that day's proceedings. Link in fact had used the same sonar testing team and had been about to go public with data identical to van Heerden's Team Louisiana findings when he got a call from the corps telling him that he might want to wait until the sheet pilings had been pulled. Sonar did not yield black-and-white results; you had to know how to interpret the readings. At first Link was indignant. Data was data, and he was going to air his no matter how disturbing. Revisions, if required, could follow. But the tipster from the corps had gone on to make a case persuasive enough to give Link pause. Somehow the same effort was not expended to spare van Heerden embarrassment.

Even knowing that sonar readings can be tricky, Link said his team was sufficiently startled by the outcome to have gone and pulled a few extra piles, just to be sure they matched what the corps had shown the press that day. And he tried to get the LSU team to point IPET to the piles that van Heerden's readings had shown were truncated. "We got zero sharing out of them," Link said. He assumed the state attorney general, Team Louisiana's sponsor, had put the kibosh on an exchange of information in case it came to litigation.

"I have yet to see a villain in all this," Link said, "unless it's the way our society has dealt with hurricane protection in the past; it's been based too much on economics." Walter Baumy, Setliff's chief engineer, likewise said he had seen no evidence of specific culpability, of individuals "acting irresponsibly." But neither man denied the gravity of the disaster. "It's sort of like coming onto a car wreck," Link said of the forensic investigation he headed. "You can certainly see that there was a car wreck and it's really bad. But it's hard to just look at mangled metal and tell what happened. What started the car accident? Did brakes fail or was it somebody on the cell phone?"

In its search for an exact understanding of the levee failures, IPET had gone so far as to build a 1:40 scale model of the Seventeenth Street, London Avenue, and Industrial canals in a huge metal warehouse at the army corps' hydrology lab at Vicksburg. The models—levee banks, peaty subsoils, flood walls, bridges, brackish water, and all—were soon to be subjected to computer-generated wave and surge action identical to the forces that had overpowered the real-world canals. "Most people just play around with surge," Link said. "We've gone to great pains to build a hydrodynamic model that follows the storm right into the structures that failed, because the real transformation of surge and waves happens when you get into shallow water."

Simultaneously, IPET was doing numerical modeling at the highest degree of resolution available to any of the teams. Higher even than LSU's? Higher than LSU's, Link said, while noting that the LSU models were for forecasting, not hindsight analysis. But Link had no lack of respect for the LSU research. In particular, he said he had found their stopped-clock data extremely helpful, the moment timepieces stopped working being a fairly strong indicator of the exact minute when flooding overwhelmed a house.

"That's the best information available on when the breaches occurred," Link said. "If levees breached before the storm reached its peak, then using peak forces is not a very accurate way of understanding their behavior."

Link had a hunch that in one respect his simulations might provide data that would disappoint those in the corps who wanted to believe that the levee failures could be blamed on uniquely vigorous wave action in excess of what the flood system was designed to handle. More likely it was going to turn out that the low-lying bridges near the mouths of the drainage canals had knocked the stuffing out of surging waves before they reached the flood wall sections that failed.

Setliff, leery as he was of critics who jumped to conclusions without complete data sets, had not been able to wait for IPET's deep analysis to be completed, no more than he could have tolerated the year or so it usually took the corps to design a major piece of infrastructure, a levee for instance. Instead, even before the corps had succeeded in "dewatering" New Orleans, first after Katrina and then again after Rita, Setliff put people in helicopters and had them scanning the hundreds of miles of levee with LIDAR, a radar-like device that used laser beams instead of radio waves to determine the height of what was still standing. "A fifteen reading, you had a pretty good idea the levee was intact. If it read zero, well . . ." And indeed, for mile after mile, the readings on submerged levees out along the Intracoastal Waterway and the Mississippi River Gulf Outlet were in the zero range. Setliff's engineers married those readings to handwritten notes they took from the air, and began guesstimating the scope and cost of the work they urgently needed to put under contract if there was to be any chance of finishing by June.

The estimates proved notably accurate, Setliff was pleased to say. The aggregate cost of the work he hoped to finish by June first: $700 million, with another $600 million available for tasks that would be completed later in the season. Chief among the later projects was—as Bob Bea and Ray Seed would be pleased to note—a belated decision to "armor" the banks of the levees with rock or concrete or possibly even a high-tech fabric version of the water-shedding reed mats that were a traditional part of levee construction and maintenance a hundred or more years ago. The challenge in armoring levees was to find a way to do it that allowed for them to be built up again after the fresh clays had settled or after the land beneath had further subsided under the levees' weight—subsidence being an ongoing process throughout southeast Louisiana. And of course, if Congress ever ordered up a Category 5 defense, one certain task would be to make the levees higher still. Much of what IPET was doing was too theoretical to be of immediate use to Setliff and company, though it could be immensely relevant if it came to building that Category 5 defense. But IPET studies that revealed where the flood barrier was susceptible to particularly strong assault by surge and rainfall flooding were already being used as a guide in determining where, on a limited budget, to armor the levees, Link said.

OCTOBER FOURTH WAS NOT OTHERWISE A MEMORABLE DAY DURING THE ALTO-gether unforgettable New Orleans storm season of 2005, but it was the day that Dean Equipment Company, working a site out along the Mississippi River Gulf Outlet in St. Bernard Parish, had turned the first sod for Task Force Guardian. The LIDAR scannings had been followed by what was for Setliff without doubt the darkest hour of his sojourn in New Orleans: the nerve-racking and frustrating wait before he could put boots—and dozers—on the ground and begin construction. Cheers had gone up among Setliff's inner circle as Dean's heavy equipment began to rumble, and the colonel, for the first time in a while, began to breathe again. Four months later, and with four months to go, a million cubic yards of soil had been moved into place at the sites where it would be compacted into levees, a heroic undertaking that had required excavating scores of borrow pits and an armada of trucks so enormous they had threatened to turn the state highways to rubble. But a million cubic yards was only a quarter of what the job was going to require.

With one hundred twenty days until storm season, Setliff's official pos-ture was unchanged: The deadline would be met.

"We're on the right glide path for all this coming together," Setliff said to a site supervisor toward the end of his tour of Industrial Canal reconstruc-tion work, "but we may have to pull the trigger and go to twenty-four hours." As he chatted amiably with Alan Darouse, Cajun Construction's man on the ground, Setliff had no reason to know or care that he was a stone's throw from the wreckage of the Lamanche Street camelback that had been home to

Patrina Peters, her parents, and her kids. And the young man silently moving waist-high orange traffic cones from one part of the work site to another was a Lower Ninth Ward neighbor of hers, for whom the fifteen dollars an hour that Cajun Construction was paying day laborers was better money than could be imagined in any other legal enterprise that had come his way.

Inspections completed and with a two-thirty PM meeting scheduled back downtown, Setliff was striding across the dusty, debris-filled grounds of a cement plant struggling back to life along the Industrial Canal. What's this, Setliff asked, cocking his chin toward a car-size chunk of Styrofoam that had washed up onto the grounds. On inspection, it turned out to be a giant elephant's head, the trunk broken off and lying alongside it. "Mardi Gras, sir," an aide advised the colonel. And for a few seconds of inscrutable silence in a city long since inured to the surreal, the commander of Task Force Guardian stood in silent contemplation of his commander in chief's party mascot.

At the midafternoon meeting with his in-house staff, Setliff studied charts color-coded to establish the status of nine major contracts for rebuilding the St. Bernard levees. Two of them were colored blue for "project completed," the jobs for preparation of the levee foundation and borrow pit, which had been let to Dean Equipment way back in October. The priciest job on the menu, a $14.5 million restoration of the Mr. Go levee in the area of Bayou Dupre, was marked red: "Danger of Missing 1 June," as were three others of lesser magnitude. Another was yellow—"Behind Schedule," and two others, totaling about $2 million, were white: "Project Not Started."

"I'm pretty happy where we are on January thirty-first. It's not where we want to be, but we've exceeded expectations," Setliff said gamely to his staff. "We're at a transition," he added, putting as good a spin as he could on what he was seeing, "an acceleration point. We may need to go to twenty-four hours."

Whether or not the corps was inclined to be vindictive toward its critics in the wider world, it could not be said that Setliff denied his own staff an environment in which they felt free to speak their minds. And one of them now piped up with some statistics not on the chart. Color them a dismal gray. "We've allowed twenty-five days for wet weather in the one hundred twenty days between now and June first," he said blandly. "In the past two years there were forty-six days and forty-five days respectively during this time period, and in 1991 there were fifty-five wet days."

Privately, away from the contractors and the cajolery and hand-holding, Setliff was willing to admit that even round-the-clock scheduling could fall short. His staffer had touched a nerve. Wet weather could be a problem. Rain stole days from you as surely as on-site accidents. "The moisture content of the soil is a big litmus test," Setliff said. "It can be too wet. With a dry winter, we'll be confident we can finish by June one, or even ahead of schedule." So far, the winter had been dry, favoring Setliff as, for so many years, wayward hurricane trajectories had favored New Orleans.

TWENTY-FIVE

Summing Up

TRUMPETER KID MERV CAMPBELL'S HEART STILL BELONGED TO NEW OR-leans, but it was not good for the city's recovery prospects that a half year after Katrina, he and Katy Reckdahl and their baby, Hector, had found no reason to tear themselves away from Arizona, and some good reasons not to. The weekly where Reckdahl had emerged as one of New Orleans's more compelling investigative reporters had laid everybody off after the storm, and, based on visits back home, she was dismayed by the slow pace of recovery. "New Orleans is just not getting it back together," Reckdahl said over coffee with a friend in early February.

Alvin Crockett had left Houston and the apartment he shared with Clayton and Cindy McKinnis—the couple who plucked him out of the milling throng by the Astrodome—but not to return to his Algiers stomping ground. For all the good intentions and Christian fervor on both sides, it was probably inevitable that the McKinnises' apartment would prove to be only a way station in Crockett's life. When the seams began to split on the air mattress they rolled out for him, the young couple had called Cindy's father, a furniture dealer in Fort Worth, and arranged for the purchase of a bed. And Alvin had been doing well, topping off his interrupted secondary education at a Houston high school and warming to the idea of going on to a local college. He had resisted wardrobe upgrades suggested by his hosts, but the worst tension developed around the Internet. Clayton McKinnis set up an e-mail account for Alvin so he could keep in contact with his friends and family, and just to make sure that's all it was used for, McKinnis imposed very tight security on the system. "The next thing I know, our desktop computer won't even boot up because of some virus he downloaded," McKinnis said. The corker was the time McKinnis arrived at work, plugged his laptop into the docking station, and found pictures of naked men and women in amorous entanglements. That some of the men were black and the women white did nothing to soothe the soul of a man who had been worried the minute the buses started arriving from New Orleans that the ruffians he had seen on TV might pose a threat to Cindy. "I thank God I was there before anyone else could walk by and see it for themselves," McKinnis said of the laptop porn.

"He's black, my wife is white, and there is absolutely no possibility of me letting my wife's safety be compromised," he added. "We had committed to him that he was welcome to stay with us until he finished high school and went off to college, but if my wife has to walk into her own home fearful for her safety, and I have to live with the fear of my wife being violated by someone we had taken into not only our home but to our families' homes— then I will go back on my word and I won't be ashamed of it, no doubt."

Alvin was deeply dismayed by his fall from grace, appalled that his young man enthusiasm for sexy pictures could be mistaken for ingratitude toward his benefactors—or worse. He and the McKinnises patched things up, but it was definitely time to move on. Katrina had been like that, a stirring of the social pot that had made for some unexpected encounters and brief alliances. Now those who had been caught up in the maelstrom were settling back into former lives with more familiar companions. In early January, Alvin hopped a flight for Vegas to see what his brother was up to.

STEPHANIE WYMAN HAD DECIDED AGAINST GOING BACK TO NEW ORLEANS, but it was not because she intended to stay on in Texas, teaching in the Webster school system. In March, she and her husband, Lt. Rob Wyman, got word that the coast guard was transferring him to the Northeast, most likely to the Washington, D.C., area.

Saundra Reed, on the other hand, was going back. In spite of the stingy insurance settlement, repairs on the Central City house next door to her sister Yeolonda's were due to be completed by June. Even Yeolonda's son Whitman would be returning. For a time, he and his wife and their two young sons had stayed on in Houston. But when his employer, Boys and Girls Clubs of America, had offered him a good opportunity with their Oklahoma City branch, he had turned it down. New Orleans was home.

RAMOLA BURNES WASN'T SO SURE. FROM THE REVEREND BISHOP FRANK Washington's church she and her daughter, Lakesha, had found their way to one of the giant trailer parks FEMA had set up for evacuees in the Baton Rouge area. They had settled in quite comfortably when the feds called one day to ask if they'd like one of the little travel trailers set up in the yard in New Orleans so they could begin repairs on the house they had fled in young Farrell's caravan of hot-wired cars. After pondering the offer, Burnes turned it down. Lakesha was in a new high school in Baton Rouge, Glen Oaks, and liked it. And to be honest, thinking about her old Uptown neighborhood kind of gave Burnes the creeps—the drugs, the tensions. Her insurer had come through with about $6,000 for mold and mildew in the house. But, frankly, she wasn't keeping up with the mortgage payments on the place and realized there was a chance she might lose it. Well, she hadn't owned it long, didn't have much equity. It just wasn't something she really wanted to deal with just then.

"I'm living a Christian life," she said in a chat with a friend in late February. "I'm trying to find myself. I'm at peace here." She wanted the same for Lakesha, and for that reason had been delighted when she managed to ease Farrell out of the trailer and on to Houston—something she hadn't felt she could do until he reconnected with his mother, who was now housing him in Texas. Oh, but that boy did want her daughter. They were adorable together, Burnes had to agree, two teenagers all glowing with their youth. And when it was time for Lakesha's sweet sixteen ball at Glen Oaks, Farrell had come all the way over from Houston—suit, haircut, the whole nine yards. "He is dying to come back," Burnes said. But she had resolved not to put up with it, not under her roof.

GRADUALLY OVER TIME, AS THEY YO-YOED BACK AND FORTH BETWEEN NEW York and New Orleans, it became less and less clear to Steven Bingler and Linda Usdin just which end of the string was home. But when the girls finished up their spring semesters at Columbia Prep and Trevor Day, there was no question what was happening next: New Orleans. The girls had been furious when their parents decided against returning to New Orleans as Anya's and Josephine's schools reopened after the new year for the first time since Katrina. The girls had tried everything, including the silent treatment, but their parents had hung tough. Now there was no holding the girls back, and Bingler and Usdin by then were just as eager to get home for good.

WITH THE INTERNATIONAL HOUSE BACK ON ITS FEET, HOTELIER SEAN CUM- mings had been able to turn his attention to a long-simmering project in his capacity as head of the New Orleans Building Corporation, the agency that handled underused or vacant city property. The goal: regaining control of a long stretch of riverfront and wharfage largely abandoned by the maritime interests in the past thirty years. Cummings envisioned a miles-long string of parks and museums, stretching from a point just below the French Quar- ter all the way upriver to Jackson Avenue, where the Garden District began. After rounds of shuttle diplomacy on Cummings's part, port officials and the Nagin administration finally signed a memorandum of understanding that went through what Cummings estimated as some four dozen drafts. In ex- change for giving up the land, the port would get 25 percent of the revenues the city collected as the swath was developed. And just to sweeten the pot, Mayor Nagin agreed to commit $150 million of federal block grants to sup- port the project. At the top of Cummings's wish list: a centerpiece structure by a world-class architect—perhaps something like the wildly daring opera house Santiago Calatrava had designed for the waterfront at Tenerife, with the cresting wave in pure white concrete that swept to a height of two hundred feet above the roof. This assumed, of course, that Cummings's patron survived the reelection fight that had already encouraged a field of twenty-two candidates to think they could deny the storm-battered mayor a second term.

MALIK RAHIM AND COMMON GROUND WERE STILL GOING STRONG. AS SPRING break swept over the nation's college world, upward of ten thousand students opted against Florida beaches or other more traditional hangouts and pitched in as volunteers in the New Orleans recovery. Common Ground fed and sheltered about two thousand, as did the People's Hurricane Relief Fund. What was conceived as an ad hoc relief effort had evolved into a multi-pronged social-services operation, a template for the kind of do-it-yourself communitarianism that adherents hoped might one day supplant the clumsy and crumbling bureaucracies that had served New Orleans so poorly, before and after Katrina. Or would the philanthropic community, like Congress, weary of Katrina and move on, leaving Malik and his volunteers to their memories of a year like no other down South?

FOR KIERSTA KURTZ-BURKE, IT TOOK A WHILE TO ACCEPT THAT THE GRAND OLD art deco mausoleum that was Charity Hospital wouldn't be opening any time soon. Just as the spirit of that place had haunted so much of life in New Orleans ever since the Great Depression, for a time after Katrina it assumed an equally spectral existence as a figment of the city's future. Rumors abounded that it was about to reopen. One day, Kurtz-Burke and a group of her colleagues showed up at a Wal-Mart in Kenner, out near the New Orleans airport, on the strength of intimations that the hospital was reopening there. Kurtz-Burke was by herself the time she visited a navy hospital ship along the riverfront. Word had spread that it was Charity's new home. For a time she set her sights on trying to open a health clinic in St. Augustine Church, a beautiful old ark of a place that had been the center of African American Catholicism for many residents of Treme, across Rampart Street from the French Quarter. And then, in a move that shocked its congregation and pastor, the archdiocese made an announcement. As part of a sweeping consolidation of its schools and churches, St. Augustine was being merged with another, more prosperous, church and would no longer be its own parish.

Kurtz-Burke's husband, Justin Burke, had stabilized the couple's finances by resuming his career as a physician at a hospital in Jefferson Parish. His wife picked up work at the Veteran's Administration Hospital down the street from what had been Charity—there being no lack of spinal cord injuries and other trauma among the wounded soldiers coming back from Iraq. And when a satellite clinic opened up under the Charity banner, her offer to assist there as a volunteer medic was quickly accepted. Other parts of the Charity operation also were revived at scattered sites in Orleans and Jefferson parishes, but it worried Kurtz-Burke that people weren't fully cognizant of the long-term impact of not having a centralized facility in downtown New Orleans: "More people will die from closing Charity Hospital than died from Katrina," Kurtz-Burke said. "People will die slow deaths from untreated diabetes, HIV, you name it." The biggest loss, as Javier Aguilar had discovered, was a subtle deprivation. Medical interventions that could be scheduled—however urgent the need—were no longer available locally to the patients without resources of their own that Charity had treated since the 1930s. The scattered New Orleans outposts would treat trauma, heart attack, stroke—emergency conditions. But for open heart surgery to prevent that next thrombosis: Try Baton Rouge—and figure out how to begin commuting to the preparatory doctor's appointments.

FEMA COULD CLAIM A VICTORY. IN LATE MARCH, THE AGENCY LOCATED THE last of 5,192 missing kids and could announce that only 12 of them had died. The last of the surviving children to be found was a four-year-old named Cortez Stewart. Separated from her family in the chaos of an evacuation that carried her mother and five siblings to a Houston apartment via the Astrodome, Cortez had been taken by her godmother, Felicia Williams, to Atlanta. FEMA eventually tracked her down—efforts by Williams and Cortez's mother, Lisa Stewart, to find each other's place of refuge having proved unavailing.

But as the post-Katrina era reached the half-year mark, a new wrinkle emerged in the FEMA trailer fiasco. Upward of eleven thousand of them, parked in Hope, Arkansas, were discovered to be modular homes of a type that FEMA rules deemed unsafe for use in a floodplain. The glitch left many in Congress, Republicans and Democrats alike, scratching their heads in stunned dismay. "So, this incompetence and this lack of capable response by FEMA and by DHS continues to this day," Senator Mark Dayton, a Minnesota Democrat, said to Chertoff, as Bush's top emergency responder was hauled before the Senate's Katrina committee yet again. "That, to me, is if anything more disturbing than the failure of the immediate response," Dayton said.

The homeless, meanwhile, had been eased out of emergency hotel accommodations. FEMA continued to provide rental assistance to those with the skills and the patience to pick their way through the agency's labyrinthine bureaucracy. The most marginalized among them had found shelter in the jumbles of flooded cars, another cleanup challenge that had been stalled while Nagin's city hall played footsie with contractors. Bushvilles, someone dubbed these clusters of backseat bedrooms, a throwback to the Hoovervilles of the Great Depression.

Flooded-out homeowners, whatever their temporary digs, remained in financial limbo. Congress was not expected to approve the block grants for housing recovery until May, and already, rival states, as Don Powell feared, had begun defying the efforts of a lame-duck president to keep $4.2 billion on track for Louisiana. The money wasn't expected to start flowing until after the storm's first-year anniversary, and even then, FEMA would not have completed the flood maps that would finally confirm how high above the ground it would be necessary to raise housing on flood-prone lots.

But real estate investor Gregory Richardson could take stock of his situation in late March and assert more confidently than ever that he was not going to lose his holdings to creditors. As the insurance settlements on his forty-nine units finally began to flow, he found that under close supervision his crew was able to rehab the apartments at a cost to him of about $50,000—little more than half what the insurers were paying. Late March brought tragedy—an attempted suicide by one of the young men in Richardson's family, after a woman left him. The despondent man, a veteran of the Iraq war, was pulled off a Mississippi River bridge and hospitalized after a friend saw him on the verge of jumping. Two days later, on the last Saturday in March, the family was able to lay Richardson's father to rest—ending a seven-month struggle to wrest his remains, all but mummified in FEMA's red tape, from the morgue at St. Gabriel. And two weeks later, a milestone of another sort was passed as Richardson moved tenants into the first of his apartments to be restored to commerce.

"It's a mountain, but I'm hitting it every day," Richardson said, settling down to a night of bookkeeping in the bedroom, in a house full of her relatives, that he and his wife called home. And the FEMA trailer, so promisingly delivered to one of Richardson's lots on Thanksgiving Day five months earlier? The city and the local utility still had not managed to inspect the hook-up and turn on the electricity.

As THE NEXT HURRICANE SEASON DREW NEARER, RAY SEED, IVOR VAN HEERden, and others probing the levee collapse had yet to identify a "smoking gun," the single act of incompetence or corruption at the heart of the worst engineering failure in American history. Rather, their analyses were leaning in the direction of a more complex syndrome of failure. Perhaps as close as the forensic engineers got to a prime cause of the catastrophe was a cross-sectional drawing to which soil testing data had been transferred faultily. The error concealed the presence of the unstable peat layer well below the depths to which sheet pilings had been driven on the east side of the Seventeenth Street Canal. Was the error deliberate, a way to spare the corps or its contractor the added expense of the deeper pilings, or merely careless? That had not become clear and, in any event, shed light only on a single two-hundred-foot breach in a levee system that had been punctured in dozens of places, some of them miles long. The intellectual jousting remained vigorous, however. In March, the army corps task force studying the army corps levee failure came out with an interim report declaring that the particular type of failure mechanism it had identified in the breaches along the drainage canals could not have been foreseen. What had happened, the task force concluded, was that under the pressure of rising water, the concrete flood walls had tipped outward just slightly, allowing water to slip into the tension crack between the sheet piling and the levee soils. That exerted pressure on a lower stratum of weak soils, causing them to slip to the landward side and blow out the levee. Within two days, Bea and Seed had fired off a formal rejoinder. Not only was the failure foreseeable, the corps itself had studied the exact phenomenon and written a report about it back in 1986, a report well circulated before the levees were topped with flood walls in the early 1990s.

The corps evidently had had enough. On a Wednesday in early April, the corps' commanding officer, Lt. Gen. Carl Strock, surrendered. The flood-wall engineering was a botched job, he conceded. The corps had screwed up. "We have now concluded we had problems with the design of the structure. We had hoped that wasn't the case. But we recognize it is the reality," Strock told the Senate appropriations subcommittee. The concrete flood walls had indeed been pushed out of alignment by the rising surge, creating a crevice that pulled water deep into the earthen levees below.

Apparently confession was in season. Days later, the corps owned up to another gaffe: Its cost estimate to bring levees in southeast Louisiana back up to pre-Katrina strength had been a bit shy of the mark. It would cost about $9 billion, three times the figure Don Powell had convinced Bush to back. Whether Congress would agree to the appropriation was anybody's guess as May gave way to June and the official opening of the 2006 hurricane season.

THE YEARNING FOR A CONCISE, SINGLE-BULLET EXPLANATION FOR KATRINA WAS not limited to the forensic engineers, of course, but the months had only complicated the search, confounding those among the true believers still open to argument. Was New Orleans treated to second-rate flood protections and a lethargic federal response to disaster because it was a majority-black city? Or was it political partisanship, the partisanship that played out so blatantly in Mississippi's early success in securing disproportionate federal grants, that numbed FEMA's crisis response to a Democratic city under a Democratic mayor and governor. Was Katrina best explained as a weatherman's warning to a federal establishment in denial about the long-range implications of global warming and the greenhouse effect, or was it God's finger wagging at a city with a famously casual approach to personal and political morality? Had the focus on terrorism blinkered America to other threats just as grave? Had the Bush administration's enthusiasm for "down-sized" and "outsourced" governance created a political culture in which truly effective governmental intervention on the domestic front was tanta-mount to the betrayal of these principles? Had deficit spending and the war on Iraq made vigorous response to domestic catastrophe an impossibility? Or was Katrina simply more than even the richest and most powerful coun-try on earth could handle?

That most all of those questions could be answered in the affirmative suggested that no one of them was an adequate key to Katrina's historical implications. The hurricane was a huge one—but one that blessedly by-passed New Orleans before delivering its full fury on the less fragile land-scapes of Mississippi. The army corps' admission that its designs were at fault still left room to ponder just what sequence of cost considerations, en-gineering compromises, and bone-headed mistakes had led to the levees being constructed as they were. The federal budget offered ample proof that indeed FEMA—and the corps, for that matter—had been bled of resources that were then reapplied to war abroad and the struggle against homeland terrorism. That the bureaucratic culture was also dysfunctional seemed less certain from Mike Brown's scathing criticism of his boss, Mike Chertoff, than that someone like Brown had been put in charge of FEMA in the first place. Katrina may not have lent much support to the Bush administration's infatuation with privatizing government functions, but it went a long way toward demonstrating the implicit contention that there were a lot of things government couldn't do very well. At least not any more.

New Orleans flood defenses, its pumps and massive river levees, had once been the envy of the engineering world. Now the state-of-the-art was overseas, in Holland, and Washington had qualms about even attempting to build a comparable system in Louisiana. Maybe America's historical mo-ment had passed and the Katrina response was a harbinger of how it was going to be in a country that had lost its way in the world and squandered the financial clout that for a century had let America have its way even when policy was flawed.

New Orleans found itself in a strange place as the 2006 hurricane sea-son rolled around. It had the feeling of a city on the brink, whether of revival or more permanent decline was the question. Only this much seemed certain: The seeds of whatever future lay ahead had been sown. The levees around the core of the city had been made strong enough to withstand a storm like Katrina in an age when much more serious storms were in every season's forecast. A moment for bold political leadership had come and gone without anything remotely like leadership emerging from among the gaggle of politicians at city hall. Perhaps it was just as well. Perhaps a concise plan to reengineer New Orleans—to true its "footprint" to the resources available to a city with its population and its tax base cut in half—would have been just another government fiasco. Perhaps it was better to let the city's revival continue helter-skelter and hope that the result was not the shantytown and plunging property values predicted in those portions of the city's 116,000 acres that failed to regain the population density an urban infrastructure requires. Perhaps the market would work its magic, suddenly remembering a city that had lain fallow for decades before Katrina, its working people idled, its children sinking deeper and deeper into poverty and lawlessness. Perhaps it would do so within the lifetimes of the men and women and children who had survived the hurricane.

PATRINA PETERS RETURNED TO HER HOUSE IN THE LOWER NINTH WARD FOR A final time before it was bulldozed. Keia came along on the ride down from Reserve and so did Peters's cousin the Reverend Eric Lewis, assistant pastor to the scattered congregation of Battleground Baptist. Damond's school, Desire Street Academy, had relocated to temporary quarters in Florida, but he'd be back at the end of the semester to patch the hole they felt in their lives without him. There were few signs of progress in the Lower Ninth. In mid-March, the huge barge that had thundered through the breach and onto the streets below the Industrial Canal had been cut apart and sold for scrap. But the wrecked houses were only just beginning to be hauled away and the appalling thing was that as the debris-removal jaws bit into the wreckage, corpses were still being unearthed—three in one day in late March.

Peters's ambition, aside from a need to just give the place a last look, was to get into that camelback somehow and retrieve a few things from her closet: a strongbox, a purse—assuming no one had snuck in there ahead of her and looted the place. One look at the ruins on Lamanche Street reminded her that even the part of the house left standing was close to complete collapse, and she lost her nerve. Lewis was willing to give it a try, though, and in short order he had climbed up onto the pancaked front roof and stepped through the upper-story window. Soon he was handing things out to Peters and Keia: Damond's sports trophies, a picture of Peters's beloved brother, Kevin. The mementos of a past life eased her pain and under her breath Peters thanked God for letting them be salvaged. Emboldened, she and Keia climbed inside and at the sight of their furniture—mangled, mud-soaked, tossed about—burst into tears.

Amid the rubble, Keia found some clothing and her diplomas. She also found her mildewed leatherbound copy of *The National Dean's List for 2001–02,* and leafed through it until she found her entry: Dakeia Johnson, Southern University at New Orleans. Her mother spotted a coffee can in which she had stored loose change and small bills—$200 at last count. But when she grabbed the can, the rusted bottom fell out and coins rained down and skittered into cracks in the splintered wood flooring. She salvaged about $100. There was one last item she dreamed of plucking from the rubble that day, something worth more to her than all the rest: a framed poster. It showed a bucolic strip of small white wooden houses and a church facing a grassy expanse. A little girl, African American, walked in the grass in her Sunday best. Peters found the poster, so caked with mold and sludge she could barely make out the inscription: Fazendeville, 1867–1964.

Anger and grief, a longing for what had been lost, and disgust with the world that had let it happen—Patrina Peters found herself pinioned between opposite emotions of ferocious intensity. All right, she was one of the lucky ones. She had survived. She had financial resources—the disability and Social Security checks that saw her and her parents through each month. Those assets were transportable to another town, and in Reserve they had found a bland, upriver existence. More than any of that, she had her faith. She missed the buzz of the big city, the bus rides downtown, a stroll through the Quarter on a Saturday night. What she missed more was her church, Battleground Baptist, those joyful song-filled services, the community of believers who had lingered on the steps, catching up with one another in the Louisiana sunshine. That was worth coming back for. That was life itself—and then it struck her. There was no Battleground Baptist. Yes, the maroon-brick building still stood there, but Katrina had shredded and scattered its congregation, like a Mardi Gras Indian tearing apart last year's costume before setting to work on a new one.

Acknowledgments

This book was a collaboration among the interviewers who worked with me and, in a different sense, among the clusters of people whose stories intersected in unexpected and interesting ways. Their names are listed below. A book such as this would not have been possible without their cooperation—interviewers and interviewees alike—and I thank them for it. I am especially grateful to *Times-Picayune* reporter Mark Schleifstein and Louisiana State University hurricane specialist Ivor van Heerden for sharing stories and insights with me even as they worked some of that material into books of their own—unusual generosity in a competitive world.

Jane Wholey was the linchpin in the whole production, and I can only hope that reactivating her skills in journalism—a career she pursued in her New York days—was as agreeable for her as it was useful to me. Her ability to disarm the people she interviewed and walk them through sometimes deeply upsetting experiences was crucial to the storytelling approach we adopted. She was ably assisted by the redoubtable Hamilton Simons-Jones, scion of fine journalistic stock and a man acutely sensitive to the ethical issues journalists confront in dealing with the impoverished and the disempowered. Nicole Polier gave generously of her time and talent and brought the outsider's perspective we provincials needed in order to see ourselves and our city whole.

My old comrade in arms Robert Ginna put me together with Random House and Tim Bartlett, whose editing was both deft and provocative. To

Kate Hamill, for riding herd on the project with fierce efficiency, special thanks. Auxiliary support took many forms. Andrei and Laura Codrescu took us in as evacuees and then turned the house over to us outright when the pleasures of crash-pad life began to wane for them. Special thanks as well to Marilee Baccich and the Unitarian Church of Baton Rouge, Greta Brister and the staff of the McWhirter School, Jacqueline and Bruce Blaney, Michael Victorian, Jennifer Whitney, Lisa Fithian, Beverly Rainbolt, Claudia Menza, and Bara MacNeill.

As the notes and citations reveal, my colleagues in the newspaper world, most especially at *The Times-Picayune,* had a shaping influence on this book, some through their published work, others through the osmosis of conversation. They kept me on my toes and, as they chased after the story of the century, I could only chase after them. Special thanks to three newspaper colleagues in particular, Robert Travis Scott, Gordon Russell, and Stephanie Grace, for plowing through the manuscript in an early and even more inchoate form.

For unacknowledged intellectual debts and for any errors of fact or interpretation, my apologies to all.

Interview List

Asterisk (*) indicates group interview.

Aguilar, Javier (alias)

Arend, Orissa

Atushi, Koike

Baccich, Marilee

Bea, Robert

Bertucci, Michelle

Bervera, Xochitl

Blanco, Gov. Kathleen
   Babineaux

Blanco, Raymond

Bienemy, Dynel

Bingler, Anya

Bingler, Josephine

Bingler, Steven

Brister, Greta

Broussard, Aaron*

Brown, Adell

Bruno, Joseph

Bueron, Juan (alias)

Burnes, Ramola (alias)

Carter, Denise

Carter, Eric

Cavato, Donna

Chisom, Ron

Crockett, Alvin

Cullen, Paul

Cummings, John

Cummings, Sean

Dedrick, Natasha

Derbyshire, Sandra

D'Hemecourt, Robert

Dregory, Nadora

Evans, Lance

Farrell, Earl (alias)

Fithian, Lisa

Ford, Stephen J.

Francis, Norman*

Franklin, Laurel

Freitas, Drina

Gusman, Marlin*

Hanslik, Fern

Harrison, Lynn, MD

Harvey, Robert

Hayashi, Haruo

Henderson, Alice

Henderson, Katina

Honoré, Lt. Gen.
   Russel*

Huynh, Au

Huynh-Yee, Thu

Isaacson, Walter

Jackson, Ted

Jacobs, Leslie

Johnson, Dakeia

Johnson, Yavana

Jones, Norman

Kalmus, Eliot

Kenyatta, Jon

Khalailel, Ray

Kobayashi, Ikuo

Kopplin, Andy*

Kurtz-Burke,
   Kiersta, MD

Kusuba, Ikuhiro

Lai, Jennifer

Laurie, Mary

Lee, Wing and Tung

Lemoine, Rachael

Linden, Lakesha
  (alias)

Love, Bay

Loyd, Jimmy

Luciano, Mariah

MaGree, Elaine

Major, Barbara

Maker, Tania (alias)

Mann, Bob

Marshall, Bob

Martin, Sherylnn

Martins, Sharon

Mayfield, Chris

McKinnis, Clayton

Mechanic, Scott

Morrison, Leah

Mwendo, Ukali

Nagin, Mayor C. Ray*

Neville, Charmaine

Nguyen, Tho

Nguyen, The Vien

Nicholson, Neil

Nolan, James

O'Brian, Maureen

Ohnishi, Kazuyoshi

Olshansky, Robert

Omar, Fredy

Ozaki, Nobuaki

Pederson, Craig

Peters, Damond

Peters, Patrina

Picard, Cecil

Polier, Steven

Powell, Donald*

Rahim, Malik

Rainbolt, Beverly

Ratcliff, Mary

Rattler, Cynthia

Recasner, Tony

Reed, Saundra

Rice, Glenda

Richardson, Gregory

Salinas, Umberto
  (alias)

Scawthorn, Charles

Schleifstein, Mark

Seed, Raymond

Setliff, Col.
  Lewis F. III

Sexton, Gregory

Shackett, Andrew

Sherrod, Henry

Stamps, Cindy

Stith, Shannon

Suber, Malcolm

Tarumi, Eiji

Ueno, Sadaharu

Usdin, Linda

Vallely, John
  Franklin III

van Heerden, Ivor

Walton, Alvin

Ward, Martha

Washington, Pastor
  Bland

Washington, Rev.
  Frank

Watters, Sherry

Whitney, Jennifer

Wyman, Stephanie

Zas, Robert

Zeichner, Baruch

Ziv, Barbara

Notes

THIS BOOK IS BUILT AROUND EXTENSIVE INTERVIEWS WITH A CORE GROUP OF some three dozen people, culled from a much larger group whose stories were sometimes not less interesting but were, on reflection, less representative of the events chronicled. It seemed best to obscure identities in two sections. One is the account of "Earl Farrell" and his associates; the other is "Javier Aguilar." All other names are real. The notes reflect indebtedness to the work of specific journalists or published sources. Attributions that are not annotated were drawn from interviews or from information that has been circulated widely and repeatedly enough to have obscured its link with any one source. Peter Berkowitz kindly consented to allow excerpts from a letter to his mother that has been circulated on the Web. The chapter on Kobe is adapted with permission from *The Times-Picayune* from reporting done on assignment for the newspaper.

TWO

When Wallyworld Closes at Four

25 A housing consultant named Raymond Breaux   Bruce Nolan et al., *The Times-Picayune,* August 28, 2005.

28 a mercenary consideration   Ibid.

THREE
An Imperfect Storm

41 All told, coastal Louisiana's losses   Matt Brown, *The Times-Picayune,* October 31, 2005.

42 $2.2 billion in losses   Matt Brown, *The Times-Picayune,* February 6, 2006.

42 Packs of dogs rushed   Stephen J. Hedges, *Chicago Tribune,* September 4, 2005.

42 for every 2.7 miles traversed   Robert Travis Scott, *The Times-Picayune,* October 26, 2005.

46 Helicopters dropped six hundred   "Failure of Initiative," House report, p. 95.

FOUR
Real Ugly, Real Fast

49 Mulholland aqueduct in Los Angeles   Nicolai Ouroussoff, *The New York Times,* October 9, 2005.

51 someone on the ground   Marty Bahamonde, Senate committee testimony, October 20, 2005.

57 The Reverend Anthony DeConciliis had been inaugurated   Susan Langenhennig, *The Times-Picayune,* October 22, 2005.

58 Bahamonde, the FEMA envoy   Senate testimony, October 20, 2005.

59 thirty thousand tourists stuck   Bruce Alpert, *The Times-Picayune,* October 21, 2005.

59 "You've done this before"   Senate testimony, October 20, 2005.

60 "We need your help"   Gov. Kathleen Babineaux Blanco, statement prepared for Congressional panel.

60 An emergency qualified as catastrophic   Mark Schleifstein, John McQuaid, *The Times-Picayune,* June 24, 2002.

60 "an oversized entitlement program"   Eric Lipton, Scott Shane, *The New York Times,* September 3, 2005.

60 a phone call early Monday   Ibid.

64 a dogsitter for the family pooch   Bruce Alpert, *The Times-Picayune,* November 3, 2005.

FIVE

Decaf Cigarettes and Golden Carp

74 Roy Mullet, an auto mechanic   Jeff D. Opdyke, Evan Perez, Ann Carrns, *The Wall Street Journal,* September 7, 2005.

SIX

Other Texans, Other Times

83 the president, a Texan   Howard Fineman, *Newsweek,* September 19, 2005.

85 more than a few police   "Failure of Initiative," House report, p. 247.

86 "So many of the people"   *The New York Times,* September 7, 2005.

86 Kanye West . . . Colin Farrell . . . Master P   For a fuller discussion, see Michael Eric Dyson, *Come Hell or High Water,* Basic Civitas, 2006.

88 He had not been an "outstanding professor"   See Lehr, Middlebrooks, Price, & Vreeland, Alabama Employment Law Letter, XVI, v: "Padded Resume Doesn't Soften Katrina's Blow," October 2005.

88 five of FEMA's top ten posts   Dyson, *Come Hell or High Water.*

89 "I can't force myself on people"   Hedges, *Chicago Tribune.*

89 three hundred rubber rafts   Bill Walsh, *The Times-Picayune,* January 31, 2005.

89 Members of the Florida Airboat Association   Nancy Imperiale, *South Florida Sun-Sentinel,* September 2, 2005.

90 Even the Red Cross   Ann Rodgers, *Pittsburgh Post-Gazette,* September 3, 2005.

90 A deadly extreme of bureaucratic inanity   Laurie Smith Anderson, Baton Rouge *Advocate,* September 16, 2005.

91 The failure to evacuate nursing homes   Bruce Alpert, *The Times-Picayune,* February 3, 2006.

91 When it came to FEMA   Ibid.

92 "Washington rolled the dice"   *Newsweek,* September 19, 2005.

92 "Every day she called him"   Bob Ross, *The Times-Picayune,* October 9, 2005.

92 Nagin used his Oprah   "Failure of Initiative," House report, p. 248.

93 FEMA had rushed out   Aaron C. Davis, Seth Borenstein, *The Philadelphia Inquirer,* October 10, 2005.

97 As proof of White House   Karen Tumulty, *Time,* September 19, 2005.

97 "No such request"   Ibid.

99 61,386 severely damaged homes   Louisiana Recovery Authority.

99 "It makes me sick"   Blanco to Garland Robinette, WWL-Radio, January 20, 2006.

100 four full-page ads   Michelle Krupa, *The Times-Picayune,* October 18, 2005.

100 Swain's yearning to flee   Michael Perlstein, *The Times-Picayune,* November 14, 2005.

101 "She panicked, I guess."   Ibid.

103 computer hub crashed   "Failure of Initiative," House report, p. 68.

103 troopless general said no   Phil Parr, Senate committee testimony, December 11, 2005.

105 "How many people"   Jeff Duncan, *The Times-Picayune,* September 19, 2005.

105 "The cat was living large"   Ibid.

SEVEN
Media in the Moment

108 story of the asthmatic child   Wil Haygood, Ann Scott Tyson, *The Washington Post,* September 15, 2005.

109 "First, do you believe"   House testimony, December 14, 2005.

115 a Ms. Lewis came forward   *All Things Considered,* National Public Radio, December 21, 2005.

116 "What I want people to understand"   Charmaine Neville, WAFB, September 2, 2005.

EIGHT
At Least Somebody Had a Plan

121 In another part of the city   Trymaine Lee, *The Times-Picayune,* December 18, 2005.

121 Three hundred police cruisers   Michael Perlstein, *The Times-Picayune,* December 18, 2005.

123 the officers commandeered   Ibid.

TEN
Like Bricks on Jell-O

146 "The breach at the Seventeenth Street Canal"   U.S. Army News Service, September 1, 2005.

147 *Larry King Live* appearance   *Larry King Live,* CNN, September 2, 2005.

152 essentially a hasty drive-by   Gordon Russell, *The Times-Picayune,* November 25, 2005; Frank Donze, *The Times-Picayune,* December 1, 2005.

152 Van Heerden had met Barry   *Meet the Press,* NBC, September 11, 2005.

152 Grunwald's front-page story   Michael Grunwald, Joby Warrick, *The Washington Post,* October 24, 2005.

157 first reference to the uncertain soils   Lisa Myers, *NBC Nightly News,* September 30, 2005.

159 "We tell our students"   Bob Marshall, Mark Schleifstein, *The Times-Picayune,* October 28, 2005.

159 "putting bricks on Jell-O"   Ibid.

164 Better to take the battle   John McQuaid, *The Times-Picayune,* November 13, 2005.

ELEVEN

Help Yourself

174 "Crazy black people"   Michael Lewis, "Wading Toward Home," *The New York Times Magazine,* October 9, 2005.

181 The most difficult to reunite   Bruce Alpert, *The Times-Picayune,* March 21, 2006.

183 Nativity could be called   Tulane University professor Richard Campanella, lecture at *The Times-Picayune,* March 15, 2006.

183 By year's end, Houston officials   Trymaine Lee, *The Times-Picayune,* January 19, 2006.

THIRTEEN

Reversal of Fortune

206 Nagin had agreed to provide   Bruce Eggler, *The Times-Picayune,* November 2, 2005.

209 "sure beats being plucked"   *Time,* October 3, 2005.

214 Remarks quoted in *The Wall Street Journal*   Christopher Cooper, *The Wall Street Journal,* September 8, 2005.

217 Weepy moments   Douglas Brinkley, *The Great Deluge,* William Morrow, 2006, as excerpted in *Vanity Fair,* June 2006.

FOURTEEN
In Search of Common Ground

219 five-year prison sentence for armed robbery   Michelle Garcia, *The Washington Post,* December 4, 2005.

227 On a random Friday, one of the injured workers   Javier is a pseudonym used to conceal the identity of an illegal immigrant.

FIFTEEN
If They Can Rebuild Beirut

238 a nightclub operator   Bruce Hamilton, *The Times-Picayune,* September 22, 2005.

238 There was Clarence Rodriguez   Trymaine Lee, *The Times-Picayune,* September 28, 2005.

238 Ashton O'Dwyer took up   Cooper, *The Wall Street Journal.*

238 agents of an Israeli security company   Ibid.

SIXTEEN
Crunch Time

244 "resilience" of cities   See Lawrence J. Vale, Thomas J. Campanella, et al., *The Resilient City,* Oxford University Press, 2004.

248 In fact, city officials   Jeffrey Meitrodt, *The Times-Picayune,* January 15, 2006.

249 Insured losses from Katrina   Mark Schleifstein, *The Times-Picayune,* December 2, 2005.

252 The truce between   Associated Press, December 17, 2005.

252 "Today I have joined in a lawsuit"   Ibid.

253 "I'm almost embarrassed"   Associated Press, December 18, 2005.

SEVENTEEN
Sue the Bastards

255 "It's like when FEMA"   James Dao, *The New York Times,* November 22, 2005.

259 The 1927 catastrophe was also the flood   John Barry, *Rising Tide,* Simon & Schuster, 1997.

266 The rewards of the game   Frank Donze, *The Times-Picayune,* September 25, 1994.

266 Framed replicas of several   Ibid.

269 Within a decade   Michael Grunwald, Susan B. Glasser, *The Washington Post,* October 9, 2005.

270 Indeed, and to the corps'   Stephen Braun, Ralph Vartabedian, *Los Angeles Times,* December 25, 2005.

270 The levee board lobbyists   Ibid.

272 "They didn't find anything"   Ibid.

272 no-bid fifty-year contract   Jeffrey Meitrodt, R. T. Scott, *The Times-Picayune,* February 5, 2006.

EIGHTEEN
A Comparable Catastrophe

278 On a frigid January morning   Jed Horne, *The Times-Picayune,* December 4, 2005.

280 Just over the line   Brian Thevenot, *The Times-Picayune,* December 31, 2005.

TWENTY
Blue Tarps in a Chocolate City

306 By contrast, Mississippi   John Maginnis, *The Times-Picayune,* October 5, 2005.

307 "Like looters who seize"   *The Washington Post,* September 27, 2005.

308 generated some three thousand applications   Orleans coroner Frank Minyard, WDSU-TV news, January 18, 2006.

308 the so-called Katrina Cottage   Greg Thomas, *The Times-Picayune,* March 18, 2006.

308 In the same crazy spirit   Gordon Russell, James Varney, *The Times-Picayune,* December 29, 2005.

309 When the corps yielded   Gordon Russell, James Varney, *The Times-Picayune,* February 19, 2006.

311 "We will go ahead and roll trailers"   Bruce Hamilton, *The Times-Picayune,* October 22, 2005.

312 "I don't like to use the race angle"   WDSU nightly news, December 17, 2005.

TWENTY-ONE
Shrink-Proof City

322 It had taken him to Medjugorje   Brian Thevenot, *The Times-Picayune,* March 19, 2006.

322 Fully five hundred people gathered   Frank Donze, Gordon Russell, *The Times-Picayune,* January 12, 2006.

TWENTY-TWO
Safe Enough for Cows

327 Mark Schleifstein had reached   Mark Schleifstein, *The Times-Picayune,* December 15, 2005.

331 "From the outside, that's suspicious"   John McQuaid, *The Times-Picayune,* December 18, 2005.

337 "It had become apparent"   Ray Seed, memorandum of October 11, 2005.

TWENTY-THREE
Children with Bad Timing

346 "As a former chairman"   Donald Powell, *The Washington Post,* February 2, 2006.

353 A poll in late November   R. T. Scott, *The Times-Picayune,* November 30, 2005.

354 Ben, then nineteen   R. T. Scott, *The Times-Picayune,* January 11, 2004.

359 "If consolidation of the New Orleans"   Jan Moller, Ed Anderson, *The Times-Picayune,* February 18, 2006.

359 "We're entering something new"   R. T. Scott, *The Times-Picayune,* February 17, 2006.

360 "It sends a . . . message"   Ibid.

TWENTY-FIVE
Summing Up

379 FEMA could claim a victory   Bruce Alpert, *The Times-Picayune,* March 21, 2006.

380 "That, to me, is if anything more disturbing"   Bruce Alpert, *The Times-Picayune,* February 16, 2006.

Index

activists, 218–31, 378. *See also specific
   person or organization*
African Americans. *See* race and class
   issues; *specific person*
Algiers district, 125–30, 207, 210,
   218–28, 374
Amarillo Club lunch, 345–46
American Society of Civil Engineers
   (ASCE), 148, 337, 368
Andrew (hurricane, 1992), 24, 263
Army Corps of Engineers: accomplishments of, 167; and blame for failure of
   levees, 145–48, 151–57, 159, 161–67,
   367, 382, 383; budget for, 163, 272,
   334, 335, 349; as builder of levees, 23,
   340; contractors for, 309–10; and design memoranda, 164–65, 333; and
   ERDC, 335, 336, 337; explanations of
   breaching of levees by, 331–33,
   335–37, 327–29; and FEMA, 309, 310;
   and "finite-element modeling,"
   333–34; and how best to fight flooding,
   269–70; IPET of, 367–71; lawsuits
   against, 238, 259–63, 267–68; levee
   board's relationship with, 269, 270–71,
   274; and NSF study, 335, 336–37; and
   politics of redevelopment, 347, 349,
   383; and questions about rebuilding
   New Orleans, 255, 257; and rebuilding

of levee system, 361–73; and Rita,
   209–10; shoring up of levees during
   Katrina by, 46; study of levees by, 349,
   367–71, 381–82; and van Heerden,
   261, 327–28, 332–33; and visions for
   the future, 320; and WES, 333–34,
   335, 368
Astrodome (Houston, Texas), 86, 95,
   185–86, 187, 190

Bahamonde, Marty, 51–52, 58, 59, 63–65
Baker Bill, 248, 342, 343, 344, 347
banks, 243–44, 246, 248, 302
Barbour, Haley, 27, 91, 97, 99, 252, 343,
   357
Baton Rouge, Louisiana: evacuees in, 26,
   37, 76, 104, 136, 175–78, 181–84,
   239–40, 268, 301, 376. *See also specific person or agency*
Battleground Baptist Church, 4, 213, 384,
   385–86
Bea, Robert, 148, 158, 328–33, 335–40,
   364, 368, 370, 382
Betsy (hurricane, 1965), 20, 21, 31, 83,
   84, 163, 329; impact on levees of, 269,
   335, 338; impact on Ninth Ward of, 6,
   20, 55, 66, 76, 117, 248
Bingler, Steven, 32, 33, 198, 199,
   288–93, 301, 303–4, 377

Blanco, Kathleen B.: Astrodome arrangements made by, 95; and blame game, 93–99; and Brown, 63, 95; and bus issues, 94–95; Bush's relationship with, 59–60, 91, 93–99, 121, 205, 347, 348, 352, 355, 357; congressional testimony of, 91, 346, 356; criticisms of, 93–99, 265, 349, 350, 355; early concerns about Katrina of, 14–15; and evacuation plans, 26, 27, 29, 30, 91, 287, 356; failings of, 90–91, 97, 357; family of, 353, 354–55; and federalization of Louisiana National Guard, 96–97, 98; and FEMA, 94–95, 97, 98; and Honoré, 103; and levee system, 350–51, 353–54, 359–60; and LRA, 215, 341; and media, 92, 97–98, 287, 353, 354; and medical licensure rules, 226, 356; Nagin's relationship with, 28, 29, 93, 97, 207; personal and professional background of, 28–29; as politician, 343, 351–55, 357, 359; and politics of redevelopment, 341–44, 346–53, 355–60; power of, 353, 355; and race issues, 87; reforms proposed by, 355–57; rescue operations initiated by, 59–61, 215, 221; state of emergency declared by, 15, 97, 122; Superdome visit of, 84; and trailer issue, 313

Boasso, Walter, 350, 354, 358, 359–60

boats, rescue, 61, 65–72, 89, 90, 101, 109, 113, 124, 144

brain drain, 198–99, 276–77, 295–96, 335

Bring New Orleans Back (BNOB) Commission, 199, 214–16, 238, 282, 288, 291, 303, 304, 341, 352; ULI report for, 315–20. See also footprint committee

Broussard, Aaron, 27, 28, 29, 92, 99–100, 352, 358

Brown, Michael: Bahamonde's messages to, 59, 63–64, 65; and blame, 93, 98, 265, 355; Blanco's meeting with, 95; and breaching of levees, 59; and bus issues, 95; and Bush, 59, 93, 147; Chertoff's relationship with, 59, 93; congressional testimony of, 59; early response by, 59, 63–65; FEMA appointment of, 65, 88, 383; on government bureaucracy, 310; and media/public relations, 64–65, 100; Nagin praised by, 98; and politics of redevelopment, 383; praise for, 98; priorities of, 64–65; professional background of, 88; recall of, 355; views about Bush administration of, 355; visit to New Orleans by, 63–64, 84

building permits, 247–48, 282, 283, 325

Burke, Justin, 136, 141, 142–44, 379

Burnes, Lakesha, 169–71, 175, 177, 376–77

Burnes, Ramola, 170–71, 175–76, 376–77

buses, 105, 128, 188, 209, 222, 356; and convention center, 76, 81, 94–95, 115, 174; FEMA's decisions about, 93, 95; in Houston, 187, 188, 209; stealing of, 172, 186

Bush, George W.: approval ratings of, 98; and blame, 355; and Blanco, 15, 59–60, 91, 93, 95–99, 121, 205, 347, 348, 352, 355, 357; Brown's contacts with, 59, 93, 147; budget cutting by, 334; criticisms of, 346; and levee issues, 59, 147, 382; and media, 91–92, 355; and Nagin, 96, 97, 121, 204, 205, 207; and New Orleans as "dodging the bullet," 46; and politics of redevelopment, 346–47, 352, 357, 359; Powell appointed by, 215; promises of, 205, 255, 352; and questions about rebuilding New Orleans, 256, 257; and race issues, 86; rumors about, 141; State of the Union message of, 346–47; and 2004 hurricanes, 15; visits to Louisiana by, 62, 83–84, 93, 98, 121

Bush administration: basic philosophy of, 87–88, 383; and blame, 93–99, 355; Blanco's relationship with, 93–99, 357; Brown's views about, 355; criticisms of, 245, 253, 255, 265, 276; early responses of, 59–60, 87–99; and federalization of Louisiana National Guard, 96–97, 98; management style of, 91–92; and New Orleans as "dodging the bullet," 46; and politics of redevel-

opment, 341–51, 355, 357–59, 383;
promises of, 205, 256, 293; and race issues, 85–86
business interests, 235–42, 243, 294–305,
314, 350, 359
Bywater district, 4, 12, 232–42, 297

Camille (hurricane, 1969), 20–21, 31, 36
Campbell, Mervin "Kid Merv," 30–31,
36–37, 184–85, 374
Canizaro, Joe, 214, 315–19, 321–22, 324,
325, 358
Card, Andy, 96, 347–48
cars, 170–72, 361–62, 380
casinos, 203–4, 216–17, 265, 272, 307,
351, 360
casualties, 11, 43, 44, 61, 103, 113, 131,
147; burial of, 308; at Convention
Center, 73, 80, 108, 173–74; and
FEMA, 90, 249, 379–80, 381; finding
of, 248–49; at hospitals, 138, 144;
images of, 74–75, 80; and lawsuits,
261–62; in Ninth Ward, 67, 76,
248–49; and nursing homes, 91, 92;
of trapped flood victims, 76, 79, 81,
129; unidentified, 299
Category 5 storm protection, 256–57,
273, 341–42, 349, 371
Central City, 34, 301–5
Chalmette district, 4, 44, 108, 232,
236–37, 240, 280
Charity Hospital, 59, 105, 132–37,
139–42, 143–44, 228, 276, 378, 379
Chertoff, Michael, 46, 59, 93, 147, 355,
380, 383
children: missing, 181–82, 379
Chocolate City Speech (Nagin), 97,
313–14
Christ: statue of, 47
churches, 5, 30, 172, 175–77, 181, 202,
213, 305, 378–79. See also specific
church or minister
city council, New Orleans, 215, 259,
311–12, 313, 319, 324, 325
CNN, 62, 133, 141, 142, 146, 147, 197,
297, 344. See also specific person or
program
Coast Guard, U.S., 60, 65–66, 102–3

coastal restoration, 215, 257. See also
Powell, Donald; specific organization
Common Ground, 224–29, 230–31, 378
communications system, 45, 53–54, 61,
63, 64, 104, 122–23, 126, 133, 141,
294, 298, 356
community centers/organizations, 195,
283, 284, 285, 301–5, 310–11. See also
specific organization
community development block grants, 99,
342, 359, 377, 380
Compass, Eddie, 35, 92, 108–9, 116, 121,
130, 201, 204
compensation formula, 344–46, 358
Congress, U.S.: apathy of, 272; and army
corps budget, 163, 272, 334, 335, 349;
and Chocolate City Speech, 314; and
convention center conditions, 91; and
despondency in New Orleans, 276; diminishing of interest by, 295; and federalizing the state militia, 96; and FEMA
trailers, 380; and housing recovery, 380;
and insurance claims, 252; and lawsuits,
260, 263, 267–68; and levee issues,
109–10, 163, 271, 272, 332, 334, 335,
349, 362, 367, 371, 382; lobbyists for,
229; Louisiana spending request to, 306,
307; mandates upgraded flood defense
for New Orleans, 269; Mississippi
spending request to, 306–7; neoconserv-
atives in, 334; and politics of redevelopment, 342, 359; and questions about
rebuilding New Orleans, 255, 256, 257;
report about Katrina of, 87, 309; and response from FEMA, 90; testimonies before, 28, 51, 59, 109–10, 162, 204, 217,
229, 346, 356, 380; visits to New Orleans by members of, 128, 229. See also
specific person
contractors, 241, 246, 247, 267, 271,
308–10, 361, 363–66, 371–72, 380
"contraflow" plan, 26–27, 36, 91, 118
Convention Center, Ernest N. Morial: and
blame game, 94–95; Blanco's speech
at, 348; building of, 322; buses at, 76,
81, 94–95, 115, 174; casualties at, 73,
80, 108, 173–74; conditions at, 73,
75–76, 79–80, 81; and devastation of

Convention Center, Ernest N. Morial (*cont'd*): Katrina, 84; elderly at, 80; evacuation of, 81–82, 105, 128, 173, 174, 185; food and water at, 73, 79–80, 81, 91, 115, 173; looting in, 80, 81, 173; media reports about, 74, 80, 105, 108, 114–15; medical staff/supplies at, 81, 128, 228; National Guard at, 75, 79; police at, 80, 81; race issues at, 174; as refugee center, 73, 75; rioting at, 114; rumors at, 173–74; tourists/visitors in, 172–75; trade show in, 360; violence at, 73, 75, 80, 174
conventions, 204, 299, 314, 360
corruption, 198, 271–72, 298, 307–8, 324, 330, 381. *See also* patronage
crime, 178, 204, 233–34, 300. *See also* looting/stealing; prisoners
Crockett, Alvin, 187–90, 374–75
cruise ship: FEMA's renting of, 130–31
culture: and visions of the future, 288–94, 319
Cummings, John, 38, 39–40, 258–63, 295, 296, 297, 298, 360
Cummings, Sean, 38–40, 258, 294–301, 377–78

Dallas, Texas, 14, 35, 37, 109, 200, 297
Domino, Fats, 57, 101, 117
downtown area, 4, 203, 207, 210, 322
drainage canals, 46, 256, 269, 270–71, 273, 323, 337–38, 370. *See also* specific canal

East New Orleans, 4, 43, 44, 76–78, 123–24, 128, 244, 312, 324, 326, 329, 367
Ebbert, Terry, 51, 59, 61–62
Edwards, Edwin, 204, 263–64, 265–66, 271–72, 307, 348
elderly, 50, 52–54, 80, 113, 118, 129, 131, 136, 189, 190, 339. *See also* nursing homes; *specific person*
elections, mayoral, 313, 314, 352–53, 378
electricity, 45, 59, 103, 125, 240, 241, 246, 298, 381; at hospitals, 136–38, 139, 140; Nagin's efforts to restore,

207, 211; at Superdome, 50, 55–56. *See also* Entergy
emergency medical technicians (EMTs), 120, 123–25, 128–29, 130, 132–33
Emergency Operations Center (EOC), 58, 59, 60
Engineer Research and Development Center (ERDC), 335, 336, 337
Entergy, 45, 241–42, 298, 345. *See also* electricity
environmentalists, 334, 335, 348, 382
evacuation: and blame game, 94–95; "contraflow" plan for, 26–27, 36, 91, 118; difficulties of, 25–26, 39–40; impact of, 181–84; lack of plans for, 220; legal implications of, 28; mandatory, 48, 287; and Port of New Orleans, 100–102; proposed reforms about, 356–57; regional plan for, 27; and tradition of not evacuating, 31–33. *See also specific person, location, or city*
evacuees: complaints about, 182–83; dispersal of, 183–84; FEMA money for, 181; impact of evacuation on, 181–84; impact on communities of, 183–86; and mayoral elections, 353; and race and class issues, 182–83; and religion, 189–90; and sociability, 189. *See also specific person or location*

Farrell, Earl, 168–72, 175, 177, 376–77
FEMA (Federal Emergency Management Agency): Allbaugh as director of, 60; and army corps, 309, 310; Bahamonde's warnings to Washington-based, 51–52, 58, 59; and blame, 91, 93–95, 98, 355; and Blanco, 28, 94–95, 97, 356; and body bags, 93; and Broussard, 100; Brown's appointment as director of, 65, 88, 383; and building permits, 248; and bus issues, 93, 95; Bush administration's views about, 88–89; and Bush's congratulations to Brown, 93, 147; business forum sponsored by, 227; and casualties, 93, 249, 379–80, 381; and comparison of Kobe and New Orleans, 280; contractors for, 241, 247,

308–9, 310; criticisms of, 65, 88–91, 93, 280, 310, 313; cruise ship rented by, 130–31; and despondency in New Orleans, 276; disaster drill by, 51, 147; dumpstering of chairs by, 227; EOC priority list communicated to, 59; evacuations by, 185; financial mismanagement by, 307, 308, 309; floodplain maps of, 247, 380; funding for, 88, 383; grants from, 181, 182, 241, 242, 246; and hospitals, 139; and housing, 380; insurance program of, 247, 248, 250; and levee issues, 58–61; and missing children, 379; mock disaster drill by, 51; and Nagin, 28, 94, 208, 313; political appointments to, 88; and politics of redevelopment, 346, 347, 382, 383; praise of, 98; priorities and red tape of, 240; promises of, 182; and property owners, 246, 247, 248, 250; proposed reforms for, 356; and rumors, 109; safety obsession of, 89–90; shelters set up by, 177; and Superdome, 51–52, 63, 64, 84, 109; and trailers, 246, 308, 311–12, 356, 376, 379–80, 381; and war on terror, 355. *See also specific person*

fire, 84–85, 280, 297, 301

firefighters, 120, 122–31

fishing industry, 41–42, 335, 348

flood insurance, 244, 247, 248, 250–53, 342, 346, 347

floodplains, 247, 248, 316, 318, 321, 342, 345, 380

food and water, 78, 91, 280, 304–5. *See also specific location*

footprint committee, 315–26

Ford, Stephen, 66–70

Ford Foundation, 289, 303, 304

foundations, 304, 331. *See also specific foundation*

Francis, Norman, 215, 343, 358

Freitas, Drina, 123–25, 128–29, 130

French Quarter, 4, 12, 47, 74, 84–85, 172, 207, 210, 232, 239, 286, 297

gas, 39–40, 125, 127, 211, 258, 346–47, 348–49

God: and explanations for Katrina, 314, 382

Groennou, Brunilda, 172–75

Hanslik, Fern, 191–92, 194, 197

Harrison, Lynn, 137–38, 142, 276–77

Harvey, Bob, 263–69, 271–74, 348

Hecker, Robert, 100–102

helicopters, 124, 128, 141, 142, 173, 356–57, 370

Herbert, Troy, 310

highway system, 26, 29, 39, 40, 44–45, 59, 74, 103

Homeland Security, U.S. Department of, 87–89, 309, 310. *See also* Cherthoff, Michael

homeless, 84, 188–89, 380

Honoré, Russel, 103–5

hospitals, 30, 31, 36–37, 59, 85, 114, 132–44, 184, 208, 356, 378–79. *See also specific hospital*

Hotel Dieu Hospital, 36, 137

hotels, 38–39, 44, 59, 172, 298–99, 380. *See also specific hotel*

housing: Blanco's proposed reforms for, 356; buyouts, 324, 344–45; condemnation of, 248, 270; evictions from, 245; and FEMA, 380; foreclosures on, 244, 246; funding for, 380; mortgages, 243–44, 245, 248, 302, 318, 321, 376; and politics of redevelopment, 343, 344, 346, 347, 359; rehabbing of, 245, 246, 380–81; rental, 246–47. *See also* flood insurance; housing projects; insurance

housing projects, 121–22, 185, 218, 221, 290, 313, 323

Houston, Texas: buses in, 187, 188, 209; evacuation from, 209, 356; evacuees in, 32, 37, 183, 185–90, 197, 207, 289, 353, 376–77, 379; mail service in, 207; media in, 188–89, 190; nursing homes in, 209; violence in, 183

Hubbard, Al, 342–43, 347–48

"Hurricane Pam" study, 51, 147

hurricanes: 2006 season of, 361–73, 382, 383–84
Hyatt Regency Hotel, 54, 56, 61, 63

Industrial Canal, 7, 62, 210, 339, 384; breaching of, 8, 43, 59, 67, 337–38; as division between Upper and Lower Ninth Ward, 3–4, 232; and questions about breaching of levees, 153, 167; and rebuilding of levees, 364–65, 371, 372; and rescue efforts, 71, 128; understanding of failure of, 369
inspectors, building, 245–47
insurance: claims for, 245, 246, 248, 249–50; cost of post-Katrina, 248; lawsuits about, 262; and plans for rebuilding, 242, 245, 246, 248, 249–50, 318, 380; and politics of redevelopment, 342, 345, 346, 347; and return to New Orleans, 376; and visions of the future, 298, 302. *See also* flood insurance
Interagency Performance Evaluation Task Force (IPET), 367–71
International House (hotel), 38–39, 294, 298–99, 300, 377
Intracoastal Waterway, 7, 153, 370
Iraq, 255, 256, 309, 357, 379, 383
Isaacson, Walter, 215, 255, 300, 342–43, 344, 346, 349, 358
Ivan (hurricane, 2004), 15, 27, 34

Jackson, Ted, 106–7, 110–15
Jefferson, Bill, 307–8, 347
Jefferson Parish, 21, 89, 107, 110, 126, 164, 221, 267, 379; evacuation of, 26, 27, 29, 99–100; and politics of redevelopment, 350, 351, 358, 359. *See also* Broussard, Aaron
Jesus sketch, 188, 189, 190
Jindal, Bobby, 28, 29, 349–50
Joint Task Force Katrina, 103–5
Jones, Norman, 74–76

Katrina (hurricane, 2005): as catastrophe, 59, 60; devastation caused by, 43–45, 84–91, 200–201; explanations for, 382–83; eye of, 36, 46, 179, 338; "eyewall replacement cycle" of, 18; as

flood, 249–53; fundraising for victims of, 86, 117; God's anger at America as reason for, 314; Hiroshima compared with, 43–44; landfall of, 7–8, 14, 41; New Orleans struck by, 8–10; tracking of, 10–15, 17–20, 23–25; waiting for, 6, 12–14; wind speeds of, 46–47, 102, 103
Khalaileh, Ray, 235–37, 239–40, 241–42, 244
Kobe, Japan, 278–86, 287, 325
Kopplin, Andy, 344, 346, 358
Kurtz-Burke, Kiersta, 133–36, 140–44, 378–79
Kusuba, Ikuhiro, 282, 283, 285–86

Lake Barrington area, 76–78, 247–48
Lake Borgne, 338–39
Lakeview district, 17, 43, 44, 57, 113, 212
Landrieu, Mary, 63, 92, 98, 306, 307, 346–47, 352
Latinos, 227–28, 230
lawsuits: against army corps, 238, 259–63, 267–68; and casualties, 261–62; and city council, 259; and comparison of Kobe and New Orleans, 282; against insurance companies, 252–53, 262; against levee boards, 157–58, 263–69, 273–74
lawyers, 227–28, 230, 250. *See also* lawsuits; *specific person*
leadership, 65, 280–82, 325–26, 384. *See also specific person*
legislature, Louisiana, 343–44, 348, 349–50, 351, 353, 355, 358, 360
levee boards: and army corps, 269, 270–71, 274; and Blanco's proposed reforms, 356; consolidation of, 274, 343–44, 349, 350–51, 353–54, 358, 359–60; contractors for, 267, 271; and corruption, 271–72; evacuation of members of, 267; lawsuits against, 157–58, 263–69, 273–74; Orleans, 263–74, 351, 359, 364; and politics of redevelopment, 341, 343–44, 349, 350–51, 356, 358, 359; and rebuilding of levees, 351, 359, 364

levees: activism concerning, 229; ASCE study of, 148, 337, 368; Betsy's impact on, 269, 335, 338; blame for failure of, 145–67, 369, 382, 383; and Blanco, 350–51, 353–54, 359–60; breaching of, 43, 45–46, 58–63, 117, 145–67, 367–71, 381–83; congressional questions about, 109–10, 163, 271, 272, 332, 334, 335, 349, 362, 367, 371, 382; deliberate breaching of, 109–10, 117, 245; design memoranda (1989) concerning, 164–65, 333; disintegration of, 57; federal neglect of, 90; funding for, 256, 320, 331, 350, 362, 370, 372, 382; as greatest threat to New Orleans, 19; and insurance claims, 251; by Lake Borgne, 338–39; maintenance of, 152, 270, 272, 330, 364; media reports about, 61–62, 146, 147, 149, 152–59, 161–63, 332, 338, 354, 366, 367; along Mississippi River, 335; NSF study of, 148, 158, 327–40, 368, 381, 382; and politics of redevelopment, 342, 353–54; and pumping stations, 99–100, 164, 340; as quaint, 288; reasons for failure of, 367–71; rebuilding of, 255, 256–57, 350, 361–73, 382, 383, 384; rumors about, 109–10; safety of, 327–40; sandbags for, 45–46; sinkholes near, 336–37; and "stopped-clock program," 154; studies and probes about, 148–49, 153–58, 159, 161, 162, 257, 327–40, 367–71; and taxes, 270; and tracking Katrina, 23, 24; and visions for the future, 298, 320–21, 323. *See also* Army Corps of Engineers; drainage canals; levee boards; *specific canal*

Link, Ed, 368–70, 371

London Avenue Canal, 59, 154, 156, 164–65, 167, 330, 337–38, 339, 369

looting/stealing, 84, 101, 210, 239, 279; of buses, 172; in Bywater district, 235, 236; of cars, 170–72; at convention center, 80, 81, 173; by firefighters, 123, 125; at hospitals, 85, 141; media reports about, 85, 112, 170, 174, 222; and need for more police, 96; in Ninth Ward, 71, 239; by police, 84, 114, 121, 123, 170, 207, 276, 299–300; from police armory, 101; police efforts to stop, 81, 84, 110; police views about, 236; reverse, 126; by Superdome workers, 57; by tourists/visitors, 172; by youth, 168–72

Lott, Trent, 252–53, 296

Louisiana: Blanco's declaration of state of emergency in, 15, 97, 122; corruption images of, 263, 307–8; Democratic Party in, 354; reputation of, 307–8, 310. *See also specific person or agency*

Louisiana Coastal Protection and Restoration Authority (CPRA), 350

Louisiana Recovery Authority (LRA), 215, 255, 300, 325, 341–45, 349, 354, 358, 359

Louisiana State University (LSU): Hurricane Center at, 22, 24–25, 62, 63, 146, 147, 148, 153, 159–62, 368, 369–70; Maravich arena at, 142–43; medical center at, 276

Lower Ninth Ward, 57, 364, 384–85; Betsy's impact on, 6, 20, 66, 76, 248; casualties in, 76, 248–49; devastation in, 4, 5, 248, 277; Katrina strikes, 8–10; media accounts of, 106–7; property owners in, 244, 246, 248, 250–51; rescue efforts in, 66–68, 101, 106–7, 128, 249; returns to, 212–14; and visions for the future, 323, 326. *See also* Ninth Ward; *specific person*

Maestri, Walter, 21, 100

mail service, 45, 206–7, 241

Mardi Gras, 292, 293, 360, 372, 386

Marigny district, 4, 12, 232, 238, 239, 294

Marsalis, Wynton, 214, 215, 290, 291, 293

Marshall, Bob, 149–52, 156–59, 161

Mary Queen of Vietnam Church, 229–30, 310–11, 312, 316, 317

Mashriqui, Hassan, 153

McFadden, Freddie III, 4–5, 6, 213

McFadden, James, 6–7, 213, 214
McKinnis family, 189–90, 374–75
McWhirter Elementary School, 191–99
Mechanic, Scott, 223–26
media, 82, 117, 130, 257, 297, 324; and
    activism, 221–23, 224; and bus issues,
    105; and casualties, 108, 113; and con-
    gressional visits, 128; convention center
    reports in, 74, 80, 105, 108, 114–15;
    and devastation in New Orleans, 74,
    277; ethical challenges facing, 106–8,
    112–15; FEMA's ferrying of, 89; hospi-
    tal reports in, 141, 142; and Houston
    evacuees, 188–89, 190; and impact of
    evacuees on communities, 185–86; and
    Jesus sketch, 190; lack of knowledge of
    conditions by, 61–62; and levee issues,
    61–62, 146, 147, 149, 152–59, 161–63,
    332, 338, 354, 366, 367; looting reports
    by, 85, 112, 170, 174, 222; and
    Louisiana's congressional spending re-
    quest, 307; and politics of redevelop-
    ment, 342, 349; and race issues, 118,
    174–75, 221–23; and rumors, 107–15,
    133, 142; Superdome stories in, 74, 80,
    105, 108, 114; and trailers, 312; vio-
    lence stories in, 80, 85, 92–93, 95, 108.
    See also specific person
medical staff/supplies, 85, 176, 179,
    276–77; and activism, 221–28, 230; at
    convention center, 81, 128, 228; and
    FEMA's response efforts, 89, 90; licen-
    sure of, 226, 356; and recovery efforts,
    210, 221–28, 230; at Superdome,
    51–52, 56, 142. See also hospitals; spe-
    cific person or hospital
migrant workers, 227–28, 294
Mississippi, 44, 91, 204, 311; casualties
    in, 43, 103; disaster aid for, 99, 306–7;
    federalization of state militia in, 97; in-
    surance claims in, 252–53; and politics
    of redevelopment, 342, 343, 346, 347,
    357, 382, 383; race in, 180
Mississippi River Bridge: confrontation
    on, 73–74
Mississippi River Gulf Outlet "Mr. Go,"
    153, 335, 338–39, 366–67, 370, 371,
    372

Morial, Marc, 202, 214, 296, 307
Morris, Noah, 223, 225, 226, 227
Mwendo, Ukali, 120–23, 125–31

Nagin, Ray: and blame game, 93–94, 96,
    97, 98; and Blanco, 28, 29, 93, 97, 207;
    and BNOB, 199, 214–16, 352; and
    Brown, 63, 98; and bus issues, 94, 95;
    and Bush, 93, 96, 121, 204, 205, 207,
    352; and casinos, 216–17; and Charity
    Hospital, 134; Chocolate City Speech
    of, 97, 313–14; city council's relation-
    ship with, 311–12; and Compass's res-
    ignation, 121; congressional testimony
    of, 28, 109–10, 204, 217; and contrac-
    tors, 361, 380; criticisms of, 90–91, 94,
    265, 353, 355; criticisms of federal re-
    sponse by, 91–92, 94; in Dallas, 200;
    early concerns about Katrina of, 14;
    early recovery efforts of, 204–12,
    214–17; evacuation of family of, 14,
    35; and evacuation of New Orleans, 7,
    9, 24, 27–30, 35, 73; and FEMA, 313;
    and funding for recovery, 293; Giuliani
    compared with, 200–201; Hyatt Re-
    gency headquarters of, 54, 61, 63; and
    levee issues, 61, 109–10; and mayoral
    elections, 313, 314, 352–53, 378; and
    media, 91–93, 97, 200, 201, 202, 204,
    207, 216, 314; migrant workers com-
    ment by, 227; and Neville's charges,
    116; personal and professional back-
    ground of, 28, 201–2; and politics of
    redevelopment, 341, 346, 352–53, 358;
    powers of, 204–5, 207, 311; and prop-
    erty owners, 246; and race and class is-
    sues, 87, 97, 313–14; Rahim's views
    about, 221; and redevelopment of city
    property, 377; and Reed, 303; and ru-
    mors, 108, 109; and trailers, 311, 312,
    313; and visions for the future, 316,
    318, 319–20, 325–26; weapons confis-
    cation ordered by, 238
National Guard, 97, 114, 175, 225–26,
    357; Blanco alerts, 15; at convention
    center, 75, 79; on cruise ship, 130; fed-
    eralization of Louisiana, 96–97; flood-
    ing of barracks of, 60, 121; at

hospitals, 133; rescue efforts of, 57, 127–28; at Superdome, 52, 54, 56

National Hurricane Center, 15, 17, 30

National Science Foundation (NSF), 148, 158, 327–40, 368, 381, 382

National Weather Service, 16, 46–47, 102

Netherlands, 163–64, 268, 300, 320, 327, 349, 383

Neville Brothers, 116–17, 184, 196

Neville, Charmaine, 116–19, 172, 232

New Orleans Building Corporation, 296, 377–78

New Orleans, Louisiana: commitment to excellence in, 300; congress mandates upgraded flood defense for, 269; corruption in, 198; as counterculture mecca, 232–33; despondency in, 255–58, 276–78; economy of, 203–4, 205, 276, 284, 286, 316; future of, 383–84; globalization effects on, 203; job cuts in, 205–6, 276; Kobe compared with, 278–86, 287, 325; master plan for, 281; nicknames for, 14; population of, 284, 296, 316, 384; possible outcomes for, 286–87; questions about rebuilding, 255–58; size of city government in, 205–7; streamlining of city government in, 344, 353, 359. *See also specific person, district/neighborhood, or agency*

Nguyen The Vien, 229–30, 310–11, 312–13, 316

Ninth Ward, 3–4, 43, 210, 232, 238, 240; during Betsy, 55, 117; casualties in, 67; devastation in, 44, 65–72; looting in, 71, 239; trapped flood victims in, 117–19. *See also* Lower Ninth Ward; *specific person or district*

nursing homes, 50, 61, 91, 92, 121, 209, 356

O'Brian, Maureen "Mo," 223, 226–27

Office of Emergency Preparedness, Louisiana, 103

Office of Public Health, New Orleans, 50, 51

oil industry, 14, 42, 258, 262, 286, 334, 338, 346–47, 348–49

Orleans Avenue Canal, 269, 340

Orleans Parish: activism in, 230–31; and evacuation plans, 27, 29; during Katrina, 42; medical facilities in, 379; and politics of redevelopment, 351, 359; schools in, 307, 350

patronage, 271, 349–51, 356, 359

People's Hurricane Relief Fund, 228–29, 230, 378

Peters family, 3, 4–10, 20, 43, 54–55, 70–73, 108, 212–14, 239, 250–51, 372, 384–86

planning commission, New Orleans, 324, 325

Plaquemines Parish, 167, 264, 310, 358

police: and activists, 226; and blame game, 96; breakdown in command of, 123; confiscation of weapons by, 238–39; at convention center, 80, 81; criminals passing themselves off as, 234; on cruise ship, 130–31; desertions by, 85, 121, 207; and drug dealers, 233; and efforts to stop looting, 81, 84, 110, 236; and evacuation of New Orleans, 26, 35; harbor, 101–2; as heroes, 120; and hospital workers, 143; hurricane plan of, 121; looting by, 84, 114, 121, 123, 170, 207, 276, 299–300; looting from armory of, 101; and Mississippi River Bridge confrontation, 73–74; need for more, 84, 96, 207; rebuilding of, 121; resignations and retirements among, 110, 121; scandals involving, 130–31; and sex crimes reports, 115–16; suicides among, 121, 275–76; at Superdome, 52, 124–25; and trapped flood victims, 76, 79; and violence, 75, 131. *See also specific person*

Poplarville, Mississippi, 34, 39, 178–82, 301

Port of New Orleans, 100–102

poverty, 26, 31, 85, 204, 205, 215, 303. *See also* race and class issues

Powell, Donald, 215, 255, 256, 341, 344–48, 358, 359, 380, 382

prisoners, 37, 134, 141, 178

property owners: rebuilding by individual, 243–53. *See also* flood insurance; housing; insurance; *specific person*

race and class issues, 117, 180, 215, 277, 279, 301, 303; and activism, 218–31; and Bush administration, 85–86; and Chocolate City Speech, 97, 313–14; at convention center, 174; and hospitals, 134, 135, 140; and impact of evacuees on communities, 182–83; and media, 118, 174–75, 221–23; and Mississippi River Bridge confrontation, 73–74; and politics, 29, 86; and slowness of relief response, 85–87; and trailers, 312; and visions for the future, 316, 324–25. *See also* poverty; *specific person*
Rahim, Malik, 218–26, 230–31, 238, 378
rape, 115–19
Ratcliff, Mary, 221–23, 224
Reckdahl, Katy, 30–31, 36–37, 184–85, 374
Red Cross, 16, 90, 176, 177, 191, 229
redevelopment: of city property, 296, 377–78; commercial, 294–305; and comparison of Kobe and New Orleans, 281–82, 283–84; contractors for, 241, 246, 247, 267, 271, 308–10, 361, 363–66, 371–72, 380; by individual property owners, 243–53; politics of, 247, 341–60, 382–83; questions concerning, 255–57; supplies for, 243; and visions for the future, 285, 288–305, 315–26. *See also specific person or organization*
Reed family, 33–36, 39, 85, 178–82, 300–305, 376
Reilly, Sean, 344–46, 358
Reiss, Jimmy, 214–15, 238, 320–21
relief/response efforts, 84, 219–20, 280, 293; and activism, 221–28; blue-ribbon committees concerned with, 214–17; and casino proposal, 216–17; for hospitals/medical workers, 133–44, 230;

lack of federal, 89–90, 93, 105; and race issues, 85–87; and Republican philosophical views, 87–88; and terrorism, 88–89. *See also* FEMA; Red Cross; *specific clinic/hospital or organization*
Republican Party, 85–86, 87–88, 252, 257, 263, 307, 334
rescue efforts: Blanco's initiation of, 60–61; boats available for, 89–90, 109, 113, 124; impromptu and unofficial, 65–72; in Lower Ninth Ward, 101, 128, 249; and response by federal agencies, 59–60, 89–90, 109; of trapped flood victims, 76–78, 79, 101, 112–13, 129; and violence, 85. *See also specific agency*
Rice, Glenda, 195–97
Richardson, Gregory, 76–82, 243–49, 380
"right to return," 321, 324–25
Rita (hurricane, 2005), 101, 208–10, 337, 356, 370
Rogers, J. David, 159, 331–32
Rousselle, Benny, 310, 358
Rove, Karl, 83, 93, 98, 322, 343, 357
rumors, 107–15, 133, 141, 142, 173–74, 178, 184

Schleifstein, Mark, 16–18, 19, 23–24, 61–62, 212, 327
schools, 280, 307, 350, 377; in Ninth Ward, 55, 384; and plans for redevelopment, 240, 326; as shelters, 75, 108, 118–19, 236–37; in Superdome, 198, 199; in Texas, 191–99, 375–76; and visions of the future, 289–91, 298, 300, 304
Seed, Ray, 148, 328–38, 368, 370, 381, 382
Setliff, Lewis F. III, 361–67, 370–73
Seventeenth Street Canal, 268, 272, 362; breaching of, 58–59, 61–63, 327, 337–38; explanations of breaching of, 329–30, 335–36, 369, 381; and questions about breaching of levees, 146, 149–51, 152, 156, 157–58, 161, 164, 165–66, 167, 327, 335–36, 337; re-

building of, 362, 368–69; and studies of levees, 329–30, 331, 332, 335–36, 337, 339, 381

sewer system, 45, 51, 56, 210–11, 345. *See also* drainage canals; Sewerage and Water Board; toilets

Sewerage and Water Board, 149, 150–51, 155, 164, 207, 257

Sharma, Radhey, 159

Shaw Group, 247, 308–9

shelters, 172, 175–77, 181, 191. *See also specific shelter*

snipers: rumors about, 104–5

Social Services, Louisiana Department of, 50, 53, 57

"special needs" people, 50–51, 52–54, 56, 57, 64, 71–72, 94, 124, 195

St. Bernard Parish: and comparison of Kobe and New Orleans, 280; devastation in, 8, 42, 43, 44, 60, 61; and levee issues, 167, 367, 371; media coverage of, 111–12; 1927 flood in, 259; nursing home in, 92; and politics of redevelopment, 358, 359; Violet area of, 44, 195

Starkel, Murray, 165–67

Sugar Park Tavern, 235, 237–38, 240–41

suicides, 275–76, 282, 380

Superdome: architecture of, 49; basketball game at, 12; and blame game, 94–95; Blanco's visits to, 84; and bus issues, 94–95; communications system in, 53–54; and comparison of Kobe and New Orleans, 280; conditions in, 49–56, 64, 71–72, 109, 114, 124–25, 142; early hours at, 12, 48–51, 54–57; evacuation of, 65, 103, 105, 124, 185; and FEMA, 51–52, 63, 64, 84, 109; food and water at, 49, 52, 56, 124–25; media stories about, 74, 80, 105, 114; medical staff/supplies at, 51–52, 56, 142; morale at, 56; National Guard at, 52, 54, 56; police at, 52, 124–25; population in, 57, 59, 73; rape attempts at, 116; registration process at, 53; rioting in, 109, 114; rumors about, 104–5, 109, 115;

school in, 198, 199; snipers outside, 104–5; "special needs" people at, 50–51, 52–54, 56, 57, 64, 71–72, 94, 124; violence at, 80, 92–93, 108, 115, 124

Swain, Cynthia, 100–102

Task Force Guardian, 361–67, 371–73

Team Louisiana, 149, 153–55, 159, 339, 368, 369

terrorism, 88–89, 127, 355, 382–83

Texas. *See also specific city*

The Times-Picayune, 16, 100, 110–11, 115, 150, 154, 163, 200, 308–9, 323, 350. *See also specific person*

toilets, 73, 79, 144, 193, 211. *See also* sewer system

tourists/visitors, 59, 172–75, 216, 232, 277, 286, 362

Touro Hospital, 36–37, 184

trailers, 182, 246, 254, 279, 280, 308, 311–13, 356, 376, 379–80, 381

Transportation and Development, Louisiana Department of, 155, 156, 161, 162

Trump, Donald, 12, 201, 202–3, 204, 206, 295

Tulane University, 158, 276, 293–94; Medical Center at, 133, 134, 140, 142, 296

University Hospital, 133, 137–38, 139, 142, 276

Uptown area, 4, 12, 168–72, 207, 210, 238, 244, 245, 295, 376

Urban Land Institute (ULI), 215, 315–23

Usdin, Linda, 31–32, 33, 34, 198, 289, 301, 377

USS *Bataan* (hospital ship), 89

van Heerden, Ivor, 22–25, 61–63, 145–49, 152–60, 163–64, 166, 167, 261, 327–33, 338, 339, 368, 369, 381

Veteran's Administration Hospital, 133, 379

Vietnamese, 229–30, 310–11, 316, 317, 318
vigilantes, 75, 218, 222, 225, 230
violence: and hospitals, 134, 135–36, 137; and impact of evacuees on communities, 183–84; media stories about, 75, 80, 85, 92–93, 95; and police, 75, 131; rumors about, 108, 115. *See also* *specific location*

Wagenaar, Col. Richard, 159, 160
Washington, Rev. Bishop Frank, 175–77, 376

water system, 45, 62, 207, 210–11, 345. *See also* food and water; Sewerage and Water Board
Watters, Sherry, 50–51, 52–53, 54–56, 57, 72, 124
Webster, Texas, 191–99, 375–76
wetlands, 42, 153, 335. *See also* floodplains; levees
Wildlife and Fisheries, Louisiana Department of, 60–61, 66, 71, 89
Wyman, Stephanie, 197–99, 209, 375–76

Zas, Robert, 233–40

About the Author

JED HORNE, a metro editor of *The Times-Picayune,* was awarded a Pulitzer Prize for his part in the paper's coverage of Hurricane Katrina. His book *Desire Street: A True Story of Death and Deliverance in New Orleans* was nominated for the 2006 Edgar Award for nonfiction crime writing. He lives in the French Quarter with his wife.

About the Type

This book was set in Times Roman, designed by Stanley
Morrison specifically for *The Times* of London. The typeface was introduced in the newspaper in 1932. Times
Roman had its greatest success in the United States as a
book and commercial typeface, rather than one used in
newspapers.